THE STUDY OF GLOBAL INTERDEPENDENCE

Essays on the Analysis of World Politics

other titles in this series:

The Scientific Study of Foreign Policy
The Study of Political Adaptation

James N. Rosenau

THE STUDY OF GLOBAL INTERDEPENDENCE

Essays on the Transnationalization of World Affairs

Frances Pinter (Publishers) Ltd., London
Nichols Publishing Company, New York

First published in Great Britain in 1980 by
Frances Pinter (Publishers) Limited
5 Dryden Street, London WC2E 9NW

ISBN 0 903804 60 3 Hardback
ISBN 0 903804 61 1 Paperback

Published in the U.S.A. by
Nichols Publishing Company
P.O. Box 96, New York, N.Y. 10024

Library of Congress Cataloging in Publication Data

Rosenau, James N
The study of global interdependence.
(Essays on the analysis of world politics)
1. International relations. I. Title. II. Series.
JX1395.R5735 1980 327 79-25642
ISBN 0-89397-078-6
ISBN 0-89397-079-4 pbk.

Typeset by Anne Joshua Associates, Oxford
Printed in Great Britain by A. Wheaton and Co., Exeter

for
F.B.R.

Contents

Acknowledgments

Support for the essays collected here was provided by many persons and organizations. Written at various times in the 1970s, the essays benefitted from the institutional support supplied by two universities, the Ohio State University and the University of Southern California, particularly the latter's Institute for Transnational Studies. A grant from the National Science Foundation was also instrumental in facilitating the preparation of Chapter 9. Richard K. Ashley, Elizabeth Cadenhead, Thomas Johnson, Mary Kirk, James Lebovic, Edwin P. McClain, and Lisa Nilson offered valuable advice on one or another of the essays. Gary Gartin, Edwin P. McClain, Dona Stinziano, Richard Stoddard, and Dean Swanson co-authored Chapter 10 with me.

I am enormously grateful to all of the foregoing for their help and counsel. For the various chapters and the book as a whole, however, I am alone responsible.

James N. Rosenau

Pacific Palisades, Ca.
January 11, 1980

1 The Study of Interdependence and Transnational Relations

The essays in this volume focus on change in world affairs and, no less important, on how to study and comprehend the change. Although written at different times in recent years, the essays share a preoccupation with the emergence of greater complexity in the affairs of states and the interaction of societies.

The scope and nature of the changes and the complexities to which they have given rise are sometimes referred to as tendencies toward greater interdependence, but I also find it useful to view them as fostering the transnationalization of world affairs. The concept of interdependence pervades the ensuing essays, and it is also central to the way in which public officials talk about the unfolding global scene. But its scope is so broad that often it is used to analyze circumstances and conditions in the physical world that shape and limit the course of human events. The concept of transnational relations, on the other hand, suggest dynamic processes initiated and sustained by people. Hence the juxtaposition of the title and subtitle serves to stress a concern with those aspects of mounting interdependence that extend beyond changing physical realities into the realms of individual experience, collective endeavor, and group interaction.

More specifically, by the transnationalization of world affairs I mean the processes whereby international relations conducted by governments have been supplemented by relations among private individuals, groups, and societies that can and do have important consequences for the course of events. Dynamic change, initiated by technological innovation and sustained by continuing advances in communications and transportation, has brought new associations and organizations into the political arena, and the efforts of these new entities to obtain external resources or otherwise interact with counterparts abroad have extended the range and intensified the dynamics of world affairs.

Not only has modern technology fostered a surge toward global interdependence, it also underlies the intense revolutions against dynamic change that have recently become so manifest, perhaps particularly in Iran and Islam but by no means only in that part of the world. Ironically, in other words, the trend toward interdependence has highlighted the virtues of historic values associated with independence, thereby giving rise to two powerful and yet contradictory processes on the global scene: an *integrative* process whereby societies are becoming increasingly *dependent* on each other and a *disintegrative* process whereby groups within societies are increasingly demanding autonomy for themselves. Whichever of these processes ultimately prevails (or even if they both remain equally powerful for decades), it seems clear that they represent a transformation, even a breakdown, of the nation-state system as it has existed throughout the last four centuries.

Stated differently, whatever structures of global life emerge in the future, it seems increasingly inappropriate to place them in an 'inter-nation' context. International relations still exist and will probably continue to mark the global scene for decades to come, but they now must be seen as embedded in a world comprised of nonnational as well as national entities. It is to comprehending this enlarged scope that the study of transnational relations is addressed. That is, the study of transnational relations encompasses the study of international relations. It focuses on interactions among nongovernmental entities as well as on relations among states and between states and nongovernmental entities. Stated more succinctly, it involves inquiry into how governmental and nongovernmental organizations seek, independently and interactively, to realize their goals and cope with the challenges that beset them. The new nongovernmental entities may never become as powerful as national governments, and they may never become preoccupied with as many diverse issues as do governments, but their attempts to move toward goals are salient enough features of the world scene to shape the course of events and cause governments to interact with them.

Perhaps no incident better illustrates the changing structure of the global system than the 1979 seizure of the United States Embassy in Iran. Not only did this situation violate international law and reflect a set of values antithetical to nation-states; but in its early days it also evoked a series of crisis-resolving attempts that depict the workings of a global system that bears little resemblance to the diplomacy of earlier eras. In the first place, it was not clear whether authority in

Tehran lay with the Iranian government, the student captors, both groups, or neither group. Secondly, foreign offices were by no means the only channels through which negotiations were initiated. Offers to mediate the crisis came from a variety of sources, from nongovernmental groups like the Palestine Liberation Organization, from non-nation-states like the Vatican, from such varied individuals as Pope John Paul II, Mohammed Ali, and Andrew Young, as well as from a U.S. Congressman who, on his own as a private citizen, went to Tehran to bargain with the captors and free the hostages.

All of this is not to imply, of course, that it is no longer appropriate to treat nation-states as central actors in the system. On the contrary, they continue to be viable and adaptive mechanisms for collective action. Some of their governments, in fact, enjoy near total power to frame and execute policies, and many also reap the benefits of intense nationalism — of strong loyalties to the nation-state and those charged with its welfare. Thus no amount of emphasis on rapid change and mounting interdependence should obscure the central role of national governments and states in world affairs. In another collection of essays I have elaborated on this role by treating nation-states as adaptive entities in a complex global system,[1] a perspective which serves to demonstrate both their capacities for coping with change and their power to effect change. And in still another collection of essays I have focused even more exclusively on the behavior of states by examining the sources out of which and the processes through which their governments conduct foreign policy.[2]

Notwithstanding the continuing importance of nation-states, however, it matters whether one views world affairs as a system of nation-states or as a system in which political life is sustained through a variety of dissimilar and competitive authority structures, not all of which are nation-states. The former approach does not allow for the consequences of global interdependence, whereas the latter does. Such is the emphasis of the essays in this volume. They focus on the dynamics of transnational relations and, as such, they treat nation-states as adaptive entities (particularly in Chapter 4) while also analyzing the larger context in which nation-states presently conduct their affairs. All three collections of essays, in fact, are conceived as an integrated whole, as a series focusing on one or another aspect of the same, continuous sequences that mark world affairs today. The fact that they have been compiled in separate volumes should be seen as a concession to publishing practicalities and not as a reflection of political realities.

[1] James N. Rosenau, *The Study of Political Adaptation* (London: Frances Pinter Publishers, 1980).

[2] James N. Rosenau, *The Scientific Study of Foreign Policy* (London: Frances Pinter Publishers, revised and enlarged edition, 1980).

The transnational perspective has one other advantage worth highlighting. By allowing for a multiplicity of actors who sustain global politics, it facilitates attention to the roles played by bureaucratic agencies within governments. An international perspective tends to treat governments as monoliths in which all interactions across national boundaries are initiated and maintained by chiefs of state, cabinets and foreign ministries, with bureaucracies serving as mere implementors of higher authority. However, enough data about the dynamics of 'bureaucratic politics' has surfaced to indicate that much of what transpires in world affairs derives from the initiatives and activities of governmental subunits, of bureaucratic agencies that work independently with counterparts abroad was well as through their superiors. An approach which treats global politics as a myriad of transnational relations brings these emergent bureaucratic roles more clearly into focus than do those more traditional approaches in which states are posited as the source of actions and interactions.

It follows that the analysis of world affairs from a transnational perspective is not easy. Heretofore inquiry has been organized exclusively around the foreign policies and interactions of states and, unfortunately, the paradigms, models, and concepts employed to probe these phenomena simply have not proven sufficient to the task of comprehending the changes that appear to be transnationalizing world affairs. To a large extent, therefore, the ensuing essays consist either of an attempt to revise and upgrade old concepts or of a search for new ways of analyzing one or another aspect of the global scene. Citizenship and power (defined as control and capabilities), for example, are subjected to re-examination with a view to up-dating them for application to transnational phenomena, while the authority structure, the adaptive mechanism, the aggregative process, and the transnational role are offered as new tools of inquiry that may yield greater insights.

It might be argued that the number, diversity, and (occasional) contradictions of the various concepts developed here are a reflection of irresponsibility, that an analyst has an obligation to focus on and fully develop one formulation before moving on to propose other approaches. In a period of global transformation, on the other hand, theoretical consistency may be more a hindrance than an aid to analytic progress; or at least the diversity of conceptual approaches may be a measure of the challenge that dynamic change is posing for students of world affairs. Surely the emergence of new phenomena is not readily absorbed by any field of inquiry. And surely the fact that these new phenomena supplement rather than replace the old patterns further compounds the tasks of theoretical analysis. Viewed in this context, it is hardly surprising that the search for theoretical clarification has taken us in a variety of diverse directions.

It just may be, moreover, that no single perspective is sufficient to trace adequately the complexities of transnational relations, that a multiplicity of concepts are needed to probe and depict the changes that are transforming world affairs. I am not inclined to argue this point very strongly, as I believe that it ought to be possible to develop a single paradigm that adequately accounts for the emerging world. But the possibility that multiple approaches may yield deeper understanding at least suggests that the several concepts developed here need not be viewed as mutually exclusive. The conception of nation-states as adapting entities, for example, does not preclude the treatment of nongovernmental entities as authority structures. Diverse and disparate as the concepts developed here may seem, in other words, they spring from a common set of concerns and thus may eventually prove integratable into an overarching transnational paradigm if one should ever evolve.

There is another reason why the development of a multiplicity of concepts may be advantageous. The state-centric paradigm of international relations has been with us for so long that it is not easily abandoned in favor of a more encompassing perspective. The tendencies to view governments as the only meaningful source of causation and to treat state interactions as the parameters of world affairs have become so deeply engrained analytic habits as to blind us to the dynamics of change, making them appear as challenges to the existing order rather than as forerunners of new patterns. To be sure, the changes *are* challenges to the prevailing arrangements, but they may also represent basic transformations in the structure of world affairs. And this possibility cannot be fully appreciated as long as we remain imprisoned in our own conceptual jails. A multiple-concept approach may thus prove useful at this time, enabling us to engineer a jailbreak that allows us to discern the dynamics of change more clearly and thereby to trace new causal sources and possible new parameters within which the course of events unfolds.

A preoccupation with complexity and change in world affairs leads naturally to a focus on the question of how change is to be identified and traced. At no point should methodological concerns obscure the effort to comprehend the substantive dynamics of change in world affairs, but neither should they be ignored. Progress toward greater understanding of transnational relations cannot be achieved without a continual sensitivity to the requirements of systematic analysis and the problems of measuring change. Accordingly, methodological concerns pervade all the ensuing chapters and are especially central to those of Part II.

No solution to the measurement problems is offered and none is even suggested. The essays of Part II deal more with the present state of the art than with what it ought to become in the light of changing global structures. In so doing all the essays highlight the enormous obstacles that will be encountered in adjusting the state of the art to better comprehend the transformations that are occurring. Measuring change is among the most difficult challenges to social scientific analysis and, obviously, it becomes even more acute when the change is occurring on such a large scale as would seem to mark world affairs today. If only one aspect of the global scene were undergoing transformation and the other aspects could then be held constant, it might be relatively easy to trace the direction and scope of the changes. But such a circumstance does not seem to obtain. Everything appears in flux, with each change in one area being both a response to and a source of change in other areas.

Clearly however, fluctuation and transformation on a large scale cannot be allowed to paralyze inquiry or a readiness to break free of conceptual jails. It is tempting, given so much change and the awesome task of measuring it, to shy away from the substantive implications of basic transformation and to continue reliance on conceptual equipment that treats the changes as mere perturbances in and temporary deviations from an otherwise resiliant and enduring structure of world affairs. Indeed, the methodological problems associated with continuity are so much more manageable than those linked to transformation that analytic biases in any field are always likely to favor the presumption that recurrent patterns rather than new departures sustain the course of events. Awareness of this likelihood, it seems to me, is the best solution to the measurement problem presently available. Until we are able to devise a satisfactory methodology for tracing and assessing change on a global scale, we can at least contest the impulse to ignore its implications by constantly acknowledging that our methodological biases orient us toward the measurement of continuities. It is this acknowledgment, I like to think, that constitutes the methodological concern which pervades the ensuing chapters.

I would argue, moreover, that in the context of this acknowledgment it is quite appropriate to proceed in a conceptual, even an impressionistic, fashion to evaluate and interpret the evidence that basic transformations are at work in world affairs. Hopefully in so doing we will evolve ever more precise hypotheses about the extent and depth of transnationalization that will, in turn, generate appropriate methodologies for testing them. But even if reconceptualization does not immediately suggest solutions to the measurement problem, we must not be deterred from our readiness to consider the world as undergoing transnationalization. To back away from such a perspective because we are unable to move from impressionistic analysis to systematic observation is to put methodological sensitivities ahead of substantive foci, and clearly such a priority is ill-founded at this time. Too much is at stake in world affairs to bring inquiry to a halt until better techniques for measuring change are developed. Knowledge is elusive at best, and thus surely it is preferable to develop understanding impressionistically and submit it for evaluation in the marketplace of ideas than to wait for the development of appropriate methodologies before proceeding.

Such a preference, at any rate, underlies the essays that follow. It is perhaps most evident in Chapter 7. That essay was conceived and developed with the intent of probing the processes through which the demands of the Third World are aggregated and articulated. The focus was thus a substantive one, but in important ways the inquiry turned out to be an exercise in methodological frustration. The latter pages of Chapter 7 depict this frustration and, in so doing, suggest the insufficiency of presently available methodological tools for uncovering the dynamics of interdependence.[3]

I offer no apologies, however, for the fact that all the essays, like Chapter 7, proceed impressionistically in the absence of adequate methodological tools. I would much rather that this book was methodologically sophisticated, but do not shrink from publishing it because such a sophistication is lacking. The ultimate test is how the substantive insights into the dynamics of a changing world fare in the marketplace. I would like to think they will prove challenging and useful, provoking elaboration and refinement that can eventually be subjected to more careful and systematic investigation.

[3]For a useful discussion of the methodological problems associated with probing concepts pertaining to mounting interdependence, see James Caporaso, 'Methodological Issues in the Measurement of Inequality, Dependence and Exploitation,' in S. Rosen and J. Kurth (eds.), *Testing Theories of Economic Imperialism* (Lexington, Mass.: Lexington Books, 1974).

Part One: The Impact of Change

2 International Studies in a Transnational World *

The title of this chapter is designed to be disconcerting. Here we are, it suggests, engaged in international studies at a time when the world is no longer organized along international lines. How could it be, the reader is supposed to wonder, that scholars are still probing a state-centered, international world when that world has moved on to a new set of structures in which the nation-state is no longer the only major source of action? Is it that scholars, like many others, are lagging? Or is it that the world is contradictory, with international structures still sufficiently predominant to warrant study even as transnational interactions have mounted sufficiently to warrant a new terminology? In short, where are we as students of world affairs? And where should we be?

These questions are not trivial. Profound changes in world affairs do seem to be at work, changes that challenge our long-standing assumptions, that defy our traditional concerns, that give pause to our methodological inclinations, that undermine our theoretical impulses, and that seem destined to reorient our foci of inquiry. I do not pretend to have a special comprehension of these changes and the structures towards which they are unfolding. I know only that the world scene is not what it used to be, and that therefore those of us who are professionally committed to probing international affairs are well advised to acknowledge our confusion, to ponder whether we are asking the right questions, and to identify the main problems we face.

*Reprinted from *Millennium: Journal of International Studies*, Vol. V, No.1 (Spring 1976), pp. 1-20, by permission of the Millennium Publishing Group, London.

Conceivably we are so confused that even the fact of change perplexes us. Conceivably the forms of world politics have undergone alteration while the underlying structures continue essentially unmodified. Possibly we have mistaken the evolution of new issues for the emergence of new institutions. Personally, I do not believe this to be the case. My political senses tell me that profound changes may be occurring at structural as well as immediately observable levels, but I also know that my senses have gone awry in the past and that more systematic techniques of measurement are needed if the extent and direction of underlying change is to be traced.

THREE CENTRAL PROBLEMS

This problem of measurement is, indeed, the first of three singled out here as central to any assessment of the present state of international studies. The second problem is the substantive side of this measurement question. That is, what are the phenomena that need to be measured for possible change? If we are to avoid a lag between our conceptions of the field and the field itself, we need to be clear about those processes and institutions through which underlying structures are sustained and those through which they are transformed. In the ensuing analysis I argue that the dynamics whereby authority is created, continued, and/or dissolved constitute the phenomena that need to be both more fully grasped and more adequately measured.

The third problem is more subtle. It concerns what I perceive to be our lack of puzzlement about the changing nature of world politics. We are confused by the change, but not genuinely puzzled by it. Below I attach a precise meaning to the idea of a 'genuine puzzle,' but it suffices here to note that such a puzzle is founded more on awe than confusion. Rather than our curiosities being aroused by the phenomena we observe, our defenses are heightened by them. Thus we tend to be quick to offer interpretations which explain away, or at least appear to account for, the changes that confuse us. I would — and do — argue that we are unlikely to achieve the substantive clarity and methodological precision needed to trace and comprehend the changing world scene until we allow ourselves to be puzzled — genuinely intrigued — by why the underlying patterns we discern unfold as they do. In other words, notwithstanding all the questions we pose and probe, we lack genuine puzzles comparable to Newton's bewilderment over why apples fall. In elaborating on this point, I shall have occasion to identify two puzzles that strike me as genuine and that, if solved, may go a long way towards clarifying the dynamics of authority that we need to grasp more fully.

INDICATORS OF CONFUSION

Before exploring these problems at length, it is useful to elaborate on the confusion that plagues us and the changes and contradictions that seem to have fostered it. That confusion prevails among us can be readily demonstrated if the degree to which we are surprised by developments is accepted as an indication of intellectual disarray. Virtually each day's news seems filled with surprises, with a bewildering array of developments that do not seem to fit in any of the explanatory niches on which we have long relied: we were surprised by the Nixon trip to China, by the Arab oil embargo, by the collapse of U.S. efforts in Vietnam. Arrangments that were once taken for granted now seem vulnerable to wide fluctuation: the United States could quit the United Nations, the sanctity of embassies may be violated, the bases for peace may be emerging in the Middle East. And who in their wildest speculation would have dared consider the possibility that an American president would resign, that an Egyptian president would travel to Israel, that Jawaharlal Nehru's daughter would lead India down authoritarian paths. Everywhere, it seems, established patterns have either come to an end or been greatly modified: the international monetary system has teetered near collapse, many governments have suffered noticeable declines in their mobilizing capacities, alliances have been fragmented. And, seemingly out of nowhere, new issues have suddenly emerged, issues so new and so different that much of our expertise suddenly seems tangential, if not hopelessly irrelevant. Now oceans, the biosphere, food and energy production and currency devaluations command our attention, compelling us to turn to marine biologists, physicists, argricultural economists, petroleum engineers and a host of other specialists before we can even begin to draw on our knowledge of diplomatic bargaining, crisis management and governmental decision-making to comment meaningfully about the course of events.

Admittedly I may be projecting my own confusion and surprise on to others. Conceivably most analysts have not been bewildered by such developments as the foregoing, seeing them rather as logical consequences of an increasingly interdependent and scarcity-ridden world. Yet there are signs that I am not alone in my perplexity. Recently there has been a spate of journal articles, monographs and textbooks that stress the mounting pace of interdependence and question where it might be leading, that highlight the growing influence of the multinational corporation and speculate that more than a few may come to dominate more than a few nation-states, that trace the widening range of transnational contacts across national boundaries and hypothesize that these may be replacing, as well as supplementing, intergovernmental ties, and that dwell on the new issues and question whether national governments will be able to cope with them. And even as the new actors, processes and issues are emphasized, so is the continued vitality of old ones acknowledged and described. Yet, with few exceptions, conspicuously missing from this burgeoning literature are any models or theories that seek to explain and accommodate the asymmetry of the old and the new. Instead, there tends to be a reliance on mere description, and much verbiage about it being too early to anticipate how the contradictory tendencies will be resolved, as if asymmetry must somehow give way to one or another form of symmetry. The tone is cautious, not confident; the scope is narrow, not bold; the future is presented as obscured, not shaped, by the present. The only predictions about the future explicitly made with a minimal degree of certainty is that it will be filled with unexpected developments, with surprises that cannot now be foreseen.

To be surprised by events is either to lack a theoretical perspective or to be caught with theory that fails adequately to explain and anticipate change. And to possess theory that inadequately accounts for the course of events is to be prey to the worst of analytic practices, to *post hoc* interpretation, to reification, to preoccupation with detail and the most recent occurrence, to reliance on endless narration, to reasoning by example, to pompous assertions about the hidden forces of history, to falling back on the personality, age and other quirks of leaders as explanations for changing patterns. It does not take much acquaintance with the literature of our field to realize that such tendencies abound.

Ideally, we ought not to be surprised by events. Even if our theories are insufficient, we ought at least to have developed the habit of allowing our variables to vary. If we are always inclined to ask about any structure or process, 'what other forms might it take, and under what conditions might these come into being?' then no major developments are likely to unfold that we did not previously identify. Our theories may not lead us to attach high probabilities to such developments, but our analytic habits ought at least to permit us to entertain the possibility of them. And once we entertain such possibilities, of course, we may be led to rethink our theories, rendering them more consistent with the structures that concern us. The fact that we are continuously surprised thus not only points up our confusion, it also suggests how we might move on to greater clarity, namely, through efforts to elaborate and perfect our theories of underlying structures.

ARE UNDERLYING STRUCTURES CHANGING?

Of the many underlying structures that can usefully be subjected to theoretical reconstruction, one strikes me as lying at the heart of our confusion and as being so basic that its theoretical clarification may be a precondition of progress on the others. I refer to the role of nation–states and the national governments that serve them in world politics. The post–war surge in their number, the advent of mini-states, the growth of multinational corporations, the emergence of a wide variety of other types of non–governmental associations with transnational memberships, the proliferation of supranational organizations, the surfacing of increasingly articulate and unified subnational groups demanding (and sometimes achieving) greater autonomy, the rising clamor of national publics, the deterioration of the international monetary system, the widening appreciation of the limits to economic growth, the burgeoning issues of conservation and pollution — these are but a few of the many developments that have converged in recent years to cast doubt on the ability of nation-states to command the loyalties and solve the problems of their citizens. At first glance, these developments suggest that the underlying structure of the centuries-old nation-state system is changing, that the national loyalties of individuals are no longer as intense or as state-centered as they once were, and that consequently the authority and legitimacy of nation-states has diminished. But further reflection gives rise to hesitation: have loyalties undergone radical transformation or are they merely fluctuating within a range that still accords prominence to the nation-state? If transformations in loyalty have undermined the authority of governments, where has that authority gone? Has a vacuum, so to speak, arisen with respect to the capacity to govern? Or are new authorities in the process of formation around the non-national actors that have recently emerged?

This ambivalence over whether or not the nation-state system is undergoing basic change pervades the literature.[1] At one extreme are those analysts who employ a framework in which the nation-state continues to be viewed as the prime international actor and the basis for the world's political organization, with all the other actors essentially subordinated to the requirements of the nation-state system. Those who adhere to this perspective acknowledge that nations are

[1] For a useful and thorough survey of the literature that contrasts a number of approaches to the implications of mounting interdependence, see Ann Alker and Hayward R. Alker, Jr., 'Four Interdependence Controversies: Contending Scholarly Perspectives,' in Hayward R. Alker, Jr., Lincoln P. Bloomfield and Nazli Choucri, *Analyzing Global Interdependence* (Cambridge, Mass.: Center for International Studies, Massachusetts Institute of Technology, 1974), Vol. I pp. 43–68.

increasingly interdependent and that they increasingly interpenetrate each other, that subnational groups and transnational organizations are having a greater impact on the course of events and that some supranational organizations (notably the European Community) have acquired substantial influence. Nevertheless, they contend that the instruments of coercion and violence are still basically under the control of national governments and that the authority of the nation-state thus remains supreme. Those who view the nation-state as primary argue that the advent of a multiplicity of new international actors on the world scene has not altered the structure of the global system in any significant manner. They see the new actors as supplementing, rather than supplanting, nation-states. From their point of view, interdependence ought to be treated not as a source of change in the underlying structure of world politics, but as a problem for nation-states that poses a variety of policy options. Indeed, the analysts who continue to use the nation-state framework cite a number of examples of governments opting to achieve greater autonomy and to reduce their dependence on external sources. In short, 'there is nothing automatic about interdependence . . . [It] can be onerous or promising, costly or cheap, symmetrical or asymmetrical. But in the final analysis it is not foreordained but optional.'[2] And it is national governments, those who cling to the nation-state framework argue, that exercise the options.

At the other extreme are analysts who espouse a framework in which the erosion of the authority of the nation-state is viewed as so thoroughgoing as to warrant abandoning the nation-state perspective altogether. From this point of view, the nation-state has been replaced by a world society, with the stresses, strains and structures that characterize any society. Those who espouse this framework do not contend that this newly emergent world society is peaceful or even that it is necessarily destined to be harmonious. They simply contend that greater understanding will come from treating world politics as the politics of a world society than from treating it as politics among nations. They argue further that the nation-state framework leads to the collection of data which, by the very fact of being focused on the nation-state, obscures the extent to which the nation-state has been superseded as a vital international actor.[3]

[2] A particularly clear and cogent exposition of how and why the nation-state system will continue to be viable in the face of mounting interdependence is developed by Lincoln P. Bloomfield (from whom the quote is taken, on pp. 70–71), 'Some Policy Implications,' in *ibid.*, Vol. I, pp. 64–94. See also John H. Herz, 'The Territorial State Revisited: Reflections on the Future of the Nation-State,' *Polity*, Vol I, No. 1, 1968, pp. 12–34.

[3] For a presentation of this framework, see John W. Burton, *World Society* (London: Cambridge University Press, 1972), and John W. Burton *et al.*, *The Study of World Society: A London Perspective* (Pittsburgh: International Studies Association, 1974).

A variety of perspectives can be found in the literature that lie between the nation-state and world society extremes. Of course, being somewhere in the middle of the continuum, these perspectives are especially ambivalent, particularly in their shared view that the authority of the nation-state has undergone substantial erosion even though 'governments are generally the most *powerful* actors because of their monopoly over military capabilities.'[4] Some analysts resolve this ambivalence by treating the changing capabilities of the nation-state as an opportunity to design strategies for hastening its decline and for encouraging the emergence of future world orders in which the nation-state is no longer predominant.[5] Others resolve it simply by elaborately describing the proliferation of ties across national boundaries, the implicit assumption being that the range and variety of ties must inevitably lead to a lessening of the nation-state's authority.[6] Still others resolve their ambivalence by claiming that the decline of the nation-state's authority in non-military issue areas has been great enough to justify making issues, rather than national governments, the prime analytic focus. This framework, labelled the world political process model, first identifies the issues that command international attention and then explores how they get handled or resolved by the relevant actors. Nation-states are acknowledged to be central to the processing of issues, but it is argued that by starting with the issues, one allows for the possibility that other types of actors may have as much, or even more, influence on the disposition or perpetuation of an issue.[7] Still

[4] Richard A. Falk, *A Study of Future Worlds* (New York: Free Press, 1975), p. 59. Italics in original.

[5] These analysts, from a variety of countries, are associated in the World Order Models Project. See, for example, *ibid.*; Saul H. Mendlovitz (ed), *On the Creation of a Just World Order: Preferred Worlds for the 1990's* (New York: Free Press, 1975); and Rajni Kothari, *Footsteps Into the Future: Diagnosis of the Present World and a Design for an Alternative* (New York: Free Press, 1974).

[6] Alger, for example, traces the flow of interaction across national boundaries through 'successive stages of analytic differentiation,' starting with an 'undifferentiated nation-state view' in which governments interact as 'billiard balls' that are identical in structure, and proceeding through more than fifteen stages of differentiation in which the processes of interaction among individuals, organizations, sectors, cities, non-governmental international organizations and international governmental organizations are delineated, either as they occur directly or as they unfold indirectly, via the mechanism of nation-state foreign policies. See Chadwick F. Alger, *Liberating Publics to Perceive, Evaluate and Control the International Dimension of Their Daily Lives* (Columbus, Ohio: Mershon Center, The Ohio State University, mimeo., 1975).

[7] For an elaboration of this framework, see J.R. Handelman, J.A. Vasquez, M.K. O'Leary and W.D. Coplin, 'Color it Morgenthau: A Data-Based Assessment of Quantitative International Relations Research,' a paper presented to the Annual Meeting of the International Studies Association (Syracuse: Syracuse University, mimeo., 1973). For a similar formulation, in which nation-states are seen as unwilling or incapable of paying the costs of independence, and thus as ready to pursue policies which allow for multinational regulation, see Karl Kaiser, 'Transnational Politics: Toward a Theory of Multinational Politics,' *International Organization*, Vol. XXV, Autumn 1971, pp. 790–817.

another framework through which analysts who reject the nation-state and world society extremes resolves their ambivalence involves a view that world politics are changing in the direction of greater interdependence among *both* governmental and non-governmental actors. The more transnational interactions occur among various segments of society, these analysts reason, the more do government officials in agencies other than the central foreign policy organs become involved in efforts to control the flow of events, and this enlargement of policy-making beyond the established foreign policy machinery has the consequence of making the range of interdependence of governments correspondingly greater.[8]

THE PROBLEM OF MEASUREMENT

One obvious reason why the various approaches to the changing role of the nation-state range so widely, and are either contradictory or ambivalent, is the lack of concrete indicators of the changes that are alleged to have occurred or are presumed to be occurring. All concerned agree that the world scene has been marked by substantial increases in the number of non-governmental actors and, accordingly, in the number of interactions across national boundaries in which governments are not the only participants. And they also seem to share the assumption that these increases have been of such a magnitude and scope as to alter the relative importance of governments, the dependency of actors on each other, and thus the underlying structure of the global system. Governments are still considered to be prime actors, but all the observers view their primacy as diminished and, in one case, as having moved in the direction of secondary status, yielding their influence to a multiplicity of subnational, transnational and supranational actors. In none of the formulations, however, is any attempt made to measure the changes or to develop operational definitions that yield concrete and comparable cases with which to trace fluctuations in the extent, direction and importance of the new patterns that are presumed to underlie the emergence of new global

[8] Robert O. Keohane and Joseph S. Nye, Jr., 'Transgovernmental Relations and International Organizations,' *World Politics*, Vol. XXVII, October 1974, pp. 39–62. The reasoning of these two authors, whose work has been central in focusing both theoretical and empirical attention on the emergence and role of transnational actors, is further elaborated in Robert O. Keohane and Joseph S. Nye, Jr. (eds.), *Transnational Relations and World Politics* (Cambridge: Harvard University Press, 1972), and in Robert O Keohane and Joseph S. Nye, Jr., 'International Interdependence and Integration' in Fred I. Greenstein and Nelson W. Polsby (eds.), *Handbook of Political Science* (Reading, Mass.: Addison-Wesley, 1975), Vol. 8, pp. 363–414.

structures. Given the lack of evidence descriptive of developments through time, it is hardly surprising that the several formulations derive divergent and contradictory interpretations of the nature of the changes which they commonly agree have occurred and continue to be unfolding. In the absence of a data base of comparable cases against which impressions can be checked, it is all too easy to move from identifying the emergence of new issues and new ways of processing them to asserting the superiority of a model of global politics in which issue-clusters replace governments as the central units of analysis. In the absence of comparable cases, it is all too easy to construct a logic in which the proliferation of transnational ties and actors leads inevitably to a diminution of the scope of governmental authority and the potential emergence of any one of a number of new structures of world order. In the absence of an adequate data base, it is all too easy to posit governments as still retaining ultimate authority and yet being compelled by mounting interdependence to exercise the option of yielding some authority in order to facilitate multinational management of new problems that are not circumscribed by national boundaries.

This is not to say that the efforts to probe the implications of mounting interdependence are short on evidence. On the contrary, the various studies are as much empirical as they are speculative and theoretical. But the evidence offered is not appropriate. The case for asserting the presence of change is made through the citation and elaboration of empirical examples. Often, to be sure, the examples are startling and compelling, clearly suggesting that long-standing processes and established patterns are different from what they used to be, and that non-governmental actors are having consequences across national boundaries which once would have been unimaginable. Jarring and revealing as they may be, however, examples are not proof. They reveal dynamics, but they do not depict patterns. They alert the analyst to change, but they do not trace change. Many comparable cases — i.e. cases in which the same variables and the interaction among them are portrayed unfolding through time — need to be examined before the presence of underlying patterns can be confidently asserted. One never knows whether the single example represents a central tendency or an exception, and even similarity across several examples is not ordinarily sufficient to warrant clear-cut conclusions. Many comparable cases are needed, and these need to be compiled in such a way that they depict the interacting variables at various points in time, thus allowing analysts to assess whether the observations made at each time-point represent changes from those made at the previous time-points and, if so, to trace the pace, direction and intensity of change.

I have purposely refrained from characterizing the evidence we need as quantitative data, preferring instead to refer to it as 'many comparable cases,' because the notion of quantification conjures up images of great amounts of data, perhaps running into the thousands. Such an inference could prove paralyzing, as obviously there are not enough clear-cut confrontations between non-governmental and governmental actors to establish data bases on such a scale. Faced with a call for quantified data, we might be inclined to argue that the lack of thousands of available cases means that we are probing for patterns that cannot be systematically traced, an argument that is self-defeating, profoundly contradictory (if there are patterns that cannot be traced, how is it known that they exist?), and likely to lead to reliance on only those examples that affirm prior impressions.

The key to the problem of evidence, in other words, lies in the comparability of cases and not their number. If the same variables and their interaction can be adequately and similarly measured in each of the cases examined, then the number of cases need not be very great, perhaps not running into more than the tens or hundreds, for the presence of patterns to be reliably established.[9] Surely there are enough clear-cut instances of multinational corporations at work, or other transnational actors interacting, and of new issues being addressed, to allow for comparable inquiries on such a limited scale. More accurately, if such cases do not exist in the tens or hundreds, then what is the justification for claiming that basic changes in under-lying structure are occurring? If data bases on this scale cannot be constructed, might not the compelling examples that seem to signify change be viewed simply as deviant cases, as interesting exceptions that demonstrate the continued viability of the long-established patterns?

I do not mean to imply that because the number of cases required is not very great, the task of developing adequate comparability is easily accomplished. For the variables examined must not only allow for comparison, they must also clearly reflect the structural phenomena that are of interest to us as possibly undergoing change. Accurate and reliable measurements are of little value unless they measure the proper variables; and, unfortunately, our speculations about changing global structures involve variables that are not readily observed. We are interested not only in changing patterns of inter-action, but also in the authority and legitimacy that attaches to them and the loyalties on which they rest. Such variables do not lend themselves

[9]For an important discussion in which it is shown how comparability can be achieved without excessive quantification through the analysis of 'crucial' cases, see Harry Eckstein, 'Case Study and Theory in Political Science,' in Fred I. Greenstein and Nelson W. Polsby, *Handbook of Political Science* (Reading, Mass.: Addison-Wesley, 1975), Vol. 7, pp. 79–137. See also P.G. Herbst, *Behavioral Worlds: The Study of Single Cases* (London: Tavistock Publications, 1970).

to direct observation, or at least considerable ingenuity may be needed to tease out and measure their operation, with the result that constructing adequate samples of cases that are both comparable and relevant may require extensive and painstaking effort.

I believe these measurement problems can be solved *if* we can clearly delineate and delimit the structural changes we wish to trace and the variables they embrace. The '*if*' is a big one, as it means our comprehension of global structures must be deep and thorough, allowing us to distinguish among the sequences and processes that converge to sustain them. Such a comprehension would seem to defy accomplishment inasmuch as we seek to develop it at the very time the structures may be undergoing change. Tracing the emergence of the structural changes that resulted in the nation-state system is not particularly difficult with the hindsight of centuries,[10] but we are part of the structures whose changes we now seek to understand, and attaining the conceptual clarity and analytic perspective necessary to grasp them is thus a mind-boggling challenge. Yet, rather than feeling paralyzed by the problems of measurement, we should recall that the conceptual task of disaggregating the relevant global structures so that their component parts are exposed — and thus measurable — is far more difficult than performing the empirical task of recording observations, Indeed, once these component parts are conceptually identified, it ought not to take much creativity to formulate operational measures for them that can be applied to their interaction across time and in the context of comparable cases.[11]

There is another reason to emphasize the large extent to which solution of the measurement problem is preceded by, and dependent on, the achievement of clear-cut conceptualization of the components of global structure. Such an emphasis serves to guard against the temptation of focusing on variables that are most easily subjected to quantitative analysis, but that do not adequately reflect the structural changes that provoked inquiry in the first place. The tendency to measure the growth or decline of interdependence by tracing increases or decreases in international transactions provides a useful illustration of this point. The flow of people, goods, services, money and ideas across national boundaries is relatively simple to observe. Governments and many other kinds of organizations keep statistics on such transactions, and they have been doing so for decades. Although such statistics are not always compiled exactly as the investigator would prefer, they are generally reliable and reasonably accessible. Thus analysts do not

[10] For example, see Charles Tilly (ed.), *The Formation of National States in Western Europe* (Princeton: Princeton University Press, 1975).

[11] For a discussion of how any variable that is adequately understood can be rendered operational, see James N. Rosenau, *The Dramas of Political Life* (North Scituate, Mass.: Duxburg, 1980), pp. 220–224.

have to 'make' data in the sense of bringing together a number of disparate observations.[12] They need merely gather and standardize the tabulations compiled across long stretches of time; and then, by assuming that the thousands, even millions, of transactions summarized in their standardized tabulations are reflective of the degree to which peoples and societies are interdependent, the users of such data can offer seemingly precise measurements of how underlying structures have undergone change.[13]

Useful and important as such studies are, they suffer from an inferential leap induced, as it were, by the ready availability of a plethora of longitudinal data. Transactions across national boundaries are surely an expression of interdependence (else why would the transactions occur?), but the inferential leap which equates them with interdependence is misleading if the main concern is that of tracing whether the state-centered structures of world politics have undergone alteration. Greater flows of non-governmental transactions may indeed be a prime prerequisite of an increasingly decentralized world and a decrease in the authority of nation-states; but it is not inconceivable that transnational ties can mount substantially without a corresponding decline in the importance of governmental actors. Increasing transnational ties, in other words, can be viewed as a necessary, but not sufficient, source of underlying structural change. To measure changes of this kind requires, as indicated earlier, conceptual clarity as to the nature of the structures involved and the sequences through which they can undergo transformations. Once these are clearly delineated, it should be evident that data depicting longitudinal transaction flows will not be sufficient (albeit they may still be useful in some respects) and that many cases are needed in which the transactions also reflect flows of authority, legitmacy and loyalty.

A similar, and perhaps even more dangerous, way in which a premature stress on data tends to lead inquiry astray concerns the relative ease with which economic variables can be measured in comparison with political phenomena. For obvious reasons, data depicting the dependency of consumers on producers abroad are much more abundant than those descriptive of shared dependence on the same sources of authority. Furthermore, the economic dependencies revealed by

[12] For a useful discussion on what is involved in 'making' data, see J. David Singer, 'Data Making in International Relations,' *Behavioral Science*, Vol. 10 January 1965, pp. 68–80.

[13] Indeed, a recent effort along this line, replete with impressive data depicting the flow of capital, trade, immigration, foreign students, mail, telegrams and phone-calls across national boundaries over decades and (in the case of capital) centuries, did uncover a long-term trend in the direction of greater transactions and (allegedly) interdependence. See Peter J. Katzenstein, 'International Interdependence: Some Long-Term Trends and Recent Changes,' *International Oranization*, Vol. 29, Autumn 1975, pp. 1021–34.

economic data are more self-contained and less amorphous than their political counterparts, with the result that they are also more easily understood, thereby tempting analysts to formulate their analytic problems in such a way that interdependence is conceived as confined to essentially economic processes. Indeed, I have the clear impression that most of the literature on the growing transnationalization of world affairs derives, explicitly or otherwise, from the assumption that needs and wants in the economic realm have expanded, and that the capacities of nations to satisfy these demands out of their own resources have declined. And, undoubtedly, economic interdependence has increased rapidly, perhaps even much more rapidly than any other kind. Yet it is not concern with economic interdependence that we express when we wonder about underlying changes in global structure and the relative importance of nation-states. Rather our concern is profoundly political — what actors allocate what values, and with what effects — and the more we rely on the vast amounts of economic data, cases and examples that can be easily accumulated and assessed, the more will we be forced to conceive of interdependence as an economic phenomenon, and the less will we be inclined to focus directly on the structural changes that perplex us.

THE PROBLEM OF CONCEPTUALIZATION

This is not the place to develop answers as to the nature, pace and direction of the changes that are transforming the underlying structures of world politics. Time permits only an initial effort to break down the problem into more manageable analytic components, specifying as precisely as possible what variables must vary if patterned alterations in the relative influence of national governments and transnational actors are to be sufficiently great to warrant the conclusion that we live in one of those few eras in international history that can truly be called turning-points. In short, I want to attempt to clarify what it is that has changed when our analytic sensitivities tell us that a transformation in underlying structures is taking place.

As previously indicated, disaggregation of the problem leads me to focus on authority structures — on those patterned hierarchical relationships between superordinates and subordinates, in which the directives or policies of the former are felt to be obligatory, and thus accepted, by the latter. Authority exists when those towards whom directives are issued unthinkingly modify their behavior in compliance with the actions enforcing the directives. Stated differently authority is possessed by those whose directives evoke 'legitmacy sentiments,'[14] i.e. they precipitate an unquestioning readiness to initiate or limit behavior in the prescribed ways. If directives are issued that do not evoke the habits of compliance on which legitimacy sentiments rest, and thus either fail to modify behavior or do so through the exercise of force, then either they do not emanate from an authority structure or, in the case of the use of force, they spring from illegitimate authority.

Although authority structures may be relevant to the processes whereby influence, loyalty and citizenship are established and maintained, it is important that they be not equated with any of these concepts. Authority structures differ from influence structures in that the latter can involve relationships between superordinates (such as two nation-states); and, under those circumstances, one actor modifies the behavior of another not because the directives are viewed as legitimate, but rather because the directives are judged to be reasonable, or at least preferable to others that might be issued. Authority structures differ from loyalty structures in that the latter are not sustained through the issuance of, and compliance with, directives: subordinates may feel faithful toward the superordinates to whose directives they attach legitimacy, but their loyalty can be expressed in a variety of other ways besides compliance with directives. Authority structures are different from citizenship in that the latter consists of a generalized set of rights and obligations to be found in law rather than the interaction of superordinates and subordinates.

The nation-state is central to modern history because of its ability to preside over other authority structures, to tap their loyalties and to define the scope of citizenship of their members. The individuals of a nation-state are organized into a vast array of different types of social systems — such as the family, the school, the firm, the army, the city and the region — each of which may be sustained by directives in which superordinates seek to initiate, limit or otherwise modify the behavior of subordinates.[15] In many, if not all, of these subnational units, moreover, the subordinates are likely to have developed at least some legitimacy sentiments towards at least some of the directives

[14] This useful phrase is Harry Eckstein's, as is the conception of authority as founded on directives passing from superordinates to subordinates. See Harry Eckstein, 'Authority Patterns: A Structural Basis for Political Inquiry,' *American Political Science Review*, Vol. 67, December 1973, pp. 1142–1161. My conception of authority and legitimacy, which underlies the analysis presented here and which parallels but differs in some respects from Eckstein's is elaborated in my *The Dramas of Political Life* pp. 94–99.

[15] Elsewhere, I have argued that the dynamics whereby one actor initiates, limits, or otherwise modifies, the behavior of another actor constitutes the heart of the process that distinguishes politics from other forms of activity. See James N. Rosenau, *The Scientific Study of Foreign Policy* (London: Frances Pinter Publishers, revised ed., 1980), Chapter 10.

issued by the superordinates. Workers, for example, may or may not feel loyalty with respect to their employers, but normally they habitually comply with those of the latters' directives in which their work assignments are specified and made. Likewise, the habit of compliance marks much of the behavior of children towards their parents, of students towards their teachers, of soldiers towards their officers, of city residents towards their public officials, and so on. While authority structures can thus be said to pervade nation-states, the latter are distinguished by an authority structure that has historically defined and superseded all the others. That is, the historic pattern is one in which the authorities of the nation-state have issued directives that establish the limits within which the superordinates in the lesser authority structures may issue directives, and that evoke legitimacy sentiments which supersede those evoked by the lesser authorities. Whenever the directives of nation-states and subnational actors have been in conflict, in other words, legitimacy has attached to those of the former and not the latter. Subnational actors may be the focus of deep-seated loyalties; they may often successfully influence national governments to adopt directives consistent with their goals; and on occasion they may even resort to violence in an effort to secede from their nation or overthrow its government; but the central tendency across more than three centuries is one in which the legitimacy of their authority has been confined by, and subordinate to, that enjoyed by the national system of which they are a subsystem.

But what happens when authority structures span national boundaries; when the superordinate is located in one nation-state, the subordinate is in another, and the directives issued by the former evoke legitimacy sentiments in the latter without being intercepted, revised or otherwise constrained by the governments who maintain the national boundaries? And what happens when a vast proliferation occurs in the number of such structures? These are the questions that, it seems to me, our analytic sensitivities are raising when we are led to wonder whether underlying change is transforming the global system.

It follows from the foregoing conceptualization that underlying change would result if a goodly proportion of the ever-increasing number of transnational ties were to become authority structures, and if these embraced legitimacy sentiments that superseded those directed towards the nation-state. Stated differently, the importance of nation-states relative to other actors undergoes noteworthy change when non-governmental, transnational, superordinate-subordinate relationships multiply to the extent that the directives issued by the other actors often evoke habitual compliance against the wishes of those who wield authority on behalf of nation-states.

This way of approaching the question of underlying change has a number of advantages. One, and perhaps the most important, is that it prevents analysis from being paralyzed by the capacity of nation-states to evoke compliance through resort to force. Many observers are unable to trace the changing importance of nation-states because their possession of military capabilities is seen as giving them an ultimate authority that does not change and that enables them to prevail whenever they wish. In effect, they cannot disaggregate the problem because one dimension of superordinate-subordinate relationships is viewed as overriding. By conceiving of as many such relationships as there are types of directives that evoke legitimacy sentiments, however, it becomes clear that actors can become more or less important *even though* the ultimate sanctions are wielded by national governments. For, obviously, governments cannot resort to their ultimate authority each time a transnational pattern begins to resemble an authority structure (i.e. each time those within the pattern who issue directives begin to become the focus of legitimacy sentiments). Governments may seek to interpret or disrupt the proliferation of transnational authority structures through nationalization of companies, expropriation of resources, immigration regulations, customs procedures, and a host of other laws designed to govern the flow of people, goods and money; but the diversity of these structures and the limits of their scope make continuous reliance on ultimate authority impossible. Only when the nation-state's authority over its physical security or its capacity to issue any directives is challenged, is it likely to turn to ultimate sanctions. Otherwise it can only experience an erosion of its authority if it is not able to prevent the proliferation of transnational structures to which overriding legitimacy sentiments attach.

Another advantage of probing global changes in terms of authority structures is that such an approach provides a means of assessing change in terms of substantive issue differences. If the transformation of the global system is essentially asymmetrical in that the nation-state continues to predominate in certain issue areas while other types of actors have emerged as central in others,[16] then the tendency towards asymmetry ought to become manifest in the degree to which transnational authority structures are developing in the various issue areas. Indeed, such an approach provides a handle for comparing the dynamics of issue areas, for tracing bargaining across issue areas, and for assessing the differences, the similarities and the interplay among the roles played by national, transnational and supranational actors with respect to both the traditional and newly emergent issues. In so doing,

[16] For a formulation that rests on this notion of asymmetry, see James N. Rosenau, 'Adaptive Politics in an Interdependent World,' *Orbis*, Vol. XVI, Spring, 1972, pp. 153-173 (reproduced here as Chapter 4).

this approach also serves to inhibit any inclinations we may have to reach premature and grandiose conclusions that pronounce either the end or the triumph of the nation-state system and assert either the inherent superiority or inferiority of other models of global politics. With a disaggregated approach to authority structures, we can more meaningfully trace a middle position in which the nation-state is viewed as having declined in importance even as it continues to be important.

Still another advantage of this perspective is that it facilitates analysis of confrontations between nation-states and other actors, particularly the multinational corporation. The literature on transnational politics is pervaded with discussions of how the corporate giants of the world of economics, and the national giants (and, in the case of mini-states, pygmies) of the world of politics, are unavoidably and endlessly on a collision course, but almost all of these analyses reify the colliding actors, treating them as uniform in their outlook, unvarying in their motivation and constant in their behavior towards each other.[17] By investigating the interaction between public and corporate officials as founded on directives which they issue to each other, and then ascertaining whether compliance occurs and, if so, whether legitimacy sentiments attach to it, the collisions can be examined for what they are — concrete sequences of action undertaken by identifiable individuals whose loyalties may or may not be divided and may or may not coincide with their sentiments toward hierarchical authority — rather than as metaphorical and amorphous clashes between abstract entities.

To have identified advantages in the concepts of authority and legitimacy is not, of course, to specify how they should be applied. But the above means of probing the role of the multinational corporation points the way. A wide range of transnational relationships need to be disaggregated in terms of the roles of which they are comprised, the flow of directives between the role occupants, the extent to which the directives modify behavior, and the degree of legitimacy that attaches to any compliance the directives may evoke. In each case, the parties to the relationship are presumed also to occupy citizen roles, and thus to be exposed to contradictory directives from

[17] For discussions of collisions between national governments and multinational corporations, see George W. Ball, 'Citizenship and the Multinational Corporation,' *Social Research*, Vol. 41, Winter 1974; Samuel P. Huntington, 'Transnational Organizations in World Politics,' *World Politics*, Vol. XXV, April 1973, pp. 333-369; Joseph S. Nye, Jr., 'Multinational Corporations in World Politics,' *Foreign Affairs*, Vol. 53, October 1974, pp. 153-175; Robert O. Keohane and Joseph S. Nye, Jr., 'Transnational Relations and World Politics: A Conclusion,' in Keohane and Nye (eds.), *Transnational Relations and World Politics*, pp. 372-74; and Raymond Vernon (ed.), *Big Business and the State: Changing Relations in Western Europe* (Cambridge: Harvard University Press, 1974).

nation-state superordinates on the one hand and those emanating from their transnational organizations on the other. The way in which these conflicting directives are handled — i.e. which ones prevail and under what circumstances — then serves as an empirical data point, as the material out of which each of the many comparable case studies needed to solve the measurement problem can be constructed.

Some illustrations can perhaps clarify this procedure. Consider labor leaders or workers who are asked to go out on strike on behalf of the grievances that their counterparts abroad have against another branch of the corporation: after the persuasion and bargaining has run its course, do they heed the directives of their employers and avoid the possibility of retaliatory corporate actions which, in effect, transfer their jobs out of their country, or do they opt for union solidarity and create the possibility of generating leverage against the corporation as a multinational entity? Consider corporate executives located abroad who are asked for a bribe in order to be allowed to conduct their business effectively in the host country: do they turn to the ambassador of their own country for legal support in resisting the bribe, or do they pay it and avoid risking a loss of opportunities? Indeed, how are executives of multinational corporations likely to respond when the foreign policies of the countries of which they are citizens run counter to the profit requirements of their companies? Towards which directives will their legitimacy sentiments tend? Or consider transcontinental airline pilots who are asked by their international pilots' association not to land in countries which receive hijackers, but which their country of citizenship does not wish to offend: which of the two authority structures are they likely to treat as superordinate? Consider, too, bureaucrats who are persuaded by their counterparts in foreign governments that the policies of their governments are ill-founded: do they ignore, or even work against, directives of their formal superordinates in order to serve transnational values, or do they give higher priority to their national roles? Finally, consider the contrast between the terrorist and the tourist, and what the former are likely to do when government officials order them to surrender and what the latter are likely to do when border guards order them to show their passports.[18]

The answers to these questions — and to many similar ones that could be asked about a variety of other roles — are not self-evident. The ease with which it is perhaps possible to feel confident about the response to the last two extreme examples, highlights our uncertainty about the changes that have occurred in the authority structures of the many types of transnational relationship that fall between the

[18] For an elaboration of the continuum along which the tourist and the terrorist are opposite extremes, see Chapter 5.

readiness of the tourist to abide by nation-state directives and the unwillingness of the terrorist to do so. One can imagine some labor leaders, corporation executives, airline pilots and bureaucrats — not to mention bankers, scientists, students, educators, journalists, judges, and the occupants of many other transnational roles — who emulate the tourist's habitual acceptance of the nation-state system, and others who incline towards the normative reasons (though not the practices) through which terrorists become alienated from governments and deny their legitimacy. But which pattern constitutes the central tendency is far from clear; and clarity is not likely to be achieved until many comparable cases of such role conflicts in every major occupational field and every major issue area are compiled.

So we have come full circle, back again to empirical questions and the need for empirical data. We return to these questions, however, with conceptual equipment that should facilitate answering them with greater confidence. Many methodological problems — such as the need for operational definitions that distinguish legitimacy sentiments from other forms of behavior — still remain to be resolved, but their resolutions ought to be more easily attainable now that we have more clearly established what it is that can be expected to undergo change if underlying transformations in global politics occur.

THE NEED FOR GENUINE PUZZLES

But, alas, the conceptual clarity and methodological precision needed to compile many cases do not automatically follow from a more clear-cut specification of the phenomena to be investigated. One more ingredient is needed, one that motivates us to be ever more precise and relentless in the gathering of empirical materials. The compilation of case studies can be tedious and the temptation to cut corners through imprecision can be considerable. We need, as it were, the psychic wherewithal to press on, the curiosity not to be deterred by tedium or diverted by ambiguous materials. We need, as indicated earlier, to be so genuinely puzzled by the processes we are investigating that we remain continuously in awe of them as we reduce our confusion about them.[19]

Genuine puzzles are not easily framed. They are not simply bewilderment; nor do they come into existence merely by asking what is transpiring or why it transpires the way it does. Genuine puzzles derive from general 'what' and 'why' questions, but they are more focused. They identify processes with specified outcomes, as well as

[19] For a more extended discussion of this point, see James N. Rosenau, 'Puzzlement in Foreign Policy,' in *The Scientific Study of Foreign Policy*, Chapter 9.

express curiosity about sources. It is not enough, for example, to ask what particular types of transnational actor do, or even why they do what they do. Such questions are so open-ended that they tend neither to sustain our curiosity nor press us to refine our concepts and methods. Rather they are so broad that they tend to appear overwhelming, thereby encouraging us to go our separate ways and give in to our immediate concerns and investigate whatever aspect of the problem intrigues us at the moment. Such open-ended questions, in other words, can only inhibit the accumulation of comparable cases but, even worse, they can mislead us into believing that we are engaged in comparable inquiries when in fact we are not. A number of analysts may think they are involved in a cumulative enterprise because they share interest in the initial question of why transnational actors do what they do; but since transnational actors do a variety of different things, the shared question accomplishes no more than giving each analyst the license to investigate whatever he or she finds interesting.

A question that asks about a sequence of activities that have particular consequences, on the other hand, narrows our analytic concern and imposes limits within which our inquiries must be contained. The specified consequences serve as boundaries beyond which those moved to investigate the question are disinclined to go, with the result that case studies undertaken to answer the question are likely to be disciplined and cumulative. Because such questions posit identifiable outcomes as part of the puzzle, moreover, our curiosity is not likely to lag for want of a focus. There is no need to feel overwhelmed and paralyzed by such a question because it is phrased in such a way as to be potenially answerable — i.e. it will be answered when the specified outcomes are explained — rather than being open-ended and subject to a multiplicity of answers, no one of which is sufficient.

Of course, this kind of question must also be provocative and not trivial, which is to say that it must spring from wonder that the specified outcomes occur so regularly, from an appreciation that the sources of the regularity are not simple and self-evident, and thus from a constant awe that the processes we observe give rise to the specified outcomes. If a question is provocative in this way, and if it is precise in the outcomes it specifies, I call it a 'genuine puzzle.' Newton's question of why apples fall is a genuine puzzle, one that compelled him to press on to creative conclusions because he asked about a phenomenon with a specified outcome. Had he asked 'why do apples do what they do?' — a question which lacks a precise outcome — he and his disciples might well have gone off in a variety of unrelated directions ('why do apples grow on trees?'; 'why do they sometimes host worms?'; 'why do they have yellow, red, and green skins?'), eventually to lose interest in the subject without contributing to such an important advance in our understanding of the world around us.

It is much easier to ask open-ended questions than to generate genuine puzzles. The open-ended question does not require much forethought. Since one does not have to be precise about outcomes, one can simply ask whatever comes first to mind, without pausing to consider how or why things culminate in the form that they do. The open-ended question can thus be self-deceptive: it can lead us to think we are expressing curiosity, when in fact the asking of it can be a substitute for reflection about the problem. A genuine puzzle, however, must come out of curiosity, since one has to be perplexed about an effect before one can raise questions about causation. Genuine puzzles are thus disciplining; they come out of repeated observations and they compel us to sort out of all the phenomena we observe those that are both patterned and intriguing. In other words, genuine puzzles are more difficult than open-ended questions because they force us to think, to understand our subject so well that we believe we perceive outcomes that occur regularly, or at least with sufficient regularity to be patterned.

This conception of genuine puzzles as necessary to the sustenance and disciplining of cumulative inquiry provides a good measure of the confusion and disarray that prevails in international studies today. Neither the growing literature on transnational relations nor the growing concern over underlying changes in global structure is conspicuously marked by genuine puzzles. None of the recurring questions that pervade the literature — 'has underlying change occurred?'; 'is interdependence mounting?'; 'is the nation-state still as important as ever?'; 'are there issue areas where actors other than nation-states are most influential?' — meets both criteria of genuine puzzlement. These are not only non-trivial questions, but also open-ended ones, leaving unspecified any outcomes that are preceived to flow regularly from the proliferating processes of interdependence. And much the same can be said about the queries that organize any of the major works in the field. Consider, for example, the questions posed at the outset of the highly regarded and widely cited symposium edited by Keohane and Nye, questions which the editors treat as constituting the five central concerns of their book:

> 1) What seems to be the net effect of transnational relations on the abilities of governments to deal with their environments? To what extent and how have governments suffered from a 'loss of control' as a result of transnational relations? 2) What are the implications of transnational relations for the study of world politics? Is the state-centric view, which focuses on the interstate system, an adequate analytic framework for the investigation of contemporary reality? 3) What are the effects of transnational relations on the allocation of value and specifically on asymmetries or inequalities between

> states? Who benefits from transnational relations, who loses, who controls transnational networks, and how is this accomplished? 4) What are the implications of transnational relations for United States foreign policy? Insofar as the United States is indeed preponderant in transnational activity, what dangers as well as opportunities does this present to American policymakers? 5) What challenges do transnational relations raise for international organizations as conventionally defined? To what extent may new international organizations be needed, and to what extent may older organizations have to change in order to adapt creatively to transnational phenomena?[20]

Not a single one of these questions embraces a specified outcome. All of them can be answered in a multitude of ways, many of which are contradictory and none of which is likely to encourage confidence that confusion is giving way to comprehension. At first glance they may seem like challenging questions, but the challenge is likely to wane as it becomes clear that virtually any response to them is appropriate. Indeed, on second thought, they may not even seem challenging: not one begins with the word 'why' and thus not one is even potentially puzzling.

It would be presumptuous of me to claim that the queries to which I have been led by the disaggregated approach to authority structures outlined above constitute genuine puzzles. Given my characterization of the literature as lacking in puzzlement, such a claim would imply that I have a better understanding of the changing nature of world politics than anyone else. Surely I do not. Indeed, the more I have tried to identify patterns on the current scene that are genuinely puzzling, the more confused I have become. However, the disaggregated approach does point to some aspects of the current scene that strike me as awesome, and it may be useful to conclude by noting these briefly. The phenomena I find awesome may not seem so to others, or they may not seem to fully meet the criteria established for genuine puzzles, but I am persuaded that the best method for generating genuine puzzles lies in our wonderment over the symmetry and persistence of patterns. Thus I have to display my awe in the hope of highlighting a methodology that can lead us on from confusion to puzzlement. If enough of us articulate our awe over the dynamics of world politics, perhaps some among us will come upon inherently intriguing and substantively important outcomes that are patterned and that thus serve to focus and discipline our inquiries.

My wonderment has both micro and macro dimensions. At the micro level I am in awe of the tourist and the many other occupants of roles in authority structures who always seem to comply with the directives of national governments as they participate in transnational processes. Perhaps because I am still deeply enmeshed in the nation-state

[20] 'Transnational Relations and World Politics: An Introduction,' in *Transnational Relations and World Politics*, p. xi.

model of world politics, I tend to dismiss terrorists as deviant cases best explained through psychological analysis. But I am puzzled by the regularity of the compliance at national borders of tourists, traders, financiers, and others who engage in border-crossing activities. Given the tendency of citizens everywhere to feel increasingly alienated from their governments and the equally pervasive trend toward ethnic and other subnational groups siphoning off the loyalties of their members, I am impressed with the uniformity of the compliance that marks border-crossing behavior. Such behavior strikes me as the end product of complex processes of legitimacy formation that we do not adequately grasp and that might provide greater insight into the global system's capacity for underlying change if treated as a puzzle and then solved.

My awe at the macro level revolves around the presence of national governments as key actors in all the new issues to which the mounting interdependence, expanding technology, and shrinking resources of the world have given rise. Why is it, I keep wondering, that national governments always succeed in intruding themselves into the authority structures that form around the new issues and thereby transform such issues into *their* problems? If the new issues of space, the oceans, pollution, and the like span political boundaries, and if national governments are undergoing a substantial diminution in their capacities to govern, I am puzzled that governments invariably manage to assimilate the new issues rather than turning elsewhere for their solution or being rebuffed by other actors in their efforts to cope with them.[21] Again such behavior seems awesome in its constancy. Surely if we probed the complex processes that produce such constancy we might begin to bring the dynamics of underlying system change into clearer focus.[22]

I would argue that these micro and macro concerns are not naive, that it is by no means self-evident why most border-crossing activities are marked by habitual compliance or why governments intrude upon all transnational activities that are controversial. But I recognize that they may appear naive and obvious to others. What is a genuine puzzle

[21] By the assimilation of issues I mean a process wherein high-level officials of a nation-state wrestle with the new problems, both among themselves and through diplomacy with counterparts abroad, and then pass on to subordinates the task of routinely administering the policies they develop to cope with the issues. As Keohane and Nye put it, 'Issues are unlikely, in general, to remain indefinitely at the top level of governmental attention. Politicization may facilitate the resolution of issues, or at least the establishment of new structures and new assumptions within which particular questions can be settled at lower levels of the governmental hierarchy' ('Transgovernmental Relations and International Organizations,' p. 59).

[22] My theoretical impulses tell me that the solution to the puzzle of why governments invariably co-opt new issues lies in the adaptive orientations and capacities of nations. See my 'The Adaptation of National Societies: A Theory of Political Behavior and Its Transformations', in *The Scientific Study of Foreign Policy*, Chapter 18.

for one analyst can well be no more than a trite observation for another. The degree to which my concerns constitute genuine puzzles, however, is not the point. Here the point is that we need to stand back in wonderment, letting our imaginations have free reign so that the recurrent and important outcomes of world politics can come to seem puzzling, thereby compelling us to focus our talents in disciplined and creative ways. It matters not at all whether readers find my concerns trite; what matters is that they allow themselves to be awed by their subject. What features of the world scene, I cannot resist concluding, genuinely puzzle you?

3 Capabilities and Control in an Interdependent World*

In pondering the changing nature of 'national power,' two recent but contradictory examples come to mind as indicative of profound changes occurring in the nature and dynamics of whatever it is we mean when we refer to the 'power' of nations. One example is the 'failure' of American 'power' in Vietnam. The other is the 'success' of Arab 'power' in the 1973–74 oil embargo. What kind of changes these examples indicate, however, is obscure. Do they suggest that military 'power' has diminished (hence the Vietnam failure) and that economic 'power' has become more effective (hence the oil embargo success)? Do they point up the increasing variability of 'power' considerations? Do they suggest that generalized characterizations of national 'power' are no longer reasonable? Or do they highlight the limitations of the 'power' concept, suggesting once again that it is a concept without meaningful content and with misleading connotations?

If the last question is addressed first and the parameters of the concept precisely delineated, all four of these questions can be answered in the affirmative. Such is the thrust of the ensuing pages. The ambiguous and misleading uses of the 'power' concept are set forth at the outset and an alternative formulation outlined. The latter is then applied to the changing nature of world politics, to the evolution of economic and other new, nonmilitary types of issues, and to the implications of these issues for the nature of national 'power.'

*An earlier version of this chapter was published in *International Security*, Vol. 1 (Fall 1976), pp. 32–49. Reprinted with the permission of the publisher.

THE 'POWER' CONCEPT AND ITS LIMITATIONS

To stress that conventional usage of the 'power' concept results in misleading ambiguities is not in any way to deny that profound changes have occurred in world politics and that these have greatly altered the dynamics whereby nations employ their 'power' to pursue and achieve their foreign policy goals. The changes are independent of the way in which the concept is formulated. Appreciation of their scope and direction, however, becomes difficult if they are traced with imprecise and obfuscating conceptual equipment. Vietnam and the oil embargo can thus be seen as illustrative of both substantive change and conceptual disarray.

Stated differently, the *surprises* that attended the inability of the 'mighty' United States to prevail in Vietnam and the ability of the 'weak' Arab states to induce altered postures in the industrial world regarding their conflict with Israel are but the most recent and dramatic examples supporting a long-standing conviction that the concept of national 'power' confounds and undermines sound analysis.[1] Little is accomplished by explaining the surprising quality of these events in terms of the changing nature of 'power.' Such an explanation merely asserts that surprising events occurred because unrecognized changes had transpired in whatever may have been the sources of the events. Likewise, to stress that military 'power' has given way to economic 'power' is not to enlarge comprehension of *why* American policies in Vietnam and the Arab oil embargo had such contradictory outcomes. Had the conventional usage of the concept of 'power been more precise, with its empirical referents more accurately identified, there would have been no surprise with respect to Vietnam and the embargo. Indeed, conceivably neither the war in the former nor the crisis surrounding the latter would have occurred if officials had more clearly grasped the 'power' concept and disaggregated it into its component parts at the time policies toward these situations were evolving.

The two examples clearly highlight the central problem with the concept because they both suggest that the success or failure of foreign policy efforts is dependent on the possession of appropriate resources in sufficient abundance to prevail in conflict situations. So viewed, the United States 'failed' in Vietnam because it lacked the requisite military resources and Middle East countries 'succeeded' because they had sufficient economic resources. Nothing could be more misleading. Such an interpretation overlooks the equally crucial facts that while

[1] My convictions in this regard were first developed in my essay, *Calculated Control as a Unifying Concept in the Study of International Politics and Foreign Policy* (Princeton: Center of International Studies, Princeton University, 1963), reprinted in James N. Rosenau, *The Scientific Study of Foreign Policy* (London: Frances Pinter, New York: Nichols, 1980) Chap. X.

the North Vietnamese were not overly impressed by American military resources, the Western industrial nations were impressed by the oil which Middle East states could or could not make available.

Possessed resources, in other words, are only one aspect of 'power'; actions and reactions through which actors relate to each other are another aspect, and neither aspect is alone sufficient. Put even more pointedly, whatever else it may connote, national 'power' involves relational phenomena. Whether it be considered in the bipolar period when military considerations predominated, or whether it be assessed in the present era when economic and transnational factors are more salient, national 'power' can only be understood in the context of how the actors involved relate to and perceive each other. The resources each 'possesses' may well be relevant to the way in which they perceive each other, but the outcome of the way in which they exercise 'power' toward each other is primarily a consequence of how they assess, accept, resist, or modify each other's efforts.

Stated in still another way, the 'power' of a nation exists and is subject to meaningful assessment only insofar as it is directed at and responded to by other actors. All the possessed dimensions of 'power' imaginable will not have the anticipated and seemingly logical outcomes if those toward whom they are directed perceive the possessions otherwise and thereby withhold the expected compliance. This is perhaps the prime lesson of both the Vietnam War and the oil embargo, the lesson that renders the two seemingly diverse situations highly comparable.

Unfortunately, for reasons having to do with the structure of language, the concept of 'power' does *not* lend itself to comprehension in relational terms. Without undue violation of language, the word 'power' cannot be used as a verb. It is rather a noun, highlighting 'things' possessed instead of processes of interaction. Nations influence each other; they exercise control over each other; they alter, maintain, subvert, enhance, deter, or otherwise affect each other, but they do not 'powerize' each other. Hence, no matter how sensitive analysts may be to the question of how the resources used by one actor serve to modify or preserve the behavior of another, once they cast their assessment in terms of the 'power' employed they are led — if not inevitably, then almost invariably — to focus on the resources themselves rather than on the relationship they may or may not underlie.[2]

The tendence of the concept of 'power' to focus attention on possessed qualities is clearly illustrated by the pervasive inclination

[2] For example, see James W. Howe, 'Power in the Third World,' *Journal of International Affairs*, Vol. 29 (Fall 1975), pp. 113-28; and Susan Strange, 'What Is Economic Power, and Who Has It?' *International Journal*, Vol. 30 (Spring 1975), pp. 207-24.

to rank states in terms of their 'power' as defined by these attributes. Indeed, analyzing the attributes and resources of states in such a way as to classify some as superpowers, some as great powers, others as regional or middle powers, and still others as small powers is the standard approach to the concept. Nor have changes on the world scene altered this conventional treatment of the concept. Most analysts tend to account for the changes by assessing how they affect the mix of attributes and resources states possess and then derive conclusions as to whether, say, the United States is still number one, whether China has moved ahead of Western Europe and Japan as number three, and whether all of these plus the Soviet Union form a world of five superpowers that has come to replace the bipolar world of the postwar era.[3]

There is a remarkable paradox in the compulsion to analyze world affairs in terms of rankings of relative strengths and weaknesses. As students of international politics we are primarily interested in what states do or do not get each other to do, and yet we are diverted from concentrating on such relational phenomena by our reliance on a concept that focuses on the secondary question of their attributes and resources.

This is not to say, of course, that the attributes and resources that states bring to bear in their foreign relations are irrelevant. The 'power' they possess underlies their officials' estimates of what can and cannot be accomplished abroad, just as the estimates made by those toward whom their actions are directed depend on calculations of the attributes and resources that may be operative. Furthermore, no matter how the possessed or deficient resources may be perceived and assessed, they are likely to shape what happens when states interact with each other. The more a state possesses the attributes and resources appropriate to its goals in a situation, the more its actions are likely to move it toward the objectives sought. So 'national power' can have some predictive and analytic value *if* it is estimated in the context of its appropriateness to situations — but to add this condition is to highlight again the significance of relational phenomena. For estimates of how one or another 'power' factor may be appropriate to a given situation requires attention to the resources, expectations, and likely responses of other parties to the situation.

[3] For sophisticated analyses of recent changes on the world scene that nevertheless fail to break away from the tendency to rank possessed attributes and resources, see Seyom Brown, 'The Changing Essence of Power,' *Foreign Affairs*, Vol. 51 (January 1973), pp. 286–99; and Stanley Hoffmann, 'Notes on the Elusiveness of Modern Power,' *International Journal*, Vol. 30 (Spring 1975), pp. 183–206. A somewhat more successful effort to probe systematically the relational consequences of relative changes in the possessed qualities of states can be found in Klaus Knorr, *The Power of Nations: The Political Economy of International Relations* (New York: Basic Books, 1975).

How, then, to focus on both the possession and interaction dimensions of 'power' without being driven by the structure of language to an overriding preoccupation with the former dimension? My answer to this question is simple, though its simplicity should not be allowed to obscure the degree to which it reduces ambiguity and allows us to concentrate on the prime questions that concern us. For years I have solved this conceptual problem by dropping the word 'power' from my analytic vocabulary (thus the use here of quotation marks) replacing it with the concept of capabilities whenever reference is made to attributes or resources possessed and with verbs such as control or influence whenever the relational dimension of 'power' is subjected to analysis.[4]

This disaggregation of the 'power' concept virtually compels analysts to keep their eyes on the interaction phenomena primarily of interest to them because any assessments they may make of existing or potential resources and attributes are bound to be manifestly incomplete and insufficient. Their conceptual equipment will necessitate that they inquire into how the assessed resources and attributes may or may not contribute to the control of desired outcomes or otherwise influence the attitudes and behaviors of other actors. Stated differently, modifying or preserving events and trends abroad — i.e., controlling them -- depends on a wide range of variables, only some of which involve the resources and attributes of the parties to the control relationship; disaggregation of the 'power' concept facilitates consideration of the full range of these variables.

Another important virtue of this disaggregated approach is that it facilitates concentration on the capabilities of governments to engage in cooperative action abroad. For historical reasons stemming from the independence of states in the international system, the 'power' concept has come to have conflictual connotations. 'Power' is ordinarily conceived to be applied *against* potential adversaries or any obstacles that block the path to goal achievement. It is not normally viewed as embracing resources and attributes that are employed *for* the realization of objectives through concerting efforts with other states. Consequently, analysts have long had the tendency to conceive of 'power' in military terms, military action being the last resort through which states seek to maintain their independence. Yet, as elaborated below, world politics is increasingly marked by interdependence, by new issues that cannot be addressed or resolved through the threat or use of military capabilities and that instead require cooperation among states if obstacles to goals are to be diminished or eliminated. In addition to the maintenance of physical security and territorial integrity, national

[4] For elaboration of this breakdown, see Rosenau, *The Scientific Study of Foreign Policy*, Chap. X.

'power' today must be exercised with respect to the problems of oceans, exchange rates, pollution, agricultural production, population size, energy allocation, and the many other issues fostered by mounting interdependence. The distinction between capabilities and control, being free of long-standing conflictful connotations, should facilitate more cogent analysis of the role states play in resolving (or sustaining) these issues. At least the distinction should allow for a fuller treatment of those organizational skills and knowledge bases from which spring the dynamics of these newer issues than would be the case if analysts relied on the undifferentiated 'power' concept.

To be sure, many of those who are accustomed to the 'power' concept stress that they have in mind a broad range of factors that extend well beyond military capabilities. And, indeed, frequently the concept is formulated in ways to include national morale, societal cohesion, leadership development, and many of the other intangible attributes and resources that underlie the foreign policy efforts of states. Even the more sophisticated formulations, however, frequently succumb to the historical tendency associated with the 'power' concept and analyze non-military capabilities as if they were designed only to serve conflictual purposes. It is no accident, for example, that the problems of monetary stability, devaluations, and exchange rates are frequently cast as problems of 'economic warfare.' And surely it is a measure of the extent to which the 'power' concept habitually provokes military and conflictual connotations that when the problem of agricultural production and distribution is treated in the context of national 'power,' it is typically conceived as a 'food-as-a-weapon' issue.

THE NARROWING SCOPE OF MILITARY CAPABILITIES

None of the foregoing is to say that military capabilities are no longer available to statesmen or that they have become unwilling to use force as a means of controlling circumstances abroad. To stress mounting interdependence and the emergence of new issues is not to deny that arms races mark the world scene, that weapons production and sales is a global industry, that threats by states to use force are an almost daily occurrence, or that all too frequently states seek to control outcomes by resorting to their military capabilities. Rather it is to say that for a variety of reasons, all of which sum to greater complexity within states and greater interdependence among them, the range through which military capabilities can achieve effective control has narrowed substantially in recent decades and that, consequently, a host of new types of abilities have become increasingly relevant if states are to maintain any control over their environments. Stated in conventional terms, 'national power' is today far more multifaceted than ever before.

It is important to appreciate that the narrowing scope of military capabilities is not simply a function of the advent of nuclear weapons and the deterrence systems they have spawned. The ever-present possibility of a nuclear holocaust has made officials more cautious in their readiness to resort to military instruments of statecraft. This caution is especially acute among those who preside over the foreign policies of superpowers, but it probably has also increased among officials of non-nuclear powers in the sense of a heightened sensitivity to avoiding military actions that could escalate to superpower involvement and the subsequent introduction of nuclear weapons.

The advent of the nuclear age, however, is only one reason why military capabilities have declined in relative importance. A seemingly much more crucial reason derives from the many ways in which an ever more dynamic technology and ever growing demands on the world's resources have shrunk the geographic, social, economic, and political distances that separate states and vastly multiplied the points at which their needs, interests, ideas, products, organizations, and publics overlap. Quite aside from the activities of governments, what happens within states would appear to have wider and wider ramifications across their boundaries and these proliferating ramifications have created, in turn, an ever-widening set of external control (i.e., foreign policy) problems for governments. The more societies, cultures, economies, and polities become interdependent, the less do the resulting conflicts lend themselves to resolution through military threats and actions. The threat and use of force is maximally effective, to the extent it is effective at all, when control over territory or compliance with the exercise of authority is at stake. But the new problems of interdependence involve attitudinal and behavioral patterns that have few, if any, territorial or legitimacy dimensions.

To modify or preserve these patterns governments must rely on much more variable and subtle means of control — means which are as complex and technical as the social, cultural, scientific, and economic dimensions out of which the patterns emerged and through which they are sustained. Military forms of control are most applicable in situations where issues cannot be split, refined, or redefined — where compliance gets cast in either/or terms — whereas the newer issues of interdependence are pervaded with so many nuances and subparts that control can be exercised only with respect to limited areas of behavior and can result in compliance that is not likely to be more than partial and incremental.

The narrowing scope of military capabilities can be readily illustrated by some hypothetical situations that once might have seemed logical but that appear patently absurd today. Imagine, for example, one state threatening a resort to force if another did not comply with its demand for a currency devaluation. Or consider the likelihood of two neighboring states going to war over a question of pollutants that flow downstream or downwind across their common borders. Compliance with demands in such situations is clearly likely to result from complex bargaining and the very absurdity of seeking to control them through the use or threat of force is a measure of the degree to which interdependence has fragmented the issues that comprise world politics today. Indeed, one does not have to resort to hypothetical situations to make this point. It will be recalled that during the height of the dislocation that accompanied the Arab oil embargo several analysts proposed that the West threaten, and possibly even undertake, military action in order to sustain the flow of oil from the region if a lifting of the embargo failed to occur.[5] This proposal involved control efforts so manifestly inappropriate to the situation that it failed to generate much support in or out of governmental circles.

Since it also bears on the problem of employing capabilities relevant to maximizing control over the newer issues generated by mounting interdependence, one other reason why military capabilities have become more narrowly circumscribed needs to be noted. It involves the greater self-consciousness of ethnic, racial, linguistic, and other subgroups within nation-states, a sense of identity that has led such groups to become increasingly coherent, articulate, and demanding. Few states are so homogeneous as to have avoided the contention and fragmentation inherent in the worldwide process through which subnational loyalties have come to rival, if not to replace, those directed toward national states. While it may well be that these disintegrative tendencies are both a source and a consequence of interdependence — in the sense that the proliferation of transnational relationships both stems from and contributes to heightened subgroup consciousness — one clearly discernable result of the dispersal of loyalties is that national governments are no longer as capable as they once were of mobilizing the kind of unquestioning support that is necessary for effective military operations. The American effort to effect control in Vietnam, resisted by subnational groups within the United States, not to mention the enormous mobilization problems encountered by the South Vietnamese in Vietnam, is but the most recent example of how the disenchantment of subgroups and their ties abroad have reduced the scope of military instruments available to most states.

Indeed, the declining capacity of national governments to govern is

[5] This line of reasoning was later developed more elaborately in Edward Friedland, Paul Seabury, and Aaron Wildavsky, *The Great Détente Disaster: Oil and the Decline of American Foreign Policy* (New York: Basic Books, 1975), and Robert W. Tucker, 'Oil: The Issue of American Intervention,' *Commentary*, Vol. 57 (January 1975), pp. 21–31.

not confined to foreign military undertakings. For most, if not all, governments the decline spans an entire range of issue-areas, both domestic and foreign. The greater internal division, the persistence of severe economic dislocations, the continued depletion of resources, the emergence of interdependence issues that cannot be resolved through unilateral action, the increased competence of transnational actors — these are but a few of the many developments that have resulted in governmental performances that fall short of aspirations and that further diminish the public support most governments once enjoyed. As will be seen, this generalized dimunition of the capacity to mobilize domestic support is no less central to the handling of the newer nonmilitary problems of interdependence than to the traditional issues of national security.

THE STRUCTURE OF INTERDEPENDENCE ISSUES

If, as indicated earlier, the newer issues of world politics are unlike those involving military security and do not consist primarily of territorial and legitimacy dimensions, what are their main characteristics? In the answer to this question lies the basis for assessing the changing nature of 'national power.' Four characteristics seem salient as central features of all the diverse issues of interdependence, from those involving monetary stability to those associated with food-population ratios, from the uses of the ocean to the abuses of the atmosphere, from the discovery and distribution of new energy sources to the redirection of trade and the reallocation of wealth. Perhaps the most persuasive characteristic of all such issues is the large degree to which they encompass highly complex and technical phenomena. To grasp how food production can be increased, ocean bottoms utilized, pollutants eliminated, and solar energy exploited is to acquire mastery over physical and biological processes that involve an extraordinary range of subprocesses, the interaction of which is not easily understood, much less easily controlled. To grasp how monetary stability can be maintained, population growth reduced, and wealth reallocated is to achieve comprehension of social, cultural, and economic processes that are equally complex and no less difficult to control. Most of these issues of interdependence, moreover, overlap so thoroughly that proposed solutions to any one of them have important ramifications for the others, thereby further complicating their highly technical character.

Quite aside from the politics of coping with these new kinds of issues, their structures and contents require new kinds of advanced scientific and social scientific knowledge and expertise if efforts to control them are to be undertaken and minimally successful. It is hardly an exaggeration to assert that what weapons and troops are to the traditional problems of national security, so are scientific knowledge and technological sophistication to the newer dimensions of security.

A second major characteristic of interdependence issues is the large degree to which many of them encompass a great number of non-governmental actors whose actions are relevant to issue management. This decentralized character of most interdependence issues is in sharp contrast to the conventional foreign policy situation — such as a treaty negotiation or a severance of diplomatic relations — in which the course of events is shaped largely by choices that government officials make. Indeed, virtually by definition an interdependence issue involves the overlap of many lives, so much so that the unfolding of the issue depends on decisions (or lack of decisions) made by countless individuals, none of whom is necessarily aware of what others have decided (or not decided). The actions of innumerable farmers, for example, are central to the problem of increased food production, just as many pollution issues depend on choices made by vast numbers of producers, energy conservation on millions of consumers, and population growth on tens of millions of potential parents. To be sure, governmental choices and actions can influence whether the decisions made by the multitude of persons encompassed by such issues are consistent and appropriate — which is precisely why the mobilization of domestic support has become increasingly relevant to foreign affairs. But the very fact of such decentralization renders the handling of interdependence issues very different from the standard means of framing and implementing foreign policy.[6]

A third major feature of interdependence issues arises out of the combination of their decentralized structure and the technical knowledge on which they rest. These two variables interact in such a way as to fragment the governmental decision-making process through which such issues are considered. More precisely, in the United States and other industrial societies with large public bureaucracies the link between most such issues and particular clienteles among the citizenry endows the governmental agencies and subagencies responsible for tending to the welfare of the relevant clientele with unusual degrees of authority and political clout. And this clout is further augmented by the fact that such agencies tend to acquire a governmental monopoly of the technical expertise needed to cope with the issues in their jurisdiction. Hence in the American case, for example, units of the Treasury Department tend to carry the day on monetary issues and bureaus within the Agriculture Department tend to monopolize decision making

[6] For a cogent discussion of this point, see Robert L. Paarlberg, 'Domesticating Global Management,' *Foreign Affairs*, Vol. 54 (April 1976), pp. 563–76.

on questions pertaining to the production and distribution of various foodstuffs. Whenever an issue draws on several expertises, of course, the fragmented authority that has evolved with respect to it leads to especially intense bureaucratic wrangling, or at least to the need for elaborate interdepartmental committees to handle it.

In either event, whether an issue is processed by a single bureaucratic unit or by several subunits, a main consequence of the dispersed expertise is to diminish the capacity of top officials to maintain control over it. Whereas the traditional issues of foreign and military policy are founded on nationwide constituencies and can be managed by heads of state and prime ministers through their foreign offices and military establishments, interdependence issues render the politically responsible leadership much more subject to the advice, direction, contradictions, and compromises that emanate from a fragmented bureaucratic structure. They normally do not have the time or expertise to master the knowledge necessary to grasp fully such issues and ordinarily they lack the political fortitude to resist, much less reject, the pressures from the special clienteles that seek to be served by the issues. The role of expertise, of whether the expert is on tap or on top, has long been a problem in the military area,[7] but this problem is miniscule in comparison to the place which scientists, engineers, agricultural economists, demographers, biologists, and many other types of experts have come to assume in the newer issues of interdependence.[8]

Allusion has already been made to a fourth structural characteristic of all interdependence issues that appears to have major consequences for the changing nature of capabilities and control, namely, the large extent to which the management and amelioration, if not the resolution, of such issues requires multilateral cooperation among governments. Any issue is, by definition, founded on conflict, but issues can differ considerably in the degree to which the conflicts that sustain them can be isolated, contained, or otherwise managed unilaterally by governments. The conventional diplomatic and strategic issues of foreign policy, springing as they do from conflicts over territory and legitimate authority, can often be pressed, resisted, or ignored by a government without concurrence by other governments. Hard bargaining and negotiating sessions may follow from the positions which a government adopts on such matters, but these can be broken off, suspended, or otherwise limited — and the issues thereby left unmanaged — if the government finds it expedient to do so. The newer issues of

[7] See Burton M. Sapin and Richard C. Snyder, *The Role of the Military in American Foreign Policy* (Garden City, N.Y.: Doubleday & Co., 1954).

[8] For a useful essay relevant to this point, see Allan W. Lerner, *Experts, Politicians, and Decsionmaking in the Technological Society* (Morristown, N.J.: General Learning Press, 1975).

interdependence, on the other hand, do not lend themselves so readily to unilateral action. Many of them spring from conflicts over the uses and abuses of the natural environment — the air (e.g., pollution), the land (e.g., food productivity), the water (e.g., ocean resources) — which do not conform to political boundaries and which most governments can thus neither dismiss nor handle on their own. Instead agreements among governments must be developed even as each presses positions that best serve its own interests. Such is the nature of interdependence issues, be they conflicts over the natural or the socioeconomic environment. Defiance, avoidance, rejection, and other forms of conflict behavior can be temporarily employed for tactical advantage, but the interdependence will not disappear nor will the issues it spawns be contained. Eventually knowledge has to be exchanged and some form of agreement achieved among those states independently linked by their shared reliance on the same environment.

The international monetary policy of the United States during John Connally's term as Secretary of the Treasury *from* 1970 *to* 1972 illustrates the limits of such strategy. It will be recalled that Connally took a defiant and uncompromising stance toward other states in order to win concessions in the restructuring of the international economic system. The instability of the existing economic order, however, persisted and the United States soon felt compelled to turn to a more accommodative posture. Perhaps an even better example of the way in which interdependence issues tip the balance in the direction of cooperative behavior is provided by the Organization of Petroleum Exporting Countries (OPEC). The members of that organization may have many differences over oil-pricing policies, but they must — and do — bury some of these in order to render OPEC more effective and thereby achieve their individual goals through collective action.

CAPABILITIES AND CONTROL IN AN INTERDEPENDENT WORLD

Given the narrowed scope of military capabilities, the declining capacity of governments to mobilize domestic support, and the technical, decentralized, fragmented, and accommodative structure of interdependence issues, it is not difficult to trace substantial changes in the capabilities that states bring to world politics and the extent and manner of the control they can exercise over events and trends abroad. Indeed, the problem is one of limiting the analysis to the allotted space. An almost infinite number of changes can be identified, thus confining the ensuing discussion to only those changes that seem most profound and enduring.

Turning first to the transformations that are likely to occur (and may have already begun) in the control dimension of national 'power,' several nonmilitary techniques are available for foreign policy officials to use in their efforts to modify or preserve the patterns that comprise the newer issues of world politics. Bargaining over differences, trading issues off against each other, promises of future support, threats of future opposition, persuasion through appeals to common values, persuasion through the presentation of scientific proof — these are the prime control techniques through which the problems of interdependence must be addressed. They are, of course, as old as diplomacy itself, but they have taken on new meaning in the light of the decline of force as a viable technique and in view of the complex nature of the interdependence issues. In particular, the last two of these nonmilitary techniques seem destined to become ever more salient as instruments of statecraft. The inclination to rely on appeals to common values, with a corresponding diminution in the tendency to threaten reprisals, appears especially likely to emerge as central to the conduct of foreign affairs. The fact that interdependence issues cannot be handled unilaterally, that foreign policy officials must engage in a modicum of cooperation with counterparts abroad in order to ameliorate the situations on which such issues thrive, means that the rhetoric, as well as the substance, of control techniques must shift toward highlighting the common values that are at stake.

Nor is this rhetorical shift likely to be confined to the bargaining that occurs behind closed doors. The decline of a sense of national identity and the emergence of more pronounced subnational loyalties seem likely to impel foreign policy officials to refer more frequently to share international values in their public pronouncements as well as their private negotiations. That is, appeals to national interest and loyalties seem likely to become less compelling as means of mobilizing domestic support, so that positions on interdependence issues will have to be sold internally in terms of their consistency with the aspirations of external parties to situations.

Resort to scientific proof is a second control technique that seems headed for much greater use in the years ahead. The complex and technical nature of most interdependence issues seems likely to lead officials to place heavy reliance on the data and knowledge they have gathered as they seek to persuade counterparts abroad of the soundness of their positions. To be sure, there has always been a knowledge component of sound diplomacy. Statesmen have long preferred to seek desired modifications of behavior abroad through rational argument before turning to coercive techniques of control. If goals can be advanced by persuading others of their inherent logic and validity, the costs of success are much less than is the case when the threat or use of force produces movement toward goals. Historically, however, the technical dimension of issues has not been so pervasive as it is in this era of interdependence, with the result that appeals founded on scientific proof were rarely controlling. Thus, despite their preferences, the practice of statesmen across centuries has been largely one of non-rational argumentation. But today's issues cannot be readily separated from their knowledge bases. To take positions on interdependence issues that ignore their technical and scientific underpinnings is to risk pursuit of counterproductive policies. Hence it seems highly probable that foreign policy officials will become increasingly inclined to achieve and maintain control through efforts to 'prove' to adversaries and friends alike the validity of their positions.

This is not to say, of course, that the inherent logic and validity of data bearing on interdpendence issues will necessarily, or even frequently, be persuasive and yield the desired modifications of behavior. Such issues are not free of values. They do not rest on an objective reality that speaks with a single and coherent voice to statesmen of all countries. One need only recall the persistent differences between industrial states and those in the Third World over the sources and dynamics of economic progress and dislocation to appreciate that the knowledge bases of even the most complex interdependence issues are subject to varying interpretations, depending on the perspectives and goals of policymakers. Yet, although future statesmen may thus be prone to bring their knowledge bases into line with their policies rather than vice versa, and even though they are therefore likely to resist and counter 'proofs' advanced by adversaries, these tendencies will probably become less and less pronounced as technical knowledge becomes ever more central to the conduct of foreign affairs. The inclination to proceed from and cling to scientific proof as a basis for negotiation would thus seem to be headed for much greater priority in the array of control techniques on which officials depend. And who knows, in more than a few instances perhaps the proofs will seem compelling and serve to modify attitudes and behavior that in the past could have been expected to remain unaffected by this form of control.

It must be stressed that these anticipated changes in the exercise of control are not posited as replacing the conventional practices of statecraft. To highlight tendencies toward greater appeals to shared values and greater reliance on scientific proof is not to herald the dawn of a new era in which rational discourse and harmony mark world affairs. The old issues of territorial jurisdiction and the scope of legitimate authority are not about to pass quickly from the scene and the conflicts and hard bargaining which they generate are not about to disappear suddenly as interdependence mounts. Rather the anticipated changes are seen as extensions of the art of statecraft, as broadening the mix through which officials seek to adapt to their external environments. Whether the long-run alterations in this mix will be sufficient to foster steady progress toward a more rational and orderly world can hardly be estimated at this time. The possibility of such progress is clearly inherent in the changing nature of control and the shifting capabilities of states (outlined below), but one ought not be so naive as to overlook the many variables that can perpetuate or deepen the differences among states and that can even encourage resort to nonrational techniques of control.

The advent and structure of interdependence issues also points to several important changes in the capabilities dimension of national 'power.' Again these changes are best viewed in the context of a new mix, of long-standing aspects of capabilities continuing to be crucial to the conduct of foreign affairs even as mounting interdependence has made other, previously peripheral aspects relatively more significant. The fertility of the soil, the minerals and other resources possessed, the configurations of geography, the size and skills of populations, the breadth and equipment of the military establishment — these are but a few of the attributes that continue to differentiate the strong from the weak and to shape the extent and direction of the control that states can exercise abroad. Growing interdependence has not diminished the role of such attributes — in some cases (e.g., oil reserves) it has even increased their role — but rather it has enlarged the composite of possessed qualities from which effective control derives.

The capacity to develop and apply scientific and technical knowledge is perhaps the attribute that has undergone the greatest transformation. The complexity of interdependence issues and their close link to the natural environment means that states are likely to be better able to cope with and procure benefits from their external settings the more they possess the ability to comprehend the dynamics whereby land, air, and water resources can be used and abused. The depth, breadth, flexibility, and commitment of a state's scientific establishment has thus come to rival its military establishment as a national resource. And, in turn, this attribute highlights the centrality of a state's educational system and its ability to produce a continuous flow of analytic, wide ranging, and technically competent citizens. The considerable stress states in the Third World place on establishing technological institutes and sending students abroad for advanced training is but one of the more obvious measures of the degree to which the capacity to generate and utilize knowledge has entered the ranks of prime national attributes.

Societal cohesion is another capability that has acquired prime importance. The decentralized nature of interdependence issues and the widening consequences of the attitudes and decisions of subnational groups has made external control efforts ever more dependent on the degree to which these subgroups perceive their interests as shared and served by the policies of their national governments. The greater the cohesiveness in this regard, the more does it seem likely that foreign policy officials will be able to pursue successfully those courses of action they deem essential to the management of interdependence issues. The readiness of American farmers, for example, to harmonize their production schedules with the requirements of proposed international agreements on the distribution and storage of foodstuffs constitutes a critical element in the United States government's ability to undertake successful negotiations on such matters. Of course, the degree of societal cohesion — and the mobilization potential thereby created — has always been a critical factor in the military area, but its centrality to other areas of foreign policy has not been so extensive. The emergence of interdependence issues has changed all this and, combined with the shifting loyalties of subnational groups, has rendered the cohesion attribute a major component of national capabilities.[9]

The capacity of public bureaucracies to overcome — or at least compensate for — the fragmentation inherent in interdependence issues is still another attribute that has become increasingly important in recent years. The readiness of one subagency to inform other relevant subagencies of its activities is not a predisposition that comes easily to units of a bureaucracy. On the contrary, rivalry is probably more securely embedded in bureaucratic structures than coordination, and these structural tendencies seem likely to be exacerbated by the fragmentation, decentralization, and specialization that accompanies interdependence. It follows that states that can continuously adapt their decision-making structure to mounting interdependence — that can train and utilize the relevant expertise, that can sensitize officials to the implications of their choices for other governmental units working on other problems of interdependence, that can find techniques for generating innovative proposals and for transforming destructive rivalries into creative tensions, that can develop scientific proofs which support appeals to transnational values — will bring to the conference tables of the world considerable advantages not accruing to those that conduct

[9] Much the same line of reasoning can be applied to the degree to which governments are authoritarian. This attribute can greatly facilitate or hinder the mobilization of domestic support, with authoritarian regimes having a greater capacity in this regard than democratic ones (assuming comparable degrees of internal cohesion). Presumably this relative advantage has widened as the advent of interdependence issues has increased the needs for governments to win acceptance and compliance from the relevant subgroups to back up their positions on such matters. If the assumption of internal cohesiveness is relaxed, however, this attribute of political structure emerges more as an intervening than an independent variable and is thus not singled out here as a capability that has been rendered especially compelling by the growth of interdependence.

bureaucratic politics and diplomacy as usual. The capacity to render large-scale governmental organizations relevant to existing problems has always been an important component of national 'power,' but its role would appear to be even more central as world affairs become ever more complex.[10]

Closely related to the increasing importance of decision-making variables is the capacity of officials to frame and pursue policies designed either to build new international institutions or to give new directions to long-established patterns. As previously noted, by their very nature interdependence issues tend to require multilateral co-operation among governments for their amelioration. The ability to contribute to the evolution of such institutions and patterns can vary considerably, depending on the readiness of societies, their publics, and their governments to acknowledge that their futures are inter-dependently linked and to adapt to the changing circumstances which may thereby arise. The adaptation of national societies can take several forms,[11] including maladaptive assessments of the way in which domestic life is interwoven into foreign affairs. Adaptation and mal-adaptation involve nothing less than the images which citizens and officials hold of themselves in relation to their external environments; and if these images are unrealistic and fail to account for the need to sustain cooperative foreign policies, then burdens rather than benefits are bound to mount with interdependence. Inasmuch as the images underlying the adaptive capacities of states derive from the functioning of their communication systems, the viability of their value frameworks, the flexibility of their political ideologies, and the dynamics of their educational systems, as well as the structure of their public bureaucracies, it seems quite evident that the capability for multilateral co-operation will not come readily to governments. Equally obvious is the fact that those which can enlarge this capability will achieve greater measures of national security than those which do not.

If the foregoing analysis of the changing mix of capabilities that accompanying mounting interdependence is accurate, it seems reasonable to generalize that 'national power' is on the decline, that the capacity of individual states to control developments abroad is diminishing and will continue to diminish. Some will remain relatively 'strong' and other relatively 'weak,' and some may become relatively stronger and others relatively weaker, but in absolute terms all seem

[10] For a useful elaboration of this point as it applies to the United States, see Atlantic Council, 'Decision-Making in an Interdependent World,' *The Atlantic Community Quarterly*, Vol. 13 (Summer 1975), pp. 139–57.

[11] James N. Rosenau, *The Adaptation of National Societies: A Theory of Political Behavior and Its Transformations* (New York: McCaleb-Seiler, 1970), reprinted in *The Study of Political Adaptation* (London: Frances Pinter, 1980, New York: Nichols, 1980).

likely to become less able single-handedly to modify or preserve patterns in their external environments. Why? Because it seems unlikely that any state, even the most industrially advanced, can develop a scientific community with sufficient breadth and depth to cope with all the diverse issues of interdependence; because everywhere societies seem destined to become less cohesive and the mobilizing capacities of their governments less effective; and because everywhere bureaucracies seem likely to become more fragmented. Whether the decline in overall capabilities to enhance national security will result in a corresponding diminution of international security, however, is less clear. As interdependence impinges ever more tightly, so may the adaptive capacities of states allow them to evolve a greater readiness for multilateral co-operation.[12] The years ahead may thus be witness to a profound paradox in which the decline of national 'power' is matched, and perhaps even exceeded, by the rise of international 'power.'

[12] For some stimulating discussions relevant to this possibility, see Marvin E. Wolfgang (ed.), 'Adjusting to Scarcity,' *The Annals*, Vol. 420 (July 1975), pp. 1-124.

4 Adaptive Polities in an Interdependent World*

Amid swift and profound technological and social change, we tend to forget that our time is also marked by continuity. Deep-seated habits still shape the actions of men and nations, and long-standing conventions still guide their interactions. Yet the changes are so great that we stress, perhaps even exaggerate, the presence of crisis. The world is seen as in perpetual crisis, so that a rhetoric of crisis has become an accepted part of our daily life. While this rhetoric forces us to confront many of the important changes that are occurring, it too often also leads us to ignore the continuities, with the result that simplistic, either-or conceptions of the scope and meaning of the changes abound: either we find immediate solutions to ecological problems or the world will starve and suffocate; either the nuclear stockpiles are dismantled or nuclear holocaust will follow; either societies invest new forms of government suited to an interdependent world or they will turn on each other in a futile effort to preserve their independence; either man develops a new morality to replace the norms of a scientific age or he will be overwhelmed by a surfeit of unmanageable technology.

It is the central thesis of this chapter that such polarizations are inaccurate and dangerous. We shall argue that what lies ahead is a world of ungainly asymmetries and not tidy symmetries — a world marked by change and continuity, starvation *and* sufficiency, nuclear

*Earlier versions of this chapter were presented to the Conference on the Conduct of International Relations in an Interdependent World, held at the Center for Democratic Institutions, Santa Barbara, California, January 27-29, 1971, and published in *Orbis*, Vol. XVI (Spring, 1972), pp. 153-173. Reprinted with the permission of the Foreign Policy Research Institute.

weapons *and* peaceful accommodations, interdependence *and* independence, old norms *and* new values. Some of the asymmetries may even be highly desirable. Continuity can facilitate as well as constrain change, independence can supplement as well as undermine interdependence, old norms can clarify as well as obscure new values. The greatest danger arises out of the tendency to define the present as racked by either-or crises from which there is no escape. Such a tendency leads to the conviction that we are pawns and not masters of the rapid and profound changes we only dimly perceive. This sense of powerlessness, in turn, leads to the abandonment of rationality. Once this happens, once the application of intelligence no longer seems useful, the world will have truly entered a crisis that is beyond exaggeration. Thus the emotional and intellectual wherewithal for man to find creative and humane responses to his changing world lies in the continuity of some deeply rooted and well-tested modes of thought and behavior -- those that comprise the scientific approach and are based on reason and the pursuit of understanding.

This is not to venerate habit and exalt the status quo. To regard certain habitual modes of thought and long-standing conventions as sources of emotional and intellectual strength is not to contend that change should be resisted or radical solutions avoided. Rather it is to say that the opportunities inherent in the established patterns of modern life need to be appreciated and utilized if its crisis-ridden excesses are to be surmounted. Habits, like changes, can be either oppressive or liberating, and those that are liberating should be included among the tools used to overcome those that are oppressive. The habits of communities that have culminated in the pollution of their environment need to be understood if they are to be reversed. The habits of the nation-state system that have generated the nuclear arms race need to be probed if they are to be contained. The best way to understand such oppressive habits is by using the liberating habit of scientific inquiry, which offers man perhaps the only route to the kind of understanding of his dilemma necessary for the development of radical and effective solutions. Unless account is taken of the persistence of habitual forms of organization and traditional modes of interaction, desired change cannot be effectively promoted and undesired change resisted.

It is not difficult to map out alternatives to present conditions if one ignores the customs and traditions that created and sustained them and that must be overcome for change to occur. But unless these established ways are identified and comprehended in all their depth and complexity, no solution, however compellingly it may be propounded, can be made a reality.

I

Our main goal here is to probe the asymmetries that characterize politics in our interdependent world and to do so in the context of scientific inquiry. Ironically, to propose reliance on the application of science to human affairs today is to be profoundly radical. In the current milieu the notion of using human intelligence to solve human problems has given way to impatience, to respect for impulse and emotion, to calls for a new morality that will rescue the individual and the nation from the oppressive excesses of modern life. Those who believe in analyzing what is, as well as what ought to be, and proceed by conforming to strict rules of evidence and cautious modes of interpretation, are viewed as obsolete and as threats to progress. Their attempts to observe and quantify the central patterns in the behavior of people in general are seen as failing to depict, and even worsening, the qualitative predicament of the individual. Scientific inquiry has thus come into disrepute. Both the Establishment and the advocates of radical change reject the premises of social science. Only recently, for example, the President dismissed, abruptly and unqualifiedly, the results of a serious effort to employ the methods of science to trace and explain the consequences of pornography. His reasons for doing so are no different from those of many radicals who, when confronted with the results of scientific efforts to analyze international politics, in effect say 'I will not accept facts that are contrary to what I believe.'

Social science, in short, has come to be associated with the old norms that produced nuclear weapons and a polluted environment. What was once commonplace — that one should proceed as rationally as possible and seek to understand one's environment before attempting to alter it — has become suspect or abandoned. Even the most thoughtful of observers who are dedicated to democratic institutions have been led by the rhetoric of crisis to posit new policy goals and new strategies designed to realize them, without also calling for efforts to comprehend why present goals persist or how they may be altered. But if we believe that human problems can be solved through the application of intelligence, we must confront their complexity and be ready to pay the price such a confrontation entails. To do so is to tailor moral imperatives to empirical realities, to enlighten aspiration with reason, and to allocate resources for pure research in the social sciences — adjustments which in today's crisis-ridden climate constitute true radicality.

The widespread loss of respect for the uses of reason and the consequent erosion of confidence in the capacity of the social sciences to contribute to the solution of national and international problems cannot be exaggerated. From the President of the United States to the local newspaper editor, from the halls of Congress to the ivory tower of academe, from the seats of power to the centers of revolution, from whomever or wherever thoughts about the future originate, the call is for a reordering of priorities and rededication to old values or commitment to new ones. Conspicuously missing is a concurrent call to reason and a readiness to pay the costs of its application, as if the urgency and seriousness of the normative problems have rendered the use of reason a luxury that can no longer be afforded. Many people would doubtless argue that too many important problems must be addressed for scarce resources to be allocated on the basis of a hope that the painfully slow processes of science will unravel the mysteries of international life. One can only respond that the cost of not making such an investment is greater — much greater — than the small amounts it would require. For, to repeat our central concern in still another way, research and knowledge are as necessary to clearing our environment of conflict as they are to clearing it of pollution.

II

The need for careful inquiry is plainly evident in the problem of assessing the symmetries and asymmetries that may accompany the trend toward interdependence in a world of independent sovereign nations. The argument for new priorities and aspirations can be readily posed. As technology shrinks social and geographical distances, more and more groups are developing interdependencies that transcend national boundaries. Increasingly, therefore, 'internal' events and trends are sustained by 'external' events and trends, so that the distinction between domestic and foreign policy has become increasingly blurred. Accordingly, the world can be said to be moving into a 'post-national order' in which the habitual methods of formulating foreign policy and conducting international affairs seem less and less appropriate. Diplomacy is seen as increasingly incompatible with democracy, as widening the gap between rulers and the ruled. In order to cope with the publics and issues that have been sired by growing interdependence, new policymaking procedures must emerge at the national level and new organizational arrangements must be developed at the global level. The problem is: will they? Will the profound forces at work in the world culminate, as many who argue for new priorities anticipate, in the emergence of supranational polities and the slow disappearance of national ones?

One can hardly quarrel with the conclusion that technology is shrinking distance and making the world increasingly interdependent.

Both direct experience and reliable data sustain it. Experientially one knows that the safety of air travel has become related to foreign political conflicts, that the air itself is now subject to growing contamination by industrial activities beyond as well as within national boundaries, that the groups to which one belongs are developing wider contacts with counterparts in other countries, that the goods one buys and the prices one pays for them are in part a consequence of economic developments abroad. Moreover, it takes only a cursory reading of the daily paper to know that one's own experience is widely shared. We learn that American students recently concluded a 'treaty of peace' with their counterparts in North Vietnam, that a crippling strike in one country can have similar effects in another, that foreign conflicts can underlie domestic assassinations and kidnapings, that the multinational corporation is gaining prominence as an international actor[1] — that, indeed, the variety of persons and groups at the subnational and supranational levels who contribute to the functioning of the international system and can properly be viewed as international actors is undergoing exponential growth.[2] The systematic data gathered on the extent of interdependence amply confirm one's impressions. Many of these have been brought together and cogently analyzed by Robert C. Angell.[3] Among his numerous findings relative to the postwar world is clear evidence of increasing study and research abroad, of growing penetration of other societies by businessmen, and of a steady annual growth in the number of new international nongovernmental organizations (NGO's).[4]

Similarly valid is the conclusion that the distinction between domestic and foreign policy is becoming increasingly blurred and that linkages between national and international politics are increasingly pervasive. It requires no great powers of observation to realize that the nonpolitical trends toward interdependence noted above give rise to political parallels. One need only reflect on the tendency for *coups d'état* to come in waves, and protest movements to resemble each other in timing and tactics, to appreciate the extent to which the political process of countries are linked to each other. Recognition

[1] For an interesting analysis of this trend, see Jack N. Behrman, *National Interests and the Multinational Enterprise: Tensions Among the North Atlantic Countries* (Englewood Cliffs, N.J.: Prentice-Hall, 1970).

[2] For a thorough discussion of the variety of new actors emerging on the world secne, see J. David Singer, 'The Global System and Its Subsystems: A Developmental View,' in James N. Rosenau, editor, *Linkage Politics: Essays on the Convergence of National and International Systems* (New York: The Free Press, 1969).

[3] *Peace on the March: Transnational Participation* (New York: Van Nostrand Reinhold, 1969).

[4] Angell estimates that roughly 300 new NGO's are founded every five years. *Ibid*., p. 132.

of the prevalence of linkage politics is also evident in a number of concrete ways. Within the same year, for example, the Council on Foreign Relations, an organization long devoted to an exclusive concern with international affairs, found it necessary to organize a study group on the Domestic Bases of U.S. Foreign Policy, while the Center for the Study of Democratic Institutions, an organization long committed to improving the institutions and practices of intranational politics, found it appropriate to organize a conference on the conduct of international relations.

As for systematic data depicting the nature and extent of linkage politics, these are abundantly available, albeit they have not yet been gathered together in a single volume. The scope of linkage politics is so vast and the relevant data so voluminous that all attempts to bring coherence to the subject have proved less than successful.[5] Nevertheless, the central thrust of all the data affirms the emergence of a transnational politics.

Clearly the domesticization of foreign policy and the swift development of previously unrecognized forms of interdependence have fostered pressures toward regional or subregional polities, if not broad supranational ones. The prime findings of Angell's inquiry not only point to the presence of an 'intersocietal web' but, even more importantly, amount to good evidence that there is 'a broadening stream of influence on national policy-makers toward accommodation among nations resulting from transnational participation.'[6] Likewise, Ernst Haas has compiled systematic data that depict an increasing readiness on the part of the members of one international organization (the International Labor Organization — ILO) to accept its conventions,[7] particularly in the area of human rights.[8] Systematic evidence that, in certain issue areas, similar tendencies are at work in the United Nations and the European Economic Community has also been uncovered.[9] To innumerable quantitative findings such as these can be

[5] Cf. two efforts at synthesis organized by the present writer: James N. Rosenau, editor, *Domestic Sources of Foreign Policy* (New York: The Free Press, 1967), and *Linkage Politics, op. cit.*

[6] Angell, *op. cit.*, p. 180.

[7] Ernst B. Haas, *Beyond the Nation-State: Functionalism and International Organization* (Stanford: Stanford University Press, 1964).

[8] Ernst B. Haas, *Human Rights and International Action: The Case of Freedom of Association* (Stanford: Stanford University Press, 1970).

[9] For example, see Hayward R. Alker, Jr., 'Supranationalism in the United Nations,' in James N. Rosenau, editor, *International Politics and Foreign Policy* (New York: The Free Press, revised edition, 1969), pp. 697–710; Chadwick F. Alger, 'Interaction in a Committee of the United Nations General Assembly,' in J. David Singer, editor, *Quantitative International politics* (New York: The Free Press, 1968), pp. 51–84; and Leon N. Lindberg and Stuart A. Scheingold, *Europe's Would-Be Polity: Patterns of Change in the European Community* (Englewood Cliffs, N.J.: Prentice-Hall, 1970).

added the recent pattern whereby international organizations are serving as the arena for attempts to come to grips with the new issues of the postnational order, especially the problems of protecting the ocean floor, policing outer space, minimizing air hijackings and thwarting political kidnapings.

III

The fact that the world is increasingly aware of its interdependence, however, is no assurance that national polities will prove to be obsolete and that new political arrangements will emerge to replace them. The presumption that the ascendancy of regional or global polities will lead to a corresponding decline in the authority of national polities allows one to preserve a sense of symmetry, but it may also be profoundly inaccurate. Just because the interdependence of the late Middle Ages led to the evolution of the nation-state system does not mean that the nation-state system will inevitably dissolve and a new type of system will evolve to cope with the expanded interderpendence of the nuclear age. Just because the instrument of diplomacy developed to facilitate interaction among nation-states does not mean that it will necessarily fall into disuse as the bases of interaction change. No omniscient hand guides history from epoch to epoch, always insuring that the institutions, processes and values of each epoch are different from its predecessor's. Overlap is possible, with aspects of one epoch persisting even as a new one emerges and takes hold.

This is not simply academic caution. There is considerable evidence that the nation-state is maintaining its independence and authority even as global interdependence mounts and supranational entities acquire added authority. For each of the trends depicted above contrary ones can be noted and supported with comparably reliable data. Much of the research which identifies the emergence of supranational tendencies also provides evidence of the persistence of national ones. Angell's work is a case in point. In order to follow up his finding that increasing transnational participation is subjecting national policy-makers to pressures toward accommodation with other nations, he used five varied measures to construct an 'Index of National Receptivity to World Responsibilities' and ranked ninety-one nations on it.[10] In terms of face validity, the index appears to be measuring what its title suggests (the countries ranked first, second and third were, respectively, Sweden, Denmark and Norway, and the ninetieth and ninety-first were South Africa and Albania); but it must also be noted that the

[10] Robert C. Angell, 'An Index of National Receptivity to World Responsibilities' (mimeo., 1970), pp. 1–14.

scores of the ninety-one societies varied widely and showed no signs of the convergence necessary to justify a conclusion that the world's policymakers are responding similarly to the pressures to accommodate to each other.

Haas doubts whether his data showing a growing national readiness to accept the ILO's conventions amount to anything more than 'internal posturing' and concludes that the overall thrust of his findings offers little basis for optimism: 'the authority of the international machinery is not improving; the overall record of national compliance is very poor and shows no signs of improvement; compliance is concentrated among countries least in need of international prodding, whereas those most in need remain uniformly unresponsive.'[11] In like manner the researchers who demonstrated substantial progress on the part of the EEC also found that the growth has been uneven, 'that individual sectors or issue areas [in which the EEC operates] seem to tend toward equilibrium, and that as integration proceeds, more and more sectors are likely to follow suit and the whole [EEC] system may become more resistant to growth.' They felt obliged to conclude from their data that 'Even if the French government becomes more European, and even if Great Britain gains entry, our long term projection [for the EEC] is still for an overall equilibrium situation.'[12]

Still another set of findings raising doubts about the trend toward a world polity was that developed by K.J. Holsti, who sought to ascertain, through a content analysis of 972 statements by the leaders of seventy-one governments during a recent three-year period, what roles statesmen perceive their societies to play in the international system. Holsti found that national policymakers primarily perceive their society's role in its own immediate region and that perceptions of a role in the global system are minuscule by comparison.[13] As he puts it,

> The world may be appropriately characterized as polar in terms of the distribution of military capabilities and some selected issue areas, but from the point of view of many governments, international regional issues and roles are most salient. Though many become involved in some multilateral and global issues through the United Nations, their chief concerns are much closer to home.[14]

[11] Haas, *Human Rights and International Action, op. cit.*, pp. 115, 118.

[12] Lindberg and Scheingold, op. cit., p. 305.

[13] K.J. Holsti, 'National Role Conceptions in the Study of Foreign Policy,' *International Studies Quarterly*, September 1970, pp. 233–309; in particular, see Table 2 on pp. 274–276.

[14] Ibid., p. 291. For other systematic inquiries into regional orientations of national polities, see Louis J. Cantori and Steven L. Spiegel, editors, *The International Politics of Regions: A Comparative Approach* (Englewood Cliffs, N.J.: Prentice-Hall, 1970), and Roger W. Cobb and Charles Elder, *International Community: A Regional and Global Study* (New York: Holt, Rinehart and Winston, 1970).

To a vast array of quantitative findings such as these can be added a never-ending stream of current events affirming the continued viability of the nation-state. When the United States withdraws its support from the Asian Bank and withholds it from the ILO, when the members of the EEC fail to agree on a common currency before the deadline, when the Soviet government compels one of its citizens to avoid acceptance of an international honor, such actions demonstrate that nation-states still posses ultimate authority and a readiness to use it.

IV

It must be emphasized that the problem posed by these contradictory trends is not one of assessing which of the two sets of data supporting them is the more reliable and valid. Both can be presumed to be reliable and there are also substantive reasons to have confidence in their validity. As will be seen, the conclusion that the world is presently marked by tendencies toward both centralization and decentralization need not be either surprising or confounding. Viewed from this perspective, the problem is to assess whether the contradictions indicate but a stage in the gradual deterioration of the nation-state system or a permanent condition. Do the assertions of national independence merely reflect old habits that are bound to disappear in the face of mounting interdependence? Or are the old habits likely to persist even as new ones develop to cope with the new issues created by interdependence? Are we witnessing the emergence of a global polity or a pluralistic one, part global, part regional and part national?

In the absence of a crystal ball, one's answer depends on his theory of world political processes. There are two contradictory lines of theory to which the analyst might well subscribe. One offers a basis for explaining the present scene as a transitional stage in a historic progression toward a global polity; the other provides grounds for interpreting current conditions as likely to persist indefinitely. The former, elaborately developed by a variety of scholars and claiming many distinguished adherents, is known as the functionalist model. The latter, still inchoate and supported by only a handful of somewhat apologetic researchers, has yet to win a widely accepted title. Some refer to it as the pluralist model, but here we will call it the adaptive model in order to emphasize its central concepts.

The functionalist approach anticipates the emergence of a global polity through a slow, indirect process whereby specialized international organizations perform functions not performed by the nation-state and, in so doing, satisfy human needs in the area of their specialty. Satisfaction in one area is then conceived to spill over into other areas, gradually fostering an ever-expanding community of interests and values that will weaken the authority of the nation-state and progressively narrow the range of its legitimacy. In its simplest form, functionalism posits the spill-over process as eventually creating such widespread and deep loyalties to supranational institutions that the habitual orientations toward the nation-state will erode and even the most traditional functions performed by the national polity will be taken over by 'higher' authorities.

More cautious neofunctionalists recognize that the boundaries between functional areas may be high and that integrative lessons learned in one area may circuitously 'dribble out' rather than spill over to others, but they will presume that the boundaries between issue areas are permeable and could disappear.[15] They thus inferentially accept the possibility of supranational polities and, if pressed for an interpretation, would doubtless consider the recent tendency toward international efforts to cope with the new issues of the postnational era as evidence of movement in that direction. Most neofunctionalists, for example, would probably view the International Civil Aviation Organization conference that led fifty nations to sign a convention outlawing the hijacking of civilian aircraft[16] as one more incremental step in the world's transition to a supranational polity. From the perspective of functionalist theory, the present asymmetry is a logical and necessary prelude to the demise of the nation-state system.

The outlines of the adaptive model are not nearly as clear-cut as those drawn by the functionalists. A number of researchers have questioned the premises of functionalism and suggested that the world of the future may be marked by pluralistic political forms. Nevertheless, a succinct effort to trace the theoretical bases for anticipating continued pluralism is difficult to find. What follows is thus a somewhat rough and inconsistent attempt to specify the main components of an alternative model which anticipates an interdependent world of independent nation-states.

A central assumption of this alternative model is that the adaptive capacities of the modern nation-state are considerable. While there is much about the aspirations of national polities and their policy-making orgnaizations that seems outmoded, their ability to keep the fluctuations of their essential structures within acceptable limits (my definition of national adaptation[17]) is not as fragile as the

[15] For thorough presentations of the functionalist and neofunctionalist positions, see David Mitrany, *A Working Peace System* (Chicago: Quadrangle Books, 1966); James P. Sewell, *Functionalism and World Politics* (Princeton: Princeton University Press, 1966); and Haas, *Beyond the Nation-State*, op. cit.

[16] *New York Times*, December 17, 1970.

[17] 'The Adaptation of National Societies: A Theory of Political System Behavior and Transformation,' in J.N. Rosenau, *The Scientific Study of Foreign Policy* (London: Frances Pinter Publishers, 1980), revised ed., pp. 502–503.

functionalist's model assumes. Most national polities are still able to reallocate their resources and revise their orientations,[18] and they manage to do so in such a way that their essential structures are not overwhelmed by the rapid and numerous internal and external changes with which they must presently cope. Equally important, the motivation to maintain rather than abandon the national polity as the instrument of adaptation to greater interdependence continues to derive considerable strength from established habits. Although the habits of exercising and obeying the authority of national polities may be inappropriate to the new types of issues now emerging, there remain many of the old issues — military security, internal order, selection of rulers, regulation of the mass media of communication, provision of welfare — for which the habits were designed and on which the advent of greater interdependence has had no noticeable impact.

Like any other human entity, the national polity can be conceived as pursuing one of four basic and mutually exclusive adaptive orientations if it is to maintain its essential structures and survive. It can seek to adjust its present self to its present environment; it can try to shape its present environment to its present self; it can attempt to create a new equilibrium between its present self and its present environment; or it can accept the existing equilibrium between its present self and its present environment. In order to simplify discussion, these four alternative sets of orientations have been designated as giving rise to, respectively, the politics of acquiescent adaptation, the politics of intransigent adaptation, the politics of promotive adaptation, and the politics of preservative adaptation.[19]

Each of the four sets of orientations is conceived to be the basic posture from which all policy decisions spring, and as stable and enduring as long as the relative strength of the demands emanating from within the polity and those arising in its present environment do not change. If such changes do take place, the national polity is seen as either undergoing a transformation to one of the other adaptive orientations or failing to survive. While there are instances of national polities being conquered or voluntarily absorbed into a larger entity, modern history records that they usually survive and that adaptive transformation rather than extinction is their typical response to profound social and technological change. The model posits an electoral or violent ouster of political leaderships as normally necessary to the occurrence

[18] For a cogent analysis of the continued viability of the nation-state as a form of political organization, see John H. Herz, 'The Territorial State Revisited; Reflections on the Future of the Nation-State,' in Rosenau, *International Politics and Foreign Policy*, op. cit., pp. 76–89.

[19] Present-day Czechoslovakia, South Africa, China and Great Britain are, respectively, illustrative of the four types. For a full analysis of each type, see my 'The Adaptation of National Societies, op. cit., pp. 504–26.

of any of the twelve possible transformations, and for some of them (especially the transformation from either intransigent or acquiescent to preservative adaptation), a major societal upheaval would appear to be a prerequisite.[20]

In our model, then, the cost of rapid change and mounting interdependence is more likely to affect individual officials, whole regimes, and even entire elite strata than the basic political forms through which societies conduct their affairs. Rather than being replaced by more comprehensive polities, national polities will cope with the quickening pace of interdependence and the new kinds of issues it creates through transformations of their basic orientations toward their environments. More specifically, the model posits a long-term trend in which all national polities undergo transformations in the direction of preservative adaptation.[21] In an era of more coherent, sizeable, and demanding attentive publics at home and greater dependence on resources and support from abroad, none of the other types of adaptation seems viable.

Attentive publics at home will not tolerate prolonged acquiescence to external dictation (albeit recent developments in Czechoslovakia suggest that the durability of the politics of acquiescent adaptation can be underestimated) and the changing world scene will not permit intransigent insistence on the perpetuation of domestic institutions deemed by most nations to be noxious (albeit South Africa has demonstrated that the fragility of the politics of intransigent adaptation can be exaggerated). Eventually, therefore, polities will be compelled to seek an equilibrium between themselves and their environments and, given the scarcity of resources necessary to sustain growing populations in an industrial order, will increasingly have to forgo aspirations to promote desired equilibria and accept those that are built into their geographic, historic and cultural situations. Even the United States, possessed of vast resources and an outward-looking value system, found the politics of promotive adaptation no longer possible and underwent a transformation to preservative adaptation (perhaps beginning, at least symbolically, with the showing of Senator Eugene McCarthy in the 1968 New Hampshire presidential primary).[22]

V

As developed to this point, our model falls short of a persuasive answer to functionalism. To conclude that most or all nations will

[20] Ibid., pp. 526–330.
[21] See ibid., p. 533, for the bases of this expectation.
[22] Ibid., pp. 519–21.

eventually pursue the politics of preservative adaptation is to indicate how they may be able to sustain their traditional functions in the face of mounting interdependence. This conclusion does not account, however, for the impact of the new issues and functions to which interdependence and a rapidly changing technology have given rise. The functionalist can still argue that current trends are only transitional phenomena, that preservative adaptation is merely a stage in the long process of spill-over, that even the preservatively adaptive polity will be unable to perform the functions required by the new issues, and that, consequently, the ultimate transformation will be the replacement of preservatively oriented national polities by supranational ones. This argument is countered by the very nature of preservative adaptation, especially the capacity which polities so oriented develop for distinguishing and maintaining rigid boundaries among issue areas.

Let me elaborate this further. In our model of an asymmetrical world, the preservatively oriented polity accepts the emergence of new issues, either at home or abroad, which have transnational ramifications, and it does so with the recognition that such issues cannot be handled in conventional ways. Consequently, by the very nature of its basic orientation, the preservatively adaptive national polity will not seek to redefine the new issues in terms of the traditional functions it performs but will choose instead to allow supranational institutions to develop the capacity to cope with them.

There are several reasons underlying this expectation that the politics of preservative adaptation will not lead to the classic nation-state pattern of treating emergent problems as subsumed by the traditional functions. First, the issues of the postnational order are more thoroughly transnational than has even been the case in the past. National decision-makers will find it more and more difficult to view the problems created by mounting interdependence as matters of strict national concern or as challenges which they have the authority to resolve. Increasingly they will be forced to recognize that many desired solutions require compliance by groups and publics over whom they have no authority. The interdependent nature of the issues, in other words, will be so glaring that the preservative orientations of national officials will lead them to accept the help of 'higher authorities' in coping with the issues, even while reserving the right to participate in their resolution in a supranational arena.

Second, the new issues of the postnational order are sure to be much more technical than the conventional issues of earlier eras, with the result that national decision-making agencies are unlikely to have developed the personnel and organizational competence to deal with them. Such problems as controlling pollution and developing the ocean floor require reliance on an expertise, made up of specialized personnel and of organizational skills, that most foreign offices cannot acquire. Supranational agencies, on the other hand, are in a position to develop the wherewithal to confront the new issues. Able to draw on a much larger pool of man-power and less encumbered by long-established procedures, they can recruit the personnel and develop the organizational skills a successful confrontation requires. These capabilities are added incentives for national decision-makers to let their supranational counterparts cope with transnational problems. One of James Reston's main conclusions after a recent visit to the Soviet Union bears out this idea that national decision-makers do not readily develop the same sense of competence toward newer issues that they have with respect to established ones:

> The odd paradox and ambiguity here [in Moscow] is that officials seem very confident about their ability to handle the conflicts of a divided world but not at all confident about reaching out with the United States to create a new and more dependable world order. They clearly don't want war with the United States and are prepared to talk about an accommodation on arms control and a political settlement in the Middle East, but they have nothing to say about the coming age, no wider vision of a more unified world community.[23]

Third, the rewards for flexibility on the part of national decision-makers will be heightened by the paradoxical fact that the new issues of the postnational order are highly visible and intimate as well as extremely technical. Unlike most of the conventional issues of the nation-state system, they impinge directly on individuals. Whether the air one breathes is polluted or the jet one travels on is hijacked matters more to the average person than the issues involved in maintaining the balance of power or collaborating in a foreign assistance program. The individual may not comprehend the scientific, economic and legal technicalities of the new issues, but he knows full well that their outcome affects him. As a result, postnational issues will be the focus of vigorous and sustained activity on the part of attentive publics, and since attentive publics are becoming larger and more articulate,[24] their activities will seem capable of threatening the continued tenure of national decision-makers. The latter will be glad to 'pass the buck' to supranational authorities, or, at least, will not try to maintain full control over the issues when it means contesting the preservative orientations of their publics.

This is not to say that preservatively oriented oficials will accede to all or even most demands that problems be handled at supranational

[23] James Eston, 'Nixon and Breshnev,' *New York Times*, December 20, 1970, p. E-11.

[24] For elaborate data depicting this trend, see James N. Rosenau, *Citizenship Between Elections: An Inquiry Into the Mobilizable American* (New York: Free Press, 1974), Chapter 2.

levels. Their readiness to proceed in this manner will obtain only with respect to problems of interdependence that have not been previously experienced. On issues for which there is precedent and which can be resolved within the jurisdiction of the polity, the long-established habits of decision-making are likely to prevail and national officials can be expected to cling stubbornly to their authority. The stubborn retention of authority in regard to conventional issues and the accommodative transference of it in attempting to deal with new ones is neither an attitudinal nor a behavioral contradiction for those with a preservative orientation. It is in the nature of this form of national adaptation for the boundaries between issue areas to be firmly maintained and for officials and publics alike to view the essential structures of their societies as more susceptible to fluctuation in one area and less so in another. Only in this way can the flow of domestic and foreign demands be kept in equilibrium. Only in this way can the requirements of mounting interdependence be met without violating those past arrangments that are still viable.

At the same time, an asymmetrical world of national and supranational polities will not want for attempts to bargain across issue areas. The stronger the feelings of officials or publics of national polities about issue X, the more inclined they will be to offer concessions on issue Y in exchange for compliance with their position on X. The processes of bargaining issues off against each other are by definition a more central feature of a preservative orientation than of the other three forms of national adaptation. Without such a process, the inherent balance between internal and external demands cannot be established and maintained. This readiness to bargain across issue areas, however, is not inconsistent with the aforenoted readiness to maintain firm boundaries between the new postnational issue areas and the old ones. The adaptation model posits different attitudes toward bargaining within each type of area on the one hand and between the two types on the other. Officials are conceived to view the bargaining process within the old and new types of areas as necessary and desirable, but bargaining between them as unnecessary and undesirable.

To be sure, the temptation to trade new issues off against old ones will amost certainly arise. There will doubtless be occasions when a demand on an old issue seems so threatening to some essential structure that officials will consider withholding accommodation on a new issue as a price for withdrawal of the demand. Some officials may even temporarily succumb to this temptation, but not for long, as our model posits them or their publics as being quick to realize that such a posture constitutes an even greater threat to their essential structures. Furthermore, since habitual attachments have yet to surround the values at stake in the new issues, they are unlikely to emerge as comparable to — and thus subject to trade-offs for — the values that sustain the old issues. It seems highly unlikely, for example, that even in an acute crisis over Berlin, threats by one party to withhold participation in global attacks on atmospheric pollution would succeed in evoking concessions from the other party. Conversely, it seems equally implausible that retaliation with respect to Berlin would ever be used to gain advantage in a dispute stemming from an ecological crisis.

In sum, the adaptation model acknowledges the growing interdependence of world affairs, allows for the emergence of new, supranational political entities to process the problems created by interdependence, and at the same time assumes that the nation-state system, with all its accompanying conflicts and procedures, will persist undiminished. If the model is valid, the new world politics of the future will supplement, but not replace, the world politics that has prevailed for centuries.

VI

We must ask as tough empirical questions about the asymmetrical image of world politics as we have about the symmetrical image. Most notably, we must ask whether in fact the boundaries between the two basic types of issue areas will remain high and relatively impermeable. There is little systematic evidence applicable to the question. Issue-area phenomena have been investigated at the level of local and national polities, and at these levels the data indicate that individual citizens, political organizations and governmental agencies are capable of differentiating both attitudinally and behaviorally among issue areas.[25] At the international level, on the other hand, with one possible exception there have been no systematic inquiries into the capacity of national polities and international organizations to separate and insulate their activities in one area from those in another. Voting behavior in the United Nations has been subjected to intense issue analysis,[26] but the relationships among issues have not been deeply probed and the

[25] In particular see Robert A. Dahl, *Who Governs: Democracy and Power in an American City* (New Haven: Yale University Press, 1961), and Warren E. Miller and Donald E Stokes, 'Constituency Influence in Congree,' *American Political Science Review*, March 1963, pp. 45-56. For more conceptual inquiries into the problem, see Theodore J. Lowi, 'American Business, Public Policy, Case-Studies, and Political Theory,' *World Politics*, July 1964, pp. 677-715, and my 'Foreign Policy as an Issue-Area,' in Rosenau, *Domestic Sources of Foreign Policy*, op. cit., pp. 11-50.

[26] See, for example, Hayward R. Alker, Jr., and Bruce M. Russett, *World Politics in the General Assembly* (New Haven: Yale University Press, 1965).

consequences of these relationships for more conventional diplomatic situations have been ignored.

The one exception in this regard is the study by Lindberg and Scheingold of the development of the European Community. These two researchers created a 'scale of the locus of decision-making' that ranged from a low score of 1 ascribed to issue areas in which 'all policy decisions [are made] by national processes' to a high score of 5 for areas in which 'all policy decisions [are made] by joint Community processes.' They then relied on their knowledge of the European scene

> to score the scope of European Community decision-making [in twenty-two issue areas] for four separate key dates: 1950, before the launching of the European Coal and Steel Community; 1957, just before the EEC and Euratom treaties came into effect; 1968, the time of writing; and 1970, the year when, according to the EEC and Euratom treaties, the Common Market is to be completed.[27]

These rankings are reproduced in Table 1. Assuming that their scoring is valid, their data indicate clearly that supranational polities can and do widen the scope of their authority in some areas even as national polities firmly retain their authority in others. Table 1 supports the central hypothesis of the adaptive model, that the capacity to differentiate and insulate issues is an integral part of the evolution of asymmetrical political structures. A cautious and elaborate analysis of the data presented in Table 1 led Lindberg and Scheingold to the interpretation that 'the nation-state remains the clearly dominant final decision-making locus, although its almost total monopoly has been clearly broken and the trend is in the direction of more joint activity.'[28] Nevertheless, they also predict that this trend will end and that the asymmetry depicted in Table 1 will persist into the foreseeable future.[29]

In addition to these few systematic data, one's own reading of the world scene provides considerable reason to have confidence in the capacity of national polities to maintain high issue-area boundaries when interacting with each other. The recent history of Soviet-American relations reveals a pattern in which negotiations progress in one area even as severe conflict marks another. The arms control negotiations between the two countries are conspicuous in this respect. While their pace is painstakingly slow, progress does occur, and it is clear that it results precisely because the negotiations have somehow been insulated against the many other conflicts that mar Soviet-American relations. The simultaneity of conflict and cooperation between the two superpowers is a major characteristic of present-day world

[27] Lindberg and Scheingold, op. cit., p. 70.
[28] Ibid., p. 75.
[29] See p. 60 above.

Table 1. THE SCOPE OF THE EUROPEAN COMMUNITY SYSTEM: 1950 to 1970*

	1950	*1957*	*1968*	*1970*
External Relations Functions				
1. Military security	1	1	1	1
2. Diplomatic influence and participation in world affairs	1	1	2	2
3. Economic and military aid to other polities	1	1	2	2
4. Commercial relations with other polities	1	1	3	4
Political-Constitutional Functions				
5. Public health and safety and maintenance of order	1	1	2	2
6. Political participation	1	1	1	1
7. Access to legal-normative system (civic authority)	1	2	3	3
Social-Cultural Functions				
8. Cultural and recreational affairs	1	1	1	1
9. Education and research	1	1	3	3
10. Social welfare policies	1	2	2	3
Economic Functions				
11. Counter-cyclical policy	1	1	2	3
12. Regulation of economic competition and other government controls on prices and investments	1	2	3	3
13. Agricultural protection	1	1	4	4
14. Economic development and planning	1	2	2	3
15. Exploitation and protection of natural resources	1	2	2	2
16. Regulation and support of transportation	1	2	2	3
17. Regulation and support of mass media of communication	1	1	1	1
18. Labor-management relations	1	1	1	1
19. Fiscal policy	1	1	3	3
20. Balance of payments stability	1	1	3	4
21. Domestic monetary policy	1	1	2	2
22. Movement of goods, services, and other factors of production within the customs union	1	2	4	4

Score:

1 = All policy decisions by national processes.
2 = Only the beginnings of Community decision processes.
3 = Policy decisions in both but national activity predominates.
4 = Policy decisions in both but Community activity predominates.
5 = All policy decisions by joint Community processes.

*Adapted from a combination of Figure 3.2 and Table 3.1 in Lindberg and Scheingold, op. cit., pp. 69, 71.

politics. Exceedingly graphic evidence of the pattern occurred on December 12, 1970, when the front page of the *New York Times* carried two adjacent stories, one headlined 'Moscow Cancels U.S. Visit by Bolshoi Ballet, Opera' and the other, 'U.S.-Soviet Pact on Fishing Signed.'

Nor is the Soviet-American pattern unique. Once one becomes sensitive to high issue-area boundaries in relationships, one begins to realize they are pervasive phenomena evident in widely varied circumstances. U.S.-Algerian relations, for example, broke down in 1967 when Algeria severed diplomatic ties with the United States during the Arab-Israeli war. These ties remain severed four years later, but business and commerical relations between the two countries have flourished nonetheless. Although there is no American embassy or aid mission in Algiers, the number of American businessmen and technicians in the country has tripled since 1967 and U.S. exports to Algeria increased by 21 per cent in 1969 over 1968.[30] Examination of a number of other conflictual international relationships would almost certainly yield similar findings.

It is hardly surprising that people, individually and collectively, can maintain high boundaries between issue areas. Modern relationships are generally so complex — be they formal or informal, intense or superficial, composed of two persons or of many — that functional differentiation is almost essential within them. This means that the tasks that have to be performed to sustain a relationship will require different sets of attitudes and behavior in different functional areas. Since the requirements of one area will often be in conflict with those of another area, contradictory attitudes and contradictory patterns of behavior will be required as the focus of the relationship shifts from one area to another. In order to preserve the valued aspects of the relationship, moreover, none of the parties to it is likely to allow the attitudes and behavior appropriate to the conflictual areas to contaminate the others. Anyone who has ever shouldered responsibilities in one branch of a large organization will affirm that it is possible to wrangle bitterly with counterparts in other branches over one matter in the morning and agree enthusiastically about another matter in the afternoon. Likewise, anyone who has ever enjoyed a dynamic marriage will know that anger over the performance of one task can shift easily to affectionate cooperation when attention turns to another. In short, modern individuals are adept at varying the performance of their roles in response to the many different demands of complex relationships to which they are a party.

[30] *New York Times*, December 15, 1970, p.16.

VII

The foregoing formulation contains an important normative implication, namely, that it is not only possible but highly desirable to maintain firm boundaries between issue areas in complex relationships. For sensitivity to issue-area boundaries leads also to the realization that it is characteristic of stable and/or desirable relationships to have strong boundaries and characteristic of unstable and/or undesirable relationships to have weak ones. More accurately, systems of interaction that one tends to value are not dominated by any one issue or issue area, whereas systems that one tends to loath are usually marked by one predominant issue area. The Cold War, for example, was a single-issue-dominant period of postwar history, whereas the fact that Soviet-American animosity no longer determines the outcome of all problems at the international level is perhaps the surest sign that world politics has moved into a new, multi-issue era. Similarly, the Middle East is presently dominated by a single issue, and few outsiders would deny that the Arab–Israeli dispute operates to the detriment of all the polities in the region. In like manner, unrewarding marriages, uncreative organizations and authoritarian societies tend to be single-issue-dominant systems in which the conflicts of one area undermine interaction in all areas.

The dedicated functionalist should not be too dismayed by the adaptive model outlined here. The notion that national polities will persist as authoritative in traditional issue areas and that supranational polities will emerge as authoritative in new areas, with spill-over kept to a minimum, contains the possibility of both a stable and a creative world order. Anything else might well be retrogressive. For if the boundaries between the issues of the traditional nation-state system and those of the postnational order do not hold, the habits that have sustained the former would probably overwhelm the needs that have fostered the latter, thus returning world politics to the uncreative and counterproductive procedures which have characterized it for so long. Viewed from this perspective, it becomes important that the emerging pluralistic patterns continue to grow. Odd as it may seem, there is good reason to aspire to and work for an asymmetrical future of independent national polities in an interdependent world.

5 The Tourist and the Terrorist: Two Extremes in the Same Transnational Continuum*

This chapter derives from two major concerns, one relating to the dictates of logic and the other to the stirrings of intuition. Both involve the consequences of the basic structural changes that have marked world politics in the last two decades: if it is assumed that the proliferation of those who initiate international action and a host of other changes have so greatly increased the interdependence of peoples and societies as to transnationalize the structure of the global political system, logic dictates that traces of this transformation ought to be manifest in the daily routines of at least some individuals. For reasons outlined below, I am prepared to make the assumption of significant systemic change, and thus I am concerned about the logical implications that follow from it.

But I cannot be fully secure with the assumption until traces of the transnationalizing process at the level of daily life can at least be conceptually identified. This is not possible today because the existing paradigms for studying world politics are not flexible enough to cope with the vast changes which have occurred. Although few analysts dissent from the view that the world is increasingly interdependent, and while many have written about the implications of the transformations wrought by transnationalization, corresponding paradigmatic revisions have yet to be made that allow for causal processes which

*Earlier versons of this chapter were presented at the Annual Meeting of International Studies Association, Washington, D.C., February 22, 1978, and the Workship on Transnational and Transgovernmental Relations and International Outcomes, sponsored by the European Consortium for Political Research, Grenoble, France, April 6-11, 1978. For a version translated into French, see James N. Rosenau, Le Touriste et Le Terroriste ou Les Deux Extrêmes du Continuum Transnational,' *Études Internationales*, Vol. X (Juin 1979), pp. 291-252.

both reach into and spring from the routines of individuals, families, and communities.

The major thrust of this chapter thus consists of a search for micro units of analysis — and the outlines of a paradigm in which to locate them — appropriate to the present-day study of world politics. This search is reinforced by a strong intuitive sense that national loyalties have undergone profound alteration in recent years and, if so, that the alterations are partly a result of structural changes in world politics. In searching for micro units of analysis, therefore, the ensuing discussion will consider what may be happening to national loyalties. In the end loyalty is not posited as a micro unit, but rather is treated as a possible source of variation in the performances of the micro units.

WHAT ARE MICRO AND MACRO UNITS?

The micro-macro distinction has come to pervade social scientific inquiry because it is a convenient way of differentiating between crucial dimensions of human affairs — between the parts and the whole, between entities and the patterns they form, between limited scope and large scale. Unfortunately, however, the distinction has not been applied carefully by students of politics. All too many analysts have tended to use it in a static way, as merely a means of labeling different levels of aggregation, with 'micro' usually referring to individuals and 'macro' usually designating collectivities. Such a simple equating of the distinction with levels of aggregation is bound to be static, even misleading, because there are a great variety of individuals and many types of collectivities and the only way to cast all individuals at the micro level and all collectivities at the macro level is to ignore the dynamics of their variability. Thus, in effect, when used to differentiate between individuals and collectivities the micro-macro distinction does not enhance analysis. It merely identifies levels of analysis. It implies the existence of links between lesser and greater degrees of aggregation but in no way facilitates the drawing of the links. How the whole is shaped by its parts, or the pattern by its constituent elements, cannot be inferred from micro-macro distinctions that fail to specify which aspects of the levels of aggregation they encompass.

The limitations and confusion inherent in the way political scientists have come to differentiate micro and macro phenomena can be easily demonstrated. Consider, for example, a major foreign policy initiative by the chief executive of a major power. Is this a micro or a macro phenomenon? Because it was undertaken by an individual (or perhaps a small group of individuals), it would have to be treated as a micro phenomenon, albeit most students of foreign affairs would be restless with such a conception, preferring instead to view it as state action at the macro level. Such confusion is in sharp contrast to the clarity achieved by economists when they distinguish between micro and macro phenomena. For many of them, the micro unit is the firm and the macro unit is the economy, and variations in the former (say, borrowing for expansion) can be traced to variations in the latter (say, inflation), and vice versa.

In short, in order to render the micro–macro distinction dynamic and thereby more clearly discern the links between parts and the whole, the basic units at each level of aggregation must be specified in such a way that their variabilities as well as their commonalities are identified. That is, they must have attributes and structures (as do firms and economies). A micro unit of analysis is thus an entity that (compared with the macro units to which it may be linked) is limited in scale and yet pervasive throughout the phenomena under investigation. An attribute of a micro unit is any of its prime characteristics, whereas a micro structure is the composition of a micro unit, the ways its parts form a whole. As conceptualized here, all micro units are sufficiently similar in their attributes and structures to be classified together and yet their attributes and structures are sufficiently variable to allow for distinctions among them (as an economist may distinguish between large and small or heirarchical and decentralized firms). Equally important, the variability of micro units allows for the possibility that they may undergo change, either in response to their own internal dynamics or to alterations in their environments.

It will be noted that this formulation does not equate micro actors with micro units. Indeed, no mention is made of actors. This is quite purposeful. The concept of 'actor' has also not been used carefully by students of world politics. Sometimes actors are conceived to be individuals (e.g., voters or the President) and sometimes they are treated as collectivities (e.g., the electorate or the United States). Similarly, sometimes macro structures are posited as the patterned behavior of individuals as actors, while at other times they are treated as the patterned interactions of actors as collectivities. At still other times they are conceived to be the interactions that give rise to actors as collectivities. Thus, for example, the balance of power is posited as a macro structure resulting from the interactions of nation-states as collectivities on the one hand and from the interactions of individual chiefs of state on the other, whereas in still other formulations the established interaction patterns within the macro collectivities of the balance of power constitute macro structures.

To avoid this terminological and conceptual confusion, and also to facilitate clarity in the search for micro units, the ensuing analysis makes no reference whatsoever to actors. Instead action is posited as emanating from either micro or macro units. The formation of macro units occurs whenever micro units are aggregated into organized entities (such as governments, multinational corporations, professional societies, and international organizations) with established procedures and regulations which govern the conduct and interactions of their micro units. Those who initiate or respond to the action emanating from micro or macro units are here posited in highly concrete and empirical terms: as role occupants in the case of micro units and as officials or spokespersons in the case of macro units. Only identifiable individuals, in other words, would be treated as 'actors' in this formulation if the term were to be used.

The macro units resulting from the aggregation of micro units may also be viewed as macro structures (in the sense of the patterns formed by their interacting micro parts), but I find it useful to reserve the label 'macro structure' for interaction patterns that are not regulated by organized entities. Thus in the paradigm constructed here macro structures are posited not only as, so to speak, self-regulating interaction patterns, but also as more encompassing than macro units and, in many instances, as founded on them. The paradigm conceives of the formation of macro structures as occurring in either of two ways: they consist either of the patterns that result from the separate actions of micro units (such as the population explosion) or of the patterns that result from the interaction of macro units (such as the balance of power that results from interacting governments or the international market that results from competing corporations). As will be seen, it is also useful to distinguish the two types of macro structures in terms of the aggregative processes that underlie their formation: the micro-action type involving unintended aggregation and the macro-interaction type being founded on intended aggregation.

ARE MACRO UNITS AND STRUCTURES FOUNDED ON THE BEHAVIOR OF MICRO UNITS?

The question is not trivial. The way in which we answer it is central to how we study world affairs and where we search for the dynamics of change. However macro and micro units may be identified and defined, if they are not causally linked to each other — if what a colleague calls the 'deep' macro structures of world politics[1] have become so deeply embedded in the course of events as to be virtually independent of

[1] Richard K. Ashley, 'The Modern Security Problematique: Growth, Rivalry, Balance, and the Search for a Peaceful Order' (unpublished paper, School of International Relations, University of Southern California, November 1977), how the basis of Ashley's *The Political Economy of War and Peace: the Sino-Soviet-American Triangle and the Modern Security Problematique* (London, Frances Pinter Publishers, 1980).

variations in their original micro sources — then we can probe the recent transformations of world politics without having to worry about the relevance of micro phenomena. Likewise, if the flow of causation between macro and micro units goes only in one direction, with the performance of the former influencing the latter but not vice versa (because world politics is so thoroughly dominated by states and their international institutions), again there would be little utility in investigating micro phenomena. Logic may dictate that traces of basic structural changes in international politics ought to be manifest in the routines of daily life, but there is little reason to follow these dictates if greater comprehension of micro changes does not also facilitate more penetrating insights into macro transformations.

Nor is the answer to the question self-evident. Causation does not necessarily flow symmetrically in two directions. A case for viewing macro phenomena as not founded on the performance of micro units can easily be made. If, for example, the whole is greater than the sum of its parts (as would seem to be the case in world politics[2]), then it could be argued that the sources of the difference between it and the sum of its parts derive from the dynamics of macro processes. That is, it may be that at least some significant dimensions of world politics are self-sustaining, with some of their structural elements being reinforced by interaction among them rather than by the micro units of which they are comprised.

Notwithstanding the possibility that macro units may be independent of their micro foundations and that the causal link between the two may originate asymmetrically only with the former, I am inclined to give an affirmative answer to the question of whether micro units serve as foundations of macro phenomena. More accurately, I think the strongest case can be made for a perspective in which macro and micro units are interactive, with each influencing or structuring the other in important ways that in turn become part of an endless flow of causation back and forth between them. This is not to imply a perfect symmetry. On the contrary, if the whole is greater than the sum of its parts, it seems likely that ordinarily the macro units will have a greater impact upon their micro components than vice versa. Even so, the summing of the parts is relevant. I find it hard to imagine any system, even the most system-dominant system, which is impervious to major, pervasive, and similar changes on the part of most

[2] For a discussion of this point, see my essay entitled, 'The External Environment as a Variable in Foreign Policy Analysis,' in James N. Rosenau, Vincent Davis, and Maurice East (eds.), *The Analysis of International Politics* (New York: Free Press, 1972), pp. 145–65. A more general, and extremely cogent discussion of how macro wholes become greater than their micro parts can be found in Thomas C. Schelling, 'On the Ecology of Micromotives,' *Public Interest*, No. 25 (Fall 1971), pp. 59–98.

of its micro subsystems. Macro economics takes the attributes and structures of firms as givens, but surely economies will undergo significant transformations if most of the firms they encompass experience common alterations.

Macro units and structures that are relatively stable through time, in other words, can be analyzed as if their micro components are constants and therefore not of particular analytic relevance. But this is not to say that the micro units are substantively irrelevant. The stability of the macro unit or structure can be partially traced to the constancy of its micro components, and vice versa, so that the causal flow continues to operate even though the performance of the micro units can be taken for granted. We know this because if either the macro or micro units should undergo profound change, the equilibrium between them would presumably be disturbed and the alterations in one set would presumably be traceable in the other. Thus, while the interaction between the macro and micro units may not be symmetrical, the two are not totally independent of each other. Some interaction does occur and, consequently, at least a minimal flow of causation is always operative. The search for micro units of analysis appropriate to the present-day study of world politics would thus appear to be a worthwhile enterprise as well as an exercise in logic.

Of course, not every entity that may be defined as a micro unit is necessarily caught up in the flow of causation. As will be seen, the transformation of world politics in a decentralized direction does not justify treating every member of the world's population as the micro unit of analysis. Or, more accurately, certainly these are a number of issues on the global agenda that are sustained irrespective of the performances of many potential micro units. Asian peasants or urban workers, for example, vary their performances so little that they are unlikely to be very relevant to the changing structure of world affairs in the foreseeable future.

In short, the search for appropriate micro units must be theoretically guided. The micro units must have attributes and structures that vary in ways which are conceived to be linked to variations in the macro units of which they are parts. If the analyst is hard pressed to conceive of how one or another aspect of a candidate micro unit might be a source of possible changes in macro structures, then either the analyst's theoretical insight is insufficient or the candidate unit lacks sufficient scope.

MACRO-MICRO INTERACTION: PROCESSES OF AGGREGATION AND DISAGGREGATION

To comprehend the dynamics of change in world politics we need to develop a conception of how the flows of causation between micro and macro units operate. These do not unfold in a mystical manner, as some analysts seem to imply. They may occur unbeknownst to the units affected by them, and evidence of the flows may not always be immediately apparent to the detached observer; but the ways in which macro and micro phenomena interact are concrete, identifiable, and susceptible to empirical examination. The links in the causal chain are to be found in several processes of aggregation and disaggregation, and the distinctions among these processes help focus the search for appropriate micro units.

Two of the processes channel the causal flows from macro to micro units and another two flow in the opposite direction. For want of better terms, I shall call the latter *unintended aggregation* and *intended aggregation* and designate the former as *policy disaggregation* and *indiscriminate disaggregation*.

Unintended aggregation occurs when a multiplicity of micro units undertake similar behavior to serve their own private purposes. Each action is designed to serve each micro unit's needs or to advance its goals; but because the actions are all similar even though the needs or goals may be diverse, the actions are summable. If the sum has consequences for the performance of one or another macro unit, then that sum will eventually be recognized and highlighted by spokespersons for macro units. Once it thus enters the arena of public discussion as a macro phenomenon, its components (the unrelated and yet similar micro acts) will have been aggregated. The population explosion, resource shortages, or financial crises are cases in point. A family has a child, fills its car with gasoline, or purchases a television set made abroad unconcerned or unaware that elsewhere millions of families are doing the same. At some point the cumulative consequences of these private acts (the people crunch, the energy crunch, or the trade imbalance) are discerned by journalists, researchers, public officials, or a host of other possible spokespersons for macro units, and the resulting publicity about the implications of the unintended aggregation then feeds into the structures and processes of world politics.

This is not to dismiss the very lengthy time lags that may ensue between the cumulative micro patterns and the public acknowledgement of them by spokespersons for macro units. Indeed, it is the discrepancy between unintended aggregation and its activation on the agenda of world politics that, in effect, reveals the 'deep' structures of international systems. Prior to the articulation of the aggregation, or during subsequent periods when it is quiescent as a public issue, policymakers for macro units may unknowingly encounter the opportunities and limitations inherent in the aggregated patterns while making decisions and launching undertakings relevant to the issues then on the global agenda. The aggregated consequences of the population explosion or of widespread distrust of government, for example, were surely encountered by policymakers long before their explicit recognition as a public problem was articulated, and surely they will continue to be so encountered in the future even if they are not active issues. Unintended aggregation of micro units, in other words, can operate as basic parameters of macro processes to the extent it limits or channels the scope or direction of those processes. As such, they are deep structures — unarticulated givens for policymakers that are no less important links between micro and macro phenomena for being deeply buried in the responses of macro policymakers to the issues they confront.

The distinction between micro-macro interaction that occurs when unintended aggregation is unarticulated on the one hand and articulated on the other also helps clarify how the whole becomes more than the sum of its parts. Once an unintended micro aggregation is publicly identified and enters the global agenda, it is no longer merely a sum of micro actions. The very fact of focusing macro attention upon it makes the aggregation something more — a problem or issue — than it had previously been. However accurate the macro articulation of the sum of micro units may be — and often spokespersons for macro units argue about what the correct sum of an aggregation is — it serves as the basis for that part of the whole that is more than the sum of its parts. Perhaps the classic illustration of this point is an arms race. Once decisions and counter-decisions to increase military stockpiles are publicly identified and treated as a major issue on the global agenda, an arms race acquires a momentum of its own that is more than the sum of all the decisions made by each of the parties to the race.

Turning now to intended aggregation, this consists of the same behavior by micro units undertaken at the same time and explicitly designed to have consequences for macro structures. Whether the intended effect occurs or not, aggregation ensues and causal links are forged because those seeking to organize the micro units will need to call public attention to their purposes and plans in order to concert the micro behavior and give direction to its cumulative impact. The efforts of a government to activate the citizenry for war or of opponents to generate public protests against military participation are obvious examples of intended aggregation. Indeed, many attempts to initiate the processes of intended aggregation spring from a desire to offset or undo the consequences of unintended aggregation. Advocates of new governmental policies to control rising birth-rates, for instance, are seeking to reverse or moderate the course of an unintended aggregative process. While the two aggreative processes may thus be interactive as they forge links with macro structures, they are nevertheless separable and can usefully be analyzed separately. The distinction between them is the difference between unplanned consequences and calculated organization, between latent and manifest cumulation, between individual and collective action, between diffused and mobilized behavior.

There is another distinction between unintended and intended aggregation worth noting: the former is, so to speak, leaderless, while the latter culminates with spokespersons calling attention to the aggregated behavior. That is, unintended aggregation gives rise to macro structures that are salient, perhaps even crucial, dimensions of the world scene as they limit or enhance what can be accomplished by those who move around in the global arena seeking to articulate, manage, or resolve issues on its agenda. Because the structures resulting from unintended aggregation consist of many diverse and unorganized parts, however, they neither have designated leaders nor positions in which leaders could be placed. To be sure, as previously noted, they become more than the sum of their parts when their existence is hailed or condemned by those in the global arena who work on issues. But those who have occasion to highlight the existence of unintended aggregations are spokespersons for organized macro units whose goals are served by hailing or condemning the unintended aggregation. The population explosion, for example, is a hard 'reality' of present-day global politics that simply exists. No leaders speak for it or are otherwise authorized to act on its behalf. Those who try to control it and give it direction act on behalf of such macro units as governments, U.N. agencies, and private organizations, which are not part of the demographic upheaval itself. The population explosion may respond to these control efforts, but such responses are precipitated from outside and are part of a different, intended process of aggregation.

Virtually by definition, on the other hand, intended aggregations do have leaders and spokespersons. Whether micro units are linked together in organizations or are unrelated to each other but mobilized to act in the same way for a particular purpose, the resulting macro aggregations require positions of leadership to serve the organizational goals or advance the purposes for which mobilization was initiated. Thus the world scene is pervaded with spokespersons shouldering responsibility for the orientations and activities of macro units and seeking to promote or preserve change in macro structures. Viewed in this context of spokespersons associating themselves with aggregated outcomes, much of world politics is a contest among leaders of intended aggregations over the legitimacy of their claims to allocations of the global pie. And, indeed, while the claims of the spokespersons may not accurately reflect their intended aggregations, the latter probably would not exist if it were not for the formers' efforts to mobilize micro units to undertake particular forms of behavior. No leaders or organizations intentionally precipitated the aggregative processes that brought the population explosion into being, but many can rightfully claim credit for having initiated intentional aggregative processes — e.g., with birth control educational programs — that reduced or eliminated the worst consequences of the explosion in particular countries or regions.

The causal flows from macro to micro units — the processes of disaggregation — can also be usefully subcategorized in terms of intentionality. Policy disaggregation involves those actions undertaken at the macro level that are aimed at specific micro units and designed to alter or preserve particular aspects of their behavior or structure. The implementation of a foreign aid program, a military intervention, a U.N. program to eradicate disease or upgrade nutritional levels — whatever governments or other macro units do to carry out policies directed at identifiable publics — are illustrative of this form of disaggregation. The policies may or may not achieve their intended effect upon the targeted micro units, and the chain of causation may not even reach its ultimate micro destination, but the disaggregative process that does occur is precipitated in a planned way. This makes it distinct from disaggregative processes not subjected to guidance and control. These unfold when micro units experience the consequences of interaction among macro units. The latter can seek to affect each other in a variety of ways and for a variety of reasons that do not include an intended impact on micro units. In so interacting, however, the macro units can initiate unplanned causal chains that indiscriminately link into the structures or processes of micro units. The 1973 oil embargo by Arab countries designed to enhance their position in the conflict with Israel is an obvious example of indiscriminate disaggregation. The consequences of the embargo sharply affected micro units in those industrial communities dependent on the automobile and lacking sufficient domestic oil supplies.

STRUCTURAL CHANGES IN WORLD POLITICS

In order to identify appropriate micro units and trace how they may be linked to basic transformations in world politics, we need to specify briefly the nature of recent macro changes. In so doing it must first be conceded that while all the indicators point to the unfolding of basic transformations, the reasoning underlying this conclusion is founded not so much on systematic evidence as on impressions of central tendencies. The conduct of foreign relations and the course of international affairs seem so different from the past as to justify an assumption of fundamental structural change, but empirical efforts that treat the assumption as an hypothesis to be tested are few in number and limited in scope.[3] Nevertheless, somehow most students of world politics, myself included, regard the presence of basic transformations as too self-evident not to be taken as given. Lest we slip into treating this assumption as established fact, however, it is useful to remind ourselves at the outset that a few analysts look out on the same world scene and come to a contrary conclusion. Some contend that appearances are deceiving, that all the indicators of transnationalization are merely surface and transitory phenomena, that the essential structure of the state system remains no different from what it has been for centuries, and that it will not be long (say, when the next severe world economic depression ensues) before the parameters of the billiard ball model of world politics are once again plainly manifest.[4] For reasons noted below, I reject this interpretation and fully subscribe to the transformation assumption, but such a view does alert one to the necessity for caution in tracing the outlines of structural change.

Although a multiplicity of changes accompany the basic transformation of any social system, five recent changes in the structure of world politics seem especially relevant to our concerns. One is the proliferation of macro units. A second is the substantial decline in the capacity of governments to meet challenges and, indeed, to govern. A third is the extensive mushrooming of subgroup loyalties and a corresponding growth of divisiveness in national communities. A fourth is the growing demand for a redistribution of wealth on the part of disadvantaged groups and nations. And a fifth is the broad expansion of the range of issues about which macro units conflict.

These dynamics are, of course, interactive. A demand for the redistribution of wealth may intesnsify subgroup loyalties which, in turn, reduce governmental capacities. But they are also independent

[3] Among the few systematic efforts to probe empirically for structural change on a global scale are P.J. Katzenstein, 'International Interdependence: Some Long-Term Trends and Recent Changes,' *International Organization*, Vol. 29 (Autumn 1975), pp. 1021–1035, and R. Rosecrance, et al., 'Whither Interdependence?' *International Organization*, Vol. 31 (Summer 1977), pp. 425–472.

[4] For an analysis that emphasizes the continuities of world politics and dismisses the changes as superficial, see F.S. Northedge, 'Transnationalism: The American Illusion,' *Millenium*, Vol. 5 (Spring 1976), pp. 21–27.

structural dynamics in the sense that all of them foster as well as reflect change elsewhere in the system. (All of them are also products of a dynamic technology and emerging resource scarcities, but I prefer to treat these dynamics as contextual rather than structural dimensions of the global system because they encompass nonhuman variables and are not exclusively founded on social interaction.)

Conceiving of macro units as those entities that undertake actions which have direct consequences across national boundaries, then the ways in which the structures of world politics have undergone change as a result of the recent proliferation of units are readily apparent. Unlike earlier eras, when international affairs were largely sustained by relatively few nation-states, the present period has witnessed a tripling of the world's nation-states, the emergence of many international and supranational organizations composed of governmental and/or nongovernmental members, and the surfacing of innumerable subnational groups — all of which engage in activities that span national boundaries and contribute to the formation or maintenance of issues on the global agenda. The ranks of macro units now include multinational corporations, scientific societies, trade associations, labor unions, local governments, terrorist organizations, ethnic-religious-linguistic groupings, political parties, crime syndicates, and a host of other functional and issue-based units as well as nation-states and international organizations. As a result of this proliferation, the structures of world politics are much more decentralized — i.e., the capacity to initiate and sustain meaningful actions across national boundaries is shared much more widely — than was previously the case and the processes of world politics are thus much more elaborate and circuitous.

And with decentralization, of course, has come a diminution of the heirarchical structure of the global system. Where several decades ago the system was marked by a bipolar structure that progressively loosened in the 1960s to the point where it was widely characterized as multipolar, now a vast array of outcomes are determined less by the dominance of the strong over the weak and more by bargaining among units whose capabilities are not so greatly imbalanced.

Let us anticipate the analysis to come by noting that the proliferation and diversity of present-day macro units does not intrude insuperable obstacles in the way of the search for micro units. As the subtitle of this paper implies, there is at least one common dimension — or continuum — to be found across the diverse array of old and new international units, a dimension that allows for clear-cut links between the performance of the micro units and the changing structures that sustain a more decentralized and less heirarchical global system.

Turning to the second basic change in world politics, the decline in the governing capacity and effectiveness of governments, this is not limited to particular governmental forms but, perhaps for various reasons, is rather pervasive throughout the First, Second, Third, and Fourth Worlds. Governments could never be very successful in their efforts to affect the course of events abroad — there being too many cultural, historical, and linguistic barriers between themselves and the targets of their foreign policies[5] — but now they also find it increasingly difficult to frame policies that maintain effective control over the course of events at home. Many — even most — governments preside over divided societies, communities driven by conflicting aspirations, loyalties, and demands, and their resulting weaknesses have tended to bring foreign policy issues ever more centrally into the arena of domestic politics. Where governments were once able to keep foreign affairs relatively isolated from domestic problems, now their weaknesses have hastened the breakdown of the domestic-foreign distinction which began long ago with technological breakthroughs in transportation and communications. Viewed in this context, for example, it is hardly surprising that an American president recently resorted to the rhetoric of military crisis in an effort to promote a domestic legislative proposal. If nothing else, the description of an energy policy as 'the moral equivalent of war' demonstrates how thoroughly foreign and domestic policies have become inter-mixed and how limited governments are in their ability to persuade publics to come to terms with the intermixture.

The decline in the effectiveness of governments as macro units has contributed to the transformation of world politics in several ways. It has intensified the tendencies toward decentralization and diminished hierarchy by virtue of the lessened scope of governmental authority and competence. That is, the emergence of other macro units has been facilitated by the void which the decline in governmental effectiveness has created. In the case of those governments that preside over complex industrialized systems, moreover, the weaknesses of their central authorities — weaknesses stemming from a shortage of expertises and time to cope with the global agenda as well as from societal division and a lack of confidence and trust — have also enhanced the importance of governmental micro units located in bureaucracies below the top officials.[6] The decentralization of global politics, in other words, has also been accompanied by a corresponding proliferation of relevant micro governmental units.

Equally important, the decline in governmental effectiveness would appear to have destablized the conduct of world affairs. Where the

[5] For a discussion of the severe limits to effective foreign policy, see James N. Rosenau, *The Scientific Study of Foreign Policy* (London: Frances Pinter Publishers, revised ed., 1980), Chapter 10.

[6] For a persuasive essay along these lines, see R.L. Paarlberg, 'Domesticating Global Managment,' *Foreign Affairs*, Vol. 54 (April 1976), pp. 563-577.

earlier structures of global politics were rooted in the ability of governments to make and carry through on foreign commitments decisively and unambiguously, now the structures are more fluid and less stable as governments find it necessary to pause and equivocate, perhaps even delay and avoid, when confronted with challenges and crises. To some extent, in other words, inertia has come to destablilize the structure of world politics. Issues linger longer and their endings tend to be more in the nature of temporary expedients than of permanent resolutions — not only because the newer socio-economic issues of today are more complex than the older diplomatic-military kind which dominated earlier global agendas, but also because the governmental units that process them are less able to proceed with dispatch and clarity.

But decline is not demise. Though weakened and much less able to maintain effective control over the course of events, national governments remain centers of decisions and prime movers in world affairs. A day does not pass without headlines depicting the great political, economic, social, and military power of national authorities throughout the world. And it is precisely here, in the conflicts between the expectations and demands of the proliferating non-governmental macro units on the one hand and the weakened but still powerful national governments on the other, that one's analytic intuitions sense that a profound alteration may be occurring in the nature of national loyalties. As new units, new issues, and changing modes of interaction come to prevail in an ever more decentralized world, those who contribute to the performances of the macro units and contest the outcomes of the new issues seem destined to find themselves frequently in recurring situations of conflicting loyalties. If this is so, then the ways in which the initiators of action in micro units resolve the conflicts become crucial (through aggregative processes) to the transformation of world politics as well as (through disaggregative processes) to the conduct of their daily lives. As will be seen, this reasoning provides an important guidepost in the search for the identity of micro units.

Much the same can be said about the third type of structural change on which our assumption of underlying transformation in world politics is found. It will be recalled that this involves a growing coherence and importance on the part of sub-national groups and a corresponding increase in divisiveness within national communities. For a multitiude of reasons, ranging from a heightened sense of ethnicity to a deepened frustration over the ills of an industrial order, feelings of group identity would on a worldwide scale appear to be undergoing redirection from the national level to those organizations, movements, and symbols that represent the specific and immediate ties people have to others. The Scots in Scotland, the French in Quebec, the South Moluccans in Holland, and the Blacks in the United States are but a few of the sub-national groups that are making claims on attitudes and loyalties that once were directed at national entities. This fragmentation, of course, has contributed substantially to both the proliferation of macro units and the decline in governmental effectiveness. No less important, it has also altered the basic structures of world politics by bringing questions pertaining to the internal fabric of societies much more fully onto the global agenda. Where the rights, welfare, and aspirations of sub-national groups were once strictly domestic matters, now they are an integral part of the global system, rendering its structures more volatile as well as adding to the tendency toward decentralization.

As the salience of sub-national groupings mounts, the dynamics of loyalty again becomes central to the identity and performance of micro units. What might be called 'sub-groupism' has, in effect, become a strong rival of nationalism as a basis for their key orientations toward macro units. Indeed, as noted below, sub-groupism can operate as a prime variable in the course followed by the processes of intended aggregation and, accordingly, in the degree of stability of global structures.

The fourth change assumed to be at work in world politics, a growing and more persistent demand for a redistribution of wealth on the part of disadvantaged groups and nations, has also contributed to the decentralization of world politics and the lessened imbalance of its hierarchical structure. Sensitive to growing disparities between the rich and the poor and emboldened by the bargaining leverage and redistribution successes attained through the manipulation of oil prices, the countries of the Third World are pressing hard in a number of ways for a larger share of the world's bounty. Where once both donor and recipient nations emphasized the need for aid in order to facilitate economic development, now the latter stress that aid is a matter of distributive justice, and this reformulation of the issue has further broadened the global agenda and weakened the hierarchical structure that for centuries enabled the strong to prevail over the weak.

The fifth structural change in world politics relevant to the search for micro units involves the emergence of a wide range of new socio-economic issues that have come to supplement — and often influence, even compete with — the military-security issues that have traditionally dominated the global agenda. Largely products of dynamic technologies and growing resource scarcities, these new issues have all surfaced with the ever-mounting interdependence among societies which marks the last quarter of the twentieth century. Not until now has the global agenda been crowded with such problems as monetary stability, polution, energy shortages, terrorism, ocean jurisdictions and space explorations, and weather control — to mention but a few of the myriad issues that have accompanied greater and greater interdependence. These issues have affected the structure of world politics in several important ways. They are partly responsible, of course, for the entry of many new macro units into the world's political arena. The banks that handle the flow of money, the industries that pollute the air and water, the oil companies and producer organizations that manage the flow of energy, the terrorists groups that control the spread of a particular form of violence, and the scientific and legal agencies that work on the uses of oceans and space are illustrative of how the newer issues of interdependence have swelled the population of macro units.

Equally important, many of the newer issues overlap both each other and the older military–security issues. Space and oceans, for example, can be battlegrounds as well as resource sites and this defense component can exert a strong pull on the way in which the contests for resources in the air and sea unfold. Thus, even as the newer issues have further decentralized world politics by adding to the ranks of macro units, so has the overlap among them made global structures more intricate. It may seem like a contradiction in terms to conclude that a tendency toward decentralized complexity underlies the course of events, but that is surely one of the major structural changes at work in world politics today.

Still another structural consequence concerns the large extent to which the new issues of interdependence have broadened the knowledge base from which the conduct of world affairs springs. Not long ago it was possible, for example, for a foreign service to train its recruits as generalists and presume they could be readily reassigned to work on any problem in any area of the world. But the newer issues have made the concepts and findings of physics, geology, biology, agronomy, demography, oceanography, and many other specializations so relevant to the course of events as virtually to render the generalist obsolete. Indeed, as indicated elsewhere, the newer issues have elevated expertise — its development and application — to the status of a major element of power in world politics today.[7]

Another possible structural consequence of the newer interdependence issues concerns a potential increase in the cooperative behavior of leaders and spokespersons for macro units. On the face of it the new issues seem likely to foster multilateral cooperation among governments, perhaps even more so than among non-governmental organizations. As indicated in Chapter 3, such issues involve disputes over the natural environment which are not readily circumscribed by political boundaries and which thus most governments cannot manage through unilateral action. While at first governments may be inclined to find their own solutions, eventually it may become

[7] See Chapter 3 above.

clear that independent policies will not resolve interdependent problems. Accordingly, it seems likely that some form of agreement will eventually have to be evolved among those states interdependently linked by their shared reliance on the same environment. To be sure, this shared reliance may not be perceived or it may be sacrificed in favor of narrow definitions of national interests. It is in this sense that structural tendencies in the direction of more cooperative interaction can presently be viewed as only a possible development. Should it occur, however, it would further confound the dynamics of change in world politics, for it means that the pressures toward decentralization are accompanied (perhaps even offset) by others that foster integration.

The fact that the newer interdependence issues may pose alternative directions for the future evolution of world politics serves to underscore the search for relevant micro units. Plainly the question of whether cooperative structures are to become more prominent features of the global system will depend to a high degree on the performance of micro units. For notwithstanding the diverse nature of the newer issues, they do share several qualities — the absence of long-standing precedents and the presence of complex expertises — that can have integrative or disintegrative consequences for world politics if they evoke common responses on the part of micro units.

THE SEARCH FOR MICRO UNITS

In order to place the search for micro units in an appropriate perspective, it is useful to note briefly what micro phenomena have served as basic units of analysis in the two paradigms of world politics that preceded the present, transnational model: namely, the billiard ball or realist model of an undifferentiated state system that was most widely applied prior to the late 1950s and the differentiated state model that came into vogue in the 1960s. These earlier paradigms differed considerably in their specification of micro units. For users of the realist paradigm the search was easy. Because only the actions of nation-states were considered to have significant consequences, and because all states were conceived to respond to the same stimuli in the same ways for the same reason (like billiard balls hit from any angle with any degree of force), the realists had no difficulty specifying nation-states as the micro units. These all have attributes and structures, and they also meet the test of being both sufficiently similar to allow for meaningful aggregation and sufficiently different to allow for variability and change.

More accurately, the realist model conceives of nation-states as varying in their attributes and structures while being identical in their orientations. Their variable sizes and resources underlie variations in their attributes while different cultures, histories, and political institutions underlie variations in their structures. Whatever these differences, however, the realist model treats all nation-states as moved by the same orientation, that of acting to advance their interest in terms of the power (i.e. attributes and structures) available to them. By thus defining the behavior of individuals and sub-national groups as irrelevant to the conduct of world affairs, the realists can focus exclusively on nation-states as micro units, as entities governed by the same rules when responding to each other and to the macro balances or imbalances they form through processes of aggregation. Different states are acknowledged to have different power bases and their responses to the prevailing balance of global power may differ accordingly, but the realist model has rules that systematically allow for such differences — rules, for example, that indicate when weak states should join alliances and when strong states should eschew them, or when each type should demand, concede, arm, fight, or otherwise engage in a variety of foreign policy behaviors on behalf of their national interests.

It was precisely because the micro units of the realist model no longer seemed adequate that the differentiated state paradigm came into vogue. As the global structure became increasingly multipolar and the countries of the Third World gained statehood in the late 1950s and throughout the 1960s, such changes evinced too much variability in both state behavior and macro structures for observers to feel comfortable treating nation-states as undifferentiated in their responsiveness to common stimuli. For many (and eventually most) analysts it seemed evident that the different attributes and structures of different states had come to underlie varying processes that produce different definitions of national interests and, accordingly, variability in foreign policy behavior that does not necessarily conform to the same, system-wide rules of conduct.

Two quite unalike micro units were developed and utilized by those analysts who came to prefer the differentiated state model over the realist paradigm. Some sought to trace the variability deriving from different attributes and structures by defining the state in terms of its duly constituted officials and then treating foreign policy decisions as the micro analytic unit out of which macro structures are aggregated. This approach allows for assessments of the effects of variations in public opinion, cultural values, historical precedents, and the many other domestic attributes and structures that can underlie decisions. And, by reconstructing the world as decision-makers perceive and experience it, this approach also permits comparisons of the relative importance of internal factors on the one hand with external stimuli on the other.

The second micro unit developed by analysts who opted for the differentiated model did not go so far in breaking down state behavior. Instead the foreign policy event was posited as the micro unit and conceived in such a way as to account for variability stemming from different attributes and structures. In most event–data schemes events are defined as a particular form of action undertaken by a state toward a specified target. By applying such a formulation to one or more public information sources, such as *The New York Times*, the variability in state attributes and structures can be traced through an analysis of the type of states that initiate events, the form their initiated behavior takes, the agencies within their governments responsible for the behavior, and the targets of their behavior.

Whatever the merits and defects of decisions and events as micro analytic units, they share one important trait. Both are founded on a perspective that treats world politics as resulting primarily from the actions and interactions of states. In one instance the variability of state behavior is laid bare through an analysis of phenomena that precede and lead to choice, whereas in the other case it is uncovered through a comparison of the sources, qualities, and outcomes of the actions that follow choice. Thus, notwithstanding the considerable differences between decisions and events in terms of their scale, scope, duration, and complexity, both micro units are analyzed as products of the same type of macro unit. Neither version of the differentiated state model attempts to account for behavior undertaken by non-governmental or non-state entities. Consequently, in their present form neither version is adequate to the analysis of the transnational world and its varied macro units that have emerged in recent years.

Nor does it seem fruitful to retain decisions or events as micro units by analytically proliferating the population of micro units to correspond with the proliferation of non-governmental macro units whose leaders make choices and initiate events. Such a strategy suffers from the fact that oft-times — i.e., whenever unintended aggregative processes are operative — the transnational consequences of the behavior of micro units do not stem from decisions or events that were undertaken for transnational purposes. Hence any transnational paradigm founded on decisional or event units would preclude examination of important dimensions of the dynamics whereby macro structures persist or change. Moreover, decisions and events initiated by governments are widely reported and therefore relatively easy to research. But the choices and actions of many of the micro units that contribute to macro structures are so widely dispersed and (in a conventional sense) so unnewsworthy that a massive, expensive, and unwieldy survey instrument would be required to investigate them.

It follows that new micro units clearly need to be formulated if the transformations that have rendered world politics both more decentralized and more complex are to be effectively probed. But how to proceed? How do we identify a micro unit that will reflect changes in macro structures even as it also facilitates meaningful analysis across the multitude of diverse macro units that presently mark the world scene? How can we develop a basic micro unit which can serve as a common analytic foundation for comparing the vast range of issues that have lately come onto the global agenda? Dare we develop a formulation that reaches so deep into the fabric of societies and the daily life of communities as to be relevant to hundreds of millions of potential micro units? Can we absorb such a jump in the scale of our analytic efforts? And, if so, can such an increase in the scope of our research be accomplished without corresponding increases in the costs of undertaking it? That is, how do we insure that our proposed transnational paradigm does not become unmanageable, with every individual being treated as a micro unit? How do we maintain the coherence of a paradigm that must allow for an almost infinite diversity of attributes and structures among the millions of micro units that contribute to the processes of aggregation out of which change at the global level stems? In short, how do we theoretically guide the search for analytic units in such a way that such unalike persons as the tourist and the terrorist can be treated as micro units?

I am not sure of the answer to these questions. The ensuing discussion offers an answer, but I am not yet persuaded that it is a satisfactory answer. The task is monumental and it may exceed the present theoretical capacities of any individual, or even the field as a whole. Yet, since it plainly needs to be undertaken, I dare to offer a possible point of departure. If nothing else, what follows can at least serve as an illustration of the magnitude of the problem.

TRANSNATIONAL ROLES AS MICRO UNITS

Several considerations encourage me to believe that a paradigm in which the macro structures of world politics are conceived to be founded on two types of transnational roles as micro units can provide adequate, or at least tentative, answers to the foregoing questions. In this paradigm any transnational role exists apart from the person or persons who occupy it. Thus, like any role, it can outlive individuals and endure as long as the macro unit or structure of which it is a micro part endures. Transnational roles, in other words, are not created by individuals. Rather they are located in macro units and structures and defined by the expectations attached to them by the other units that sustain the macro structures. While the expectations cannot be directly observed, they can normally be inferred from both the performances of a role's occupants and their interaction with other role occupants who comprise the macro units or structures. In effect, the expectations consist of those formal and informal requirements evolved within the macro unit or structure for its own continuance and/or change. Because considerable deviation in the performance of micro roles is usually tolerated within most macro units and structures, the expectations that attach to the roles tend to be general and allow leeway for individual discretion. But they are never so general as to permit total discretion. Each transnational role has limits (which define its boundaries), and performances which exceed these limits signify either that the occupant will exit from the role (via dismissal or resignation) or that the macro unit or structure in which the role is located has undergone change.[8]

As an example of how the expectations and limits of transnational roles operate, consider an executive of a multinational corporation, let us say in the field of office equipment. Both the corporation and the field are part of a macro structure which frames the responsibilities

[8]For an elaboration of the formal, informal, and discretionary dimensions of political roles, as well as of how role boundaries set limits to behavior, see James N. Rosenau, *The Scientific Study of Foreign Policy*, (London: Frances Pinter Publishers, revised ed., 1980), Chapter 7.

and duties of the executive's position, requiring any of its occupants to formulate policies and undertake actions that promote the sale of computers abroad, maintain cordial relations with host governments, or otherwise enhance the corporation's foreign operations and profits. These formal role requirements are supplemented by the informal expectations which emanate from daily interactions within the corporation's home office, with colleagues abroad, and with counterparts in other corporations or organizations relevant to the conduct of business in the computer field. Taken as a whole, the formal and informal expectations tend to promote certain commitments to the corporation, certain attitudes toward competitors, and certain patterns of behavior both within and outside the field. Yet the commitments, attitudes, and behavior patterns can range widely, allowing each executive that occupies the role as much leeway in the quality and direction of his or her performance as is consistent with the limits of the role. But if sales are persistently too low, employees too unproductive, host governments too inhospitable, or for any other reason profits too small — i.e., if performance falls short of expectations — then at some point the role's boundaries will be judged to have been exceeded and the executive will be reassigned, relieved of certain responsibilities, or otherwise removed from the position.

Or consider the terrorist. The expectations and tasks of this role are set by the group or organization formed for anarchistic or political purposes. Often the assignments appear to be specified in great detail even as the occupants of the role are given discretion to cope with unexpected emergencies as they see fit. Should their performances be inconsistent with the role's requirements, however, they will either be dropped (or eliminated) by the terrorist organization or captured (or eliminated) by the targets of their terrorism.[9]

The drinker of coffee offers another kind of example. Here the expectations are very simple. The coffee market and the economies of which it is a part demands of its consumer roles that their occupants pay a particular price for their coffee and that they be prepared to continue to purchase coffee even as its price goes up. However, if the price rises beyond a certain point, or if medical research reveals that the costs of coffee are not only financial, the coffee drinker may not be able or willing to maintain performances consistent with the role and will be forced to exit from the role or switch voluntarily to drinking tea.

Because both the multinational executive and the terrorist may be consumers of coffee, these examples also help illustrate the next

[9] Or, if terrorists are so consistently successful that governments become more compliant with their demands, basic changes in the macro structures of world politics will probably begin to occur.

important point in specifying the micro aspects of the paradigm, namely, that an individual can, knowingly or otherwise, simultaneously occupy more than one transnational role. Indeed, everyone occupies a number of roles that are located in a number of macro structures other than those that sustain world politics. Most occupy roles in family, work, educational, religious, and community systems — to mention but a few of the structures from which social roles stem — and the expectations of many of these roles overlap, sometimes in a reinforcing fashion and sometimes in a conflicting, even mutually exclusive, way. The same behavior can thus conform to the expectations of more than one role or it can be consistent with the requirements of one role and negate those of another.

The simultaneous occupancy of more than one role and the resulting possibility of role conflict facilitates a major step forward in the search for micro units. It facilitates a distinction between two basic types of transnational roles: what I shall designate as *primitive* and *derivative* roles. The former refers to roles in macro units that, clearly and unmistakably, have transnational concerns among their purposes and activities. Primitive roles are micro parts of macro units which would not exist if their activities did not span national boundaries. The terrorist and the multinational corporate executive are illustrative of occupants of primitive roles inasmuch as they are located in organizations that directly and explicitly participate in interactions across borders that divide states. Some roles, on the other hand, are located in macro structures that do not depend on transnational interactions for their existence even though performances in them do have transnational consequences. The transnational expectations attached to such roles are thus only derivative of their origins in other macro structures. The housewife who purchases coffee because of her family's expectations exemplifies a derivative transnational role. Her contribution to aggregative processes that sustain macro transnational structures in the realm of coffee production and distribution is indirect and implicit, perhaps not even known to her as she fulfills the expectations of her family.

This distinction between primitive and derivative transnational roles is important for several reasons. In the first place, it enables us to develop a paradigm founded on variable rather than fixed micro units. Some macro structures and issue situations consist mainly of primitive roles, while others embrace both primitive and derivative roles.[10] The advantage of this variability is that it allows for the analysis of the newer interdependence issues which may encompass hundreds of millions of persons without requiring that our paradigm treat all

[10] It is hard to imagine any macro structure comprised exclusively of derivative roles.

individuals in the world as micro units. Any inquiry based on this formulation proceeds by identifying the primitive and derivative roles subsumed by the questions under examination, and their occupants then become the only micro units that need to be assessed. In the case of issues involving the production and distribution of scarce resources, for example, analysts can exclude from their concern all mass publics and focus only on those who consume the resource. There may be hundreds of millions of coffee drinkers, but there remain large segments of the world's population that can be ignored when analysts focus on issues raised by the scarcity of coffee.

A second reason for distinguishing between the two types of transnational roles is that the dynamics of the newer interdependence issues can be more clearly discerned. This is so because the distinction clarifies the task of macro leaders who aspire to mobilize support on behalf of particular solutions to the issues. The outcome of many of these issues is affected by the aggregate behavior of large masses of producers (e.g., farmers, parents) or consumers (e.g., car drivers, home owners) who occupy derivative roles, and it is the task of the mobilizers to persuade these many producers and consumers to treat their derivative roles as primitive roles. If coffee drinkers can be mobilized to view the macro transnational structure in which their coffee drinking is a micro unit as just as important as the other systems in which their consumption of coffee is relevant, they would then be more willing to boycott coffee or otherwise participate in such a process of intended aggregation. Those in the Third World who work on birth control education and other policies to contain the population explosion will recognize that this need to transform derivative into primitive roles is more than an academic formulation.

The concept of derivative transnational roles also provides a means for systematically including distrust of government as a variable in present-day world politics. It will be recalled that the declining effectiveness of governments is one of the major changes unfolding in the global system and that this is partly a result of citizenries losing confidence in public officials and what they can accomplish. The degree of trust (or distrust) citizens bear toward their governments is derivatively relevant to the conduct of world affairs inasmuch as it underlies their responsiveness (or unresponsiveness) to efforts to mobilize their support for stances taken on the newer issues of interdependence. In the energy field, for example, it seems evident that distrust of government has shaped the unresponsiveness of Americans to attempts to get them to conserve resources and treat their gas-consuming activities as part of a primitive rather than a derivative transnational role. To the extent that the role of citizen involves a readiness to respond to governmental appeals on interdependence and foreign policy issues, in other words, it too can be seen as a micro unit in the transnational paradigm.

Another reason for distinguishing between primitive and derivative transnational roles springs from the aforementioned concern for tracing macro structural changes in the routines of daily life. Logic dictates that such traces ought to be discernible, and yet at first glance people seem to be living their lives as they always have. If many facets of everyday behavior are conceived as expressive of derivative transnational roles, however, then micro traces of the macro transformations in world politics begin to come into view. People do not necessarily occupy derivative roles unknowingly. On the contrary, as the world becomes increasingly interdependent they probably become increasingly aware of their derivative roles and the tensions between these and their roles in other, nontransnational systems. Thus arguments in families over whether to purchase a Toyota or a Ford, discussions among co-workers over whether to form a car pool, or thoughts shared among friends over whether or not to vacation abroad can become micro traces of macro structural change. To be sure, if people unknowingly occupy their derivative roles (as doubtless most coffee drinkers do), then the traces cannot be empirically observed and must be conceptually imposed by the analyst who treats the transnational consequences of daily patterns as reflective of unthinking behavior in derivative roles.

Stated in another way, derivative transnational roles contribute to the 'deep' structures of world politics. Embedded in the daily patterns of many people, and yet not a prime basis for their daily activities, derivative transnational roles serve, through the processes of unintended aggregation as the basis for macro structures because behavior in them tends to be constant, or at least as constant as the stability of the other systems that sustain daily routines. If derivative roles can be viewed as the micro units of 'deep' macro structures, moreover, so can primitive roles be posited as the micro units of the more 'visible' structures of world politics. (It hardly seems appropriate to call the latter, antonymically, 'shallow' or 'surface' structures.) That is, the dynamics, situations, patterns, and crises of world politics unfold in the context of the parameters set by the responsibilities, obligations, and expectations attached to the roles of those who act on behalf of the proliferating macro units in the global arena.

Still another virtue of the distinction between primitive and derivative roles is that it helps insure a central place for governments in the paradigm. There is a danger, to which more than a few observers have succumbed, of so emphasizing the recent proliferation of non-governmental entities as to overlook the continued importance of governments in the course of events. Obviously public officials — elected, appointed, or tenured bureaucrats in the foreign policy-making system — are occupants of primitive roles whose presence in virtually every situation cannot be ignored. There may now be issues and interaction patterns largely sustained by non-governmental entities, but their predominance under these circumstances is never so great as to justify treating officials as irrelevant. No matter how diminished the authority of nation-states may have become, their representatives can still act in such a way as to enhance or limit the capacity of non-governmental entities to achieve their goals. This point is not likely to be overlooked in the context of our transnational paradigm because any inquiry it guides must start by specifying the relevant primitive and derivative micro roles, and analysts are unlikely to proceed without pausing to consider how public officials may contribute to the structures of interest to them.

A final advantage of defining the two types of transnational roles as the micro units of analysis is that it clarifies and simplifies the tasks of research. By focusing on the attributes and structures of these roles the investigator narrows the field of inquiry in manageable ways. All those aspects of role occupants that are peripheral to their behavior in response to (or against) role expectations — and there are many such peripheral aspects — can be excluded from the analyst's purview. To be sure, it is always possible to stretch the analytic net in such a way as to treat every characteristic of role occupants as relevant to their transnational actions, but the probabilities of carrying reductionism to absurd extremes seem much less when roles rather than individuals are treated as micro units. To delineate role expectations, for example, is to render personality traits as peripheral and thereby greatly ease the research task without giving up relevant phenomena. Moreover, it seems reasonable to believe that with a clear-cut specification of the relevant roles and how their sum contributes to macro units and structures, the analyst need not rely on massive and prohibitively expensive research techniques. While some derivative roles may have hundreds of millions of occupants, the scope of the roles are so narrow that standard compilations of economic, social, and political statistics can usually be used to observe the behavior of their occupants and standard sampling procedures can usually be employed in order to reduce to manageable proportions the attributes and attitudes that need to be probed. Much the same can be said about analyzing the primitive roles of many of the new macro units spawned by mounting interdependence. It ought not require a prohibitively large sample of bankers, for example, to facilitate greater comprehension of the contribution of banking institutions to issues of monetary stability in the First World and economic development in the Third World.

THE LEGITIMACY-AUTHORITY CONTINUUM

To feel secure about the distinction between primitive and derivative transnational roles, however, is not to complete the search for micro units. Earlier it was noted that an adequate formulation requires specification of both the similarities and the variabilities among micro units. We have implicitly allowed for variability by indicating that the expectations comprising both types of roles can be issue-specific. Because there is great diversity in both the traditional and newer issues of world politics, the variability inherent in the multiplicity of roles that underlie present-day world politics is surely enormous. It remains to identify the attributes and structures that the two types of roles have in common and that can serve as a basis for introducing coherence and theory into our transnational paradigm. More specifically, since this is a long-run task that cannot be completed here, it remains to point the way to further development of the paradigm by identifying at least one continuum on which all transnational roles can be located and along which their occupants can vary.

In a sense, of course, I have already begun this task. In specifying that each transnational role is located in a macro unit and structure, that it consists of numerous expectations, and that these expectations can often conflict, I have already identified major characteristics of any micro unit. But along what continuum might these vary? One seems especially relevant to all five of the changes in world politics previously outlined. It is founded on the conception that the occupants of any transnational role also occupy many other social roles and the presumption that inevitably this multiple occupancy accords some degree of legitimacy to the transnational role and a corresponding degree of authority to the macro unit or structure in which it is located. That is, by virtue of the overlap among their multiply occupied roles, individuals have to develop a notion of the relative importance of each role they occupy and a set of priorities as to the order in which the expectations of each will be filled. The place of each of their transnational roles in this hierarchy is the legitimacy accorded to it. In short, whatever the issues involved, and irrespective of whether they are primitive or derivative, all transnational roles can be located on a continuum of greater or lesser legitimacy. If the overlap among the roles is extensive and involves mutually exclusive expectations in the form of prescriptions or proscriptions that must be followed, then the legitimacy accorded each role is likely to be closely linked to how much authority is possessed by each of the macro units from which the conflicting expectations emanated.

This legitimacy-authority continuum of transnational roles is especially relevant to the recent changes in world politics because the legitimacy of each such role can come into conflict with the legitimacy of the citizen role and the authority of the nation-state. No matter how much governments and their authority may have declined, there is no issue of world politics which unfolds without governmental policies, regulations, or laws being evoked and laying claim to the allegiance of the occupants of transnational roles. Every individual is viewed by some government as under its jurisdiction. Even terrorists who totally reject state authority are legally regarded as citizens by some state somewhere, if not by their place of birth, then through their need to show a passport when crossing state boundaries. Conflicts between the expectations of transnational roles and the obligations of statehood are thus always potentially operative. And, if 'subgroupism' has mushroomed and the disadvantaged are demanding a redistribution of wealth, and if new non-governmental units have proliferated and become increasingly relevant to the course of events, the frequency, intensity, and duration of such conflicts can be presumed to be growing rapidly.

Presumably, for example, executives of multinational corporations increasingly confront situations in which the policies of their companies and their countries are at odds. Presumably homemakers increasingly encounter discrepancies between purchases that will please their families on the one hand and undermine their countries' trade or energy policies on the other. Presumably the members of trade unions, ethnic groups, and professional associations are subjected to more and more tension over whether to heed the appeals of their subgroup or governmental leaders.

I use the word 'presumably' because hard data on such role conflicts are virtually non-existent. The literature on international production, trade, marketing, and monetary processes is pervaded with observations about the activities of banks, but not about bankers; about import–export firms, but not about importers or exporters; about automobile companies, but not about their managers or union leaders; about international airline associations, but not about airline pilots; about flows of scientific knowledge, but not about scientists; and so on. In effect, what I am designating as macro units most analysts have treated as the micro units of analysis, with the result that data relevant to the legitimacy–authority continuum are scarce.

For reasons already noted, I do not think it is excessive reductionism to suggest that organizations, societies, and associations be recast as macro units and the roles that comprise them be defined as micro units. I would argue that the role conflicts identified above can be resolved in too many ways to assume that all the occupants of the same transnational role — say, all bankers, all traders, or all corporate managers — make the same contribution to aggregative processes. And if variability can mark performances in the same roles, so can variability mark the outcomes of the aggregative processes, thereby yielding changes in world politics that we will not adequately comprehend until we investigate roles as micro units.

One way of launching such a research strategy is that of developing, probing, and testing hypotheses as to where various transnational roles are located on the legitimacy–authority continuum. A point of departure is suggested in the subtitle of this chapter. Terrorists are hypothesized to be at one extreme of the continuum because they accord total legitimacy to their transnational roles and treat their organizations as the only source of authority to which they will respond. At the other extreme are tourists, who are hypothesized to comply with customs procedures or otherwise accede to state authorities during their travels.[11] Most other transnational roles would seem to fall somewhere between the two extremes, the exact location being determined by the degree to which primitive roles incline their occupants to seek ways around state authority whenever they can and the degree to which the occupants of derivative roles are habituated to making their performances consistent with the policies of their governments. As occupants of primitive roles, for example, traders are disposed to pay duties, complete forms, or otherwise to bow to official regulations and are thus probably much closer to tourists than to terrorists on the continuum, whereas multinational corporation executives tend to be trained to view state authority as impeding the carrying out of their responsibilities and therefore are probably located closer to the middle of the continuum. Such a comparison is somewhat more difficult in the case of derivative roles, since much depends on the extent to which governments seek to intrude their policies on the occupants. Energy consumers offer a good illustration. Governmental efforts to get them to form car pools, buy smaller automobiles, drive slower, or otherwise conserve gasoline can vary greatly and, as they do, energy consumers will fluctuate back and forth on the continuum as their habits of compliance with state authority are more or less evoked by the stringency or leniency of their government's policies.

The differences between traders and corporate executives, or between energy consumers and coffee drinkers, may not be very great, but they may be quite relevant to an understanding of the dynamics of their transnational behavior. Much the same can be said about comparisons of any two transnational roles, though their relative location on the continuum may prove hard to pinpoint.

[11] Admittedly some tourists are not averse to minimizing the goods they declare or falsifying the papers they prepare, but most accord legitimacy to their national citizenship roles and habitually comply with state authority.

TRANSNATIONAL EXPECTATIONS AND NATIONAL LOYALTIES

It is here, in speculating about the way in which occupants of transnational roles resolve the conflicts between the demands of their citizen and transnational roles, that intuitions about the changing nature of national loyalties become especially intense. More accurately, the foregoing formulation provides a basis for explaining the intuitive sense that the feeling of unquestioned commitment to 'country' — the habit of unthinkingly abiding by the directives of duly constituted national leaders — may be attenuating on a large scale — if not on a global scale, then at least in those parts of the world where compliance with national policies is not achieved through the constant use or threat of force. The conventional explanation for possible changes in the intensity of national loyalties focuses on the failure of national governments to provide solutions to basic problems. That is, the declining competence of governments is posited as a basis for people losing faith in their country and its institutions (with the deceptions of Vietnam and Watergate providing additional impetus for the loss of faith in the United States). But this explanation suffers from failing to indicate how people forego the habits of loyalty for the processes of semi-rational assessment that lead to the conclusion that national policies no longer merit unthinking acceptance. Given the traditional intensity and depth of national loyalties in many countries, it might be expected that declines in governmental effectiveness would lead to a search for scapegoats or a demand for reform rather than diminished belief in the 'rightness' of country and lessened emotional attachment to its historic symbols. Yet this does not appear to have occurred; or at least there would seem to be much more evidence of reduced national loyalties than intensified reaffirmations of loyalty through a search for scapegoats and demands for reform. (In the United States, for example, there has been no clamor for an investigation into the 'errors' made in Vietnam, as happened in the cases of Pearl Harbor and Korea.)

A perspective that posits a world in which proliferating transnational roles are increasingly in competition with national roles, however, offers insights into why a diminution rather than a resurgence of national loyalties seems to be underway. Part of the insight lies in the greater specificity of transnational roles and the more appealing rhetoric that attaches to efforts to mobilize performances in these roles. Whereas national citizen roles seem constraining in the sense that spokespersons for the state stress the obstacles to progress and offer few immediate and tangible rewards, transnational roles appear liberating in the sense that spokespersons for their macro units emphasize the personal advancement and organizational gains to be achieved through appropriate performance in them. While the state calls on citizens to shoulder the burdens of distant concerns such as national defense and collective welfare, the transnational organization urges its members to accept responsibility for enhancing seemingly more concrete self interests. Thus the rhetoric of the state is founded on sacrifice, on giving up, whereas the rhetoric directed toward transnational roles is based on accumulation, on getting. Surely this difference makes it easier for many people to undergo subtle changes in their habitual responses to various authorities.

But there is, I think, an even more persuasive and direct reason why national loyalties may be undermined by the proliferation of transnational roles. As efforts to convert derivative into primitive transnational roles mount, as attempts to transform unintended aggregative processes into intended aggregation intensify, and as role conflicts involving transnational expectations otherwise become more frequent and acute, so must individuals devote more time and thought to calculating their priorities. And calculation, of course, contravenes the persistence of habit. Because national loyalties are non-calculative and spring from long-standing predispositions which require no thought, they seem bound to erode as citizens find themselves in more and more conflicts over which role expectations to accord the highest priority.

To be sure, the resolution of such conflicts need not be highly conscious and can also become a matter of habit. However, in an era of rapid change in which unfamiliar choices may often arise and old patterns may often seem out of place, it seems likely that the question of priorities will increasingly push its way into consciousness and thereby promote processes of semi-rational assessment. It hardly seems an accident, for example, that recent decades have witnessed a redefinition of many issues as matters of conscience. For all the commentary on how alienation from society is growing, more and more people seem to be assuming the right to decide for themselves whether to accept prevailing societal norms with respect to military service, group prejudices, paying taxes, interpersonal relations, and the like. Indeed, many of the newer issues of interdependence, such as energy conservation and atmospheric pollution, are defined as matters of conscience when spokespersons for macro units seek to convert derivative transnational expectations into primitive roles.

Stated differently (and without trying to fathom the psychological dynamics whereby habits give way to semi-rational calculations), the proliferation of transnational roles has made it easier to exit from the role of loyal citizen.[12] Or at least the advent of

[12] For a dicussion of how loyalty can affect the probability of individuals exiting-from roles, see Albert O. Hirschman, *Exit, Voice, and Loyalty: Responses to Decline in Firms, Organizations, and States* (Cambridge: Harvard University Press, 1970).

proliferating macro units has increased the number of sources from which people obtain the psychic supports and tangible benefits once considered to be supplied only by nation-states.

THE TASKS AHEAD

Much remains to be done if a new paradigm appropriate to the study of world politics in a transnational era is to be elaborated. To have identified a viable micro unit is only to begin the task. Now the identity, attributes, structures, and processes of the various roles that can usefully serve as micro units for the analysis of different global issues need to be conceptualized, as do the ways in which each type of role gets aggregated as the basis of macro units or structures. Obviously, too, variations among the micro units in addition to their distribution along the legitimacy–authority continuum need to be specified and empirical inquiries then undertaken that identify more accurately the relative location of each type of micro unit on the several continua.

It must be stressed, however, that these conceptual and empirical refinements of the micro units are needed because of our interest in the changing structure of world politics and our assumption that both the continuities and changes of the global system are partly founded on the behavior of micro units. As students of world politics, we are not interested in micro units *per se*. We do not particularly care why a few people become terrorists or why many become tourists. These are surely fascinating questions from many perspectives, but our perspective is that of changing macro structures as they build upon and are limited by the variabilities and aggregations of their micro parts. Thus we are interested in terrorists only as their role performances contribute to the balance of payments, the diffusion of cultures, and other macro structures.

To be sure, there may be reason to investigate the motivational sources of micro units if our concern for macro structures goes beyond comprehension to efforts to hasten, slow, or redirect change in world politics. Such an activist orientation would involve us in estimating how to precipitate processes of policy disaggregation that alter the behavior of micro units and, obviously, such estimates would require some knowledge of why people occupy the relevant transnational roles that they do. Even with this activist intent, however, our concern for individual motivation would be guided by and limited to our focus on macro structures.

Much the same can be said about loyalty and the other continua in which micro units may need to be located. As students of world politics, we are not interested in the many moral and legal questions posed by conflicts of loyalty and their varied resolutions. Rather we need only explore the aspects of loyalty that shape those performances in transnational and citizenship roles which are aggregated into macro units and structures. Activists who seek to promote greater citizen involvement in public and world affairs exemplify this point. Their efforts to associate loyalty with greater involvement spring not from a conviction that people would feel better about themselves as citizens if they were more informed about the course of events. Rather they seek to elevate the level of public information because they assume that the processes of intended and unintended aggregation would then result in sounder public policies and more desirable macro structures.

It follows that the central tasks that lie ahead involve conceptual specification and empirical probing of macro structures that parallel efforts to enlarge comprehension of micro units. We need to delineate more clearly the macro structures that sustain change and continuity in world politics, to outline more precisely the boundaries and the overlaps of the various issues that comprise the global agenda, to trace more thoroughly the processes of aggregation and disaggregation that link the macro and micro phenomena, to differentiate more exactly between the aggregate behavior of macro structures and the behavior of spokespersons for macro units, and otherwise to develop more elaborately a basic theoretical framework that is suitable to the study of a decreasingly centralized and yet increasingly interdependent system of world politics.

6 Toward a New Civics: Teaching and Learning in an Era of Fragmenting Loyalties and Multiplying Responsibilities *

The title of this paper is intended to suggest irony. Or at least tension: tension between the mounting burdens of good citizenship and the splintering orientations of those who are supposed to practice good citizenship.

And this tension is, in fact, the central thesis of what follows. I shall argue that the tasks of educators have undergone change as the world becomes more interdependent. I shall seek to show that mounting interdependence has so transformed world affairs as to alter profoundly the nature of democratic citizenship, the dynamics of national loyalty, and the structures whereby authority is acquired and exercised. I shall contend that high levels of information and interest are no longer sufficient to the practice of good citizenship. I shall suggest that modern citizenship now requires of individuals that they relate themselves to the remote worlds of public affairs with the same sensitive and sophisticated sense of self that makes for good ties to their personal worlds. If these contentions are correct, it follows that those of us who teach the young, and thereby participate in the complex processes whereby new generations of Americans are socialized politically, must ponder anew the content of our courses and the kind of learning we want our students to experience.

Put in more dire terms, it is my central thesis that our conceptions of citizenship need to be updated, that the responsibilities of citizen-

*Earlier versions of this chapter were presented at the First Assembly of the Institute for the Advancement of Teaching and Learning, California State University, Northridge, December 9, 1977, and the Annual Meeting of the American Political Science Association, Washington, D.C., September 1, 1979. It is scheduled for publication in *Comparative Political Analysis*, Vol. I, No. 1 (Fall 1980); reprinted with permission of the publisher.

ship in these complex times are far more extensive and elaborate than our textbooks, mass media, and civic action groups appear to realize. Indeed, I would contend that the United States is unlikely to make a thoroughgoing adaptation to the changing circumstances of our ever-more interdependent world unless the conception of citizenship to which succeeding generations of students are exposed is brought into line with the choices that greater interdependence imposes on individuals in all walks of life.

Let me acknowledge at the outset that there are good reasons to wonder whether a modernized conception of citizenship can be developed in time to prevent the breakdown of community. Loyalties may prove to fragment more rapidly than our capacity to highlight multiplying responsibilities. On the other hand, the analysis that follows is essentially upbeat. It discerns unique opportunities for a new civics in the very same processes that are fragmenting loyalties and multiplying responsibilities. The dynamics of complex interdependence are brilliantly exposing to the naked eye the aggregative processes through which individuals are being ever more closely linked to the worlds around them. While the life of communities has always been founded on the aggregation of individual actions, never before has the transformation of individual behaviors into collective problems been so plainly and so poignantly self-evident. There are a multitude of occasions each day to be aware of ourselves as links in causal chains, as contributors to aggregative processes. Whether it be when we start our cars, turn on our air conditioners, or buy our groceries, it is hard not to have a fleeting thought that the very act of pressing the accelerator, raising the thermostat, or purchasing bread is part of a world-wide process. To be sure, some among us repress such thoughts. It is easier to blame oil companies or incompetent politicians for problems than to acknowledge that one is part of the problem. And it is also true that others among us are keenly aware of the aggregative processes, but seek to insulate ourselves from them by ignoring, cheating, hoarding, or otherwise acting irresponsibly with respect to them and then justifying the self-serving behavior on the grounds that everyone else is doing it and thus no one individual can turn the tide. But such scapegoating and self-serving responses are, of course, what makes our tasks as educators so challenging. If relevant civic education means anything, surely it means that we must highlight the multiplying responsibilities that attach to life late in the Twentieth Century.

To grasp this educational challenge one needs a clear-cut conception of democratic citizenship on the one hand and an understanding of the sources and ramifications of global interdependence on the other. Once one begins to specify the nature of responsible citizenship and the dynamics of complex interdependence, it should become clear that the fit between the two is extraordinarily intricate and is far removed from long-standing and conventional notions of what constitutes good citizenship training.

CITIZENSHIP AS PARTICIPATION IN AGGREGATIVE PROCESSES

Citizenship, be it before or after the advent of complex interdependence, refers to the decisions and actions through which individuals link themselves, knowingly or otherwise, to public affairs. The degree to which these decisions and actions are undertaken self-consciously and purposively determines whether or not the individual is practicing good or poor citizenship. Good citizens are those who seek to be aware of their ties to the community and act to sustain the ties in terms of their own values. Poor citizens are those whose decisions and actions relating to public affairs are made unknowingly and unintentionally.

By public affairs and the community (I treat these terms as synonymous and use them interchangeably) I mean those arenas of action and interaction where the collective needs and wants of individuals who do not know each other, are recognized, addressed, and managed. Individual citizens are tied to these arenas in two basic ways. One involves the actions through which citizens serve their needs and wants: these are experienced by community leaders (through direct observation, statistics, journalistic accounts, pressure tactics, etc.) and then aggregated by the leaders (through public speeches, policy proposals, stubborn demands, tough bargains, etc.). Secondly, the resulting conflicts and decisions that comprise public affairs shape the quality and pace of daily life and, in turn, alter or sustain the needs and wants of citizens that are aggregated at the next moment in time. Thus do the processes of aggregation whereby the collective needs and wants of those encompassed by the community come into existence, persist, and change form a seemless web. They are constantly unfolding and, as such, give direction and structure to public affairs. They set the limits beyond which community leaders cannot extend their management of public affairs. Whether it be democratic or authoritarian, in other words, the community could not exist without the aggregative processes that link the collectivity to the individuals who comprise it.

Thus citizenship, being the contribution that individuals necessarily make to the aggregative processes, is always present for each member of the community. He or she may not be aware of all the arenas to which his or her actions are linked and the impact of the decisions made in those arenas may not always intrude on personal affairs in highly visible ways, Nevertheless, the links do exist. The remote worlds of public affairs are aggregations, the terminal points of a chain that originates in the close-at-hand world of daily life. The links that forge the chains may be frayed or they may be firm, but they are always operative. Accordingly, neither through ignorance nor disdain can the individual get out of citizenship, if only because noninvolvement and inactiön also have consequences for the processes of aggregation. This is why the key difference between good and bad citizenship lies in the self-consciousness and purposiveness of the individual's behavior. Since participation in the aggregative processes of public affairs is unavoidable, the manner of the participation is a critical factor in determining the shape of public issues and the course of public affairs. Little wonder, then, that training for citizenship has traditionally focused on alerting individuals to their responsibilities to become informed about and active in politics. Information and involvement were considered the prime prerequisites to participation in the aggragative processes. As will be seen, the prerequisites to good citizenship have expanded considerably with the advent of complex interdependence.

Since the needs and wants of individuals are aggregated at several levels, they are members of several communities. Some of these are 'horizontal' communities and others are 'vertical' communities. The former are presided over by governments or other public authorities at the local, national, and international levels, while the latter are dominated by non-governmental actors. The two types of communities are distinguished by the breadth of the issues they span and process. Horizontal communities, being geographically bounded, embrace a broad range of issues and thus deal with all the concerns of citizens. Vertical communities, being comprised of such unofficial groupings as corporations, ethnic minorities, trade unions, and professional associations that are functionally rather than geographically based, span a narrow set of issues (the corporation's product, the minority's ethnic heritage, the union's trade, the association's profession) and thus focus on the same selective needs and wants of the persons they encompass. One of the hallmarks of complex and mounting interdependence is the increasing degree to which the boundaries of horizontal and vertical communities are overlapping and conflicting, thereby confounding the practicies of citizenship and the holding of multiple loyalties.[1]

Each level and type of community embraces difference aggregative processes to which individuals may contribute in various ways.

[1] For a more elaborate discussion of horizontal and vertical communities and the overlap between them, see James N. Rosenau, *The Scientific Study of Foreign Policy* (London: Frances Pinter Publishers, revised ed., 1980), pp. 155–64.

A few examples are suggestive of this variety. One's readiness to strike or go on 'sick outs' is part of the aggregative process whereby those who preside over unions or professional associations are encouraged or hesitant to press demands. One's adherence to subcultural norms is part of the aggregative process whereby those who speak for ethnic minorities resist or acquiesce to the requirements of an industrial order. One's acceptance of new driving speed limits is part of the aggregative process whereby those who frame energy policies are made aware of the limits within which they must choose. One's purchase of a foreign-made good is part of the aggregative process whereby those who conduct international affairs are confronted with alterations in the patterns of world trade and monetary exchange. One's vote in a local election is part of the aggregative process whereby those who govern the community are selected. One's letter to a Member of Congress is part of the aggregative process whereby those who govern on the national level are apprised of public sentiment.

Whether the remote worlds of unknown others are horizontal or vertical communities, of course, their aggregative processes contrast sharply with the interactions of identifiable and known others who make up daily life in family, social, and work situations. Personal affairs are distinguishable from public affairs by their lack of an aggregative process that carries the course of events beyond the individual's scope of direct experience. The same individual action (such as the purchase of a foreign-made good) can contribute to both the patterns that make up the close-at-hand world and the processes that sustain the remote worlds, but citizenship is practiced only with respect to the latter kind of contribution. If actions designed to enhance personal affairs inadvertently have beneficial consequences for public affairs, they are not therefore viewed as reflecting good citizenship. Responsible persons are not necessarily responsible citizens. In making judgments here about responsible behavior I have in mind only the self-consciousness and purposiveness of behavior directed at horizontal or vertical communities. What individuals direct at their personal world is not of concern in citizenship training, much as one might wish that more people acted as responsibly in the public arena as they do at home or on the job.[2]

Nor does the concept of good and bad citizenship refer to the

[2] While there undoubtedly is an interaction between the ways in which many people conduct themselves in the worlds of personal and public affairs, with the practice of responsible citizenship feeding back to enhance (or undermine) personal life (and vice versa), this is clearly too complex a matter to be taken up here. For a formulation that posits interaction between the experiential consequences of activity in the personal and public worlds, see Harry Eckstein and Ted Robert Gurr, *Patterns of Authority: A Structural Basis for Political Inquiry* (New York: John Wiley, 1975).

content of the activities through which individuals link themselves to the various communities in which they are members. It would be sheer arrogance if as teachers we sought to train students to pursue certain goals and oppose others when they enter the public arena. Rather, to repeat, responsible citizenship involves a sensitivity to the ways in which decisions and actions may become part of the processes of aggregation that give direction and structure to public affairs. Our educational task is to highlight these aggregative processes so that students can be aware of their participation in them and, depending on their values, act self-consciously and purposively to sustain, redirect, or negate the processes. As citizens ourselves we may prefer that certain processes be ended, but as educators we will have performed our tasks well if we train our students to be cognizant of their roles in various communities and they then attempt to perpetuate the processes we oppose.

Later I will elaborate on this conception of citizenship and suggest how its scope has been greatly expanded by mounting interdependence. First, however, it is useful to indicate briefly where loyalty fits in the citizen's relationships to the various horizontal and vertical communities to which he or she belongs. While citizenship involves the ways in which individuals do or do not establish contacts with these communities, loyalty pertains to those attitudes whereby citizens attach priorities to the claims of the various worlds in which they live. More specifically, the loyalties of citizens provide them guidance as to which worlds they will favor with supportive behavior when confronted with conflicting demands from two or more of them. Normally it is possible to hold multiple loyalties — to be predisposed to support, or at least not to oppose, the activities of the leaders of several communities — and to do so without strain or calculation. Normally, too, the priorities among multiple loyalties are clear-cut and do not trouble citizens. Loyalties ordinarily become habits — unthinking inclinations to respond to and/or conform to certain community policies and as such there are usually no problems in knowing where to attach the highest loyalties, where to direct the next highest loyalties, and where to fix the other supportive tendencies one has. However, these are not normal times. Complex interdependence has undermined the traditional habits of loyalty, rendering the priorities among them obscure and often posing the need to reaffirm calculatively one loyalty at the expense of another. In pondering the tasks of modern citizenship training, therefore, we need to develop ways to sensitize students to their feelings of loyalty and to how they might go about resolving conflicts among them even as they preserve the capacity to maintain multiple loyalties.

Let me recapitulate my reasoning thus far and anticipate where it will take us. I have said that citizenship involves the degree and manner of participation in the aggregative processes that create and sustain public affairs. I have also said that good citizenship occurs when the participation in these processes is self-conscious and purposive. By the simple examples cited, moreover, I have implied that traditionally good citizenship was relatively easy to practice. Prior to the advent of complex interdependence the number of aggregative processes that meaningfully linked individuals to more remote communities were comparatively few. Public affairs were sustained mainly by governmental actors and thus a few simple acts such as voting and writing letters to officials were viewed as enough to practice good citizenship. As will be seen, however, mounting interdependence has so extensively complicated public affairs, giving rise to an enormous proliferation of relevant aggregative processes that link us to an ever-expanding range of remote communities, that good citizenship can no longer be practiced through a few simple acts. Likewise, mounting interdependence has enormously complicated the task of sorting out priorities among multiple loyalties. The number of communities claiming loyalty has proliferated and so has the overlap among them, thereby giving rise to a greater frequency of situations in which conflicts of loyalty can arise.

MOUNTING AND COMPLEX INTERDEPENDENCE

To stress that world affairs are marked by growing interdependence is not to imply that heretofore individuals and groups were self-sufficient and independent. People have always been interdependent. The tendency to rely on others for basic services that sustain individual and community life is as old as human history itself. What is new about interdependence is the global scale on which it is presently unfolding. For centuries the work and lives of people have been organized around and through the nation-state. In recent decades, however, rapid scientific and technological advances have precipitated profound changes that are transforming relations both within and among nation-states. Advances in transportation have shrunk geographic distances and advances in communications have shrunk social and political distance, making peoples and groups ever more interconnected and rendering legal and traditional boundaries ever more obsolete. Today issues are so interconnected that two states may be allies in one issue-area and antagonists in another, trading concessions in the latter for continued support in the former. Today situations are so complex that bureaucrats in several countries may form a coalition to oppose convergence among their respective chiefs of state. Today so many nongovernmental actors have become important in world affairs that we accept as commonplace such a recent development as students taking over an embassy in Teheran.

At a personal level, too, the interconnectedness of global life can be all-encompassing. Today an event or trend in one part of the world can have repercussions for daily routines in every other part. An assassination in Dallas is, within minutes, a searing experience in Buffalo and a painful one in Buenos Aires. A new technique of nonviolent protest in Bombay is emulated in Oakland. A presidential dinner in Peking is a vicarious culinary experience, if not a welcome political occasion, in Tucson. A presidential speech to the Knesset in Jerusalem is, in no time, an uplifting experience in Boise and a startling one in Brussels. A distant political struggle, or a stranger's tormented psyche, results in a luggage search for plane passengers in Minneapolis. A conflict in the Middle East precipitates murder at a sporting event in Munich, an oil shortage in Muncie, and mandatory energy cutbacks in Los Angeles. An effort to enhance national security in Seoul gives rise to scandal in the U.S. Congress. A currency devaluation in Tokyo is a job threat in Trenton and a purchasing opportunity in Tampa. An upheaval in Iran is a lowered thermostat in Indianapolis.

In short, world affairs have become so much a part of personal and domestic life that the globe can fairly be said to be entering a new era as the Twentieth Century enters its final decades. It is an era in which international relations are being supplemented by transnational relations, by interactions across national boundaries that are being sustained by business firms, professional societies, labor unions, voluntary associations, and a host of other private groups as well as by governments.

To be sure, nation-states and their governments continue to be centers of decision and prime movers in the affairs of men. A day does not pass without headlines depicting the great political, economic, social, and military power of national authorities throughout the world. Yet national governments can no longer handle and channel all the relations that mounting interdependence has spawned. New ties, loyalties, and modes of interacting are proliferating among people in different cultures and professions, supplementing and (in some instances) by-passing the conduct of affairs by national governments. It is too soon to assess whether these new and expanding transnational relations will eventually foster new forms of government or whether they will continue to proliferate alongside national governments. In either event it seems unmistakably evident that the future will be marked by greater diversity and intensity in the contacts of people. The emergence of the multinational corporation, the onset of the energy crisis, and the havoc wrought by terrorism are but three of the more obvious developments that mark the world's passage into a new era of transnational relations.

Stated differently, just as mounting interdependence has fostered greater complexity within and among nations, so has it altered the identity, motives, and capabilities of those who act and interact on the world stage. The number of individuals is growing at a rapid rate and, accordingly, so are the organizations through which they seek to concert action on a large scale. The number of nation-states has tripled since World War II and, as indicated, the increase in nongovernmental actors who engage in activities within and across national boundaries is so great as to be beyond precise calculation.

To grasp the challenge we face as educators responsible for citizenship training, however, it is not enough to comprehend that human affairs have been transnationalized on a global scale. To appreciate the processes whereby technology has lessened geographic and social distances is not to be sensitive to all the dynamics presently at work that are fostering complexity and that may thus be central to the updating of our conceptions of citizenship training. For the challenge of interdependence is multiple, deriving from a great many interactive factors and posing a seemingly endless array of interactive problems. Scientific and technological advances may be the root cause of change, but many of the ensuing changes have in themselves become sources of change and, as such, they are part of the complexity and the challenge. As suggested in previous chapters, several dynamics seem especially relevant to teaching and learning in a transnational world: (1) the advent of an era of scarcity; (2) the growing demands of the disadvantaged for a redistribution of wealth; (3) the emergence of divisive subgroup loyalties; (4) the declining effectiveness of governments; and (5) the shift of attention in world affairs away from military-security issues and toward social-economic issues.

The end of abundance and the onset of pervasive scarcities is clearly linked to the world's mounting interdependence. Not only have dynamic technologies rendered human lives ever more interwoven, so have they facilitated and encouraged faster economic development and more complex industrialization, processes that in turn have consumed natural resources at a greater rate — with the result that technological breakthroughs are then generated in order to offset the emergent resource shortages. Experts differ on the extent to which various resources are being depleted, but virtually all agree that depletion is occurring and that the future will be marked by increasing scarcities. Be it local, national, or international, every social system must thus function in situations of scarce resources. None can be self-sufficient. None can insulate itself from the outside world and at the same time move toward its goals.

From a citizenship perspective, increasingly acute resource shortages mean more and more points at which sensitivity to aggregative processes can occur. There is a limit beyond which blaming nature's calamities or the oil companies begins to ring hollow and an awareness of what depletion implies begins to intrude. And to begin to appreciate the processes of depletion is to begin to understand a system at work and to project into the future a picture of one's self as a system participant, as a part of the aggregative process that sustains the depletion. A resource scarcity, in short, is an incisive and profound form of citizen education, albeit the lessons it teaches may be as much those of heightened self-interest as those involving the need for collective endeavor and individual restraint.

Partly as a consequence of mounting resource scarcities and partly for a variety of other reasons, the motives of actors on the world stage have proliferated as much as have their numbers. Most notably, the underprivileged are no longer content with their lot. They want the affluent to start sharing their wealth and both within and among nations their demands for redistribution of resources and status mount steadily. The poor and minorities within nations are increasingly restless and their restlessness has brought them together in organizations that are increasingly effective. Similarly, the nations of Africa, Asia, and Latin America have become increasingly aware of their poverty and have organized to press those in the West for a new economic order. And as motives change and become more self-conscious, so do long-established relationships among individuals, groups, communities, and states undergo both subtle and radical shifts. Oft-times it is no longer clear who is leading and who is following, who is dominant and who is subordinate, who is astride the wave of the future and who is riding the crest of the past.

With the proliferation of actors and the changes in their motives, and with the continued advances of technology and the unending consumption of resources on which its advances rest, comes equally profound alterations in the capabilites through which the various actors pursue their goals, reinforce their motives, and maintain their relationships. More organized and more cohesive, many subgroups in many societies are better able than ever before to back up their demands with the stubborn persistence that accompanies a sense of purpose and a confidence that goals are attainable. And as the capabilities and dedication of subgroups grow, corresponding declines often follow in the authority of governments, reducing their capacity to govern and further altering the pace of change and the relative strength of the actors contesting its direction. Thus many governments are increasingly less able to maintain order, solve problems, plan ahead, or otherwise cope with the transformations at home and the challenges from abroad.

In a like manner the relative capabilities of nation-states have undergone profound alteration. The superpowers are not as super as they once were and some of the small powers are not as small as they once were. Oil, its availability and its scarcity, has altered the balance among the strong and the weak, and the distribution and utilization of a number of other resources bid fair to further transform such balances in the future. Likewise, the breakdown of authority within nation-states is paralleled by the fragmentation of ties among them, so that grand alliances are no longer grand and their leaders can no longer be sure their allies will follow their leads. The bipolar world has thus given way to the multipolar world and to the possibility of forms of world order that have yet to mark human history.

From a citizenship perspective, the growing demands of the under-privileged, the increased coherence of subgroups, and the changing capabilities of governments and nation-states also mean a heightened awareness of the processes of aggregation and disaggregation. Whatever else they may portend, the swelling chorus of claims in the Third World and the splintering of subgroups in the First World is good civic education. Fragmentation highlights the dilemmas of conflicting loyalties and multiplying responsibilities. It forces citizens to ponder their priorities; it sensitizes them to ask where they fit and where their sympathies lie as collective entities get restructured and communities get restratified. The bumper stickers recently affixed by independent truckers blockading truck stops in protest against high fuel prices exemplify the dilemmas of fragmentation as they carry word of conflicting loyalties across the nation's highways: 'I'm fed up, but I love America.'

And to all the emergent changes in historic values, perceptions, motives, capabilities, and relationships must be added those generated by the new issues of interdependence. Indeed, by virtue of being new, issues of this kind are perhaps especially challenging. Many political actors have had some experience in responding to the rising demands of subgroups and the declining competence of governments, to the shifting structure of alliances and the realignment of the international pecking order, but there are few precedents for coping with currency devaluations, lines at gas pumps, air hijackings, and the many other events that seem to originate in far off places and yet daily seem to intrude on the routines of life.

One consequence — and to some degree a source — of all this change is the dislocation of economies. At local, national, and international levels economic growth rates have slowed and inflationary pressures have proved resistant to control. In turn, such economic difficulties have added to the restlessness of disadvantaged groups and the caution of economic elites whose capital investments might help stimulate a resurgence in growth rates.

Again citizen education is a beneficiary. Surely nothing heightens awareness of self in aggregative processes than economic dislocation, with all that this means for pocketbooks, living standards, and daily routines. And the issues derived from mounting interdependence add further to this awareness. Being socio-economic in origin, they reach much more deeply into the fabric of everyday life than do those of high politics. They call attention to our intangible possessions, such as the air around us and the safety of our travel, in the same penetrating way that economic dislocation highlights our material possessions.

In sum, like the individuals who comprise them, political and social systems are everywhere under duress, besieged by internal challenges to their integrative capacities and by external demands on their adaptive capacities. The ways in which different systems respond to the challenges of interdependence will doubtless vary considerably, but the challenges are global in scope and relentless in intensity, allowing no system the luxury of relying on long-standing traditions to sustain its values and move toward its goals.

TEACHING AND LEARNING IN A TRANSNATIONAL WORLD

And this imperative, of course, returns us to the central problem: to meet the challenges of interdependence they must be perceived for what they are, and to be so perceived traditional perspectives must give way to transnational ones. More specifically, the attitudes, loyalties, and participatory behavior of citizens must undergo profound transformations. Interdependence is laden with potential for citizen education, but it is a potential that has yet to be realized. There have been, to be sure, some changes in recent years. As exemplified by the growth of consumer groups and the intensified activities of conservation organizations, the perspectives of citizens have not been immune to the dynamics of mounting interdependence.[3] But such changes in the orientations of citizens is minimal in comparison to what is needed. If for no other reason, large educational tasks still remain because of the ways in which the choices citizens must make and their grasp of important economic, social, and political problems are shaped and confounded by the mass media. The event-centered approach of the media often creates jumbled and confused perspectives that are woefully lacking in the coherence and flexibility that the challenges of interdependence require.

To make matters more difficult, many of the challenges of

[3]For a discussion of the changing orientations and activities of citizens, see James N. Rosenau, *Citizenship Between Elections: An Inquiry into the Mobilizable American* (New York: Free Press, 1974), Chapter 2.

interdependence are not immediately apparent. Even if the mass media were to alter their ways, the capacity to recognize the transformations that are unfolding cannot be easily developed. The deep-seated changes that are at work are obscure. Their sources are multiple, their scope unlimited, their direction variable, their impact extensive, their influence pervasive, and their consequences profound. It is simply not clear what personal, community, national, and international life is going to be like in the years ahead. We know only that it will be different and that as educators we need to shoulder the task of preparing our students to conduct themselves responsibly under these conditions of uncertainty, complexity, and transformation. How do we restructure our courses and reorient our teaching so as to equip our students for life in a transnational world? How do we sensitize them to the dynamics of change? How do we alert them to recognize the many ways in which world affairs impinge ever more closely upon their daily lives? How do we enable them to fill more responsibly the new and varied transnational roles they seem bound to occupy, to discern the aggregative processes to which they contribute, to think more clearly about the choices that they and their communities will have to make, to appreciate more fully that opportunities as well as threats are inherent in change? How do we contest apathy and foster confidence in the potentials of human intelligence and political action? How do we do a better job in preparing young people for citizenship in a world where nation-states are no longer the only central actors and governments no longer omnicompetent, where the dynamics and responsibilities of citizenship are in transition and no longer as evident as they once were, where traditional values and loyalties are no longer as relevant as they once were, and where new values and loyalties have yet to emerge with compelling clarity? How, in short, do we help young people realize the full measure of their talents and sensitivities in a fast-changing world that fosters uncertainty, invites unease, and seems ever more ominous?

There are, obviously, no easy answers to these questions. The fit between the responsibilities of modern citizenship and the dynamics of mounting interdependence is clearly an ungainly one and not easily achieved. However, if my analysis of the transformations at work in world affairs is correct, and if the foregoing notion of citizenship as self-conscious and purposive involvement in the aggregative processes of remote communities is meaningful, some guidelines as to how we need to reorient our educational efforts emerge with clarity. First, it seems plain that the citizenship training we undertake can no longer be confined to the person-in-the-street. As more and more nongovernmental organizations form more and more vertical communities, the number of occupational and social roles to which transnational dimensions and responsibilities attach proliferates accordingly. Our students, in other words, are destined to find themselves in many more situations that relate them to public affairs than was the case for their predecessors. Hence we have to assume that not only will they be voting in future elections, but also that many will be occupying positions in business, legal, communications, labor, and other types of organizations that are linked to a wide variety of the aggregative processes through which the transnationalization of world affairs is taking place. The ways they conduct themselves in these roles — their judgments about the causes and consequences of the various decision choices open to them — thus fall within the purview of our concern as educators of future citizens.

Second, and perhaps most important, the foregoing discussion of interdependence suggests that our task is not simply a matter of providing new and up-dated information about the human condition. Ideally, to be sure, it would be desirable to expand student knowledge about the activities of multinational corporations, the demands of Third World countries, the imbalanced trading patterns of the United States, and the growth of dissident movements in Iran, Canada, and the Soviet Union. Yet, higher levels of factual information do not necessarity conduce to good citizenship, at least not in a time of mounting interdependence. For recognition and comprehension of the proliferating, complex aggregative processes in which all of us have become participants is not a matter of knowing the facts. It is rather a matter of possessing the analytic skills with which to trace the innumerable links in the innumerable causal chains that entwine our lives. To know, for example, that the United States consumes daily more oil than it produces and that it does so through increasing imports from the Middle East is not necessarily to be able to appreciate how daily choices in getting to work, discarding old newspapers, buying new appliances, or keeping money in savings accounts might thereby be relevant. To understand that Italy's politics are divisive or that few governments of the industrial world are run by clear-cut majorities is not necessarily to be able to grasp how one's actions upholding or contesting the policies of one's union, ethnic association, or veterans organization might further enhance or diminish the stability of one's government. To be acquainted with the fact that the underpriviledged in Third World countries are restless and demanding a redistribution of the wealth is not necessarily to be able to discern the implications for Ghana in drinking cocoa for breakfast or for Brazil in drinking coffee at dinner. To have insight into the growing importance of multinational corporations in world affairs is not necessarily to be able to sort out one's loyalties if one is a businessman whose company's policies in a foreign land conflict directly with those of one's country. To be informed that everywhere subgroups are pressing for more autonomy is not necessarily to be able to cope with requests that one support professional colleagues abroad if one is an international airline pilot urged to protest insensitivity to hijackings in Algeria or a scientist pressed to condemn oversensitivity to intellectuals in the Soviet Union. To understand that governance is more complex than it used to be is not necessarily to appreciate why a chief executive can treat energy policies as 'the moral equivalent of war' or to have reactions to students who take over an embassy.

In short, information and knowledge are in themselves no longer adequate guides to action. They may have been sufficient when the variety and kinds of actions necessary to the performance of responsible citizenship were limited in number and narrow in scope. Now, however, a broad range of activities have consequences for public affairs. Aggregative processes are pervasive, encompassing many of our family decisions and undergirding many of our work or job-related choices. Thus good citizenship training more than ever involves development of the ability to analyze as well as the capacity to absorb information. Students need the tools with which to process information, give it coherence and meaning, both as to its empirical implications and its ethical imperatives.

Before turning to a discussion of what the analytic talents appropriate to good citizenship may involve, let me suggest a third guideline for the reorientation of our educational responsibilities that can be readily derived from the mushrooming of relevant aggregative processes. It is a guideline that involves the exercise of restraint in our efforts to motivate students to act more responsibly as citizens. I refer to the temptation to arouse them by treating the long-term trends underlying mounting interdpendence as threatening and bound to overwhelm and subvert the values they cherish. Such outcomes are, of course, possible, but they are far from certainties. Yet, it does not require much imagination to perceive the long-term trends as ominous and the world as inescapably headed toward disaster. The data on population growth relative to increases in food supply can readily be depicted as eventually leading to famine, just as the decline in the capacities of government and the rise of subgroup loyalties can easily be portrayed as ultimately culminating in upheaval and chaos. Whatever the accuracy of such projections, they offer fertile opportunities for those of us who are inclined to use scare tactics as a means of engaging apathetic students. 'Unless you become interested and active,' we may be tempted to reiterate in our classes, 'you and your generation will be engulfed by catastrophe.'

Not only is it dubious that the reiteration of this theme is unlikely to motivate lethargic students, but, even worse, it may well give them an erroenous picture of the aggregative processes in which they are participants. While scare tactics do highlight the existence of the aggregative processes by stressing that undesirable outcomes are likely to ensue in the absence of action, such tactics are hardly conducive to a deep understanding of the dynamics of aggregation. By portraying doomsday to students, it seems to me, the aggregative processes emerge not as concrete and multiplicative sequences subject to social and political control, but rather as unseen hands at work, as hidden forces that are undermining long-established and comfortable routines and that are inevitably forging the chain of events along paths from which there is no escape.

How, then, to motivate students to want to probe and shoulder their widening citizen responsibilities? The answer, I think, also lies in the need to conceive of citizenship training as involving refined analytic skills as well as high levels of information and motivation. If students can learn to recognize, trace, and interpret the many aggregative processes in which they necessarily participate, then they are likely to have a greater sense of control over their own destinies and, accordingly, to be readier to relate themselves self-consciously and purposively to public affairs.

THE TOOLS OF CITIZENSHIP

But what are the analytic skills and tools that can foster good citizenship in an interdependent world? What should we be emphasizing in our teaching in addition to providing relevant information and stimuli to learning? How do we sensitize our students to recognize an aggregative process when they are caught up in one?

I have compiled a list of eighteen tools that may be appropriate to training for citizenship in an ever more interdependent world. Long as the list is, I do not offer it as an exhaustive compilation. There are surely many more tools that could be added to the list and much more that could be said about the ones identified below. Hopefully, however, what follows will serve as a useful contribution to a much-needed dialogue on the problem of modern citizenship training.

Although I regard all the tools on my list as important and thus offer them in a rather random order, certainly high on any list would be the capacity to trace the flow of influence. We should organize our curricula and courses in such a way as to sensitize our students to the complex processes whereby one actor gets others to engage in behavior they would not otherwise undertake, to differentiate between those behaviors that are the result of prior influences and those that would have been undertaken in any event, to discern how each stage in an aggregative process shapes and limits the aggregation that can occur at the next stage. Tracing the flow of influence has always been pervaded with difficulties and pitfalls, but the task has been rendered even more arduous by mounting interdependence and the multiplicity of new transnational actors who can exercise influence in one or another situation.

A second tool we need to provide our students is the ability to discern and assess unintended consequences. With so many new actors engaged in so many new and varied activities, considerable skill is required in distinguishing those events and trends that are the result of planning and effort from those that are unanticipated and unwanted and that can therefore lead actors and the aggregative processes of which they are a part in directions quite contrary to the desired goals. To be sure, our students as citizens might opt to serve their personal wants even as they know these will contribute to undesirable aggregative processes for the community (say, by choosing to buy a gas-guzzling car instead of a compact even though their family can manage easily with a small car), but surely they are better citizens by virtue of having consciously made such choices rather than being unable to recognize the unintended consequences of yielding to their personal preferences.

A third tool on which we need to focus our teaching talents is the concept of role. We need to equip students with the ability to see behavior as springing from the requirements and expectations of roles as well as the idiosyncracies and impulses of individuals. If they are to be professionals, association members, producers, consumers, tourists, and a variety of other transnational role occupants, they will need to be alert to the limits and potentials inherent in their roles just as they may already be learning the limits and potentials they possess as individuals. If they are to recognize the process whereby discrete actions are aggregated and culminate in community policies, they will need to grasp that often what is aggregated is not random and coincidental behavior on the part of widely scattered individuals, but is rather common and expected behavior attached to occupational, socio-economic, and political roles that all concerned perceive as systematically and narrowly linked to each other. If they are to make sound judgments as to which of their multiple loyalties should prevail in response to the demands of complex transnational situations, they will need to grasp that the choices confronting them involve sorting out role behavior is hardly easier than tracing the flow of influence or the advent of unintentional consequences, but the ability to do so would appear to be more and more central to the skills of modern citizenship as the world becomes more and more interdependent.

A fourth tool both builds upon and reinforces the sensitivities to influence, consequence, and role phenomena that we help our students develop. It consists of the ability to recognize patterned behavior and the social systems to which the patterns give rise. Such an ability is truly an analytic talent, since neither the patterns nor the systems exist in nature and come into being only through the operation of our minds. Large organizations such as multinational corporations and large collectivities such as nation-states may be the focus of emotional energy and they may have legal status, but empirically they acquire form and structure only as observers discern patterns in individual actions. Once they acquire a sensitivity to patterned behavior and systemic attributes, many of our students may well be stunned and exhilerated by how their analytic capacities permit them to infuse some order into the change and chaos that mounting interdependence seems to portend. And as they gain confidence in their ability to identify social systems and assess their strengths and weaknesses, so may many students begin to develop judgments about where they fit in the patterned processes of transnational aggregation that encompass their lives.

The fifth tool to which we need to address our teaching talents concerns the role of history. We need to enable students to differentiate between the historical trends that are repeated in the present and the current dynamics that cut off the flow of the past and give rise to the break-points of history. As previously implied, we may be living through one of the great break-points of history. If we are, those who conduct themselves as if historical continuities are unfolding may fail miserably as responsible citizens seeking to cope with the challenges that lie ahead.

A sixth tool is the opposite of the ability to discern the limits of historical patterns. It involves the capacity to recognize the limits of change. We need to alert our students to the large degree to which habit pervades human affairs, inclining individuals, groups, and nations to perceive, evaluate, and otherwise respond to events as they always have. Patterned behaviors and aggregative processes are probably more pronounced and discernible than many students realize. People become so habituated to certain practices that they neither think about nor are aware of their behavior, with the result that many historical patterns are maintained even as they become increasingly inappropraite. Thus does inertia mark history; and thus do periods of transformation tend to be marked as much by incremental as by drastic change. Our students need to appreciate these limits of change imposed by the deep-seatedness of habit if they are also to comprehend the limits of history.

A seventh tool necessary to modern citizenship involves an appreciation of the power of industrialization and the dynamics of large-scale organizations. We need to build into our courses a capacity for grasping the range of profound impacts that follow from the processes of industrialization and the large economic, social, and political organizations to which an industrial civilization inexorably gives rise. While such an emphasis has long been necessary to good teaching, it takes on added importance as the processes of industrialization have begun to create large-scale organizations that transcend national boundaries. The emergence of multinational corporations is, I would argue, only the first wave of complex transnational organizations that the march of industrialization will leave in its wake. Comparable entities in science, education, health, communication, religion, and other walks of life seem likely to proliferate, if they have not already, and understanding the ways in which they do proliferate, creating new transnational roles and reshaping old relationships as they multiply and grow, is surely a prerequisite to effective citizenship training.

An eighth tool we need to provide students concerns the ability to know when to be outraged and when to suspend judgment. The complexity of world affairs heightens the importance of being able to avoid premature closure until all the elements in a situation fall into place, of knowing when and how to apply one's values to new and unfamiliar issues. It is all too tempting to fall back on simplistic standards and be outraged when rapid change gives rise to unexpected and perplexing developments. It is not difficult, for example, to redefine incidents of transnational role conflict as issues of patriotism. Instead of suspending judgment until the scope and consequences of such incidents become manifest, one can more easily resort to moral condemnation when a transnational occurrence does not readily fit into one's comprehension of public affairs. Our students seem likely to be faced with an endless series of such seemingly surprising developments. Hence, we need to alert them to the possibility that they may have to revise and reorganize their conceptions of proper and improper behavior if their analytic talents are to lead them into deeper levels of understanding. Obviously the ability to probe aggregative processes is not likely to grow if, with each accretion to an aggregation, one is inclined to reach value conclusions. This is not to suggest that one ought never apply high ethical standards or render moral judgments because the world has become complex. On the contrary, the proliferation of transnational actors who add to the claims on our loyalties (and whose performances thus need to be evaluated) would seem to expand the degree to which our value systems are relevant to good citizenship. But the need to apply values to unfamiliar situations should not be seen by our students as justifying the substitution of value judgments for analytic tools whenever they appraise the aggregative processes in which they participate.

There are at least ten other tools of modern citizenship that strike me as worthy of emphasis in our teaching, but space limitations prevent even a brief elaboration. So let me just enumerate them here as an agenda for future consideration. These ten additional tools include enabling our students to distinguish between individual motives and group requirements, to differentiate between stable and unstable patterns, to separate the political from the legal, to discern how past actions feed back over time into present behavior, to know when leaders lead and when they follow, to distinguish between ideology as rhetoric and ideals as motivation, to recognize the difference between easy scapegoats and complex explanations, to delineate between political and organizational responsibility, to differentiate between expressive and instrumental action, and to recognize the ways in which conflict derives from cooperative endeavor.

To elaborate on the educational tasks that lie ahead is not, of course, to ensure their performance. Indeed, there is so much to be done that doubtless adequate performance will be wanting in a variety of ways. But let me stress that we have some things going for us. Most notably, unbeknownst to our students, they have had considerable subconscious experience in participating in aggregative processes, experience that we can build upon in our teaching. From the chain letters they are asked to perpetuate as children to the traffic jams in which they are caught as young adults, from the boycotts they may be asked to join to the water shortages they are asked to alleviate, our students have had ample first-hand exposure to the links between individual and collective behavior. Whatever they may do, they have learned that a failure to send the letter on to five new names will break the chain. Whatever they do, they have learned that the traffic jam is worsened rather than improved when in their franticness not to be late they move forward at every opportunity and their car is forced to stop in a north-south cross street, blocking traffic going east and west. So they basically know that individual actions can cumulate in aggregate outcomes, and our task is to extend this analytic capacity into new realms, heightening their sensitivity to the flow of cause and effect and refining their ability to distinguish between the manifest and the latent, the intentional and unintentional, the implusive and the reflective, the continuity and the discontinuity.

And if all else fails, if our efforts to build upon the curiosities and past experiences of our students fall on deaf ears and we have to justify our stress on analytic skills, we can always fall back on an instrumental approach and exploit their career orientations. We need only point out that employers are as concerned about the analytic skills as the expertise of those they recruit and promote, that the most lucrative and distinguished careers accrue to those whose capacity for analysis is refined and incisive, that neither luck, nor family connection, nor a winning personality, nor technical training is as effective a means of getting ahead in any field as the ability to trace influence, discern unintended consequences, assess systemic performance, or creatively apply any of the other skills I have mentioned. And if our students are skeptical about this evaluation of the dynamics of the job market, we need only read them this excerpt from a recent advertisement of no less a prestigious employer than the Mobil Oil Company:

> We have learned by experience that when we are looking for a man or woman with executive ability to promote. . . an individual's ability to deal with abstract problems involving judgment and the ability to reason is often more significant at that juncture than any technical knowledge . . . What is critically important in the long term is the broader dimensions of knowledge and insight that enable people to deal successively with a variety of social and economic problems.[4]

A PRESCRIPTION FOR CITIZENS OR FOR LIFE?

In conclusion let me acknowledge that my elaboration of our educational tasks and the skills needed for citizenship in an ever-more interdependent world would seem to amount to a prescription for the training of more than citizens, that it amounts to nothing less than the cultivation of broad-gauged human beings. To the extent that we in the teaching profession consider ourselves as possessing refined analytical talents and sensitivity to the dynamics of social systems, it might be argued that we are trying to remake our students in our own self-image, by encouraging their growth as thoughtful individuals, constantly probing who they are, where they are going, and where they fit in the worlds evolving around them. There is some truth to the argument. We do aspire to enabling our students to move more sophisticatedly and self-consciously in their future roles. We do hope they will become more aware of nuances, of underlying complexities, of subtle relationships. And we do seek to facilitate their sense of their own values and how these may be articulated in the larger scheme of things. But we do so not to promote our self-images. We strive to achieve these educational goals not because we want to commend the virtues of sensitivity and the life of the mind to our students. We do so because responsible citizenship in a transnational world requires a delicate and humane use of the senses and an imaginative and disciplined use of intelligence.

[4] Quoted by Richard F. Ericson in his 1979 Presidential Address to the Society for General Systems Research, in *General Systems Bulletin*, Vol. IX, No. 2 (Winter 1979), p.42.

Part Two: The State of the Art

7 The Concept of Aggregation and Third World Demands: An Analytic Opportunity and an Empirical Challenge *

When paradigms crumble, they crumble very quickly. The slightest inroad into their coherence opens gaping holes and the collapse of each of their premises raises further doubts about their adequacy. Before long everything seems questionable, and what once seemed so orderly soon looms as sheer chaos.

Such a process of paradigm deterioration, I believe, is underway in the study of world affairs. And while this can lead to an exciting sense of venturesomeness, so can it result in enormous difficulties and confusion.

Thus these are hard times for those who theorize about world affairs and foreign policy. No sooner had we successfully come through several decades of enormous theoretical progress than the world which we began to comprehend manifested unmistakable signs of profound change, rendering our hard-won theoretical sophistication increasingly obsolete. No sooner had we replaced the 'billiard ball' model of the realists with a differentiated state model that focused on decisional processes and the domestic sources of foreign policy than the

*An earlier version of this paper was presented at the Conference on Constancy and Change: The Political Economy of Global Differentiation, sponsored by the National Science Foundation and held in Ojai, California, November 14-17, 1979. I am deeply grateful to James H. Lebovic for his help in developing the empirical materials used in the analysis. The more theoretical parts of the ensuing analysis were first developed in James N. Rosenau, 'Muddling, Meddling, and Modeling: Alternative Approaches to the Study of World Politics in an Era of Rapid Change,' a paper presented to the Seminar of Theories of International Relations and Theories of Knowledge, Department of International Relations, The Australian National University, Canberra, July 27, 1978, and revised for presentation at the Conference on International Relations Theory, New Delhi, India, May 17, 1979.

competence of governments began to decline and their capacity to sustain effective foreign policies underwent further deterioration. No sooner had we moved significantly forward in understanding the dynamics of arms races and the premises of strategic theory than new problems of interdependence began to rival the older questions of diplomatic and military strategy as issues on the global agenda. No sooner had we started to link the machinery of foreign policy formulation to the external behavior of states than a host of important transnational entities appeared on the world scene that were not governments and did not conduct foreign policies. And no sooner had we perfected new methodologies for analyzing decisions and tracing the pattern of events than relevant decisions and events began to spring from the behavior of multinational corporations and other types of nonstate organizations that could not be readily examined through the application of the hard-won methodologies.

In short, nothing seems to fit. Our great strides in theory and research during the 1950s, 1960s, and 1970s no longer correspond well to the world they were intended to describe. Authority has been too widely decentralized and societies too thoroughly fragmented to be adequately handled by even our most refined concepts. Consider for example, these recent events reported in the Los Angeles Press:

> The Navahos and 21 other Western Indian tribes enter into discussions with the Organization of Petroleum Exporting Countries (OPEC) in an effort to get advice on the development of energy resources.
>
> President Sadat of Egypt consults with Jesse Jackson, a private American citizen on a five-nation trip to bring peace to the Middle East.
>
> The University of Southern California and the government of Bahrein sign a contract in which the former agrees to provide the intellectual resources needed by the latter.
>
> Ministers of the Quebec separatist government undertake a series of tours of California in an effort to gain understanding and build support for their independence movement.

How does one analyze such transnational developments? In what niches of the post-realist, differentiated, and multipolar state model can they be placed? The answer strikes me as obvious as it is distressing: such events have no home in our current formulations. We could, of course, discuss them as isolated, inconsequential, or transitory phenomena, a reaction that would then allow us to treat them as random incidents and to muddle through in spite of them. I doubt, however, whether we will long be able to muddle through our analyses as if basic and profound changes in the structures of world politics were not at work. The evidence that such transformations are underway seems too extensive to ignore. The Navaho may never get the aid they want. Jackson and Sadat may never get the peace they want, Bahrein may never get the guidance it seeks, and the Quebec separatists may never generate the private support abroad they desire; but aspirations, efforts, and activities of this kind seem likely to become more rather than less pervasive and salient in world politics. Or at least this possibility seems too great to justify an analytic posture of muddling through.

BEYOND MUDDLING: MEDDLING AND MODELING

Another possible reaction to the indicators of underlying change involves acknowledging that structural transformations are at work and attempting to accommodate them by meddling with our current formulations. Indeed, this would seem to be the prevalent analytic posture in the field today. Aware that the dynamics of change are too extensive to dismiss, many analysts have understandably sought to tidy up their conceptual equipment to account for the transformations.[1] Explorations have been sought through emphasis on the mounting interdependence of groups and societies (hence Bahrein and USC), through stress on the proliferation of nonstate actors (hence the Navahos and the Quebec separatists), and through the notion that transnational relations have come to rival interstate relations as dominant features of the world scene (hence Jackson's five-nation tour of the Middle East). But such meddling will not do. The tidied up formulations are too ungainly to yield a deeper understanding. To posit greater interdependence is not to explain complexity. To allow for a much greater variety and number of significant international actors is not to account for the direction and pace of decentralization. To conceive of transnational phenomena as more salient is not to grasp what moves the course of events.

A third reaction to the presence of pervasive change is possible. Rather than preserving our current formulations either by dismissing the change or by absorbing it, we could treat it as so fundamental as to welcome the deterioration of existing paradigms and to warrant the construction of entirely new models. Such an analytic posture has been adopted by a few analysts who have gone well beyond tidying up and offered whole substitutes for the post-realist, differentiated, and multipolar state model. Most notably, the underlying structural changes have been located in the context either of an issue paradigm that depicts the complexities of a decentralized world[2] or of a global

[1] For a succinct review of a variety of efforts to employ the meddling approach, see Kal J. Holsti, 'A New International Politics? Diplomacy in Complex Interdependence,' *International Organization*, Vol. 32 (Spring 1978), pp. 513-30.

[2] For example, see J.R. Handelman, J.A. Vasquez, M.K. O'Leary, and W.D. Coplin, 'Color it Morgenthau: A Data-Based Assessment of Quantitative International Relations Research,' a paper presented to the Annual Meeting of the International Studies Association (Syracuse; Syracuse University, 1973).

society that subsumes and manages an ever more interdependent world.[3] But these paradigmatic endeavors are also wanting. For the world appears to be both more decentralized and more interdependent, thereby requiring a paradigm that posits an overall global structure which imposes coherence on diverse issues without presuming the orderliness of a society.

PUTTING FIRST THINGS FIRST

The foregoing rests on two basic convictions that can usefully be explicated. One is that no amount of muddling or meddling through can prevent the collapse of a paradigm that has started to go. Thus I see no choice for us but to start afresh with the modeling approach. I shall return to the question of what this choice might involve.

Secondly, I am convinced that neither epistemological nor methodological problems are the source of our difficulties in the field today. The need to develop a new paradigm springs not from the failure of quantitative techniques or the insufficiency of qualitative modes of analysis. Rather our dilemmas derive from substantive sources, from the dynamics of change that are rendering the world ever more complex as the twentieth century nears an end. Whether one is inclined to rest inquiry on scientific practices, on Marxian dialectics, on historical-interpretive approaches, or on the methods of analytic philosophy, one still has to contend with the mushrooming of resource scarcities, the declining capacity of governments, the rise of new issues, the advent of new actors, and the many interactive effects that derive from mounting interdependence in an increasingly fragmented world. These substantive dynamics are at work no matter how we proceed. And they are not going to become any less perplexing if our methodological disputes are resolved and our epistemological differences clarified.

I suppose it is conceivable that some of the substantive dynamics lend themselves to greater clarification through one epistemology or methodology than another, but this would be hard to demonstrate and the energy invested in such a debate does not seem worth any gains that might result. Much more is to be gained, I would contend, by presuming that all the available epistemologies and methodologies have something to offer if more appropriate paradigms can be developed.

[3] Examples here are John W. Burton, *World Society* (Cambridge: Cambridge University Press, 1972); Richard A. Falk, *A Study of Future Worlds* (New York: Free Press, 1975); and A.C. Simpson, 'International Relations in a World Society: Living with Cobwebs,' paper delivered at the Seminar on Theories of International Relations and Theories of Knowledge, Department of International Relations, Australian National University, Canberra, September 7, 1978.

Such a presumption seems reasonable. The realist–idealist and science–nonscience debates have spent themselves, I think, and one senses that an acceptance — if not a tolerance — of diversity has set in. We in the international relations field probably contested methodological and epistemological issues more intensely, more stubbornly, and more thoroughly in recent decades that did those in any other subfield of political science, but thus we may also be able to move on more quickly. Or at least the philosophical and methodological debates now unfolding elsewhere in the discipline somehow seem antiquated. We have covered that ground and few among us still have a need to assert the importance of such matters.

I have wondered for a long time why methodological introspection seemed so much more endemic to the study of international relations than to other fields of political analysis. The answer would not seem to be in the recruitment process — in the kinds of combative personalities that are attracted to study international phenomena. Rather it is to be found, I think, in the elusiveness of international phenomena — in the great distances from which we must observe them and the tough cultural barriers through which our observations must pass. But now it seems clear that these very difficulties are also an advantage, since they have inhibited the emergence of orthodoxy and encouraged the perfection of diverse methodologies.[4]

This is not to say there is no need to be methodologically aware of epistemologically sensitive. Obviously such matters will continue to be important — if only because the advent of new nongovernmental actors may require the development of new techniques of analysis — and clearly inquiry will be more incisive the more sophisticated it is in these regards. But our hard-won tolerance of diversity does allow us to put methodological concerns in perspective and to converge on the central problem. This is, to repeat, the problem of theory, of constructing paradigms that more adequately account for the changing structures of world politics.

AN AMERICAN DISTORTION?

Reactions to earlier versions of the foregoing reasoning have made me keenly aware that the process of pervasive change are not self-evident, that many observers do not perceive a need for new paradigms because they view the structures and dynamics of world politics as essentially undifferentiated from the past. The wealthy elites still

[4] For a useful discussion of this point, see Jeffrey Harrod, 'International Relations, Perceptions and Neo-Realism,' *The Year Book of World Affairs*, Vol. 31 (1977), pp. 289-305.

dominate the working classes (say the Marxists), the superpowers still dominate the international scene (say the power theorists), and nongovernmental actors have always limited the capacities of governments (say the post-realists). The trends and developments that strike me as reflective of basic transformations, in other words, are seen by others as peripheral, as mere perturbations in long-standing, deeply rooted historic patterns.

This criticism has been voiced primarily by nonAmericans, who contend that the perception of pervasive change is not so much an empirical observation as it is a conceptual bias of scholars.[5] The decline of the United States' role in world affairs, supplemented by an inclination toward pragmatic and nonhistorical analysis that sometimes amounts to faddism, are said to have predisposed American students of international relations to be much too quick to treat marginal fluctuations as central changes and much too ready to ignore the possibility that things are the same as they have always been except for a substantial lessening of their country's influence over the course of events. It could be. The question of how much change constitutes basic change is more a conceptual than an empirical question. Or at least the empirical attempts to measure change have not yielded such clearcut and convergent findings as to promote widespread agreement on whether fundamental transformations are at work.[6] And surely American scholars have long been biased toward keeping their studies of world affairs consonant with their images of world affairs.[7]

[5] For an analysis that emphasizes such a bias and argues that the changes are superficial in comparison to the continuities of world politics, see F.S. Northedge, 'Transnationalism: The American Illusion,' *Millennium*, Vol. 5 (Spring 1976), pp. 21-7. For a perspective in which pervasive change is acknowledged and yet not requiring the construction of new paradigms (there being two basic and enduring paradigms, the pluralist and the structuralist, that have both proven flexible enough to accommodate the changes), see Ralph Pettman, 'Competing Paradigms in International Politics,' a paper presented at the Seminar on Theories of International Relations, Australian National University, August 17, 1978.

[6] For some systematic attempts to assess the degree of structural change in the global system, see P.J. Katzenstein, 'International Interdependence: Some Long-Term Trends and Recent Changes,' *International Organization* Vol. 29 (Autumn 1975), pp. 1020-34; R.R. Kaufman, H.I. Chernotsky, and D.S. Geller, 'A Preliminary Test of the Theory of Dependency,' *Comparative Politics*, Vol. 7 (April 1975), pp. 303-31; and R. Rosecrance, A. Alexandroff, W. Koehler, J. Kroll, S. Laqueur, and J. Stocker, 'Whither Independence?' *International Oranization*, Vol. 31 (Summer 1975), pp. 425-72.

[7] Two observers, for example, note that the study of 'international relations is an American invention dating from the time after World War I when the American intellectual community discovered the world. Like most American essays in regard to the word, it has been enthusiastic, well-financed, faddist, nationally-oriented, and creating more problems than it solves.' Fred Warner Neal and Bruce D. Hamlett, 'The Never-Never Land of International Relations,' *International Studies Quarterly*, Vol. 13 (September 1969), p. 283.

To dismiss the indicators of change as an American bias, however, is to fail to confront the central question of whether world politics is undergoing transformation. Such a dismissal may even be expressive of a nonAmerican bias in which European and Oriental scholars presume that nothing basically new can ever be found in history. To be sure, one can always identify incidents in the past that correspond in some salient ways to any present event. But history also records breakpoints, watersheds, transformations, redirections, and the like, with the result that the presumption of historical continuity can be just as prejudiced and self-deceptive as the assumption that profound changes are occurring. Furthermore, it is the very nature of paradigms that they are so encompassing as to be entrapping, preventing us from seeing their increasing inappropriateness because they are founded on premises that can absorb and explain any contradictions. This is why paradigms seem to crumble quickly once they start to crumble: when we finally break free of them enough to get an inkling of their inappropriateness, they are already far gone and thus appear to crumble quickly.

How, then, does one proceed? Assuming the problem is conceptual and not empirical, what presumption does one make as to whether profound changes are transforming world politics or whether deep-seated continuities are preserving the existing structure? My answer is already clear. I find it safer to proceed as if the changes are occurring than to treat them as peripheral. In this way we can at least allow for the evolution of a new paradigm which may, subsequently, prove insufficient because not that much change has occurred. But if we muddle or meddle through by stressing the deep-seated continuities, we run the risk of missing out on the prevailing dynamics of our field. I admit to being insufficiently grounded in history and I acknowledge the possibility that my perspectives are too grounded in American biases. Yet I find the indicators of change (such as those noted on p. 130) to be so impressive and so pervasive that I cannot back away from the conclusion that trying to develop new paradigms is energy well expended.

MUDDLING, MEDDLING AND MODELING IN INTERNATIONAL POLITICAL ECONOMY

Perhaps nothing has revealed the insufficiency of our present paradigms more clearly than the emergence of international political economy (IPE) as a field of inquiry and as a label for a vast cluster of recently salient global issues. In the United States the rush to embrace IPE has been swift and thoroughgoing: in less than five years courses in IPE have been added to most undergraduate and graduate curricula, an IPE subfield has been added to many Ph.D. programs, conferences on the teaching of IPE have been held, the U.S. Office of Education has sponsored programmatic development in the field, workshops devoted to identifying the boundaries and central problems of IPE have been convened, IPE journals have been founded, research monographs and articles on the subject have proliferated at a dizzying pace, and — by no means least — IPE texts have been published and have received such a warm reception as to come out again in revised editions.[8] Indeed, the evolution of IPE as an intellectual focus has been so widespread that already it has undergone fragmentation into subfields of its own, with some scholars specializing in monetary, trade, or commodity issues, others focusing on such IPE actors as UNCTAD or the multinational corporation, and still others concerning themselves with the problems of such broad global subdivisions as the North–South dialogue or the merits of such comprehensive analytic schemes as the liberal, mercantile, and Marxist approaches to IPE.

These myraid activities and specializations derive, of course, from comparable developments in world affairs. The pervasive repercussions flowing from the breakdown of the monetary system, the rising demands of the Third World, and the energy crunch are but the most obvious examples of the large extent to which the changing global scene has converged around problems of political economy. For some analysts, in fact, such IPE problems constitute the boundaries of international relations, as if the world's mounting interdependence involves only (or, at least, mainly) economic dynamics as they have come to impinge upon various processes of political management. While this has always struck me as an excessively narrow view of what interdependence encompasses, certainly there can be little doubt that the 1970s have been marked by economic issues emerging to rival traditional political and diplomatic conflicts for the top spots on the global agenda. The emergence of IPE as a scholarly field is thus neither fluke nor fad. Its roots are embedded deep in the soil of global change, and its central concerns are also those of statesmen, bureaucrats, and publics.

But the IPE-dominated world is a bewildering one, for both those who are active in it and those who analyze it. As one observer who examined a series of IPE events in the mid-1970s notes, '. . . interdependence *had* changed many of the conditions that decision makers had to deal with, and it had diminished the liklihood that the

[8] See David H. Blake and Robert S. Walters, *The Politics of Global Economics Relations* (Englewood Cliffs, N.J.: Prentice Hall, 1976), and Joan Edelman Spero, *The Politics of International Economic Relations* (New York: St Martin's Press, 1977).

conventional wisdom would continue to provide satisfactory answers.'[9]

Much the same can be said of the wisdom of analysts. Or at least the world of IPE is perplexing to those of us whose training in political science largely ignored economic variables while concentrating on the calculations and deliberations of individuals and small groups as they interact and conflict with each other. Relatively speaking, the political world is a micro world: it turns on self-conscious choices designed to serve self-conscious goals reached through careful planning and cost-benefit assessments. The actions and reactions of large collectivities are central to the course of political affairs, but these are ordinarily undertaken by leaders and articulated by spokespersons, thereby enabling political scientists to account for macro developments through focusing on their manifestation at micro levels. By contrast, on the other hand, the economic world is a macro world: it turns on the actions of markets, fluctuations in prices, flows of currency, shifts in trading patterns, and a host of other developments cumulated out of diffuse patterns of production and consumption. The actions are reactions of individuals are central to the course of economic affairs, but these are ordinarily reflected in large-scale trends and rarely are they articulated by spokespersons.

Stated differently, political scientists are concerned mainly with subsystem-dominant systems, whereas economists focus primarily on system-dominant systems, and this difference leads them down very different analytic paths. In studying politics one tends to posit actors as seeking to manipulate or control their environments, whereas the student of economics tends to treat environments as having their own dynamic with respect to which actors are essentially irrelevant and to which they must yield. Both political and economic actors may seek to create the parameters within which outcomes can occur, but political actors can more readily shape the course of events as they unfold toward outcomes than can their economic counterparts. This difference is so pronounced, in fact, that it is reasonable to conceive of political actors as promoting outcomes and economic actors as striving to cope with outcomes.

The essential nature of IPE can be readily derived from the foregoing considerations: to bring the disciplines of political science and economics together in the study of political economy is to commit oneself to *the analysis of self-conscious efforts to shape, control, or otherwise manage the large, impersonal forces that infuse configurations and direction into the structure and functioning of global life.* And this task is one for which neither the political scientist nor the

[9] Robert L. Rothstein, *Global Bargaining: UNCTAD and the Quest for a New International Economic Order* (Princeton: Princeton University Press, 1979), p. 13 (italics in the original).

economist seems to be temperamentally suited or conceptually equipped.

Students of international politics, for example, are bewildered by how shifts in the price of gold and the value of the dollar occur despite the efforts of governments to shore up currencies. They can understand the elementary economics which, say, explains why gold rises when the dollar falls, but the unsusceptibility of these processes to firm control is hard to grasp. Each shift in a currency seems to be the product of so many separate decisions by so many unknown actors (located somewhere in that amorphous arena called 'international banking circles') that none of the conventional tools of analysis, such as the concepts of authority, power, or strategy, seem to fit. Why even the organizational structure of the IPE world is ungainly and confusing: one of its most important organizations (GATT) is called a 'general agreement' and another (UNCTAD) is a 'conference,' hardly titles that suggest an ongoing structure of authority or constitutional arrangements for making decisions. Then there is the way in which national actors are treated in the IPE literature. Trained to avoid using reified and anthropomorphic designations and instead to give empirical specification to those who undertake action, the political scientist is put off by the broad abstractions that pervade the IPE literature. The Americans seek trade expansion, the Germans press for monetary reform, the Japanese maintain protectionism, and only rarely are such actors depicted in terms of the individuals, cabinets, or administrations that engage in the specified actions. No less disconcerting, a bewildering array of international actors are depicted as moving about on the IPE stage as if they were individuals interacting, but without any indication of the processes from which their actions derive: there is the EEC which is unwilling, the OECD which investigates, the West which is concerned, the South which makes demands, the Group of Eminent Persons which calls for change, the MNCs which seek markets, the Committee of Twenty which succeeded the Group of Ten and which serves a crisis management function, the IMF which offers advice and exerts influence and the CAP which assures protection for European farmers, the IBRD which strives to prevent economic nationalisms, Comecon which coordinates trade, the IPC which facilitates resource transfers, the Group of 77 which now numbers more than one hundred, and so on through a seemingless endless cast of acronyms that crowd the IPE stage with their goals, conflicts, and procedures.[10]

[10] One survey of the field facilitated movement through the IPE world by appending a list of 'Abbreviations' employed throughout the work. All told, these came to eighty-two different entities. See Robert W. Cox and Harold K. Jacobsen (eds.), *The Analysis of Influence: Decision-Making in International Oranization* (New Haven: Yale University Press, 1973), pp. x-xiii.

While many political scientists have turned to meddling or modeling as a way of coping with IPE-induced change, a number have sought to muddle through. Some have done so by denying that the world is any more interdependent than it ever was and dismissing indicators of transnationalizing processes as 'illusions.'[11] Others have acknowledged the existence of profound changes, but have posited them as changes in scale rather than as transformations of essential structures: as Tucker puts it in discussing the demands of Third World countries, '. . . we are standing on familiar terrain. The stage is much larger than it has ever been. There are more actors than ever before. Even so, the actors are still states, their conflicts occur in a society that remains dominated by the institution of self-help, and they are contending over goods states have regularly contended over in the past.'[12]

Still others have unknowingly resorted to muddling through the IPE world by appearing to meddle with their conceptual equipment. Not disposed to be self-conscious about their analytic tools and yet aware that changes may have occurred for which they ought to account, such analysts do not really meddle with their formulations but, instead, are content to proceed by distinguishing between 'high' and 'low' politics. The former are said to describe the traditional issues of diplomacy and military strategy, whereas the newer, IPE issues derived from mounting interdependence are said to constitute low politics. If it has any particular reference, the distinction between high and low apparently denotes the governmental level at which issues are handled and decisions made with respect to them. Historically diplomatic and military challenges are the responsibility of those high in decision-making structures — cabinet officers, prime ministers, and presidents — and the task of coping with socio-economic problems has been left to subcabinet, bureaucratic, and other lesser officials. The form of muddling through by appearing to meddle follows readily: the emergence of the IPE world is posited as an elevation of low politics into high politics, thus only requiring of analysts that they treat the newer socio-economic issues as they have always examined the conflicts that comprise the global agenda. For all its apparent elegance, in other words, the high-low distinction is specious and deceptive. It conveys the appearance of conceptually accounting for changing circumstances, but in fact it makes no allowance for the new types of actors, motives, processes, and structures that have accompanied the IPE-induced transformation of the global agenda.

A number of analysts, however, have been unable to deny or ignore the structural changes that have brought about the IPE-dominated

[11] See Northedge, op. cit.

[12] Robert W. Tucker, *The Inequality of Nations* (New York: Basic Books, 1977), p. 65.

world. They accept the fact of profound change and the need to make corresponding conceptual adjustments. Accordingly, they have self-consciously and systematically resorted to meddling by attempting to tailor established analytic tools to the confounding world of IPE. Caporaso has sought to 'relate' dependence and dependency 'to more familiar concepts,' particularly to the concepts of power, capability, and bargaining.[13] Rothstein has used a bargaining context to extensively examine negotiations over commodity problems within UNCTAD.[14] Cox and Jacobson have edited a compendium of eleven essays that probe the functioning of international organizations relevant to IPE in terms of decision processes and the structure of influence.[15] Then there is Keohane and Nye's elaborate and extensive effort to develop the concept of 'complex interdependence' and apply it to the dynamics of regime change in two major issue areas.[16] Indeed, this attempt is so thoroughgoing that some might regard it more as a modeling than a meddling response to the transformations occurring in world politics. Not much familiarity with their formulations is required, however, to realize that it is founded on long-established analytical tools (such as power, issue structure, hierarchy, and leadership) and that its central thrust is more analytic than paradigmatic, thereby rendering it more a conceptual framework than a theoretical mode. Keohane and Nye examine a number of key variables and often indicate the range across which they vary, but at no point do they explicitly offer integrated hypotheses as to the circumstances under which the variables vary in one way rather than another.

Although meddling efforts such as the foregoing provide useful insights and often yield important findings, they raise more questions than they answer with respect to the underlying dynamics at work in IPE. Decision-making and bargaining are clearly practiced and power and influence are clearly operative in the IPE realm, but the relevance of such phenomena, the larger context in which they unfold, is far from clear. Like Keohane and Nye, none of the works purport to be theoretical and thus none offer interrelated hypotheses as to the casual sequences underlying IPE. More than a few, in fact, admit to confusion as to how theory-building in IPE should proceed. As one analyst puts it, 'Intellectual uncertainty seems to me to be one of

[13] James A. Caporaso, 'Dependence, Dependency, and Power in the Global System: A Structural and Behavioral Analysis,' *International Organization*, Vol. 32 (Winter 1978), pp. 13–43.

[14] Ibid.

[15] Robert W. Cox and Harold K. Jacobson (eds.), *The Anatomy of Influence: Decision Making International Organization* (New Haven: Yale University, 1973).

[16] Robert O. Keohane and Joseph S. Nye, *Power and Interdependence: World Politics in Transition* (Boston: Little, Brown Co., 1977).

the most critical behavioral characteristics of the current international system . . . Perhaps one of the problems is that if interdependence has decreased the autonomy of national decision making, it has also decreased the autonomy of the intellectual constructs that attempt to explain such decisions.'[17]

Some analysts, aware that neither muddling nor meddling will do, have sought to cope with the dynamics of change and the intellectual uncertainty it has fostered through modeling. Most of these efforts, in turn, have been founded on the premise that macro economic phenomena are located at the heart of world affairs and that it thus ought to be possible to avoid a lengthy process of paradigm replacement by starting from a Marxist perspective, or what one analyst prefers to call 'historical materialism' (since 'Marxism carries so many conflicting connotations of doctrinal orthodoxies and political lines').[18] Adherence to a Marxist paradigm strikes me as likely to mark increasing numbers of international relations analysts in industrial democracies. It is, after all, a coherent and yet flexible paradigm, with all the attractions offered by any comprehensive integrated theory and with the added advantage of being able to account (through class conflict) for the behavior of the new actors and the dynamics of the new issues of interdependence that underlie disenchantment with the differentiated state model. The mounting of North–South tensions and the demands for a New International Economic Order, not to mention the prominent role multinational corporations have come to play as rivals to governments in world politics, can readily be interpreted in a historical materialist framework as the differentiated state model seems increasingly inappropriate. Moreover, since 'Marx is capable of a wide range of interpretations . . . each perfectly consistent within itself,' and since there are thus 'many Marxes,'[19] the handling of monetary crises, famine, trade imbalance, and many of the other new interdependence issues on the global agenda may be just as easily cast in one or another Marxist framework as any fledgling non-Marxist paradigm that may evolve.

I wish it was so simple. Building paradigmatic foundations is so arduous and tenuous that ready-made formulations as incisive as those to be found in Marx are tempting replacements. As I understand the four essential elements that the many historical materialist

[17] Rothstein, *Global Bargaining*, pp. 241, 242.

[18] Robert W. Cox, 'Ideologies and the New International Economic Order: Reflections on Some Recent Literature,' *International Organization*, Vol. 33 (Spring 1979), p. 289.

[19] Robert L. Heilbroner, 'Inescapable Marx,' *The New York Review of Books*, Vol. XXV (June 29, 1978), p. 34. Cox also notes (*Ideologies and The New International Economic Order*, p. 290) that 'the historical materialists are divided among themselves,' with the differences revolving around 'three main cleavages.'

formulations have in common,[20] however, the fit does not seem sufficient to yield to temptation. Though it surely needs to be done by many observers, this is not the place to undertake an analysis of how the dynamics of change may or may not be shaping a world that conforms to Marxist paradigms. Suffice it to note that I find too much diversity in the fragmentation of authority, as well as in the structures, social bases, and aspirations of the new nonstate organizations through whom the fragmentation is occurring, to accept the Marxist emphasis on class struggle as the prime motor of historical change.

Nor can one rest content with the models developed by those who opt for that variant of Marxism which stresses IPE phenomena as well as class conflict. Perhaps articulated most forcefully by Wallerstein, this variant has been especially attractive to American analysts, who are impressed with the need for new models but unwilling to found them exclusively on economic variables. The Wallerstein paradigm is attractive because it does downplay the role of states, positing them as linked into the world economy in such a way that their policies and institutions are dictated by the processes of production and distribution that sustain the global economic system.[21]

Furthermore, although the various materialist models have the virtue of being comprehensive, integrated theory that allows for and explains change, they are so wedded to deriving explanations from the operation of the global economy that their models do not focus on the kinds of phenomena that I have identified as central to IPE. That is, if IPE involves the analysis of self-conscious efforts to shape, control, or to otherwise manage the large, impersonal forces that infuse configuration and direction into the structure and functioning of global life (as I argue on p. 137 that it does), the historical materialist models do not pose questions addressed to such processes and efforts. Their concerns involve the evolution and unfolding of historical forces, with questions about the policy conflicts and control decisions that intervene to sustain the forces treated largely as peripheral phenomena.

The conclusion that past IPE-modeling efforts are insufficient and wanting is hardly unique. Leaver, for example, asserts that model-building '. . . is noticeably absent within international relations, where theoretical tardiness has characterized the development of political economy. It appears that the very factors which have hastened the development of a political economy of international relations have had an important adverse effect — to abort any inclinations toward

[20] Heilbroner, 'Inescapable Marx', p. 35.
[21] See, for example, Immanuel Wallerstein, *The Modern World-System: Capitalist Agriculture and the Origins of the European World-Economy in the Sixteenth Century* (New York: Academic Press, 1974).

theory.'[22] Similarly, Rothstein concludes that 'dissatisfaction with the results produced by traditional conceptualizations in international relations (and economics) is growing, but consensus on the nature of existing problems, the questions to be asked, and the goals to be pursued does not exist.' Indeed, Rothstein refers to this theme at the end of a lengthy examination of negotiations within UNCTAD over a new order in commodity trade, noting that

> A good part of the uncertainty can be attributed to the failure of existing concepts or approaches to provide satisfactory explanations for behavior in the North-South arena . . . But these failures are even more consequential when we move from specific concepts to paradigms or the intellectual frames of reference (theories would be far too strong a term) that we use to provide guidance and predictability in the current international system. None of the prevailing paradigms appear to provide an adequate explanation for the results of the negotiating process in commodities.[24]

SOME ESSENTIAL COMPONENTS OF NEW PARADIGMS

Having worked within the post-realist differentiated state model for nearly three decades, I am in no position to offer a new and coherent paradigm. To recognize the rapidity with which a paradigm crumbles when it starts to go is not to discern the outlines and basic premises of those that might evolve in its place. One is, of course, highly conscious of the reasons for the collapse, but these may point only to some of the essential components of a new paradigm rather than to the organizing assumptions and causal links that render it coherent and all-encompassing. A long period of disarray and tension may have to ensue before the essential components of a new paradigm are pieced together into a structured and parsimonious whole.

Does it follow that students of world politics are in a helpless situation? If they are impressed with the rapid pace of change and the fruitlessness of coping with it by muddling through or meddling, and if they are also dissatisfied with the existing paradigms for integrating the change even as they also feel incapable of replacing them, are they bound to founder, trapped in rich empirical materials without any hope of giving them coherence? My response is to emphasize that it is unrealistic to expect the kind of paradigm that is needed to be fashioned by a single individual, but that the individual can contribute a great deal by clarifying the essential components of which

[22] Richard Leaver, 'Towards the Political Economy of International Relations: The End of the World as We Know It?' a paper presented at the Seminar on Theories of International Relations, Australian National University, Canberra, October 26, 1978, pp. 5–6.

[23] Rothstein, *Global Bargaining*, p. 13.

[24] Ibid., p. 242.

any workable paradigm is likely to be comprised.

But where to begin? How do we know the essential components of such a paradigm when we come upon them? What criteria should we use to select the building blocks of appropriate new models? My answer to these key questions is twofold. In the first place, we need to develop concepts that focus on dynamic rather than static phenomena, that are organized around the processes of interacting entities rather than their attributes. If we can construct the outlines of a world in which the course of events is sustained by processes rather than actors, we need not fear that our paradigm will be rendered obsolete by the declining capacities of governments, the advent of new issues initiated by new organizations, the fragmentation of authority, or the growth of interdependence. For all these tendencies are processes, and they ought to be subject to investigation irrespective of whether they are maintained by states, bureaucracies, nongovernmental entities, or transnational bodies. Secondly, it follows that we need to begin with building blocks that are developed at such a high level of abstraction that they enable us to analyze both the processes presently at work and any that unfold in the future. Highly abstract concepts, moreover, can help free us from the differentiated state paradigm to the extent they involve new words, labels, and ideas that may inhibit our inclinations to fall back into old analytic habits.

But what processes should be the focus of our modeling effort? Here I derive the answer from what strikes me as the most elemental dynamic common to both the changes and the continuities at work in world politics, namely, that dynamic or set of dynamics whereby individual actions are summed and thereby converted into collectivities and then, at subsequent points in time, converted over and over again into more or less encompassing collectivities. Such dynamics underlie the emergence of new issues and actors, both those that result from the fragmentation of authority and those that stem from cooperative integration. And they also undergird the decline of old issues and actors as well as those that remain unaltered by changing circumstances. I shall refer to these most essential dynamics as aggregative or disaggregative processes, since the summing of actions into more or less encompassing collectivities can be readily seen as transformations through which behavior is more or less widely aggregated.

To anticipate what follows, this line of reasoning leads to a world populated by a great variety of aggregations that are macro wholes summed out of micro parts. In this world some of the aggregations are formal organizations, others are loose coalitions, and still others are comprised of unorganized individuals whose actions sum to recognizable wholes; but all of them are subject to events that alter their parts and thus the sums to which they cumulate. As a result, all of the aggregations are posited as either undergoing formation and leaderless or as established and led by authorized or self-appointed spokespersons who seek to mobilize the parts or otherwise articulate and advance their interests.

Although the ensuing analysis treats aggregation at a very high level of abstraction and as a series of never-ending processes, I would not claim that it is otherwise sufficient as a building block for a new paradigm. Such a conclusion requires a much more extended inquiry than is set forth here, not to mention the identification of the other building blocks out of which a viable conceptual structure can be fashioned. But at least this formulation is suggestive of what may be involved if we opt for modeling rather than muddling or meddling.

THE CONCEPT OF AGGREGATION

As indicated, an aggregation is conceived to be a whole (or macro unit) composed of parts (or micro units) whose actions are sufficiently similar to be summable into the whole, and an aggregative process refers to the interactions whereby such transformations occur. The smallest micro unit in world politics is the individual, but all aggregations of individuals — from two person groups to nation-states to international organizations — can also be viewed as micro units if they are treated as parts of more encompassing wholes. All the aggregations, of course, can also be treated as macro units if there are no reasons to focus on how their actions are transformed into larger wholes. Thus, for example, bureaucratic agencies are macro units embracing individuals as micro units, whereas from a broader perspective the agencies are micro units embedded in such macro units as governments, large corporations, or international organizations.

But the important point is not that the varied collectivities of world politics can be viewed as either macro or micro units. Rather, for reasons developed below, the key to making a full break with the differentiated state paradigm and contructing new ones to replace it lies in the readiness to treat all collectivities as susceptible either to aggregative processes that transform them into larger wholes or to disaggregative processes that transform them from wholes into parts.[25] For these processes are nothing less than the causal flows in international relations, the dynamics through which action is initiated,

[25] That the ensuing analysis deals only with aggregative processes is not meant to imply that there need be no concern about the causal flows from macro to micro units. On the contrary, as noted in Chap. 5, the processes of disaggregation are also central to any paradigm-building effort. Aggregative and disaggregative processes, however, differ in certain key respects, albeit space limitations permit probing only the former here.

sustained, redirected, or terminated on the world stage. Thus, whether one is concerned with a state's foreign policy, the population explosion, a balance of power, an arms race, the Third World's demands for greater equity, or a resource scarcity, its place in the larger scheme of world politics becomes more elaborately and more incisively manifest when it is viewed as the product of or a contributor to any or all of several aggregative processes.

Three aggregative processes strike me as especially fundamental. One results in *unintended* aggregations, another in *articulated* aggregations, and the third in *mobilized* aggregations, the differences among them being due to the ways in which their micro parts come together into macro wholes.

In the unintended process the micro parts are aggregated whenever the similarity of their parts is recognized but not acted upon (e.g., migrations), whereas in the other two processes recognition is accompanied by action on the part of spokespersons (e.g., immigration regulations). Leadership activities do not accompany unintended aggregations because the similar actions of their micro parts may stem from a variety of sources. Indeed, their similar actions may be undertaken for very different, perhaps even conflicting, private purposes. Yet, being the same, they are summable. These unintended sums may be recognized by journalists, scholars, and/or other observers who have occasion to take note of the separate but similar actions that comprise the aggregation in the course of performing their responsibilities. For reasons suggested below, however, the unintended aggregation is not the basis of action on the part of those who sum its parts through recognition. It is simply a structural feature of the world scene that may play a crucial if passive role in the course of events. A resource scarcity typifies an unintended aggregation. It results from individuals or groups consuming the resource for their own private reasons and, in so doing, creating a scarcity. None of the micro units intended the shortage, but their separate actions aggregated to such an outcome. The growing scarcity may have long been recognized by various observers, but it remains an unintended aggregation as long as their observations do not provoke action by spokepersons for other aggregations that have previously been converted into collectivities.

Frequently, of course, the actions of micro units are undertaken for similar purposes. If so, obviously they will also be similar in content and recognized as aggregating to a larger whole. Less obvious is that the similarity of the purposes of the micro units leads them to permit or select spokespersons to act on behalf of their summed actions. That is, the micro units intend — or at least allow — their aggregation and they intend for it to be recognized and organized in such a way that action can be continuously taken on behalf of their collective interests. It is this process that I refer to as an *articulated* aggregation. It is exemplified by the activities of multinational corporations, rebel movements, trade unions, professional societies, or international organizations, all of whose spokespersons seek to promote and preserve the concerns of their stockholders, members, followers, and any other micro units of which they may be composed. Most notably perhaps, an articulated aggregation is illustrated by the foreign policies of a state, which are framed and advanced by its spokespersons on the basis of the prior and continuing actions of its citizens that permit their aggregation into the state. The spokespersons and those toward whom their policies are directed presume that through aggregation they enjoy sufficient support of the citizenry — micro units — to articulate its interests. To be sure, on rare occasions the actions of foreign policy officials are lacking a support base and thus do not represent accurate summations of the micro units. But these exceptions also reveal the nature of articulated aggregations since they normally result in the ouster of the officials (as proved to be the case when Anthony Eden aggregated inaccurately and launched an English invasion of the Suez Canal in 1956 or when Lyndon Johnson did the same in 1965–67 and escalated U.S. involvement in Vietnam).

The third basic type of aggregative process occurs when the similar actions of microparts are stimulated by spokespersons who seek to sum them into a particular whole for a particular purpose. Normally an articulated aggregation is the focus of such efforts (as when states go to war or when some leaders of the Third World generate support among their colleagues in the Group of 77 to reinforce demands for a New International Economic Order); but sometimes an unintended aggregation is the target of the stimuli (as when spokespersons for governments try to get people to conserve energy or when aspiring politicians attempt to seize leadership of a grassroots revolt against high taxes). Whichever may be the target of the efforts, it is the result of this process that I call a *mobilized* aggregation.

It is important to stress that the summing of the micro units of an aggregation into a macro whole is a process undertaken and sustained not by the micro units themselves, but by observers and/or leaders (i.e., spokespersons) who recognize, articulate, and/or mobilize them. The collective consequences of individual actions, in other words, only become aggregations when they are identified as cumulative sums. And they only become *politically relevant* aggregations when their sums are both identified and used by spokespersons to advance, resist, or otherwise contest claims *vis-a-vis* the community. Individuals might band together to press a claim, but even their concerted actions do not become those of an aggregation until their summed demands are articulated by their leaders and acknowledged by those of whom the demands are made. Spontaneous street mobs, organized protest marches, impulsive buyer resistances, or planned consumer boycotts, for example, do not become summed aggregations until the summing is experienced and reacted to as a collective action.

It follows that the relationship between the micro units of an aggregation and its macro spokespersons can vary greatly, from a tight, one-to-one relationship in which the latter do not act without the consent of the former to a loose, tenuous relationship in which the spokespersons need not be particularly concerned about the accuracy of their sums. Most aggregations are of the loose, tenuous type (thereby giving rise to the need for creative and effective leadership), but even here there can be great variety, depending on how well the leadership calculates, articulates, and mobilizes the sums.

Much more often than not the spokespersons are likely to be inaccurate in the sums they calculate, but their inaccuracies are rarely so serious as to provoke the micro units into collective actions that relieve them of their statuses as spokespersons. Tolerance of the inaccuracies is the norm partly because the calculation of objective sums tends to be impossible (if only because many articulated aggregations consist of parts, such as attitudes and motives, that are not readily quantifiable), partly because of the considerable leeway built into most processes through which summation occurs (i.e., most groups allow their leaders discretionary authority in asserting claims on their behalf), and partly because the links between the micro units and their macro spokespersons are so circuitous and cumbersome that the former are often unaware that the latter are acting on their behalf.

Usually, of course, macro spokespersons try to be as accurate as possible in the sums they calculate. The more accurate they are, the more are they likely to be in touch with their support base and thus the more effectively can they cite evidence supporting their claims. There may be times when the aggregated sums are intentionally exaggerated or underplayed for tactical purposes, but in the long run spokespersons have much to gain through maximizing the accuracy of their aggregated sums.

Whatever the accuracy with which the parts are summed, there is one sense in which inaccuracy is bound to occur: the aggregated whole is bound to be larger than the sum of its parts whenever the similar actions that comprise an aggregation are articulated or mobilized by its spokespersons and their assertions and activities thereby become the basis of issues in the political arena. At such points the needs and wants of the aggregation acquire an existence apart from its micro units. The aggregation becomes an entity unto itself, capable of pressing, resisting, bargaining, and accommodating demands, and in so acting its spokespersons render it into a whole that exceeds the sum of its parts.

USES OF THE CONCEPT

Crude as it may be, this initial formulation of the several types of aggregation can serve the paradigm-building task in a number of ways. One is that it lends itself to close empirical examination. The several aggregative processes consist not of hidden hands that somehow mystically transform individuals into collectivities. To be sure, the interactions of masses of people are so circuitous, complex, and subtle that they are not easily discerned. Nevertheless, in this formulation the ways in which micro units cumulate into macro units are concrete and identifiable; aggregation occurs when similar actions are recognized, summed, and articulated. Recognition and summation are manifest in birth rates, agricultural outputs, industrial production figures, election outcomes, trade patterns, and a host of other indicators that are regularly published or readily compiled; similarly, articulation is empirically manifest in the activities of spokepersons who continuously recognize and sum the aggregations for which they act.

Secondly, by conceiving of the collectivities that sustain world politics as aggregative processes rather than structural parameters, we allow for the dynamics of change at all levels of analysis and under all possible circumstances. Viewed as aggregations whose formation depends on the convergence of similar behavior, collectivities appear less as enduring constants and more as being in constant flux. If we can discipline ourselves to see the world not as a cluster of nations, alignments, or publics, but as a cluster of everchanging aggregative processes — of parts forming wholes, coming apart, reforming, and doing so in such a way that the wholes are sometimes roughly equal to the sums of their parts and sometimes greater than the sums — then we ought to be better able to pick up and rearrange the pieces of the paradigms that collapsed under the weight of pervasive change.

The capacity of the aggregation concept to render us more sensitive to the dynamics of change is especially relevant to the longstanding practice of viewing certain circumstances as the 'realities' of world politics — as those deeper structures comprised of longstanding habits, cultural tendencies, economic imperatives, and sociological necessities entrenched in the environment that are beyond manipulation and yet profoundly condition what people do and how communities function. As considered here, however, all such 'realities' are unintended aggregations that, being composed of recognizable parts, may be susceptible to manipulation (i.e., to transformation into articulated or mobilized aggregations). The energy problem, for example, is often posited as consisting of realities embedded in the interaction between the world's oil reserves and the consumption patterns of an industrial civilization. Recent efforts in the West to get people to change their energy utilization habits constitute an attempt to render an unintentional aggregation into a mobilized one and, notwithstanding the apparent failure of such efforts, it suggests the emergence of a readiness on the part of spokespersons to undertake manipulation of what not long ago had been regarded as unmanipulable. Much the same can be said about ocean problems, food shortages, currency fluctuations, and the population explosion. These are but a few of the many unintended aggregations that have lately become salient on the global stage as foci of endeavors to convert them into articulated or mobilized aggregations.

The ability to distinguish among the several aggregative processes, therefore, can greatly facilitate analysis as the world becomes more decentralized and as we search for ways of identifying those of its features that are becoming permanent and those that are undergoing fundamental change. It virtually compels us to reconsider the 'realities' of world politics and assess the extent to which these collapsed with our paradigms. By viewing them as unintended aggregations rather than as deep-seated, habitual and immutable tendencies of people in a complex world, we at least allow for the possibility that altered circumstances may redirect the processes by which wholes get aggregated out of parts. For, to repeat, aggregations are processes composed of discrete and separable parts and, as such, they are susceptible to alteration, a characteristic which does not obtain if the same phenomena are viewed as fixed and permanent.

Fourthly, and relatedly, by treating aggregative processes as parameters of world politics, we put the individual person more centrally onto the global stage. Aggregations begin with and build upon concrete and identifiable individuals who, through recognized and articulated similar behavior, become groups, communities, governments, nations, international balances, and the like. Putting the person onto the global stage is important because the decentralization of authority, the fragmentation of societies, and the emergence of interdependence issues takes the origins and dynamics of politics into the homes and jobs where individuals make choices and undertake actions. The population explosion is perhaps the clearest example of how aggregative processes can be traced back to the individual level, but the relevance of the motorist, the banker, the farmer, the fisherman, and the terrorist to, respectively, the energy crunch, monetary instability, food shortages, ocean problems, and political upheaval is indicative of the large degree to which the structures of world politics have become ever more solidly rooted in the soil of individual orientations and behavior.

Indeed, the declining competence of governments can be traced partly, if not primarily, to mounting distrust to public institutions on the part of citizens.

A fifth advantage of this formulation is that it can hasten our break with any paradigm that relies on states as the prime sources of causation. By focusing on aggregations and their spokespersons, we allow ourselves to analyze varied behavior on the global stage without having to presume the importance of states or implicitly ranking them as more significant than other types of actors. Indeed, this formulation enables us to get away not only from states as abstract actors, but also from the very notion of action being the product of any abstraction. As conceived here, action is located where empirically it originates and is maintained, i.e., in and by individuals. For the only actors in this formulation are the individuals who comprise aggregations and those who serve as spokespersons for them.

Sixth, the notion of spokespersons for aggregations offers the potential of a fresh approach to analyzing the policy-making process. Instead of being forced to treat such processes as bounded by the political and legal constraints of states, we can focus on the dynamics whereby the spokespersons experience, sum, assess, and articulate the interests of their aggregations and then interact with other spokepersons of other aggregations. Sometimes these interactions occur within governments (thus resulting in what are now called policy decisions), sometimes in bargaining between governments (thus giving rise to policy outcomes), and sometimes in the nongovernmental arena where political parties, interest groups, professional associations, and other groups compete for the support of citizens and the attention of officials. But mostly aggregations extend across the boundaries that separate agencies within governments, that divide governments from each other, and that differentiate governments from the private sector. Thus the consequences of mounting interdependence and fragmented authority are likely to be built into any analysis of what happens when spokespersons articulate and mobilize their aggregations.

A seventh reason why the concept can serve as a useful building block for a more appropriate paradigm is that its several types provide a uniform basis for analyzing any of the diverse issues that may be on the world's agenda at any moment in time. Any issue can be viewed as a problem posed by an unintended aggregation or as arising out of a competition among articulated or mobilized aggregations. Whatever its aggregative foundations, the issue can be dissected and probed by examining the dynamics — the motivations, presumptions, and/or habits — whereby the actions of individuals allow for and lead to their aggregation and the articulation of their collective needs and wants. Thus, despite the diversity of their contents, the structures, overlaps, and consequences of the prevailing issues can be contrasted and compared. And, hopefully, such comparative analyses can lead to a more precise specification of a parsimonious typology of aggregative processes which, in turn, can facilitate the derivation of a few basic causal principles around which the beginnings of a paradigm can be organized.

It follows that the distinctions among the several types of aggregation should also better enable us to discern the similarities between the newer IPE issues spawned by mounting interdpendence and the old military-diplomatic issues that continue to occupy prominent places on the global agenda. Presumably any new paradigm that evolves will have to surmount the inclination to treat the IPE issues as interlopers, as unconventional aspects of world politics that require special treatment. These new issues seem here to stay and we have to begin to treat them as integral parts of world politics. The differentiation among aggregative processes offers a means for achieving this analytic integration. It allows us to view socio-economic and military-diplomatic issues in the same context — as processes of aggregation that can undergo progression from the recognition through the articulation and mobilization stages of development. To be sure, since most socio-economic issues derive from the habits and patterns of millions of persons, they evolve in different ways and at different rates than do most military-diplomatic issues. Hence the former are much less subject to articulated aggregation than are the latter and they are also less susceptible to mobilization.[26] Nevertheless, viewing both types of issues as aggregative processes at least renders them comparable and enables us to contrast them in meaningful ways.

A final advantage inherent in the concept of aggregation is that it provides a means of observing how the global agenda is formed, with issues rising and falling, some crowding their way to the top of the agenda, some lingering on its periphery, and others never making it at all. By tracing how unintended aggregations are transformed into those that are articulated or mobilized, we can begin to see how activities at various levels of organization do or do not become linked to each other and, as a result, how the linked actions can culminate in a place on the global agenda. It will be recalled that whatever may be the micro units of an aggregation — be they the purchases of citizens or the decisions of officials — they are not necessarily the basis for action once they are recognized and summed into a more encompassing macro unit. They can remain simply as an unintended aggregation recognized only by detached observers such as journalists and scholars. Even if such observers stress that the aggregation constitutes a serious social, economic, or political problem, it does not become a political issue if

[26] For a useful elaboration of this point, see R.L. Paarlberg, 'Domesticating Global Management,' *Foreign Affairs*, Vol. 54 (April 1976), pp. 563–77.

their warnings fall on deaf ears. Indeed, an unintended aggregation may even be recognized by public officials and not become a public issue. They may encounter the similar behaviors in the course of performing their responsibilities and merely take them for granted as a 'reality' of the situation that cannot be altered. For years discrimination against minorities in the United States exemplified this circumstance. It constituted aggregate behavior that was recognized by disinterested observers and public officials alike, but virtually all concerned treated it as a given social condition.

In short, the conversion of an aggregation into a public issue occurs when its recognition is followed by spokespersons for macro units who have reasons to call attention to the similar actions of the micro units and to highlight the need to respond to their collective implications (say, the importance of the patterns formed by the purchases of citizens or the significance of the policy patterns formed by the decisions of officials). The spokespersons can speak on behalf of the aggregation or they can speak about it, contending that it enhances or threatens certain values. In either case, once an aggregative process thus enters the articulation stage, it can become controversial if spokespersons for different aggregations contest the claims made on its behalf. When enough spokespersons become involved, the aggregation becomes the basis of an issue competing for a place on the agenda of a politifal system. Stated somewhat differently, the articulation of an aggregation links it to actions at more encompassing levels of organization. Whether this occurs through the parts being mobilized to form a whole or simply through articulation of the interests recognized as the sum of the parts, the result is the same: the spokespersons precipitate processes of aggregation that can move through more and more encompassing levels until they pass beyond national boundaries and culminate in transnational and international activities.

Thus, for example, do votes become electoral mandates, and thus do the decisions of officials become the policies of governments. And so, too, do electoral mandates become societal demands and so do governmental policies become international conflicts. As the processes of aggregation move on from level to level, at some point their dynamics either wane or gather more force, with the result that the aggregation either fails to push its way as an issue onto the agenda of political systems or its urgency becomes unavoidable and it becomes an issue with which systems must cope. Having long been ignored by the spokespersons of most aggregations, discrimination against minorities in the United States followed such a pattern and eventually acquired status as a civil rights issue on the national agenda. And this particular aggregative process has continued to unfold to the point where it hs now been pushed ever more securely onto the global agenda.

THIRD WORLD DEMANDS AS AGGREGATIVE PROCESSES

The advent of 'Third World demands' for a New International Economic Order affords a useful opportunity to elaborate the concept of aggregation and further assess its utility. Such is the purpose of the remainder of this paper: to explore the dynamics of the aggregative processes whereby these so-called 'demands' appear to have transformed the global agenda, a task that involves identifying the variety of sources from which the 'demands' emanate, the rhetoric through which they are articulated, the context and form in which they are pressed, and the ways in which they are aggregated into compelling public issues.

These 'demands' are perhaps especially suitable as a testing ground for new conceptual equipment because they are so closely linked to the changes in world affairs that have underlain the collapse of the realist and post-realist paradigms. At the same time they appear, at first glance, to be comprised of all those bewildering macro processes that mark IPE phenomena, those impersonal, even amorphous, forces that have somehow moved effectively and inexorably through the 1970s to a top spot on the global agenda. If the concept of aggregation enables us to give coherence to these 'demands,' to transform vague forces into self-conscious efforts to shape, control, or otherwise manage the structure and functioning of global life, it surely will have passed a critical test as a building block for new modeling efforts.

Stating the case for focusing on these demand phenomena in substantive terms, consider the long period of time that occurred between the worsening plight of the peoples of Africa, Asia, and Latin America on the one hand and the worldwide consciousness of these realities on the other. Throughout most of the post-World War II period the gaps between the developed and underdeveloped worlds have widened and the injustices suffered by the latter have deepened accordingly. Yet, the quality and direction of the relationships between the First and Third Worlds has only lately become a prime issue on the agenda of global politics. Why? What variables have undergone change sufficient to render salient problems of equity and distribution that have long been part of the global scene but are only now foci of widespread attention and contention?

The answer lies, doubtlessly, in a multiplicity of factors, ranging from the 1973–74 oil embargo and the steady depletion of other essential resources to the United States defeat in Vietnam and the comeuppance of the French, British, and other former colonial powers elsewhere in the world, from the internal dynamics of newly independent polities in Africa and Asia to the emergence of articulate intellectuals in Latin America, from shifts in the balance of payments to alterations in the patterns of trade. In and of themselves, however, such historical factors do not transform the agenda of global issues. The needs and wants of the Third World are not endowed with mystical powers that force their way into the consciousness of First World elites and publics. New trading patterns do not speak for themselves, inequities in resource allocation are not self-evident, historic injustices do not cry out for reversal. The relevance of needs and wants have to be recognized, assessed, and articulated, and then aggregated into coherent demands that attach salience to issues and crowd the political agenda. The aggregation of these demands thus constitutes a critical variable underlying the salience which has lately become attached to the links between the developed and developing worlds.

This is not to imply, however, that a self-consciously empirical approach will readily uncover the dynamics whereby the demands have been and continue to be aggregated. The notion of 'Third World demands' has become a commonplace term, used alike as a slogan by politicians, a catchword for conflict by journalists, and a shorthand for complex processes by academics. All of these usages often conjure up images of mobs in the streets of the Third World, restlessly on their feet, shouting, protesting, pleading, begging, or otherwise calling for an alleviation of their circumstances. Such an image, however, is profoundly misleading. It posits Third World demands as spontaneous responses to the conditions of poverty, as if the demands constituted an unintended aggregation, whereas in fact neither mobs nor publics in the underfed, underhoused, underemployed, and overpopulated parts of the world are in any position to vocalize and pursue claims for an improvement in their lot. Clearly their 'demands' must be voiced and pressed by leaders. Clearly, if 'Third World demands' have any empirical base whatever, they are expressive of articulated or mobilized aggregations, the actions, interactions, negotiations, bargains, assertions, and decisions of leaders.

A multi-method strategy was adopted for uncovering the demands and the dynamics that sustain them. First, it seemed advisable to affirm the assumption that processes of aggregation have occurred in the Third World. This was accomplished through a search for broad patterns among extensive quantitative data descriptive of the actions Third World countries have directed at the First World over a period of years. A total of 26,178 events, 15,324 coded as conflict events and 10,854 as cooperative events, extracted from the *New York Times* from 1966 through 1978, served as the data base.[27] Any one or more of seventy-nine Third World countries directed 13,184 of the 26,178

[27] I am indebted to Charles A. McClelland for his help in adapting the full twelve-year World Event Interaction Survey (WEIS) data set to the particular purposes of this chapter.

actions toward any one or more of forty-three industrialized countries (a measure of the flow of demands), while the remaining 12,994 actions were those that Third World countries directed toward each other (a measure of the processes of aggregation). The results of this inquiry provide support for the assumption of a rising, aggregated chorus of Third World demands, albeit the escalation of the demands is not as dramatic as might have been expected and, in some respects, the direction of the demands is quite different from what might have been anticipated.[28]

Another aspect of the multi-method strategy involved an effort to dig beneath the overall patterns and observe aggregation at work. If the concept as developed above is to be of any utility, it seems essential to uncover traces of the day-to-day steps through which Third World spokespersons have cumulated their common interests and thereby summed the micro parts into macro wholes. At the very least careful and systematic inquiry ought to yield the outline of answers to these elementary questions bearing on the internal dynamics of the aggregative process:

(a) What kinds of communications, if any, get cited as sources of Third World demands: the resolutions of organizations, the writings of intellectuals, the speeches of leaders, the results of opinion polls, etc?

(b) What kind of substantiating evidence, if any, do those making the demands offer: quantitative data, scientific proof, the statements of authority figures, the unfolding of nature's processes, economic statistics, etc?

(c) What symbols, if any, are employed to legitimate the demands, such as, for example, the will of the people, (some) God's conceptions of equity and judicial rule, the actions of top leaders?

(d) Is the Third World treated as a single entity or are its demands posited as stemming from particular sub-segments of the Third World?

(e) Are the demands specific or general? Do they spell out procedures that must be followed if they are to be met? Are they cast as threats, with time limits and specified outcomes, or simply as goals with no mention of means for implementing them? If threats are

[28] The compilation and analysis of these data was undertaken by James H. Lebovic, who wrote up the results in a paper entitled, 'Third World Demand Aggregation: A Study of Empirical Trends.' Space limitations prevent the inclusion of this paper as an appendix to the present chapter, but copies of it are available from the Institute for Transnational Studies, University of Southern California, Los Angeles, CA 90007.

used, to what extent are economic sanctions cited?

(f) Are the demands posited as mounting, as part of a groundswell, or otherwise located in processes of aggregation?

Four months — and many weary hours of microfilm viewing later — it is necessary to report an initial failure to turn up meaningful traces of the demand aggregative process. A careful, detailed scrutiny of the annual *Index* for the *New York Times* yielded only 440 articles for fifty-eight months between 1973 and 1977 that might be expected to report Third World demands in such a way as to serve as a basis for answers to the foregoing queries. And a reading of these articles resulted in only thirty-eight citing demands, five that pertain to question (a), twenty-seven to (b), three to (c), nine to (d), eight to (e), and twenty-three to (f) — hardly a conspicuous data base from which to draw conclusions about the dynamics of the demand-aggregating process. What was found, instead, was a data base depicting the consequences of the demands, the responses to them in Western capitals, in international organizations, and in the Third World countries themselves. In effect, the *New York Times* appears to treat the demands as givens, as the outcomes of interaction processes that are assumed to have occurred and, accordingly, do not require either intensive or extensive reporting. Since the interaction processes that follow the issuing of the demands can make for dramatic copy, I suspect that the *New York Times* is not alone in this respect, that the processes culminating in the demands are overlooked by the press throughout the world.[29]

Nor did the (admittedly limited) third dimension of the multimethod strategy, a search of professional journals and book-length analytic treatments, yield much information relative to the above questions. Even narrative accounts of how Third World demands crowded onto the global agenda are difficult to find. Certainly a lengthy, coherent account, one which enumerates and links the main events that transformed the agenda through the 1960s and 1970s, has yet to be compiled. Pieces of the full story can be found in various sources, but these are so scattered and brief as to provide little continuity and no sense of the momentum that must have accompanied the reshuffling of the agenda.

There are, of course, some bright spots in the literature. Nye has provided a cogent, micro account of how Raul Prebisch, UNCTAD's first secretary-general, provided intellectual underpinnings and political

[29] For a useful analysis relevant to this point, see Mort Rosenblum, 'Reporting from the Third World' *Foreign Affairs*, Vol. 55 (July 1977), pp. 815–35.

leadership to the collective claims of the Third World in the 1960s.[30] Prebisch is assessed 'one of the most successful men in the twentieth century in the use of an international organization . . . to affect governmental policies,'[31] which is another way of saying that Prebisch may have been the initiator of the agenda-transforming process. Similarly, Krasner has demonstrated how the aggregation of the Third World demands have subsequently followed two tracks, one a multilateral track in international organizations (á la Prebisch) designed to reduce 'the LDC's vulnerability in the international system" and the other a bilateral track outside international organizations where "they have pursued goals related to economic well-being,'[32] A useful insight into the first of these tracks is provided by Smyth, whose analysis of U.N. voting patterns reveals Third World countries to be an issue-by-issue coalition that is most unified on 'laudatory symbols.'[33] Likewise, although short on empirical referents, Haas has diagrammatically traced how increases in the number of weak states and declines in the influence of hegemonic states have resulted in the 'evolution of global issue-areas,' both in terms of a 'structural explanation with tactical linkages' and a 'cognitive explanation with substantive linkages' among issues and states. Haas is more concerned with the formations of regimes in issue areas than the global agenda-building process, but his formulation will surely prove invaluable in any effort to use Third World demands as a basis for refining the concept of aggregation.[34]

Exceptional analyses such as these, however, do not begin to provide the data needed to shed light on the internal dynamics of the aggregative process. They suggest the complexity of the process and they clearly affirm the importance of investigating it. But, taken alone or collectively, they are more in the nature of hypotheses about than evidence of how the global agenda has been reshuffled.

In short, the study of Third World demands in the context of aggregative processes presents an enormous methodological problem: is it possible to observe them unfold, or are the data descriptive of them too sparse and too elusive to permit close empirical investigation? To explore this question is to ask why such a seemingly crucial dimension of world affairs should be so underdocumented. Two interrelated

[30] Joseph S. Nye, 'UNCTAD: Poor Nations' Pressure Group,' in Cox and Jacobson (eds.), *The Analysis of Influence*, pp. 334–70.

[31] Ibid., p. 348.

[32] Stephen D. Krasner, 'North-South Economic Relations: The Quests for Economic Well-Being and Political Autonomy,' in Kenneth A. Oye, Donald Rothchild, Robert J. Lieber (eds.), *Eagle Entangled: U.S. Foreign Policy in a Complex World* (New York: Lougman, 1979), pp. 123–46 (quotes from p. 124).

[33] Douglas C. Smyth, 'The Global Economy and the Third World: Coalition or Cleavage?' *World Politics*, Vol. XXIX (July 1977), pp. 584–609.

[34] Unpublished manuscript, Chap. 4.

explanations come to mind. One is that the demand-aggregating process is, for all practical purposes, undocumentable. That is, it occurs primarily in the cloak-rooms, hallways, and other informal settings of international organizations and foreign affairs that are not readily available to outside observers. Indeed, even if it occurs in the formal deliberations of international organizations, verbatim accounts of the debates are not likely to be recorded or accessible.[35] A second, equally plausible explanation for the sparseness of demand data concerns the diffuse, uncoordinated, even haphazard nature of this particular aggregative process. Conceivably the Third World's demands were initially aggregated in an extremely disjointed and circuitous fashion, with diverse and distant leaders articulating and mobilizing their aggregations unaware that their counterparts elsewhere in the world were moved by similar aspirations to engage in comparable activities. Only toward the end of the aggregative process, in other words, may the various spókespersons for a new economic order have converged and coalesced in diplomatic cloakrooms and hallways prior to collectively asserting what are now called the demands of the developing world. If this is the case (and, to some extent, it doubtless is), it is hardly surprising that data descriptive of the aggregative process are sparse and elusive.

Whatever the dynamics of the process, however, empirically-oriented analysts cannot be so deterred by the apparent lack of data that they unknowingly yield to the premise that 'somehow,' say, in the logic of the situation, the Third World demands came into existence and inexorably crowded their way on to the global agenda. If new and more appropriate paradigms of world affairs are to be developed, efforts to flush out the aggregative process must be undertaken. It is not enough to presume that because the peoples of the Third World have suffered injustices, their demands are justified and therefore inevitably and logically moved to the top of the global agenda. Rather, it must be presumed that traces of the aggregated process are uncoverable and observable if the concept is to be of any utility. Even more important, if the dynamics of First World–Third World relations are to be meaningfully grasped, it seem crucial that insights into the processes of aggregation through which the Third World has acquired coherence be treated as a subject of inquiry rather than as a slogan, a catchword, or a shorthand for an urgent agenda item.

But how to proceed if appropriate data prove too elusive to develop fully at an early stage in the inquiry? The answer is obvious: the multi-method approach must be expanded. Interview surveys need to be

[35] I understand that UNCTAD meetings are an exception in this regard, albeit I have not had an opportunity to get to Switzerland to check the adequacy of the accounts for research purposes.

constructed and conducted, collections of speeches by Third World leaders need to be compiled and content analyzed, and narrative case studies of the evolution and aggregation of particular demands need to be developed. In addition, so as to guide the application of these methods, hypothetical dialogues among Third World spokespersons need to be fashioned. One can readily imagine, for example, a dialogue such as the following as a basis for the formulation of interview questions, content analytic categories, and case-study episodes:

Third World Actor A: For a variety of reasons we'd like to join you in your quest for *X*.

Third World Actor B: Welcome aboard. You appreciate, don't you that we're only prepared to press for *X*-1.

A: Yes, I understand and I accept that if you'll accept pressing for *Y*.

B: Fine, that's what it will be. We'll join together on behalf of *X*-1+*Y*.

A: That's a deal. (Aside: I'm really not sure *X* will serve us well, but we'll never get *Y* unless we agree to join the chorus of demands for *X*.

CONCLUSION: FROM BUILDING BLOCKS TO THEORY BUILDING

On the basis of the analysis to date, it could be concluded that the concept of aggregation is a blind alley, leading not to more incisive paradigms, but to more ambiguity and bewilderment over the dynamics of the IPE-dominated world. Indeed, given the inconclusiveness of the data gathered and examined here, one might well be justified abandoning the study of political economy as self-conscious efforts to shape, control, or otherwise manage the large, impersonal forces that infuse configuration and direction into the structure and functioning of global life.

Such a conclusion, however, would be premature. The data examined here are obviously too scant to serve as a test of the aggregation concept. Surely the many other possible dimensions of a multi-method strategy indicated above would have to be exhausted before abandonment of the concept is warranted.

Furthermore, even if the methodological problems can be surmounted, the concept of aggregation is not in itself a sufficient foundation for a new paradigm. As formulated, it is just a building block, subject to any of a number of possible uses. If one is so inclined, for example, it could readily be integrated into a Marxist framework. Unintended aggregations could well be treated as instruments of the class struggle, unrecognized by both the dominant and the subordinate classes but nonetheless present as expressions of the latter's resistance to the former's control. Likewise, a Marxist would have no trouble viewing articulated and mobilized aggregations as reflections of imperialism, as the basis on which the ruling classes expand and secure their domination.

In short, necessary as the concept of aggregation may be to a new, nonMarxist paradigm, it is not sufficient to do the job alone. Other concepts are needed and so is the inspired creativity that can weave them together into a theoretical cloth. Among others, the concepts of role, authority, and legitimacy ought to be considered in this regard. The first can be viewed as the source of the similar behavior out of which aggregations are formed and the last two can serve as the stitching, so to speak, that links the micro parts of aggregations once they have been recognized and their interest articulated.[36] Developing these concepts for this purpose, however, will take some work. This is especially so in the case of authority. Although there is a vast and rich literature on the concept that ought to be consulted, it needs to be supplemented and enlarged with fresh thought. Virtually all the existing literature treats authority in a legal context, whereas the goal of the modeling approach is to free us of state-centric paradigms by allowing for aggregative processes that do not necessarily sum to relevant collectivities based on formal legal structures.[37]

As for the inspired creativity that can cement the building blocks into a coherent and parsimonious model, here one can only reiterate that modeling is preferable to muddling or meddling and urge that recourse to creativity be an endless commitment. The various types of aggregation need to be played with in our minds, imagined as responses to different conditions, fostering different outcomes, and governed by different lawful properties. And perhaps we should toy around with the possibility of treating the global agenda as an overaching structure that imposes coherence on diverse issues without presuming the orderliness of a society. A playful mind may not be enough to capture and discipline all the changes that are transforming world politics, but it surely is a necessary prerequisite to paradigmatic progress.

[36] For an initial effort to probe how the concept of authority might be used as a building block for a new paradigm, see Chap. 2. An initial formulation of the role concept in this context can be found in Chapter 5.

[37] For a cogent analysis that notes the difficulties inherent in applying the concept of authority to the nonlegal structures that sustain international phenomena, see Harry Eckstein, 'Authority Patterns: A Structural Basis for Political Inquiry,' *American Political Science Review*, Vol. 67 (December 1973), pp. 1142–61.

8 Theorizing Across Systems: Linkage Politics Revisited *

Although the great breakthroughs in empirical political theory have yet to occur, the last decade of theoretical effort has been marked by forward movement. At least it is now possible to discern what the nature and shape of the great breakthroughs will be. Stated succinctly, breakthroughs will be characterized by theoretical constructs which specify how and under what conditions political behavior at one level of aggregation affects political behavior at another level. Recent years have witnessed substantial clarification of the dynamics that underlie political behavior at the individual, local, national, and international levels, but the capacity to move predictively back and forth among two or more of these levels is presently lacking. Yet, the rapid advances at the several levels have revealed that more theorizing is needed, that across-systems-level theory has much greater explanatory power than within-systems-level theory.

So it is a good time to take stock. Having taken great strides, we can usefully pause to assess the problems that may hinder progress toward the bright theoretical future that is now in sight. The across-systems breakthroughs may still be decades away, but it is not too early to consider what conceptual and methodological equipment they may require.

*Earlier versions of this chapter were presented at the Annual Meeting of the American Political Science Association, Chicago, September 7, 1971, and published in Jonathan Wilkenfeld (ed.), *Conflict Behavior and Linkage Politics* (New York: David McKay Co., 1973), pp. 25-56.

I

It must quickly be stressed that we are interested in middle-range theory and not in across-systems breakthroughs which can be applied to any two system levels. While the sense of forward movement is evident at all levels of analysis, our concern here is confined primarily to the strides that have and will be taken in theorizing about the interaction of national and international systems. No doubt some future Einstein of political science will eventually break through to across-systems theory that is applicable to any two levels, but my knowledge of recent progress is limited mainly to the national-international realm, thus restraining the impulse to move beyond the middle-range.

It is possible, however, to state the nature of across-systems theory in general terms. Consider figure 1 as outlining four levels of aggregation at which political behavior accurs. The least aggregated level is represented by the *X*s. The organization and analysis of clusters of *X*s leads to the *A* level of aggregation and a similar process gives rise to the *B* level. The latter in turn may be aggregated in such a way as to create the *C* level. Depending on the perspective of the analyst, of course, a virtually endless number of levels can be used as the basis for inquiry. Whatever the number of levels regarded as relevant, the actors at each level — the *X*s, *A*s, *B*s, and *C* in figure 1 — are viewed as having some common attributes and as engaging in behavior that is to some extent recurrent. In terms of empirical theory, therefore, their actions and interactions are posited as possessing lawful properties that the researchers seek to uncover and explain. Within-systems theory presumes that these properties can be adequately explained by examining the similarities and differences that characterize the actors at each level. Whether his data base is a case (say, an *A* in figure 1) or a comparative sample (say, an A, A_1, A_2 and A_3), the within-systems theorist thus limits his efforts to predicting to the behavior of the actors in the system and/or explaining why they behave as they do. He may well take note of the antecedents of their behavior, but the scope of his theoretical concerns extends neither to the systems in which the antecedents are located nor to the systems into which the behavior of the actors is projected. In explaining the actions of voters, for example, the within-systems theorist may specify the factors which predispose them to vote in one way or another, but he will not be interested in either the personality systems through which their predispositions were shaped or the policy-making systems created by the outcome of their vote. Similarly, the within-systems theorist who focuses on public policies at the national level may identify the private groups that press for and are affected by the policies, but he does not theorize about the

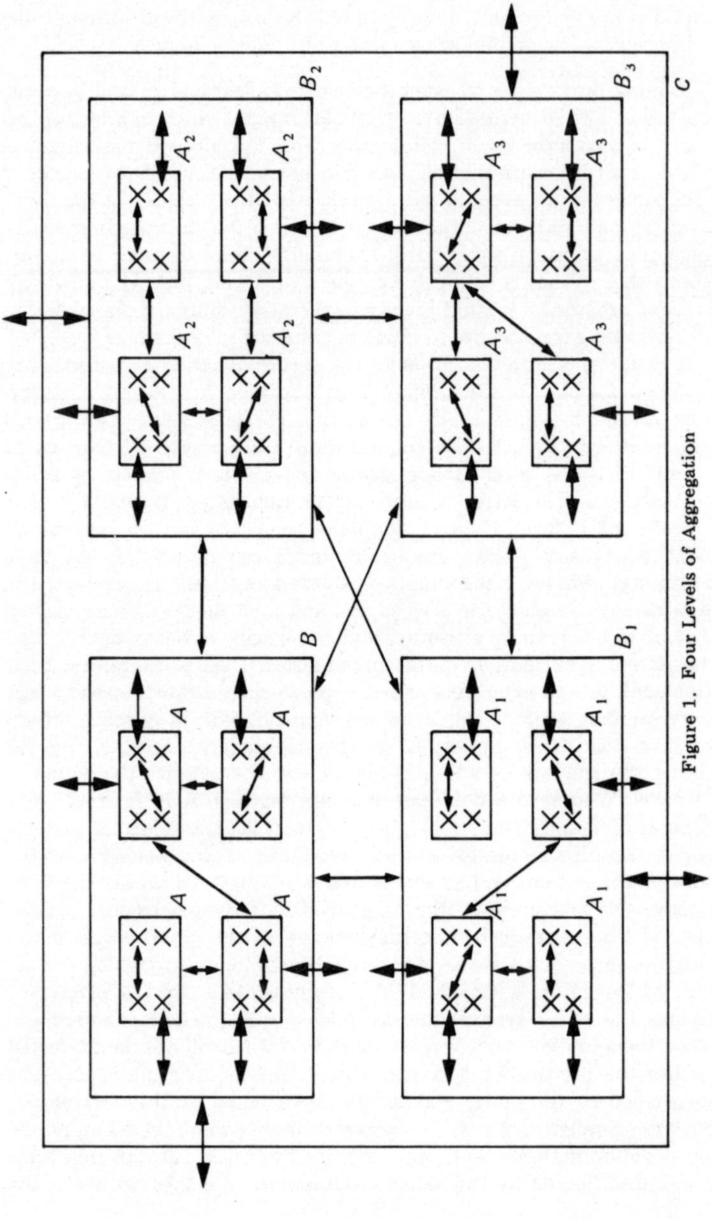

Figure 1. Four Levels of Aggregation

variations in the dynamics that sustain or transform the groups and that may be systematically linked to variations in public policy.

The across-systems theorist, on the other hand, aspires to explanations in which actions and interactions at one level are at least partially accounted for by attributes and behavior at another level. He is not content to presume that the properties that are lawful at the level of aggregation that interest him can be adequately explained by holding other levels constant. He is so impressed by the number and variety of system levels in which individuals and groups occupy roles that he is impelled to expand his explanatory net beyond the dynamics operative at the level to which his hypotheses predict. Stated differently, the dependent variables comprising his theory all concern phenomena at the same systemic level, but his independent variables will be drawn from lesser or greater levels of aggregation as well as from the same level. Put in terms of figure 1, his efforts to account for the actions and interactions of, say, the *A*-level actors will include propositions that allow for variation in the nature or behavior of those at the *X* or *B* levels (the thick arrows in the figure). Conceivably, if his talents are truly Einsteinian, they might also allow for variability at the *C* level, but it seems reasonable to anticipate that across-systems theory will develop first across adjacent levels of aggregation. Such theory is difficult enough to formulate without attempting to skip over levels and accounting for phenomena greatly removed in time, space, or function.[1]

[1] The question arises as to whether across-systems theory is likely to develop in one particular direction, either that in which the independent variables predict to phenomena at a greater level of aggregation or to a level involving smaller units. In terms of figure 1, will theory development move from explanation of the *A*s in terms of the *X*s, to the *B*s in terms of the *A*s, and to the *C*s in terms of the *B*s, or will the progression move from the *C*s to the *B*s, the *B*s to the *A*s, and the *A*s to the *X*s? It might be argued that since empirical theorists aspire to ever more encompassing constructs, they will primarily follow the first course. Such an argument, however, misreads the nature of scientific parsimony. The effort to develop theory that embraces ever more encompassing bodies of data does not necessarily require moving to new, more comprehensive levels of aggregation. To be parsimonious as a theorist is to reduce the number of independent variables needed to account for variation in a set of phenomena. Parsimony need not also entail adding to the range of phenomena encompassed by the dwindling number of explanatory variables. To search for 'master' variables that account for most the variation in the *A*s of figure 1 is not to require exploration of the impact of the *B*s upon them. As long as the across-systems theorist is able to move toward the replacement of many independent variables with a few 'master' ones, he remains true to his aspiration for parsimony, and it does not matter whether some of the master variables are located in less aggregated systems or whether they are dimensions of more aggregated systems. The choice as to which direction an across-systems theorist should move depends, in the final analysis, on the kinds of phenomena that interest him and the questions they lead him to ask. If, for example, his focus is that of the national political system, a variety of considerations can lead him to search for master variables among the sub-systems that comprise the national polity and equally varied concerns can lead him to look to international systems for constraints that

II

That across-systems theoretical breakthroughs still lie in the future is hardly surprising. Formidable problems confront those who seek to build such theory in the realm of politics. Most notably, the analyst is faced with the need to comprehend the dynamics of actors at two levels of aggregation so well that he can trace variations at one level to variations at the other. Such a task is awesome because few among us ever feel that our comprehension at one level is sufficient and thorough enough to identify the master variables that account for varying phenomena at that level. A lifetime of concentrated inquiry often seems necessary to the acquisition of parsimonious theory at a single level, so that to achieve such competence at two levels looms as a fine but unobtainable aspiration. More concretely, across-systems thory at the national and international levels appears to require the knowledge and conceptual equipment of both the area specialist and the discipline generalist. More accurately, if the theory involves the behavior of actors in several geographic or cultural areas, it requires the knowledge of several types of area specialists as well as that of the generalist.

The problem of acquiring adequate skills at two levels of aggregation is further compounded by the seemingly endless variety of actors and actions that sustain the processes of politics. The variety is so great that the political analyst, unlike the economist, cannot readily presume that certain attributes or behavioral predispositions predominate at one level and thus concentrate his efforts at the other level. Rather he must allow for wide variability at both levels, with the result that time and energy must be devoted to probing a multiplicity of actors. This important difference between economics and politics has been succinctly summarized by Susan Strange, who notes that

> . . . the study of politics — whether local, national, or international, whether ancient, Renaissance, revolutionary, or contemporary — impresses the student with the unlikeness of the actors involved, with the variety of generative ideas by which they are influenced, by the quirks and oddities of the systems within which they act. The study of economics impresses the student with the likeness to one another of consumers, or of producers, or of markets and mechanisms from Toledo to Timbuctoo. The units along the economic scales are essentially equivalent and undifferentiated.[2]

In view of this difference, it is hardly surprising that across-systems theory has been abundantly developed in economics but has yet to appear in political science. Compared to the political scientist, the

shape behavior at the national level. Indeed, his temperament and curiosity may encourage him to look in both directions, albeit Einsteinian talents may be required to develop viable theory which spans the levels of aggregation immediately adjacent to both sides of the level that encompasses the phenomena he is trying to explain.

[2] 'The Politics of International Currencies,' *World Politics* 22 (January 1971): 224.

economist simply does not have to probe as many variations at one level in order to make statements about how they may be systematically linked to variations at another level.

Stated differently, most political systems are subsystem dominant, whereas economic systems tend to be system dominant. That is, the behavior of two or more actors in most political systems can substantially alter the structure and dynamics of the system in which they act, but such is not the case in many economic systems. The United States, for example, can alter world politics unilaterally by changing its diplomatic positions, but few of its postwar efforts to cope with world monetary crises prevented continuous upheavals in the world's financial structure.

In short, the problem of variability in politics becomes more acute the greater the levels of aggregation at which across-systems theory is sought. Students of elections or legislatures who seek partial explanations of public policy through variations in the distribution of votes do not need to examine every voter or every legislator because these actors are known to share attributes and predispositions that can be subdivided into relatively few categories. Thus relieved of the task of probing the nature of many of his independent variables, the analyst can devote most of his efforts to examining variations in the dependent variables. Students of national and international systems, on the other hand, cannot proceed to the dependent variables so readily. Each of the actors treated as independent variables must be carefully examined to determine the extent to which they are similar to each other, and these similarities, along with the differences among them, must then be taken into account in any across-systems theory that is developed.

III

Despite these obstacles to across-systems theory, recent years have been marked by intellectual stirrings that may well be the prelude to theoretical breakthroughs that sweep them aside. The signs of forward movement are still faint, but they are unmistakaable and, more importantly, they are characterized by one element essential to any breakthrough, namely, a readiness to ignore long-standing conceptual boundaries and think anew about interaction across different levels of aggregation. Insofar as the interaction of national and international systems is concerned, forward movement is manifest in an emerging preoccupation with a host of concepts that denote such interaction.[3]

[3] An empirical indication that this preoccupation has become widely shared can be seen in the survey finding that more than three-fourths of a sample of 101 distinguished students of international phenomena believe that more research designs

Interdependence, penetration, linkage, intervention, emulation, integration, adaptation — these are typical of the concepts that some students of national and international politics have begun to take seriously. As discussed below, these are not different labels for the same phenomena, but concepts that are differentiated by important nuances of meaning and, in some instances, even by inconsistent empirical referents. Yet common to all of these concepts is a focus on some form of interaction between national and international political processes. The emergence of this shared focus is certainly a significant development, especially as it has evolved less than a decade after students of the two fields were impressively warned that efforts to conduct research simultaneously at both levels were bound to fail.[4]

The reasons for this growing preoccupation with concepts that facilitate across-systems analysis are varied, ranging from a concern in the case of the linkage concept to bring two fields of inquiry closer together,[5] to an effort in the case of the concept of integration to give meaning to idealism,[6] to an attempt in the case of the concept of intervention to clarify immediate policy questions.[7] One source of this emerging focus, however, stands out. Technology is rendering the world smaller and smaller, so that the interaction of national and international systems is becoming increasingly intense and pervasive. The conceptual tidiness achieved through analyzing the two types of systems separately is thus no longer compelling. There is simply too much evidence of overlap between them for analysts to conduct research at one level blissfully ignoring developments at the other.

The various concepts which may become elements of eventual theoretical breakthroughs can be differentiated in a number of ways. They can be distinguished in terms of the scope of the phenomena they encompass, with the concepts of interdependence and linkage having the widest scope and intervention and emulation the narrowest. They differ in terms of whether an event, an actor, or a process serves as the central analytic focus, with intervention, adaptation, and linkage exemplifying, respectively, these three foci. They vary substantially in the

ought to be characterized by across-systems analysis in the future. Cf. James N. Rosenau, *International Studies and the Social Sciences* (Minneapolis: International Studies Association, 1971), p. 106.

[4] J. David Singer, 'The Level-of-Analysis Problem in International Relations,' *World Politics* 14 (October 1961): 77–92.

[5] See, for example, James N. Rosenau, *Of Bridges and Boundaries: A Report on a Conference on the Interdependencies of National and International Political Systems*, Research Monograph No. 27 (Princeton, N.J.: Center of International Studies, 1967).

[6] Stanley Hoffmann, 'International Organization and the International System,' *International Organization* 24 (Summer 1970): 389.

[7] Symposium, 'Intervention and World Politics,' *Journal of International Affairs* 22 (1968): esp. 198–207, 217–46.

degree to which specific relationships are hypothesized or assumed at different system levels, with the concept of integration being perhaps the most, and that of interdependence the least, theoretically developed. They diverge considerably in the extent to which violence and hierarchy are treated as central dimensions, intervention and penetration being the concepts most pervaded by these dimensions and linkage and adaptation the least. They vary in terms of the amount of planning posited as antecedents to the across-systems processes, intervention and linkage being the two extremes in this regard. They are also marked by differences in the extent to which attitudinal or behavioral phenomena are the organizing focus, with emulation and adaptation more illustrative of the former and penetration and integration more reflective of the latter. Finally, the various concepts differ in terms of whether the posited dependent variables are located in a more or less aggregated system than the one which contains the independent variables. The concepts of adaptation, intervention, and penetration, for example, are concerned with the nation-state as the site of the dependent variable, while integration models posit international systems as the arenas in which outcomes are to be observed and measured. In the case of the linkage concept, on the other hand, both national and international systems are treated as levels at which outcomes are located.

Notwithstanding all these differences, however, it bears repeating that the several concepts are all parallel in that they all share a concern with across-systems phenomena. While none of them may ever actually serve as the basis of the breakthroughs that lie ahead, they are guiding us down the right road. Nothing in the ensuing analysis of the insufficiencies of the concepts should be permitted to obscure this common and crucial quality.

IV

While the main purpose here is to assess theory and research associated with the linkage concept, it is useful to look briefly at the uses and limits of the other concepts concerned with across-systems phenomena. In each case several criteria of evaluation can fruitfully be applied: Has consensus developed with respect to the precise nature and scope of the phenomena delimited by the concept? Has the concept been formulated in such a way that variations at one level of aggregation are systematically associated with variations at another level? If not, does it readily lend itself to the derivation of such associations? Has the concept served as a tool of empirical inquiry? If so, do the operational definitions of it allow for quantitative analysis or have its applications been tailored to particular case histories? In short, have theoretical and empirical efforts based on the concept yielded any generalizations and findings that can serve as building blocks for further inquiry?

These questions are most easily answered for the concept of interdependence. In each case clear-cut negative answers are in order. Interdependence is perhaps the most generic of all the concepts in the growing lexicon of across-systems theory and, as such, it is used in an extremely loose fashion, with little effort being made either to give it precise meaning or to specify empirical referents which distinguish phenomena that are interdependent from those that are not. Indeed, so general is the concept that it is rarely defined and is instead usually presumed simply to refer to any phenomena in one system, the functioning of which cannot occur without some events or processes occurring in one or more other systems. Interdependence does not necessarily connote direction, regularity, purpose, or even interaction insofar as across-systems processes are concerned. Interdependencies can originate or culminate in international organizations or in nation-states; they can occur spasmodically or continuously; they can be intended or unintended; they can sustain desirable tendencies or regretted ones; they can involve specific transactions or simply perceived dependence. It follows that no variables are widely regarded as signifying the presence of interdependent phenomena and, consequently, that uses of the concept rarely, if ever, involve the specification of associations between independent and dependent variables. In itself, in fact, interdependence is not usually posited as being causal, but is rather treated as the context in which phenomena at one level may be posited as fostering outcomes at another level.

Plainly, the concept of interdependence, as it is presently construed, does not hold out much promise as a foundation of across-systems theory. To identify an interdependence between national and international systems is to begin to account for the shrinkage of social and geographic distance, but it is not otherwise to differentiate among phenomena or to provide guidance for further theory and research. Since analysts do not tend to attribute great explanatory power to it, it is not a concept which can be said to hinder inquiry, but neither can it be viewed as an especially useful tool in the storehouse of across-systems analysis.

In sharp contrast to the minimal utility that attaches to the concept of interdependence, work on the concept of integration has advanced rapidly and yielded an extensive body of theoretical and empirical materials. Those collected over the past fifteen years with respect to regional integration have recently been succinctly summarized[8] and

[8] Ernst B. Haas, 'The Study of Regional Integration: Reflections on the Joy and Anguish of Pretheorizing,' in Leon N. Lindberg and Stuart A. Scheingold, eds.,

relative to the other concepts analyzed here, the summary depicts an impressive array of hypotheses and findings pertinent to a wide variety of across-systems phenomena. Not only have 'enormous quantities of information . . . been uncovered about common markets, parliamentarians, regional interest groups, trade and mail flows, attitudes of masses, self-definitions of interest by elites, career patterns of civil servants, role perceptions, relations between various kinds of economic tasks, links between economic, political, and military tasks, and the influence of extra-systemic actors,' but close analysis of these data reveals that they are 'by no means randomly collected information.'[9] On the contrary, it proved possible to identify thirteen 'empirical generalizations,' six of which are 'global' in their application to regional groupings of nation-states, while 'socialist groupings,' West European nations, African nations, and Latin American nations are each the subject of one generalization (consisting of several parts) and 'the external world' of the regional groupings is the focus of three generalizations (each consisting of two parts).[10]

This is not the place to enumerate these findings, but suffice it to note that they all involve interaction between attributes or behavior of units at one level of aggregation (usually the nation-state) and outcomes for units at another level (usually the regional grouping). To be sure, in summarizing the findings Haas finds cause for concern about their limitations as well as satisfaction in the progress they represent. He notes that important definitional differences still prevail among students of integration,[11] that 'only a few' of the generalizations 'rise above the level of verifying simple hypotheses based on readily observed behavior,[12] and that therefore many gaps remain and much needs to be done to move work on regional integration into and beyond a pretheoretical stage.[13] In particular, Haas is uneasy about 'the indefinite nature of the end state or the terminal condition to which regional integration is supposed to lead.' He sees work on the concept as sometimes positing a process and sometimes an outcome as the end state, a distinction which is 'appealing . . . because it sidesteps the definitional problem,' but which at the same time holds back the development of theory:

It is not only a question of whether we wish to explain the process, necessarily stressing a time dimension, whereby relationships change between nations and actors or to describe the terminal condition (which could be conceived in static terms) to which the process is likely to lead. The job is to do both; but the task of selecting and justifying variables and explaining their hypothesized

'Regional Integration: Theory and Research,' *International Organization* 24 (Autumn 1970). 607–46.

[9] Ibid., p. 613.

[10] Ibid., pp. 614–21.

[11] Ibid., pp. 610–11.

[12] Ibid., p. 621.

[13] Ibid., p. 622.

interdependence cannot be accomplished without an agreement as to possible conditions to which the process is expected to lead. In short, we need a dependent variable.[14]

While the lack of clarity and consensus on the dependent variables embraced by the concept certainly indicates that its full potential has still to be realized, there is good reason to believe that this problem will not resist solution for long and that students of regional integration will continue to contribute to across-system theory. The concept lends itself to such progress because, unlike interdependence, it is precise in specifying the kind of phenomena at the national and international levels which have either been conceived or found to be systematically associated with each other. The fact that theory-building is plagued by definitional differences and confusion over the identity of the dependent variables is not a cause for serious concern, since the progress toward specification of empirical referents has been so pronounced and continuous for well over a decade. One need only peruse the essays comprising the symposium for which the aforementioned summary serves as an introduction to know that the concept of integration will long operate as a stimulus to across-systems theory and research.[15]

Notwithstanding this potential, however, it must be noted that the concept of integration can never make more than a limited contribution to across-systems analysis. This is so because its scope is restricted to a particular set of phenomena, namely, those encompassed by noncoercive efforts to create 'new types of human communities at a very high level of organization.'[16] Stated more succinctly, 'the main reason for studying regional integration is . . . normative.'[17] This means that while a wide variety of actors, attitudes, and behaviors are of interest to students of integration, they will nevertheless ignore the many phenomena which are important aspects or determinants of across-systems processes but which are unrelated to the norms that sustain their inquiries. To be sure, their models are not so naive as to be confined only to processes which promote integration. Most students of the subject allow for a full range of variation in their key variables, including those which operate to hinder integration or foster disintegration. More than a few studies have straightforwardly (albeit regretfully) interpreted data as indicating tendencies

[14] Ibid., p. 622.

[15] For especially provocative analyses that demonstrate the stimulating character of the concept, see part 2 of the symposium (Lindberg and Scheingold, "Regional Integration, pp. 649–916) and, in particular, Leon N. Lindberg, 'Political Integration as a Multidimensional Phenomenon Requiring Multivariate Measurement,' pp. 649–731.

[16] Haas, 'Study of Regional Integration,' p. 608.

[17] Ibid.

away from integrationist attitudes and patterns.[18] To allow for a wide range of variation in the variables of a model, however, is not necessarily to probe a wide range of variables. And in this respect the integration theorists operate within narrow limits and can be counted on to enrich only a small proportion of the dimensions of across-systems processes that mark present-day world politics. Most notably, in addition to eschewing coercive phenomena in their formulations, their foci are such that they are unlikely to contribute to across-systems processes that culminate at the national level of aggregation. The attributes and dynamics of national actors are crucial to their research, but only as independent variables and what happens to the nation-state as a consequence of the role it does or does not play in regional integrative or disintegrative processes is essentially beyond the pale of their concerns. For all of the abstract models founded on it, in short, the concept of integration would seem to be capable of producing only partial understanding and limited breakthroughs in across-systems theory.

Researchers who have sought to tailor the concept of adaptation to the needs of across-systems analysis have to a large extent avoided the foregoing limitations inherent in the concept of integration. More accurately, the foci and purposes that guide inquiry into adaptive phenomena are quite different from those that direct integration research. Stated succinctly, adaptation focuses on the national level of aggregation; it is not limited to noncoercive phenomena; and it is not a concept that arises out of normative concerns.

To the extent that it has been developed for the analysis of phenomena aggregated at the national level, adaptation refers to the efforts and processes whereby national societies keep their essential social, economic, and political structures within acceptable limits. It posits fluctuations in the essential structures as stemming from changes and demands that arise both within and external to the adapting society. All the factors, coercive as well as noncoercive, which keep (or fail to keep) these fluctuations within a given set of acceptable limits are considered to be adaptive (or maladaptive). Four basic modes of keeping the fluctuations within acceptable limits have been posited as available to societies and any of the twelve possible shifts from one of these modes to any of the others are viewed as adaptive transformations.[19] Since both the adaptive modes

[18] For example, see Leon N. Lindberg and Stuart A. Scheingold, *Europe's Would-Be Polity: Patterns of Change in the European Community* (Englewood Cliffs, N.J.: PrenticeHall, 1970).

[19] For an elaboration of these major components of the adaptation concept see James N. Rosenau, *The Adaptation of National Societies: A Theory of Political*

and transformations involve the nature of the balance that is achieved between conflicting internal and external needs, the concept readily lends itself to across-systems analysis. Indeed, it facilitates analysis across three levels of aggregation, the subnational level at which internal demands arise, the international level from which external demands emanate, and the national level at which the demands are or are not reconciled. To comprehend either a nation's capacity for adaptation or its actual persistence through time, therefore, the analyst must probe phenomena at several levels of aggregation and his theories must account for the interaction between at least two of the levels. Inescapably, in short, the concept of adaptation forces across-systems analysis.

Although frequently misinterpreted as reflecting a concern for the preservation of the status quo at any moment in time, the main reason for studying national adaptation is not normative. Interest in adaptive phenomena does not require the analyst to posit end states or anticipate terminal conditions. It can be as appropriate to investigate national actors which fail to adapt as those which successfully cope with their environment. As long as an adapting entity manages to persist, adaptation is conceived to be a never-ending process, one which can include military aggression, revolutionary upheavals, dictatorial repressions, or integration into larger federations as well as rational calculations, democratic elections, peaceful transitions, or policies of intransigent isolation. Life in an adaptive national society can be restless or content, static or dynamic, stable or chaotic; but whatever the prevailing conditions, the study of national adaptation concerns itself with the fluctuations in the society's essential structures to which both internal and external demands give rise. The researcher who focuses on the phenomena of adaptation is led to do so not by normative concerns, but by an intellectual fascination with the question of why and how most national societies adjust to a rapidly changing world and why some fail to make it. Thus, unlike his counterparts who focus on integration, the student of national adaptation is not constrained by his central concept to ignore any phenomena which may operate as important aspects or determinants of across-systems phenomena. Admittedly, analysts or policy makers who venerate the nation-state may be inclined to view adaptive phenomena in a normative context and use the concept as a guide to efforts to maintain a desired status quo. Such an approach, however, is not inherent in the way the concept has been formulated. It is essentially a tool of basic research, whatever the applied purposes to which it might be put.

System Behavior and Transformation (New York: McCaleb-Seiler, 1970, and in *The Scientific Study of Foreign Policy*, 2nd edition (London, Frances Pinter, 1980, New York, Nichols, 1980) pp. 501–34.

On the other hand, this is not to say that the concept of adaptation stands up well against all the evaluative criteria set forth above. In the first place, work on it is only a couple of years old and is thus not nearly as advanced or cumulative as that which has been done on integration. Virtually no empirical case studies, much less any quantitative analyses, have been underaken,[20] so that presently the literature consists primarily of two main theoretical formulations,[21] both of which have been rigorously criticized.[22] Thus it is too early to reach any conclusions as to whether the apparent theoretical utility of the concept will in fact pay off. It would seem, unlike the concept of interdependence, to provide the basis for observing how variables at two or more levels of aggregation vary in relation to each other, but the observations have yet to be made and unforeseen methodological difficulties may well lie ahead.

A second limitation of the concept of adaptation is that it is exclusively centered on the nation-state. That is, just as the integration concept is limited by the fact that all its dependent variables are posited as operative at the international level, so are all the dependent variables in the study of national adaptation confined to measures of change or constancy within the national society whose adaptive behavior is the focus of attention. Subnational and extranational factors, to the extent that they are the sources of demands made upon the adapting society, are treated as independent variables. They may even be manipulated as intervening variables if the adaptive model allows for feedback processes whereby the adapting society's domestic and foreign policies foster responses abroad and at home that in turn produce demands that cause fluctuations in its essential structures. In the end, however, the student of national adaptation concentrates on the fluctuations and his interest in phenomena at the subnational and extranational levels ends once he ascertains the way they operate in relation to the various modes of adaptation. To be sure, the concept of adaptation could readily be applied to regional groupings or subnational entities. But such applications have yet to occur (perhaps

[20] W. Scott Thompson of Tufts, however, is presently undertaking a comparative analysis of the Philippines and Thailand in the context of the adaptation model.

[21] Rosenau, *The Adaptation of National Socieities*, and Patrick J. McGowan. 'Toward a Dynamic Theory of Foreign Policy,' mimeographed (Syracuse, 1971). Also see an earlier paper of McGowan's, 'A Formal Theory of Foreign Policy as Adaptive Behavior,' mimeographed (Paper presented at the annual meeting of the American Political Science Association, Los Angeles, 1970).

[22] Peter A. Corning, 'Toward an Evolutionary-Adaptive Theory of Politics,' mimeographed (Paper presented at the annual meeting of the Midwest Political Science Association, Chicago, 1971). For an elaborate presentation of Corning's own use of the adaptation concept, see Peter A. Corning, 'The Biological Bases of Behavior and Some Implications for Political Science,' *World Politics* 23 (April 1971): 321-70.

in the case of the former because their essential structures are still so unformed), and thus the concept's potential contribution to across-systems analysis is presently limited to a narrow (though important) set of phenomena.

Although it has been the focus of numerous inquiries, the concept of intervention is narrower in scope than either adaptation or integration.[23] In its most common usage it refers to an action and not a process—to a single sequence of behavior, the initiation and termination of which is easily discernible and the characteristics of which are dependent on the use or threat of force. An intervention begins when one national society explicitly, purposefully, and abruptly undertakes to alter or preserve one or more essential structures of another national society through military means, and it ends when the effort is either successful, abandoned, or routinized.[24] Some analysts prefer to conceive of intervention in much wider terms and posit any sequence of behavior, military or nonmilitary, as interventionary if it involves one actor's intentional efforts to affect the domestic affairs of another. In effect, these broad formulations equate intervention with influence. While the lack of definitional consensus in this regard has proved troublesome and is likely to persist,[25] the tendency to use military phenomena as the empirical referents for the concept is becoming increasingly pronounced. Agreement on the precise nature of interventionary phenomena may never be unanimous, but such widespread concurrence has emerged with respect to the military formulation that it is reasonable to confine the ensuing discussion to it.[26]

Two reasons for the growing readiness to focus on the narrow, military conception of interventionary behavior are worthy of note. One is that increasing attention to across-systems phenomena has led to greater definitional specificity and, in turn, to a proliferation of concepts designed to account for what were once regarded as simply the nuances of a single concept. Thus, in the case of intervention, those phenomena associated with the prolonged and routinized processes whereby one society is consistently involved in the domestic affairs of another are increasingly brought under the rubric of the concept of penetration (see below), leaving abrupt, overt, and coercive

[23] Indeed, in one formulation intervention is seen as but one form of adaptation. See James N. Rosenau, 'Foreign Intervention as Adaptive Behavior,' in *Law and Civil War in the Modern World*, ed. John Norton Moore (1974), pp. 129-151.

[24] For a lengthy discussion of this and other conceptions of intervention, see James N. Rosenau, 'Intervention as a Scientific Concept,' *Journal of Conflict Resolution* 13 (June 1969): 149-71.

[25] The reasons why definitional differences are likely to persist can be found in James N. Rosenau, 'The Concept of Intervention,' *Journal of International Affairs* 22, no. 2 (1968): 165-76.

[26] For evidence of this emerging consensus, see Rosenau, 'Foreign Intervention as Adaptive Behavior,' pp. 2-6.

efforts to affect domestic affairs abroad to analysis by students of interventionary phenomena.

The second reason for equating interventionary and coercive phenomena is that threatened or actual military interventions seem increasingly likely to mark world politics as rapid social change within national societies intensifies the extent and frequency of internal violence and as shrinking social and geographic distance between societies intensifies the degree and frequency of outside involvement in domestic upheavals. Or, if the actual number of interventions is no greater than in the past, these factors make their importance and consequences seem greater, with the result that the attention of both students of national and international systems has been attracted to them. Students of national systems are not so much concerned with across-systems phenomena as they are with the applied problem of how to improve the quality of foreign policy to the point where the need for interventionary behavior can either be avoided or made more effective. These policy analysts are primarily, if not exclusively, preoccupied with phenomena at the national level, either those that underlie the intervening nation's behavior or those that shape the outcome in the intervened nation. To be sure, some theoretical insights and considerable data relevant to across-systems phenomena have been generated by the policy analysts,[27] but these consist largely of uncoordinated case histories and do not systematically posit patterns of association between variations at two levels of aggregation.

The analysts who have approached interventionary phenomena from an international perspective, on the other hand, have developed the concept in such a way that it does lend itself to the derivation of across-systems propositions. Their perspective leads them to pose the problem in terms of the interplay between internal and external violence — that is, the conditions in the international system that conduce to interventions and those aspects of domestic upheaval that attract interventions — and once posed in this way, they are led to prove how variations at one of the levels interact with those at the other. Stated differently, once internal war and domestic violence came to be recognized as pervasive phenomena of crucial relevance to the study of politics,[28] the processes by which such phenomena

[27] For example, see Alexander L. George, David K. Hall, William R. Simons, *The Limits of Coercive Diplomacy: Laos-Cuba-Vietnam* (Boston: Little, Brown & Co., 1971): Graham Allison, Ernest May, and Adam Yarmolinsky, "Limits to Intervention,' *Foreign Affairs* 48 (January 1970): 245-61; Max Beloff, 'Reflections on Intervention,' *Journal of International Affairs* 22, no. 2 (1968): 198-207.

[28] Perhaps with the publication of Harry Eckstein, ed., *Internal War* (New York: Free Press, 1964).

become internationalized quickly became a major focus of analytic attention.[29] It did so both for those in the field of international law with an applied interest in the creation of a more stable world order[30] and for those interested in basic research into the dynamics of international politics and foreign policy.[31] Indeed, the interaction between internal and external violence has proved so stimulating to theory-building that those interested in this dimension of interventionary behavior have been able to generate quantitiative data and test hypotheses which depict across-systems processes that both originate and culminate in both national and international systems. In this sense, of course, the concept of intervention is actually broader than those of integration and adaptation (which, it will be recalled, focus only on dependent variables that are located, respectively, at the international and national levels). It is much narrower, however, in the sense that it is limited to single sequences of coercive behavior.

That curiosity about the dynamics and consequences of internal wars led students of intervention to derive findings and generalizations that may contribute to across-systems analysis can be readily demonstrated. In the first place, as will be seen below, such a focus has encouraged the development of models in which the concept of intervention is treated, in the larger context of linkage politics, as one form of penetration. The interest in across-systems phenomena has led not only to a proliferation of concepts designed to differentiate among them, but, even more significantly, it has resulted in the proliferation of concepts that bear close relation to or subsume each other. Second,

[29] See, for example, James N. Rosenau, ed., *International Aspects of Civil Strife* (Princeton, N.J.: Princeton University Press, 1964).

[30] Cf. John Norton Moore, 'The Control of Foreign Intervention in Internal Conflict,' *Virginia Journal of International Law* 9 (May 1969): 209-342; and Symposium, 'Foreign Intervention in Civil Strife,' *Stanford Journal of International Studies* 3 (June 1968): 1-122.

[31] For example, see C.R. Mitchell, 'Civil Strife and the Involvement of External Parties,' *International Studies Quarterly* 14 (June 1970): 166-94; John W. Eley, 'Intervention as Transnational Behavior: A Critique and a Proposal,' *International Studies Quarterly*, forthcoming; Metin Tamkoc, *International Civil War* (Ankara: Middle East Technical University, 1967); Charles Tilly, 'Research on the Relations Between Conflict Within Polities and Conflict Among Polities,' mimeographed (Ann Arbor, 1970); Andrew M. Scott. 'Military Intervention by the Great Powers: The Rules of the Game,' mimeographed (New York, 1968); David W. Paul, 'Soviet Foreign Policy and the Invasion of Czechoslovakia: A Theory and a Case Study,' *International Studies Quarterly* 15 (June 1971): 159-202; George A. Kelly and Linda B. Miller, *Internal War and International Systems: Perspectives on Method*, Occasional Paper No. 21 (Cambridge: Center for International Affairs, Harvard University, 1969); George A Kelly and Clifford W. Brown, eds., *Struggles in the State: Sources and Patterns of World Revolution* (New York: John Wiley and Sons, 1970): Frank J. Popper, ,Internal War as a Stimulant of Political Development,' *Comparative Political Studies* 3 (January 1971): 413-24; and John W. Eley, 'Internal Wars and International Events: An Analysis of the Internationalization of Internal Wars' (Ph.D. diss., University of Maryland, 1969).

at least a few quantitative studies have become available in recent years. In a cross-national survey Sullivan used a number of indicators of national attributes to probe the 'international consequences of domestic violence.'[32] Hazlewood has used a factor analysis of a series of variables to probe the interaction of domestic violence and attributes of the international system.[33] Collins has used the same technique to explore similar interactions for thirty-three independent countries in Africa.[34] And Eley has collected data on thirty internal wars as a means of investigating the dynamics whereby such conflicts become internationalized.[35] Third, these empirical inquiries have resulted in a number of hypotheses, some tested by the data and some derived from them, that posit variations at the two levels as systematically associated with each other. Eley, for example, tested some twenty-nine preliminary hypotheses, from which ten emerged as more advanced propositions. The following are illustrative of his derivations:

1. There is a significant positive relationship between the type of responses stimulated by internal wars and the type of internal war involved.
   1.1 Any internal war is more likely to be marked by at least material support for one of the belligerents if it is a revolutionary war or a political civil war than if it is a war of independence.
2. There is a significant negative relationship between the type of responses stimulated by internal wars and the power rankings of the responding actors.
   2.1 Small or medium power actors are more likely to intervene in internal wars than are great power actors.[36]

Notwithstanding its potential for across-systems analaysis, however, the concept of intervention cannot in itself provide the basis for major theoretical breakthroughs. The exclusive concern with coercive phenomena is a severe constraint on theory-building. What is needed is a more generic concept which allows for both coercive and noncoercive phenomena as well as for across-systems processes that originate and culminate at both the national and international levels.

Although below we conclude that it is too early to reach a judgment about the theoretical utility of the linkage concept,[37] it may

[32] John D. Sullivan, 'International Consequences of Domestic Violence,' mimeographed (Paper presented at the annual meeting of the American Political Science Association. New York, 1969).

[33] Leo A. Hazlewood, 'Informal Penetration, Systemic Constraints, and Political Violence,' mimeographed (1971).

[34] John N. Collins, 'Foreign Conflict Behavior and Domestic Disorder in Africa,' chap. 9, this volume.

[35] John W. Eley, 'The International Dimensions of Internal Wars: A Preliminary Analysis,' mimeographed (Paper presented at the annual meeting of the Southern Political Science Association, 1970).

[36] Ibid., pp. 19-20.

[37] The original formulation of the linkage concept in which its components were specified in considerable detail was first presented at the 1966 annual meeting of the American Political Science Association and later published in James N. Rosenau, ed., *Linkage Politics: Essays on the Convergence of National and*

meet the test of a generic concept. At least it seems especially free of the deficiences of the concepts examined thus far. Moreover, despite early doubts and even an attempt to dismiss it as incapable of generating research,[38] it has evoked some interest and exploration. Thus it is to the efforts along this line that our attention now turns.

V

As previously noted, the linkage concept was not developed in response to either normative pressures or sheer intellectual curiosity. Rather its initial formulation arose out of a conviction that students of comparative and international politics were needlessly and harmfully ignoring each other's work. The world had become so small, it was argued, that specialists in comparative (i.e., national and subnational) politics could no longer hold international variables constant in their models and, conversely, those who specialized in international politics could no longer afford to treat domestic variables as constant features of the world scene.

To facilitate the convergence of the two fields, it was proposed that a 'linkage' serve as the basic unit of analysis, 'defining it as any recurrent sequence of behavior that originates in one system and is reacted to in another.'[39] The original formulation stressed that a single reaction did not constitute a linkage. Only those sequences of behavior in one system that, in the process of unfolding, are recurrently linked to phenomena in another system were so defined. Since boundary-crossing sequences could occur through 'processes of perception and emulation as well as . . . direct interaction,'[40] allowance was made for intermittent as well as continuous linkages. No operational definition of intermittency was offered, but it was plainly emphasized that the scheme was designed to uncover the more enduring dimensions of politics and not to analyze isolated historical events.[41]

The original formulation also posited the initial and terminal stages of a linkage as, respectively, outputs and inputs for the national

International Systems (New York: Free Press, 1969), pp. 44–63. For an earlier, less elaborate formulation, see Karl W. Deutsch, 'External Influences on the Internal Behavior of States,' in *Approaches to Comparative and International Politics*, ed. R. Barry Farrell (Evanston, Ill.: Northwestern University Press, 1966), pp. 5–26.

[38] James N. Rosenau, 'Adaptive Strategies for Research and Practice in Foreign Policy,' in *A Design for International Studies: Scope, Objectives, and Methods*, ed. Fred Riggs (Philadelphia: American Academy of Political and Social Science, 1971), pp. 218–45.

[39] Rosenau, *Linkage Politics*, p. 45.

[40] Ibid.

[41] Ibid., p. 48.

or international system in which the sequence of behavior either originated or culminated. In this way, across-systems analysis that could be undertaken from either a national or international perspective was made possible. Indeed, analysis based simultaneously on both perspectives was built into the framework by identifying the existence of a 'fused' linkage — one which

arises out of the possibility that certain outputs and inputs continuously reinforce each other and are thus best viewed as forming a reciprocal relationship. In other words, a fused linkage is one in which the patterned sequence of behavior does not terminate with the input. Stated in positive terms, a fused linkage is conceived to be a sequence in which an output fosters an input that in turn fosters an output in such a way that they cannot meaningfully be analyzed separately.[42]

Three basic processes were posited as providing the means by which outputs and inputs get linked together. A '*penetrative process* occurs when members of one polity serve as participants in the political processes of another.'[43] A '*reactive process* is the contrary of a penetrative one: It is brought into being by recurrent and similar boundary-crossing reactions rather than by the sharing of authority.' The third process is in turn a special form of the reactive one. Referred to as an '*emulative process*.' it 'is established when the input is not only a response to the output but takes essentially the same form as the output.'[44]

In order to make the ensuing analysis clear, one final component of the original framework should be noted here. It consists of a 24 by 6 matrix compiled out of 'twenty-four aspects of polities that might serve as or give rise to outputs and inputs . . . [and] six aspects or (from a polity perspective) subenvironments of the international system that might generate or receive outputs and inputs.'[45] The derivation of the components of the matrix was admittedly arbitrary:

In the case of the twenty-four polity subcategories, we have merely listed some of the more obvious determinants of outputs and inputs, trusting that their general characteristics are self-evident. The listing includes phenomena that sustain behavior at different levels (actors, attitudes, institutions, and processes) and that unfold in different settings (the government, the polity, and the society). Likewise, in the case of the environmental categories, we have proceeded on an equally simple and impressionistic basis. The only rationale for the categorization is the impression that both actors and observers tend, often unknowingly, to think about international phenomena in terms of the units represented by the six subenvironments. Again no claim is made that these six are exhaustive or

[42] Ibid., p. 49.

[43] For a more elaborate development of the concept of a penetrated political system than is provided in the original linkage framework, see James N. Rosenau, 'Pre-Theories and Theories of Foreign Policy,' in Farrell, ed., *Approaches to Comparative and International Politics*, pp. 65-92. For another, slightly different elaboration of the nature of penetrative processes, see Andrew M. Scott, *The Revolution in Statecraft: Informal Penetration* (New York: Macmillan Co., 1967).

[44] Rosenau, *Linkage Politics*, p. 46.

[45] Ibid., p. 49. The matrix itself can be found on p. 52.

mutually exclusive. Further inquiry may well reveal that other output or input phenomena, such as those of a legal, technological, and military kind, are so important as to justify the establishment of additional categories. We do contend, however, that these six environments are operative in the minds of actors and that they are thus at least a meaningful sample for our purposes here.[46] The six proposed categories of the international system are the 'Contiguous Environment,' the 'Regional Environment,' the 'Cold War Environment,' the 'Racial Environment,' the 'Resource Environment,' and the 'Organizational Environment.'[47]

While it was readily conceded that the 144-cell matrix was crude and that not all of the cells would yield interesting or important findings, it was argued that the scheme offered a number of possible advantages as an agenda for research. It was suggested that students of linkage phenomena had a variety of options open to them: they could undertake comparisons of different societies within any cell; they could engage in comparative analysis of one or many societies across one or more of the rows (i.e., how the same or different aspects of the same society or different ones are linked to the various polity attributes); and they could pursue any one of multitudes of other combinations and permutations of these options. Moreover, through the listing of a series of substantive questions, it was asserted that any or all of these options seemed likely to pay off in intriguing insights, and perhaps solid findings, about the interaction of phenomena at the national and international levels.[48]

The initial effort to apply this framework systematically to empirical materials fell far short of the claims made for it. Twelve scholars spent two full days in January 1966 discussing the main features of the framework, clarifying the components of the matrix, and reaching agreement on which of its dimensions they would all use in applying the approach to the comparison of two or more national societies. Despite these self-conscious efforts at coordination, however, the resulting essays[49] failed to yield comparable findings. The linkage dimensions they were all to investigate turned out to have different meanings for each of them. Indeed, the task of actually applying the original formulation apparently proved so vexing that a few of the participants in the initial discussions abandoned it entirely in their essays. Taken as a whole, moreover, the resulting essays proved to be a methodological hodgepodge, with some founded on quantitative data, some on journalists' observations, and some on overall impressions. Some tested hypotheses and others provided historical narrative. All in all, the editor of the essays was compelled to conclude that the

[46] Ibid., pp. 51-53.

[47] For an elaboration of the boundaries and nature of each subenvironment, see ibid., pp. 60-63.

[48] For the case made for the linkage framework, see ibid., pp. 53-60.

[49] Ibid., chaps. 4-12.

provision of a loosely designed, atheoretical typology was a failure as a research strategy.[50] The resulting volume did contain useful descriptions of the interaction of national and international systems, but as an instance of comparative inquiry into such phenomena it was painfully unproductive.

The editor, however, also made clear his conviction that the lack of comparability was the fault of the research strategy and not of the participants in the project. Reflection on the reasons for the failure to achieve a coordinated set of essays led to the recognition that the original framework — and especially the 144-cell matrix — was simply a typology that was totally lacking in theory.[51] The cells were created by the convergence of national and international variables, but there was no specification of the phenomena that might be found in them. In the absence of any guidance along these lines, it is hardly suprising that the essays were marked by variability rather than comparability. At the time, therefore, it seemed clear that a different research strategy ought to have been used:

> If some predictions about the phenomena embraced by each cell of the matrix had been hazarded, those using it would have at least had some guidance as to the kinds of questions to explore and the kinds of data to gather. Comparisons might have then revealed that the predictions were erroneous or far-fatched, but at least extensive analysis would have been undertaken and a clearer picture thereby obtained of the conditions under which linkage processes are inoperative. Bad theory, in other words, would have been better than no theory — both as a means of achieving coordinated effort and as a way of extending comprehension.[52]

In sum, the noncomparability of the original essays suggested that the strategy used would prove counterproductive, that the massive framework intended to stimulate a variety of across-systems analyses would in fact stifle investigation, demonstrating through its very massiveness and lack of direction the wisdom of continuing to confine theory and research to a single analytic level. Indeed, without going so far as to agree with one critic who contended that circulating an atheoretical matrix known to lack mutually exclusive categories is irresponsible and a 'scandal,'[53] the desirability of burying the framework was publicly asserted.[54]

[50] This conclusion is elaborated in ibid., pp. 15-17. For a similar assessment, see the cogent book review by Dina A. Zinnes, *Midwest Journal of Political Science* 14 (May 1970): 344-47.

[51] It is thus no accident that in recounting here the development of the linkage concept, it has been labeled as constituting a 'framework' or a 'formulation'; the label of 'model' or 'theory' has been carefully avoided.

[52] Rosenau, *Linkage Politics*, p. 16.

[53] Marion J. Levy, 'Does It Matter if He's Naked' Bawled the Child,' in *Contending Approaches to International Politics*, ed. Klaus Knorr and James N. Rosenau (Princeton, N.J.: Princeton University Press, 1969), p. 105.

[54] See note 38.

VI

Yet the linkage concept did not die. The original prognosis may prove correct, but a variety of researchers have pursued it in a variety of directions. Indeed, five years later the concept was still regarded as sufficiently viable to justify devoting a panel at the annual meeting of the American Political Science Association to an evaluation of the problems, progress, and potential of national-international linkages as foci and tools of inquiry.[55]

Perhaps most of the investigations into linkage phenomena have been nation-state centered, with one or another external environment being treated as the source of outputs and the national society as the locus of inputs. That is, many researchers have employed the concept in an effort to explain behavior at the national level. In some instances single countries have served as the analytic focus. For example, Manley has concentrated on Guyana,[56] Clark on Venezuela,[57] Hodnett and Potichnyj on the Ukraine,[58] Bunker on Peru,[59] and Couloumbis on Greece.[60] In other instances one or two nations have been intensively examined or contrasted with a view to generalizing beyond the single case. Wahlbach has examined Finland in such a context[61] and Meadows has contrasted Indonesia and the Philippines for the same purpose.[62] In still other cases linkage phenomena involving types of nation-states have served as the basis of comparative analysis. Reid is looking at micro-states,[63] Sonneberg at 'pariah' states,[64] Lewis

[55] The panel was organized by Albert F. Eldridge, Jr., of Duke University and, in addition to an earlier version of this chapter, included presentation of the following papers: Sheldon W. Simon, 'Further Reflections on a Systems Approach to Security in the Indian Ocean Arc'; Terry L. McCoy, 'External Outputs and Population Policy Making in Latin America'; and Curtis E. Huff, Jr., 'Regional Patterns and Changes After Military Coups D'Etat: The Foreign Relations of African States.'

[56] Robert H. Manley, 'Linkage Politics: The Organizational Environment for Guyanese Nation-Building,' mimeographed (Paper presented at the annual meeting of the International Studies Association, San Juan, 1971).

[57] Robert P. Clark, Jr., 'Economic Integration and the Political Process: Linkage Politics in Venezuela,' mimeographed (1969).

[58] Grey Hodnett and Peter J. Potichnyj, *The Ukraine and the Czechoslovak Crisis* (Cranberra: Australian National University, 1970).

[59] Rod Bunker, 'Linkages and the Foreign Policy of Peru, 1958–1966,' *Western Political Quarterly* 22 (June 1969): 280–97.

[60] Theodore A. Couloumbis, 'The Foreign Factor in Greek Politics,' mimeographed (1971); also see idem, *Greek Political Reaction to American and NATO Influences* (New Haven: Yale University Press, 1966).

[61] Krister Wahlbach, 'Finnish Foreign Policy: Some Comparative Perspectives,' *Cooperation and Conflict* 4 (1969): 282–98.

[62] Martin Meadows, 'Theories of External-Internal Political Relationships: A Case Study of Indonesia and the Philippines,' *Asian Studies* 6 (December 1968): 297–324.

[63] George L. Reid, 'Linkage Theory in Application to Micro-States,' mimeographed (Ph.D. diss. prospectus, Southampton, N.Y., 1970).

[64] Milton Sonneberg, mimeographed paper (Ph.D. diss. prospectus, Cleveland, 1971).

at small states,[65] Grundy at the black states of Southern Africa,[65] and Blong at 'political systems exhibiting high versus low levels of external penetration.'[67]

Although a minority, some analysts have centered their inquiries at the international level. Hoadley and Hasegawa have investigated the postwar linkages between two proximate nations, China and Japan.[68] McCoy has probed international population programs, with a variety of international, national, and subnational agencies external to Latin America being treated as the sources of outputs and the twenty-one nation-states of that region as the loci of inputs.[69] Hazlewood, as previously noted, has similarly treated outputs and inputs in order to investigate 'the impact of certain kinds of international behavior as predictors of domestic political violence.'[70] Edmondson, Feld, Korbonski, and Dominguez, on the other hand, have compared across international levels (i.e., across subenvironments, in the terminology of the linkage framework), with the outputs and inputs they treat being located at different levels of international aggregation: Edmondson confines his attention to transnational racial phenomena;[71] Feld focuses on the links between the national societies of Eastern Europe and the European Economic Community (EEC);[72] Korbonski probes the links between roughly the same East European societies and the Council of Mutual Economic Assistance (COMECON);[73] and Dominguez explores the interaction among the central international organizations, and (especially)

[65] Vaughan A. Lewis, 'The Structure of Small State Behavior in Contemporary International Politics' (Ph.D. diss., Jamaica, W.I., 1971).

[66] Kenneth W. Grundy, 'The Foreign Policies of Black Southern Africa,' mimeographed (Paper presented at the Symposium on International Law and National Development in Southern Africa, Los Angeles, 1970). Also see idem, 'Host States and the Southern African Liberation Struggle,' *Africa Quarterly* 10 (April-June 1970): 15–24.

[67] Clair Karl Blong, 'A Comparative Study of the Foreign Policy Behavior of Political Systems Exhibiting High Versus Low Levels of External Penetration,' mimeographed (Ph.D. diss. prospectus, College Park, Md., 1971).

[68] J. Stephen Hoadley and Sukehiro Hasegawa, 'Sino-Japanese Relations 1950–1970: An Application of the Linkage Model of International Politics,' *International Studies Quarterly* 15 (June 1971); 131–57.

[69] Terry L. McCoy, 'A Functional Taxonomy of International Population Programs,' mimeographed (Paper presented at the American Society of International Law Regional Meeting, Charlottesville, 1971).

[70] 'Informal Penetration,' p. 1.

[71] Locksley Edmondson, 'Africa and the African Diaspora: Interactions, Linkages, and Racial Challenges in the Future World Order,' mimeographed (n.d.).

[72] Werner J. Feld, 'National-International Linkage Theory: The East European Communist System and the EEC,' *Journal of International Affairs* 22, no. 1 (1968): 107–20.

[73] Andrzej Korbonski, 'Theory and Practice of Regional Integration: The Case of Comecon,' *International Organization* 24 (Autumn 1970): 942–77.

international subsystems on the peripheries of world politics.[74]

Doubtless other inquiries into linkage phenomena have been completed or are underway,[75] but the foregoing sample is sufficient to suggest some major trends in the development of the concept. In the first place, one is struck by the extent to which the various studies, each in its own way, are concerned with hierarchical phenomena. Both the case studies and the comparative analyses focus on linkages between superiors and subordinates. It would seem to be no accident that Latin American and East European societies are predominant among the case studies, since many of the linkages discussed therein involve outputs originating with nearby superpowers. The same emphasis pervades the comparison of micro, pariah, and small states, Even the studies cast at the international level, especially Dominquez's, focuses on hierarchical links between the strong and the weak. Conspicuously missing are analyses of linkages in which, say, the twenty major national actors in world politics are loci of inputs.[76] Topdog-underdog comparisons appear to pervade use of the linkage concept, perhaps because they involve more immediately self-evident phenomena. While such a trend is not necessarily regrettable, since world politics is surely marked by significant hierarchical differences, neither is it entirely welcome. It indicates that those who study only the major national and international actors presume that the foci of their inquiries have somehow remained outside of the linkages that have grown with the decrease in the world's social and geographic distances.[77]

[74] Jorge I. Dominguez, 'Mice That Do Not Roar: Some Aspects of International Politics in the World's Peripheries.' *International Organization* 25 (Spring 1971): 175-208.

[75] And surely the growing sensitivity to such phenomena can also be found in many studies that are not explicitly cast in a linkage framework. Such a sensitivity, for example, is plainly evident in the finding that' . . . the major explanatory variable in understanding the new Romanian conception of bloc relations and conflict resolution is party institutionalization.' Kenneth Jowitt, 'The Romanian Communist Party and the World Socialist System: A Redefinition.' *World Politics* 43 (October 1970): 38-60. For other recent inquiries sensitive to linkage phenomena that were received too late to incorporate into the text of this essay, see Frank C. Darling, 'The Traditional Polities of Asia: A Macro-Analytical Approach,' *Pacific Community* (Winter 1971): 52-76; Albert F. Eldridge, 'Foreign Policy and Discrimination: The Politics of Indigenization,' mimeographed (1971); Martin and Joan Krye, 'Experimental Application of the Linkage Concept to Military Occupation: The Okinawan Case,' mimeographed (1972); and R.K.C. Tung, 'External Dependence and Internal Underdevelopment: Politics of Penetration and Permeability,' mimeographed (Paper presented at the Fifth Nordic Conference on Peace Research, Norway, 1972).

[76] A partial exception here is the Hoadley-Hasegawa inquiry into Sino-Japanese linkages. See Hoadley and Hasegawa, 'Sino-Japanese Relations.'

[77] A possible exception here is Bruce M. Russett, 'Indicators for America's Linkages with the Changing World Environment,' *The Annals* 388 (March 1970): 82-96. However, Russett used the notion of linkage more as a means of measuring relationships than as a concept of analyzing the processes on which relationships are founded.

Such a presumption seems exceedingly risky and, accordingly, it is regrettable that the linkage concept may come to be seen as primarily a tool for the analysis of hierarchical links across national and international levels of aggregation. It is certainly no less reasonable to presume that linkage processes are as dynamic, if not more so, in situations of relative equality as they are in those where heirarchical considerations are crucial.

The amenability of the linkage concept to topdog-underdog relationships would appear to underlie another tendency in the aforementioned studies, particularly those in which the inputs occur at the national level. This is the fact that most of them focus mainly on the penetrative process and ignore the reactive and emulative processes. Bunker starts from the 'primary assumption' that 'Peru is a thoroughly penetrated society,'[78] just as Couloumbis's first paragraph asserts that 'Greece has been, is and probably will continue to be "a penetrated political system." '[79] Likewise, Lewis argues that penetrative processes are 'the *base* elements from which internal and external linkages can be derived'[80] and Grundy posits them as a central strategy which the black states of Southern Africa could employ toward each other or toward the white South African states.[81] Indeed, the concern for penetrative processes has even led one student of linkage phenomena to investigate on a comparative basis the foreign policy behavior of polities differentiated by the degree to which they are penetrated systems.[82] To a large extent, in short, linkage and penetration have come to be used synonymously.

Another characteristic of many of the linkage studies is the readiness of their authors to tailor the original framework to the specific foci of their research. Clark, for example, broadened the 'Cold War' environment into a 'center-periphery' category,[83] while Manley found the need to retitle it as the 'East-West' environment and to add two other external environments, the 'ideological' and the 'North-South.[84] Similarly, Reid found good reasons to identify a special type of insular polity, 'the archipelagic,'[85] and to differentiate between the 'emulative'

[78] 'Linkages and Foreign Policy of Peru,' p. 281.
[79] 'Foreign Factor in Greek Politics,' p. 1.
[80] 'Structure of Small State Behavior,' p. 263.
[81] 'Foreign Politics of Black Southern Africa,' pp. 37–38.
[82] Blong, 'Comparative Study of Foreign Policy Behavior.'
[83] 'Economic Integration,' p. 5.
[84] 'Linkage Politics,' p. 1.
[85] Consisting of islands 'which form a chain,' such as those found in the Caribbean, and which 'may experience linkage phenomena which emanate from outside the geographical area but which are transmitted through the chain by being received first in that island which is more receptive to the phenomena and subsequently dispersed among the others through the channels of social communication which are relatively more intense between members of the chain than between members and nonmembers' ('Linkage Theory,' p. 9).

process of linkage and one he calls the 'imitative' process.[86] In a like manner Dominguez's concern with international subsystems led him to delineate a particular kind of fused linkage process.[87] Conceptual innovations of this kind are, of course, welcome. The original framework was admittedly crude and arbitrary, and it is hardly surprising that its application generated revision. Furthermore, the innovations themselves would seem — at least in the case of those identifying new linkage processes — to be creative and to enlarge the explanatory capacity of the linkage concept.

Unfortunately, the empirical data thus far generated by the linkage framework have not been as innovative as the conceptual revisions. As previously implied, most of the data that have become available describe specific historical developments in particular countries and are not readily usable in contexts other than those in which the authors used them. Bunker's detailed, almost month-by-month account of how events internal and external to Peru got linked[88] is typical of the linkage data that comprise the presently available literature. There are exceptions, as the aforementioned studies by Hazlewood and Eley demonstrate,[89] but for the most part the concept has yet to yield a rich data base that can be used to explore the interaction of the many variables through which linkages get formed and sustained. Indeed,

[86] 'Some states may be appropriately regarded as being affected by emulative processes in the sense that they undertake activity with the objective of seeking to equal or excel in the attainment of some end state which is seen to be possessed by actors of similar resource capabilities. Other states may, then, be regarded as being involved in imitative behavior if they seek to achieve similar conditions as are perceived to be possessed by actors whose resources are significantly greater' (ibid., p. 3).

[87] 'Fusion occurs when there is a rise in simultaneous violent conflict in geographically contiguous subsystems previously indifferent toward each other. A precondition for fusion is that the local subsystems must already be relatively autonomous from the international center at least in the issue areas to be fused. Linkage through fusion takes place through local centers. A linkage through the center (whether systemic or subsystemic) means: (1) significant direct relations between the linked countries are few; (2) these countries are now relevant to each other primarily because they are significantly affected by the friendly or hostile actions of a given center power in their competition for resources which can be used in the local subsystem or in the countries themselves; and (3) only the linking center is a member of the two or more linked subsystems' (p. 187).

[88] 'Linkages and Foreign Policy of Peru,' esp. pp. 285–95.

[89] Another exception is the data creatively generated by McCoy, 'A Functional Taxonomy.' These are derived from tables in which each column represents one of the 21 Latin American countries and each row one of the international, national, and subnational agencies that support family planning programs somewhere in Latin America. The data consist of entries in the relevant cells of the tables indicating the fact or kind of support which the various agencies give to the various countries. A horizontal examination of the tables gives a clear picture of which are the most active agencies, whereas a vertical perusal provides a quick insight into which countries are likely to be the site of the most extensive national-international linkages in the population issue area.

since the comparative inquiries noted above are still largely conceptual and have yet to move into an empirical phase, one is compelled to note that not even faint traces of such a data base have become discernible and that, after all, it may be that the linkage concept will prove incapable of serving as a building block for further across-systems theory.

On the other hand, it can be argued that it is premature to anticipate an outpouring of linkage data, that the concept is too new and the phenomena it depicts too elusive for abundant quantifiable materials to have already become available. At least, such an argument would stress, the linkage framework has stimulated the consideration of phenomena, processes, or problems that had not previously been investigated. If this is so, then a clue as to the long-run utility of the linkage concept is to be found in the kinds of theoretical insights that the several years of inquiry have yielded. Even if the case histories do not provide data for further analysis, they and the more conceptual efforts that together comprise the presently available literature on linkages ought at least to have resulted in a series of generalizations about across-systems phenomena which will eventually stimulate the generation of appropriate data and the subsequent development of across-systems theory. Here the record is a mixed one. Some of the studies have not yielded anything resembling a generalization or hypothesis susceptible to empirical refinement. Their authors may have been led by the 24 by 6 maxtrix to investigate factors that might otherwise have been ignored — as Bunker did in Peru, Hodnett and Potichnyj in the Ukraine, and Clark in Venezuela — but the results were nonetheless bound by time and place. Bunker, for example, examined generally overlooked aspects of Peru, but his conclusions that 'Peru has a penetrated political system,' that 'there are instances when Peru has an effective foreign policy,' that 'interest groups in Peru do influence its foreign policy,' that 'national economic growth is often the issue that initiates a foreign policy response,' and that 'international actors other than nation-states have important roles in the formation of the foreign policies of Peru'[90] hardly exert pressure for further research. Similarly, Hodnett and Potichnyj were led by the framework to probe the attitudes, communicatons, institutions, and actors operative in the role played by the Ukraine in the Czechoslovak crisis of 1968, but their intepretation of this role as amounting to a fused linkage process[91] is not likely to serve as the basis for additional inquiry. Nor is the fact that Clark uncovered support for his hypotheses that 'the configuration of linkage components' in Venezuela were such as to prevent or render meaningless that country's participation

[90] 'Linkages and Foreign Policy of Peru,' pp. 295-96.
[91] *Ukraine and the Czechoslovak Crisis*, pp. 115-25.

in multi-national economic integration in Latin America'[92] likely to serve as an element of future across-systems theory. No less discouraging are those studies employing the linkage framework which derive generalizations that are so broad as to be irrefutable, and thus useless as a building block. Manley's derivation from his work on Guyana of the proposition that 'external factors can have either a positive or negative impact on the nation-building process'[93] is an example of this failing.

In short, it would appear that to some extent the linkage framework has merely provided a new rhetoric with which to analyze old problems and, to the extent that this becomes its predominant use, it can hardly be counted on as a route to future theoretical breakthroughs. To repeat, however, the record is a mixed one. Some of the studies subjected to scrutiny were laden with interesting propositions, as a result either of examining data or readying the concept for the collection of data. The hypotheses derived by Eley cited above (p. 179), are indicative of the former process and the work of Blong and Reid is illustrative of the latter process. Blong deduced from his reasoning three challenging and general hypotheses relative to the dynamics of penetration that he plans to test on empirical data.[94] Reid's prospectus, although it does not formally identify any propositions, is pervaded with general expectations about the linkages that will be found to sustain the politics of microstates. Noting that the prime ministers of such societies tend to hold several cabinet posts, for instance, Reid observes that this can give rise to important role conflicts, an observation which leads him to hypothesize that 'Where domestic issues are highly salient, and where the decision-maker has little previous experience in formulating purposive strategies of response to external phenomena, there will be an increased probability that foreign policy considerations will be dealt with in the context of more longstanding domestic issues, and foreign policy may thus play a subordinate role in the total policy matrix.'[95] Similarly, while indicating the many ways in which oceanic microstates are especially weak, Reid's reasoning also leads him to hypothesize about important ways in which the insularity of such societies enhances their strength: '. . . for even weak insular polities there is a delay in the transmission of linkage phenomena across the national boundary which will provide the decision-makers with a greater degree of time to contrive a response than would be available to leaders in even

[92] 'Economic Integration,' pp. 2–3 (for the hypothese) and 38–40 (for a summary of the findings).

[93] 'Linkage Politics,' p. 3.

[94] 'Comparative Study of Foreign Policy Behavior,' pp. 13–15.

[95] 'Linkage Theory,' p. 14.

relatively larger continental polities.'[96] Plainly, propositions such as these are sufficiently intriguing and specific to stimulate types of inquiries that might not otherwise be undertaken.

VI

So it is really too soon to reach a firm judgment about the theoretical utility of the linkage concept. It appears to have surmounted the major problem inherent in an atheoretical framework, that of failing to spark and guide further inquiry. In addition, it seems to offer advantages over a number of other concepts that have across-systems connotations. At the same time there has yet to develop convincing evidence that it lends itself to the derivation of interrelated propositions that systematically link variations at one level of aggregation with variations at another level. Some hypotheses and data do exist, but these are unrelated to each other and are a long way from comprising an integrated across-systems theory. Whether they will eventually prove to be building blocks of such a theory or merely isolated insights based on a common terminology is as yet undetermined. Either outcome seems possible on the basis of progress thus far.

Lest the aspiration to an integrated linkage theory be abandoned because it was not defined clearly enough, it is perhaps useful to outline briefly what such a theory might look like if it were to develop. The ensuing effort does not purport to be other than merely suggestive and is offered only as an example of the kinds of interrelationships that may be used to break through to the construction of across-systems theory. What follows is exceedingly crude and simplified, partly because clarity is best served through simplicity, but mainly because the conceptual and empirical equipment necessary to frame incisive linkage theory has still to be developed.

To illustrate the possible contours of viable linkage theory, we will use East Asia and the behavior of four national societies toward it as an example.[97] China, Japan, the United States, and the Soviet Union are the four societies, and each is assumed to have a main goal in East Asia, the pursuit of which is presumed to be measurable on a five-point intensity scale ranging from 'vigorous' to 'halfhearted.' The primary goals ascribed to the four countries are as follows:

[96] Ibid., pp. 16–17.

[97] The idea for this example originated with a reading of Robert E. Bedeski, 'The Prospects of Crisis in East Asia: Dimensions and Approaches,' mimeographed (Columbus. Ohio, 1971).

		Intensity Scale 1 2 3 4 5	
China:	vigorous maintenance of sovereignty	. . . . .	halfhearted maintenance of sovereignty
Japan:	vigorous securing of markets and resources	. . . . .	halfhearted securing of markets and resources
U.S.:	vigorous maintenance of balance of power	. . . . .	halfhearted maintenance of balance of power
U.S.S.R.:	vigorous defense of eastern border areas	. . . . .	halfhearted defense of eastern border areas

In addition, the theory assumes that the domestic life and structure of each society can be summarized in terms of fluctuations along one central dimension, which in turn is one of the two prime determinants of the degree to which the main goal in East Asia is being pursued vigorously or halfheartedly. The central domestic dimension is also assumed to be measurable on a five-point scale, referred to as a structural scale, and is listed below for each society, with the characteristic at the left being the one that tends to foster vigorous pursuit of the main East Asian goal and the one at the right being the basis of halfhearted pursuit:

		Structural Scale 1 2 3 4 5	
China:	centralized leadership	. . . . .	decentralized leadership
Japan:	economic growth	. . . . .	economic stagnation
U.S.:	interventionist tendencies	. . . . .	isolationist tendencies
U.S.S.R.:	singular leadership	. . . . .	collective leadership

The other major determinant of the degree to which each society's East Asian goal is pursued vigorously or halfheartedly is the interaction pattern that results from the way in which all four pursue their respective goals at any moment in time. That is, different combinations of vigorous or halfhearted pursuit of the four goals are presumed to give rise to different degrees and forms of stability and instability in the East Asian international system, and these are in turn likely to encourage increased or decreased vigor in the pursuits of the goals by each power.

Linkage theory becomes relevant when one attempts to develop propositions about how the degree of stability of the East Asian system will affect each society's location on the structural scale and how location on the structural scale will affect the degree of vigor with which each society pursues its external goals, thus affecting the nature and structure of the East Asian system. Given five-point scales, the possible permutations and combinations in this regard are too numerous to record here. They can readily be calculated with the aid of a computer, however, so that the only obstacle to viable linkage theory is the obvious inadequacy of the assumption that societal goals and structures can be reduced to single dimensions. Leaving this inadequacy aside, the example is pervaded with linkages. First, there are the linkages in which the outputs are found in the various domestic structures and the inputs in the East Asian system. The Cultural Revolution in China, for instance, moved that country toward the decentralization extreme, with the result that international politics in East Asia entered a new era of stability. Second, there are the linkages in which the outputs are located in the East Asian international system and the inputs in the domestic structures of the major powers. One can readily imagine, for example, how instability in that region would foster movement toward the interventionist extreme of the U.S.'s structure and the singular leadership extreme of the Soviet Union's structure. Third, there are the linkages in which the vigor of each society's effort to achieve its East Asian goal operates as the output and the locations on the structural scale of the other three societies are viewed as inputs. That is, not only may one or another aspect of the domestic structures of each of the four be systematically linked to East Asian systemic factors, but they may also vary systematically with changes in the vigor with which each of the other societies pursues its external goals.

In short, an integrated linkage theory posits a vast feedback system. Variations at each level are seen to be systematically linked to variations at the other levels in such a way as to feed back into and become part of the behavioral sequences at the original level. The links and the feedbacks are not the only — or even the most important — determinants of behavior at any level (there are other determinants of East Asian stability besides the vigor with which the major powers in the region pursue their East Asian goals). Yet, if theory along these lines could ever be developed, it ought to be possible to anticipate and trace the global repercussions of events and trends in an ever smaller world. Another cultural revolution in China, the ouster or death of another Khrushchev in Russia, another racial flare-up in the United States, another resurgence of the birth rate in Japan, another exacerbation of tension in East Asia — such developments would be data that fit readily into, rather than undermine, the across-systems theories toward which our emerging conceptual tools are inexorably leading us.

9 Success and Failure in Scientific International Relations Research*

For more than a decade, foundations and government agencies have funded large scientific inquiries into various aspects of international relations (IR). The most obvious results have included an increasing use of quantification, mathematics, and computers, a methodological self-consciousness, and a vast outpouring of new models, hypotheses, data, and findings. These developments, in turn, have attracted considerable interest, if not status, in the IR field. It is by no means clear, however, exactly what this newly won prominence of the scientific mode represents. To gain attention is not necessarily to achieve theoretical or empirical breakthroughs. To acquire status is not necessarily to initiate a cumulative knowledge-building process. To stimulate interest is not necessarily to persuade the many investigators in the field who are committed to other research traditions that the scientific mode provides them with an additional and important avenue to deeper understanding of international phenomena. Prominence may merely reflect a vogue in which quantitiative analysis serves as a substitute for, rather than as an instrument of, creative theorizing and rigorous hypothesis-testing.

In short, what have all the funds invested in the U.S. community of IR researchers bought? Or, more accurately perhaps, what do they

*An earlier version of this chapter was written in March, 1974, as a Report to the National Science Foundation, which funded the workshop on the Successes and Failures of Scientific International Relations Research in Ojai, California, June 1973. The papers presented at the Workshop were later revised and, along with a summary of the Report, were published in James N. Rosenau (ed.), *In Search of Global Patterns* (New York: Free Press, 1976), Part One. The excerpts from the papers and the Report included in this chapter are reprinted with the permission of the publisher. Copyright © 1976 by the Free Press, a Division of The Macmillan Company.

presently seem to be buying? What has been accomplished and what remains to be accomplished? In what ways is the field better off today as a consequence of all the talent and energy mobilized by the large research programs? Are there ways in which it is worse off? Has progress been more apparent than real? How should energy and inquiry be directed in the future?

It is to questions such as these that the Workshop on the Successes and Failures of Scientific International Relations Research was addressed. Supported by the National Science Foundation[1] and attended by fifteen scholars, all of whom had received funds for large-scale research programs,[2] the Workshop was convened in June 1973 at the Ojai Valley Inn in Ojai, California. In that spectacular setting, where the air was invigorating and the scenery stimulating, penetrating discussions and often heated arguments ensued for three days. What follows is an account and assessment of these deliberations and the written materials which many of the participants developed both in preparation for and subsequent to the Workshop. While the results reported here are not as spectacular as the circumstances under which they were generated, hopefully they provide a measure of where the field stands today and, in so doing, will invigorate and stimulate thought on where it ought to go in the future.

I. AN IMPORTANT CAVEAT

It must be stressed at the outset that any assessment of a field depends crucially on what the assessors are looking for, on their conceptions of cumulated knowledge, on their definitions of progress, and on what they want the field to become. Criteria for the assessment of research activity are far from standardized in the IR field.[3] As a result two participants in the same workshop or two readers of the report on it can come away with very different conclusions as to what

[1] Through a grant (GS-37340) to the Ohio State Research Foundation.

[2] The participants were Chadwick F. Alger of Ohio State University, Hayward R. Alker, Jr., of the Massachusetts Institute of Technology, Edward E. Azar of the University of North Carolina, Nazli Choucri of the Massachusetts Institute of Technology, Alexander L. George of Stanford University, Harold Guetzkow of Northwestern University, Charles F. Hermann of Ohio State University, Ole R. Holsti of Duke University, Charles A. McClelland of the University of Southern California, John Mueller of Rochester University, Robert C. North of Stanford University, Richard Rosecrance of Cornell University, R.J. Rummel of the University of Hawaii, Bruce M. Russett of Yale University, J. David Singer of the University of Michigan, and the present writer.

[3] For one attempt to develop assessment criteria, see James N. Rosenau, 'Assessment in International Studies: Ego Trip or Feedback?', *International Studies Quarterly*, Vol. 18 (June 1974), pp. 339-67.

the deliberations revealed. The workshop summarized here is no exception. Its proceedings readily allow for both great optimism and deep pessimism over what has been accomplished in a decade of work. Using excerpts from the comments of the participants, I have tried to depict these contradictory themes in as fair and detached a way as possible; but the reader should ponder his or her own criteria of assessment before reaching any judgments about the present state and future potential of scientific inquiry in the IR field.

II. THE LARGER CONTEXT

Neither this report nor the Workshop itself are the first effort to assess the state of the field as a scientific enterprise. On the contrary, the ensuing account must be seen in the context of a series of recent attempts to describe and evaluate the trends and findings of research undertaken since the late 1950s. The preference for scientific procedures and quantitative analysis grew so rapidly in the 1960s that a number of observers were provoked to scrutinize, and even to challenge, the utility and rationale of the headlong rush to operationalize variables and quantify data. Acceptance of the philosophical premises underlying scientific inquiry did not come easily to a field whose investigative practices had long been shaped by diplomatic historians, international legal scholars, and experienced statesmen. So it was only natural that a number of debates about the applicability of scientific methods to international phenomena accompanied (and also fostered) a spate of efforts simply to assess the divergent trends in the field.[4]

[4] Some of the philosophical debates will be found in Klaus Knorr and James N. Rosenau (eds.), *Contending Approaches to International Politics* (Princeton: Princeton University Press, 1969), while the following should be consulted for more general assessments of the field: Hayward R. Alker, Jr., 'Research Paradigms and Mathematical Politics' (mimeo., 1973); Hayward R. Alker, Jr., and P.G. Bock, 'Propositions About International Relations: Contributions from the *International Encyclopedia of the Social Sciences*,' in James A. Robinson (ed.), *Political Science Annual: An International Review* (Indianapolis: Bobbs-Merrill, 1972), pp. 385-495; W.T.R. Fox, *The American Study of International Relations* (Columbia: Institute of International Studies, University of South Carolina, 1968); John H. Herz, 'Relevancies and Irrelevancies in the Study of International Relations,' *Polity*, Vol. LV (1971), pp. 26-47; K.J. Holsti, 'Retreat from Utopia: International Relations Theory, 1945-1970.' *Canadian Journal of Political Science*, Vol. 4 (1971) pp. 165-77; Norman D. Palmer (ed.), *A Design for International Relations Research: Scope, Theory, Methods, and Relevance* (Philadelphia: American Academy of Political and Social Science, 1970); E. Raymond Platig, *International Relations Research: Problems of Evaluation and Advancement* (Santa Barbara: Clio Press, 1967); Robert L. Pfaltzgraff, Jr., 'International Studies in the 1970s,' *International Studies Quarterly*, Vol. 15 (March 1971), pp. 104-28; Charles A. McClelland, 'On the Fourth Wave: Past and Future in the Study of International Systems,'

Few of these assessments, however, were made by those who directed the large research projects through which the movement toward scientific analysis gained momentum and visibility. Instead the assessors were mainly scholars whose own work had been conducted along more traditional lines but who welcomed diversity and sought to reconcile the older and newer approaches to the field. What such assessments thus lack is the benefit of close familiarity with the pleasures and pains of generating, managing, and analyzing great amounts of data. Those who had this familiarity tended not to divert energy from their projects to taking a hard, systematic look at what the collective surge toward scientific inquiry was and was not achieving. They joined actively in the debates over the merits and potentialities of quantification[5] and many of them also evaluated their own projects in the process of publishing their findings and reporting to funding agencies.[6] Self-reports of research in progress lack perspective, however, Understandably they seek to highlight the virtues rather than the flaws of a research design.

So it is that the Ojai Workshop offered a unique opportunity. While it was not the first attempt to assess recent research in the field, it was probably the first occasion when builders of scientific models and managers of extensive quantified data engaged in a prolonged and critical discussion of what their collective effort had accomplished. With the wrangles over whether IR could be studied scientifically largely (though not entirely) behind them and with the legitimacy of their enterprise securely (though not universally)

in James N. Rosenau, Vincent Davis, and Maurice East (eds.), *The Analysis of International Politics* (New York: The Free Press, 1972), pp. 15–40; Harry H. Ransom, 'International Relations,' in Marion D. Irish (ed.), *Political Science: Advance of the Discipline* (Englewood Cliffs: Prentice-Hall, 1968), pp. 55–81; James N. Rosenau, *International Studies and the Social Sciences: Problems, Priorities, and Prospects in the United States* (Beverly Hills: Sage, 1973); Bruce M. Russett, 'International Behavior Research: Case Studies and Cumulation,' in Michael Haas and Henry S. Kariel (eds.), *Approaches to the Study of Political Science* (Scranton: Chandler Publishing Co., 1970), pp. 425–43; Richard C. Snyder, 'Some Recent Trends in International Relations Theory and Research,' in Austin Ranney (ed.), *Essays on the Behavioral Study of Politics* (Urbana: University of Illinois Press, 1962), pp. 103–72; and Ronald J. Yalem, 'Prolegomena on the Post-Behavioral Revolution in International Studies,' *Orbis*, Vol. XVI (Winter 1973), pp. 1032–42.

[5] For example see the chapters by Singer and North in Knorr and Rosenau (eds.), *Contending Approaches to International Politics*, pp. 62–86 and 218–242.

[6] Examples of self-evaluations can be found in Harold Guetzkow, 'A Decade of Life with the Inter-Nation Simulation,' in Ralph M. Stogdill (ed.), *The Process of Model-Building in the Behavioral Sciences* (New York: W.W. Norton, 1970), pp. 31–53; R.J. Rummel, 'Some Empirical Findings on Nations and Their Behavior,' *World Politics*, Vol. XXI (January 1969), pp. 226–41; and J. David Singer, "The 'Correlates of War' Project: Interim Report and Rationale," *World Politics*, Vol. XXIV (January 1972), pp. 243–70.

established, some of those who had enjoyed large-scale support for their research could focus — at least for a few days — on what a decade or more of sustained work had produced.

Lest this brief synopsis of the context in which the Workshop was convened be misconstrued as implying that the turn to scientific inquiry in the 1960s was initiated by the advent of large-scale funding, it must be stressed that this development sprung from many sources, probably the least of which was the availability of substantial financial support. The funding agencies greatly sustained the movement, but they did not create it. Rather its origins can be traced back to the effects of World War II and the subsequent evolution of several different schools of thought with a common predisposition to move beyond the legal and institutional approaches of the past. Overwhelmed by the horrors of the war and the totalitarian terror that preceded it, some scholars drew heavily on the behavioral sciences and dedicated themselves to pluralistic peace research, while others became concerned with the practical problems of the Cold War, such as deterrence and arms control, and developed a variety of concepts and models designed to cope with such problems. Thus both peace researchers and cold warriors arrived at the intellectual premises out of which the commitment to scientific procedures could (and often did) evolve.

In addition to the breakdown of the international system during the 1940s, the behavioral revolution that occurred in the social sciences, and particularly in political science, during the 1950s also fostered the inclination to apply scientific methods to international phenomena. With notable exceptions such as Harold Guetzkow and Charles McClelland, most of the individuals who self-consciously introduced the scientific perspective into IR research and/or launched the large data gathering projects were trained as political scientists. Being familiar with the foundations of the behavioral revolution, they naturally sought to subject the international phenomena in which they were interested to the more rigorous and systematic procedures of scientific inquiry.

While the stirrings of science in the IR field thus had a variety of sources, they had the common outcome of leading a number of researchers to seek financial support to implement their research designs. At the same time, and for similarly diverse reasons, government agencies and private foundations became increasingly interested in developing more incisive knowledge about world affairs. As a result, many of the requests for funding support developed by U.S. scholars in the late 1950s and early 1960s were well received and a number of research programs launched.

The fact that the initial impulses toward scientific IR research originated within the scholarly rather than the funding community is a major factor accounting for some of the communications difficulties evident during the Workshop. Because individuals came to the funding agencies with proposals, rather than vice versa, the funding process was highly individualistic. Not only were a variety of agencies involved, each with its own conception of the kind of knowledge that ought to be developed and the process through which to generate it, but the various researchers sought support for the investigation of very diverse substantive problems. Some projects focused on individual-level phenomena, others on the dynamics of governmental policy-making, and still others on international system processes and institutions. Methodologically, too, diversity characterized the proposals, with some committed to data-making techniques such as simulation and aggregate data generation, others to the derivation and application of mathematical models, and still others to statistical techniques such as factor and correlational analysis. In short, not even the bare outlines of a shared paradigm characterized the advent of scientific IR research. All that those who launched the early projects had in common was a commitment to the proposition that world affairs could be more penetratingly and thoroughly grasped through the identification of recurring patterns, a commitment that required implementation through the compilation of quantitative data and/or the construction of mathematical models. Whether, and to what extent, a more widely shared paradigm has evolved in the intervening years is a question to which we shall return, but it seems clear to me that the diversity of foci and methodologies in terms of which scientific IR research was launched still hinder communication among otherwise like-minded scholars.

III. THE IMMEDIATE CONTEXT

A brief account of the intellectual tasks the participants took on when they accepted the invitation will facilitate an appraisal of the results of the Workshop. The original invitation stressed that the deliberations would be 'wide-ranging and free-wheeling' with a minimum of formal structure and a maximum of spontaneous interchange. Indeed, in a subsequent memo clarifying the procedures of the Workshop, a rationale was offered for avoiding 'a format in which sessions have designated chairmen, paper-givers, and discussants, with the thrust of all subsequent remarks being a disarrayed function of when the speakers got their names on the chairman's list rather than a coordinated, cumulative discussion'[:]

> I wish to avoid simply another conference. I would like this conference to be different, a landmark occasion which will — through the dissemination

of its conclusions and taped proceedings — stimulate renewed and revised effort. I think the time has come for intellectual leadership to be exercised in the field and I think the circumstances of the Ojai Conference allow us to dare to exercise it. If we can break out of established ways of interacting at conferences and instead concentrate on integrating our separate research experiences into a coherent whole, I think we can come up with some kind of manifesto for future inquiry that will have a profound impact. We are sufficiently few in number to sustain intense and focused discussions, sufficiently like-minded not to waste time rehashing old issues, sufficiently free of status concerns with each other to permit the interruptions and departures from agenda that make for genuine intellectual advance, and sufficiently restless to be motivated to try out a new format that may yield worthwhile results.[7]

The suggested alternative to the conventional format was to organize the deliberations around a series of substantive foci and questions (noted below), with a discussion chairman responsible for 'seeing to it that we stick to the main subject and that only one person is speaking on it at any time' and with a commitment to moving from one focus to the next 'when we agree that a particular focus has been adequately examined — or, even better, when we reach clear-cut, succinct, and shared understandings about a particular focus that can be included in our post-conference manifesto.' As will be seen, this procedure did not yield a manifesto or even an orderly consideration of the suggested foci, but it did foster vigorous discussion and expose subtle and important differences in perspective and emphasis.

The substantive challenge to the participants came in two stages. The initial invitation raised a series of questions that it was proposed the Workshop discussions would address. In addition each participant was asked to prepare a short paper in advance of the Workshop that 'succinctly and yet candidly' discussed the questions in terms of his or her particular research project. The questions listed in this first communication were as follows:

In what ways is our comprehension of the dynamics of international politics different because of the large-scale and systematic research programs that have been undertaken? Have our efforts evidenced the signs of a 'normal' or a 'revolutionary' science — or are both characteristics inapplicable in the IR case? What concrete findings, if any, have been uncovered that have become the basis of widespread intersubjective consensuses in the field? What theoretical models and/or perspectives have been rendered obsolete and what new ones have been generated that serve as organizing paradigms for the field? How reliable and generalizable is the knowledge resulting from our systematic inquiries? What new methodologies, with what potentialities and limitations, have been fostered by the research programs? Among the original motives that led to the various research projects, what was the balance between curiosity and the availability of research funds? More important, in what ways, if any, did the process of carrying out the programs alter this balance? How widespread has been diffusion and scholarly utilization of the research? What

[7]Memorandum dated April 25, 1973.

> evidence can be cited indicating that each research program either initiated or contributed to a cumulative knowledge-building process? What unanticipated policy or teaching spin-offs, if any, of the work can be identified? Where should scientifically oriented IR research go from here?[8]

The invitation to the Workshop provoked one of its recipients, R.J. Rummel, to respond that while 'your list of questions are central and will, indeed, involve all of us in a vigorous and fascinating dialectic,' the Workshop could not be sufficient to the task of coping with the foregoing questions and that therefore a second, follow-up conference comprised of IR specialists 'not especially involved at a project level' ought to be part of the original planning. Rummel indicated that his suggestion came out of

> . . . a fear that all of us at this coming conference may be wary of trumpeting our own horns on the one hand, or getting involved in invidious comparisons with other projects. Consequently, I doubt that we will be able, in any thoroughly gutsy way, to evaluate ourselves and the movement of which we are a part. This I think could be left to those in a second conference who do not have a personal stake in a project themselves and who don't have to worry about collegial and research relationships with other projects and their directors or investigators. Of course, I may simply be misreading my colleagues and the culture of which we are a part. However, what we are about to do does seem somewhat like the leaders of the Students for a Democratic Society getting together to evaluate their successes and failures.[9]

Rummel's letter suggesting a second conference was circulated to the invitees and, in turn, evoked a response from G.R. Boynton, then the NSF's Program Director for Political Science, who used the occasion to clarify his thinking about why the National Science Foundation was supporting the Workshop. Because the Boynton letter was also circulated in advance and thus contributed to the context of the Workshop, its relevant paragraphs are reproduced here:

> . . . I agree that this may not be the group of people to do the kind of overall evaluation of the research that Rummel has in mind. It is very difficult for an individual or group to be completely objective in evaluating their own research. There is also the problem that there are no objective standards against which to measure the accomplishments of this research in the field. However, this does not persuade me that the conference will not be productive. My own concerns are somewhat more limited than the kind of evaluation he seems to have in mind. Let me try to articulate my basic concern and then go on to some subsidiary concerns.
>
> One of the outstanding characteristics of research in political science during the last several decades has been its non-cumulativeness. At the simplest level I would take cumulativeness of research to be the following: a second research effort on a topic can rely on findings of a first research effort in such a way that it does not have to start from scratch. This can take two forms (oversimplified for brevity). It can be formalized in one or another mathematical

[8] Letter dated January 12, 1973.
[9] Letter dated January 22, 1973.

form. At the verbal level it might be something as simple as: (research #1) the dependent variable can be explained by an independent variable; (research #2) the dependent variable can be explained by the independent variable under one condition but is independent of the independent variable under condition two.

This 'verbal' type example could of course be formalized through statistical or some other mathematical technique which would provide a good deal more precision.

Let me illustrate the non-cumulativeness that I have in mind from research on political participation — a topic I know something about. The non-cumulativeness takes two forms. First, research is just repeated. There must be hundreds if not thousands of studies that have established that the more highly educated are more likely to participate in politics. That simple hypothesis is among the most over-validated findings in captivity. However, the work is not cumulative in that it really does not go beyond the initial finding. Second, research on political participation is non-cumulative in the sense that most studies have added new variables to our list of predictors without specifying the relationship of the new independent variable to old independent variables.

I have taken a rather simple example of cumulative research — one in which energy was concentrated on explaining a single dependent variable. Another and more complex example would be one in which there was a rather complex system of relationships specified. Different researchers worked on different parts of the model to improve that specific part, but the work of each researcher could be added back into the model. My impression is that econometric modeling is much like this.

One of the questions that I am interested in is — to what extent is the research of this fifteen or so researchers cumulative. Are the topics of their individual research efforts close enough that each can build on the work of the others or is each working on such a different topic that there is little or not building. If the latter is the case, why is it the case? If the latter is not the case how might the situation be changed? Would such a change be good? In other words I see a significant problem for our discipline. I seem to feel that they share some common goals as well as a common type of data. And I wonder if they have been able to overcome the problem — at least a little.

There is also a much simpler task that I think can be performed by the conference. This is essentially descriptive — what do we know now that we did not know before all of this research started? This does not require any assumption about one set of research building on another, but is a process of summarizing what has been done.

Finally, there is the business of a collective setting of goals or coming to agreement on what should be done next, given what you have discovered. What is it really important to know — what kind of priorities should there be for this subfield of the discipline?[10]

Boynton's stress on cumulativeness was incorporated into, and became a central part of, a second letter that was sent to the participants in order to clarify and specify more precisely the substantive foci of the workshop and the pre-Workshop papers. This letter offered four 'premises (and ground rules) as the basis for the [Workshop] discussions':

[10] Letter dated February 8, 1973.

1. Whatever qualms we may have about the legitimacy and inherent potential of quantitative analysis and a science of international relations, for present purposes we ought to assume both the legitimacy and the potentials of such an enterprise. This assumption underlies the funding of our research programs and there is no reason to abandon it prematurely. Nor is there any reason to devote precious time to a reconsideration of it; the literature is filled with recent efforts along this line and there is no need to add to it.
2. The ultimate measure of the growth of a science is the substantive knowledge that it cumulates and not the methodology it perfects. Thus we should avoid discussions of methodological problems except insofar as they are necessary to the clarification of substantive questions.
3. Our prime focus should be on the dynamics of cumulation — what do we know cumulatively with respect to the central foci of the field (see below) and, in each case, what are the impediments to a more rapid process of cumulation.
4. Indeed, the cumulative nature and status of our knowledge should not only constitute the underlying thread of our discussions, but it should also serve as the main thrust of our subsequent manifesto. Science is essentially a consensual process in which all concerned seek to converge around and extend a shared understanding of empirical reality. Thus, to give *intellectual leadership* to a *field* is to point out the ways in which those it encompasses can more effectively cohere and build on each other's efforts.

Turning to the question of what phenomena should be considered in the context of cumulativeness, this second letter offered three suggestions for the organization of the Workshop discussions and pre-Workshop papers:

1. Each of the following should serve as successive foci of discussion (allowing time for the consideration of additions and deletions at the outset and for drawing overall conclusions at the end):

   foreign policy decision-making
      of individuals viewed psychologically
      of individuals viewed as rational actors
      of bureaucracies

   balance of power and other system models

   alliances

   issue-area and cultural differences

   domestic sources of foreign policy

   international organization

   international behavior:
      cooperative
      conflictful
      transnational
      integrative

   demographics:
      human resources
      nonhuman resources

   crises

2. More precisely, with respect to each of the foregoing we should press ourselves to come up with responses to the following queries: Has a body of knowledge cumulated? What are its main outlines? In what sense is it cumulative? Can new findings and/or theories easily upend it? If little has cumulated, why? How can the pace of cumulation be hastened? If much has cumulated, what factors account for the success and can they be adapted to other foci and concepts? Is the immediate need that of probing the independent variables encompassed by the focus, the dependent variables, the interaction among them, or all of these dimensions? Would increased funds for research into this focus yield correspondingly greater results?
3. To add to the breadth of the discussion of these queries, the brief papers prepared as the 'price' of admission to the conference should not consider the questions themselves. Rather the papers should be — to coin a term — *project autobiographical*, with emphasis on all the ways in which your project or program has been linked to researchers not connected with it and may thus have contributed to a consensual process wherein cumulation has occurred or may yet occur. Using the project files as a data base, such questions as the following might serve as the basis for the papers: Who (or how many) have requested use of your data? for what purposes? What kinds of things have they done with the data? Have any of the hypotheses derived from your project been tested by others? With what results? Has the feedback provided by the users of your data or concepts had an effect on your thinking and the evolution of the project? If so, how? If you could do it over again, equipped with your present understanding, what would you do differently? Stated immodestly (or modestly), how is the IR field better off by virtue of the funds and time invested in your project?[11]

These instructions prompted the preparation of thirteen 'project autobiographical' papers, most of which were circulated prior to the Workshop, thus further enriching the immediate context of the proceedings at Ojai. For the present purpose of summarizing and evaluating the Workshop, there is no further need to distinguish the contents of the papers from those of the Workshop discussions or of the supplemental memos that some of the participants subsequently prepared. The papers, many of them considerably revised, are available elsewhere, but the interpretations set forth below are based on the transcript of the Workshop proceedings as well as on the written materials it generated.[12]

[11] Letter dated April 25, 1973.

[12] Unless otherwise noted, the excerpted materials that follow are taken from the original versions of the papers presented at the Workshop. The revised versions can be found in James N. Rosenau (ed.), *In Search of Global Patterns* (New York: Free Press, 1976), Part One.

IV. THE CONCEPT OF CUMULATION

The Workshop's answer to the question of what a decade or more of scientific research in IR has accomplished proved to be ambiguous. As it turned out, much depended on what each participant regarded as progress. All concerned agreed that the decade had been marked by both successes and failures, but there was much less agreement as to which was which. Notwithstanding a shared commitment to scientific inquiry, some viewed as major accomplishments what others saw as stagnation. While the distinction between scientific and non-scientific modes of inquiry was not a matter of intense dispute, different conceptions of the surest way to build scientific knowledge surfaced and persisted during the Workshop. Some stressed the processes of normal science and the cumulation of reliable, replicable, and interdependent findings as the most efficient route to an ever-widening base of knowledge. But others contended that the processes of revolutionary science — the competition of paradigms and their application to new and challenging contexts — are equally, if not more, central to progress in the field.[13] Perhaps the most notable consequence of these different emphases was the persistence of differences over the meaning and importance of the concept of cumulation. Throughout the discussions — and in several of the Workshop papers as well — a reluctance to treat cumulation as the prime criterion of success was frequently manifest. More than a few of those present asserted, in effect, that there can be (and has been) considerable progress without corresponding growth in the corpus of reliable and interdependent findings.

Stated differently, a distinction developed early in the Workshop between a narrow and a broad view of the processes of cumulation. Some considered the Boynton view of cumulation (see the excerpts from his letter above) as too narrow and constricting. Those expressing this belief argued that while the aggregation of reliable, tested, and interdependent findings is an important aspect of scientific progress, it is not the only dimension of greater understanding and must be seen as but one part of a larger enterprise. The re-conceptualization of core notions, the development of diverse methodologies, the discovery and pursuit of anomalies, and the emergence of competing theories and paradigms were asserted to be as, and perhaps more, central to the growth of a science of IR as the painstaking process of empirically delineating the explanatory power of independent variables and the operation of dependent variables. And, it was claimed,

[13] For a compelling delineation of the distinction between a normal and a revolutionary science, see Thomas S. Kuhn, *The Structure of Scientific Revolutions* (Chicago: University of Chicago Press, 2nd edn., 1970).

progress during the first decade of scientific inquiry was perhaps even greater in the former respects than in substantive findings.

Nor did resistance to the narrow conception of cumulation immediately yield in response to vigorous reassertion of the notion that the ultimate measure of the growth of a science is the substantive knowledge that it cumulates. Those espousing the narrow view contended that revised and sharply delineated concepts, innovative methodologies, clarified anomalies, and competing theories are of little value unless they result in an ever-growing corpus of findings in which an ever-widening community of scholars has confidence. Why, it was asked, should the National Science Foundation or any other funding agency take the field seriously and continue to invest in scientific IR research if its practitioners were not building on each other's work and expanding the realm of established knowledge? Because, came the answer, the expansion of knowledge does not occur in neat and logical sequences. As Hayward Alker observed in his pre-Workshop paper, 'In the long run, major scientific progress is discontinuous, even dialectical.' Alker conceded that the concept of cumulation set forth in my pre-Workshop memo (see above) had some merit, but he stressed that it was not sufficient:

> Rosenau's focus on cumulative, consensual development may be appropriate within certain research paradigms (which ones?). A heavy commitment to data gathering (by Singer and others) is also appropriate for some at a pre-paradigmatic level of scientific development. But the dialectics of scientific revolutions occasioned by a combination of crisis-generating internal anomalies and external constructive critique is not suggested at all by Rosenau's language.

Similarly, Edward Azar complained that

> The criterion of cumulativeness seems overarching and monlithic, unfair to both our research mode and the scientific occupation. Insofar as 'cumulative' means serial collaboration, no problem exists. But cumulativeness can lead to or become a criterion for the *rejection* of research activities.

In short, for several of the Workshop participants emphasis on cumulation posed the danger that research practices will inhibit the growth of a revolutionary science and sustain the expansion of a normal science.

The present state of the world was another compelling reason offered for not becoming too locked into the precepts of normal science. It was argued that too many important and urgent problems marked the international arena for cumulation to be the only criterion employed in evaluating IR research. As Alexander George put it,

> I myself would assign equal, if not greater, weight to the criterion of *relevance*. *Why* do we want to develop IR knowledge and theory? What kinds of knowledge and theory about the various phenomena and processes of international relations is likely to be more useful? It is important to pose these questions

> explicitly, and to juxtapose them with the criterion of 'cumulation,' when we evaluate research performance in the IR field, if for no other reason than the fact that there can be — often are? — trade-offs between increased cumulation and enhanced relevance. Cumulation is no guarantee of relevance. If one perceives the choice clearly, would one decide to undertake additional research to enhance cumulation of that variant of IR knowledge that has little foreseeable relevance; or would one reformulate the research task to enhance potential relevance?[14]

Similarly, noting that the field had made some progress in building 'islands' of reliable findings, Bruce Russett expressed concern over the possibility of a

> . . . demand that quantitative IR research focus almost exclusively on the one or two or three islands where the cumulating model works most effectively, producing a·host of studies each making very marginal improvements (e.g., as is done in experimental gaming, or some other corners of experimental psychology). This latter would seem to me to be the worst possible course for the IR community. There are just too many and too varied phenomena, quite outside any of the scientific islands that currently are at all well developed; too many questions, vital to the survival of the race, on which we need some evidence or at least insight. The experience of other sciences, especially the behavioral sciences, that have experienced a concentration of resources on a few limited islands surely should be an object lesson to us. Similarly, it is vital that our funding agencies not insist, in a mistaken attempt to follow other sciences, that research be so focused, or that they will fund only those projects which build within a well-worn paradigm, with previous findings, hypotheses, and methodological intentions all spelled out clearly and neatly in the proposal. International relations is too important to leave exclusively to the Rummels, the Russetts, Singers, etc., when they have their cumulating hats on.

Another basis for resisting the narrow conception of cumulation was that it is premature, given the relatively brief time during which scientific work in IR has been pursued, to measure the successes and failures of the field in terms of an expanding base of substantive findings. Rummel put it this way:

> . . . as a movement the quantitative approach to IR is only about fifteen years old. This is hardly enough time to crystallize trends, methodologies, theories, and results, and to overcome the extreme variance between people in their competence, approaches, scientific sensitivity, and norms. With people of different traditions, training, skills, and perspectives working side by side, it seems scarcely appropriate or fair to assess success and failure in this first working-out-the-differences stage. At least a couple of decades more are needed to significantly lessen the impact of this generational and transitional variance on our self assessments.

Concern about the limits of quantitative analysis was still another basis for dissatisfaction with the narrow approach to cumulation and its stress on the identification of recurring patterns in quantified data. George argued that the exclusive reliance on quantitative analysis that

[14] Letter dated January 2, 1974.

launched the scientific quest in IR was 'naive and turns out to have been incorrect,' that 'part of the important learning experience with scientifically oriented IR research has been that patterns can be identified, often more easily and validly, through *qualitative* research procedures,' that there is 'no inherent incompatibility between quantitative research strategies that process a large number of cases in the sample and qualitative procedures of comparative analysis that must forego statistical analysis, given the few cases compared.'[15]

Once the many limitations of the narrow perspective were identified, some of the initial resistance to employing it as a basis for assessing IR research began to dissipate. As if all concerned realized that the stress on discontinuity, diversity, and prematurity might imply that a decade's work had accomplished little and that the field was no less disarrayed than ever, the deliberations took a sudden turn toward the end of the first session. A willingness to consider successes and failures in the development of the field from the perspective of a normal science spread among the group.[16] This culminated in a readiness to devote the remaining sessions mainly to discussions of the cumulation accomplished and the problems encountered in research on various kinds of substantive phenomena, as well as in a commitment to prepare post-Workshop memos enumerating some of the findings that could fairly be judged as cumulative. Excerpts from these memos are presented in the next section. Like the memos, the ensuing discussions focused mainly on the phenomena around which the various participants had organized their research projects, but at the same time both the deliberations and the post-Workshop memos covered, at least tangentially, many of the fifteen topics listed in the pre-Workshop agenda (see above).

Before turning to the assessment of successes and failures that followed the early resistance to such an endeavor, it may be useful to speculate about the sources of this resistance. In part, of course, it reflected the predisposition to set forth overall perspectives which dominates the opening sessions of most conferences. Doubtless, too, much of the wariness about construing the dynamics of cumulation

[15] Letter dated January 2, 1974.

[16] Subsequently J. David Singer recorded a different assessment of the extent to which a readiness to employ a normal science perspective spread among the group: 'I differ with your interpretation that we were able to leave the old and sterile 'behavioral-traditional' debates behind us. I detected a strong undercurrent of anti-scientific sentiment, and I don't mean merely anti-positivist sentiment. To my ears, many of the speeches sounded as if they had come from Hedley Bull or Hans Morgenthau, in the sense that the need for reproducible evidence was either ignored or rejected. How much longer will we believe that if one person *thinks* such and such is true, that this constitutes useful *knowledge*?' (Letter dated November 28, 1973.)

narrowly is well founded. Scientific research in the field has only just begun and there are a number of urgent problems which need to be investigated. And surely it is also the case that paradigmatic competition fosters progress as well as discontinuity.

While there are thus good reasons to be skeptical about the utility of treating IR as a normal science, another possible factor needs to be noted: most of the Workshop participants are, so to speak, first-generation scientists in the field. Most of them — and their projects — helped initiate the break with the traditional modes of investigating international phenomena, a task which required not only the perfection of new research techniques, but also the allocation of considerable time to arguing the philosophical case for scientific inquiry. As a consequence, many of those at the Workshop may have developed the orientations of the revolutionary scientist even as their work served to establish a normal science. The inclination to reconceptualize core notions, experiment with new methodologies, and construct new theoretical models became habitual for them, inclinations which run counter to the normal scientist's predisposition toward building a knowledge base in small increments through replications and extensions of previous work. Temperamentally, in short, many of the Workshop participants may be too set in their ways to practice normal science or to fully appreciate its products.

There was considerable support for this interpretation in many of the pre-Workshop papers. Taken together, these revealed that launching and managing large-scale research projects constituted profoundly personal experiences for the Workshop members. They had been asked to prepare project autobiographies, but in a number of instances the results were more in the nature of personal autobiographies, so intimate was the link between their research and their own development. The models and findings generated by the projects now stand on their own, as the products of any scientific inquiry should, but several papers made it clear that exasperation and frustration, as well as confusion and extensive revision, marked the evolution of research designs, the gathering of data, and the interpretation of results. That Charles McClelland reported that he now engages in research tasks that were 'well outside [his] abilities, skills, and interests' only seven years earlier is a measure of the depth of the impact that the projects had upon their creators. Intellectual growth of this magnitude and the deep emotional commitment depicted by many of the papers are hardly likely to be associated with easy acquisition of the patience and detachment that sustains the practice of normal science. The difficulties inherent in such development are plainly manifest in Rummel's compelling analysis of how he came into scientific IR research and why he is now dubious about its sufficiency. Or ponder Russett's admission that his research is eclectic in its approach to a number of substantive areas because there are too many urgent problems to warrant painstaking attention to a single line of inquiry and too many levels of analysis relevant to any particular problem. Or consider Alger's account of how he became increasingly (and self-consciously) immersed in the daily routines of the United Nations as his research design developed and his data accumulated. Or reflect on the present writer's work over the last decade, work that could readily be characterized as an impetuous, discontinuous, and restless moving from one concept to another — from issues to linkages to adaptive mechanisms — in search of theoretical handles.

Even more illustrative of the foregoing explanation of why the Workshop participants initially resisted the concept of cumulation is the fact that, throughout the deliberations and in the papers, relatively little attention was paid to perhaps the most significant trend in scientific IR research today — namely, the proliferation of studies and findings generated through events data analysis. Only Azar and Hermann, who were among the youngest in attendance and who might well be regarded as second-generation scientists, called attention to the existence of a mounting number of convergent (and cumulating) inquiries spawned by what has properly been called the events data movement.[17] There is, in other words, a second — and possibly even a third and fourth — generation of IR scientists who were not fully represented at the Workshop, who would have been more comfortable with the concept of cumulation, and who have compiled in but a few brief years impressive foundations for a cumulative structure.[18]

This is not to suggest that the first generation of IR researchers have ceased to be productive or that their successors are making more valuable contributions. Generational differences exist in every science and progress by any group probably cannot occur without the prior groundwork laid by its predecessors. As long as the progression from one generation to the next is not discontinuous, knowledge will cumulate. Happily, continuity can readily be traced through the few generations of IR scholars who have been committed to scientific inquiry.

[17] See below (pp. 226–28) for data which Azar compiled to show the growing number of inquiries based on events data.

[18] For a assessment of the output of the events data movement, see Philip M. Burgess and Raymond W. Lawton, *Indicators of International Behavior: An Assessment of Events Data Research* (Beverly Hills, Cal. Sage, 1972).

V. ISLANDS OF CUMULATION

Once the attention of the Workshop members turned to specifying what knowledge had been cumulated as a consequence of their research efforts, the discussions did not lag. Evident in some of the pre-Workshop papers and in the excerpts from the post-Workshop memos presented below, virtually all of the participants believed that their work had yielded reliable empirical findings about the dynamics of world politics. Viewed collectively, however, the degree of overlap among the findings is not conspicuous. Most of them amount to what Russett called 'islands of cumulation,' each substantively independent of the others and without an overarching theory or paradigm to link them. To be sure, in a few instances some of the findings of several projects converged and reinforced each other, and at no point during the deliberations did two or more participants identify findings that were contradictory. Nevertheless, as the following account indicates, the cumulated findings are better described as islands rather than continents.

The main exception to this conclusion, perhaps approaching subcontinental proportions, involves convergence around the finding that domestic or internal variables are important sources of the external behavior of states. Three participants, North, Rosenau, and Rummel, all reported consistent findings that depicted such variables as powerful determinants of international behavior. Indeed, Rummel went so far as to contend that the 'stability' of the findings on the importance of wealth, political accountability, and size were so consistent, and their ability to account for the observed variance in state behavior so 'near perfect' ('correlations over 0.9 are commonplace'), that they represent 'natural social laws.' Rummel reiterated this view, along with a number of other conclusions relative to the contribution of his Dimensionality of Nations (DON) project to the cumulative thrust of the field, in his post-Workshop memo:

> By way of background, I should stress that over DON's ten years I have emphasized accumulativeness as a central goal, whether in selecting variables, doing analyses, assessing methodological questions, or developing theory. To detail this accumulation with attention to context, qualifications, and implications, then, would be to offer again the variety of DON research reports and books, especially my *Applied Factor Analysis* and *Dimensions of Nations*, and my articles in Singer's *Quantitative International Politics*, in Russett's *Peace, War, and Numbers*, and in the 1965 *General System's Yearbook* (the middle part on conflict). But of course this accumulation can be synthesized, compressed, and the most important detailed generalizations abstracted, and I am now attempting to do so in a series of four or five volumes. Leaving details aside, however, I certainly should be able to illustrate here some specific *areas of accumulation* and some corresponding *general findings*. This task requires first unpacking the concept of accumulation.

Now, accumulation has two meanings relevant to our mutual efforts. One is to build on others' works, to 'stand on the shoulders of giants.' The results, theories, and ideas of others provide a base for extending knowledge another increment. Accumulation also means convergence towards reliable knowledge which is invariant across social scientists, across data sets, and across methodologies. The two meanings of accumulation are mutually independent: we may continue to build on the work of others but yet have little convergence towards reliable results within a scientist's idiosyncratic research program.

Regarding accumulation as building on others' works, as a rule I have infused each stage of my data collection and analyses with the results, hypotheses, and theories of other social scientists. For example, along with the variables of specific concern to me for an analysis, I normally include those indexing others' relevant findings and conclusions. On this I refer you to Table 4.3 beginning on page 194 of the *Dimensions of Nations*, which shows how DON's first large data collection and analyses were related to the relevant literature.

In this sense, others who attended our conference also are accumulating. Bruce Russett's works clearly show attention to this, as do those of Dave Singer, Hayward Alker, Harold Guetzkow, Chad Alger, Bob North, and others. So I claim no special virtue. However, when I consider the presently voluminous and multifold, quantitative-scientific IR literature as a whole, I must say that such accumulation is rare. In article after article, paper after paper, we find quantitative analyses similar in design, scope, or intention to those published years ago with no attempt to build on or relate to these previous analyses.

One example of this wide-scale practice will suffice. Within a period of six months I received two research reports from opposite parts of the country. One was an expensive and extensive attempt to define the attribute dimensions of nations factor analyzing around ninety attributes. The other research report similarly carried out a broad-scale factor analysis on some fifty nation attributes and behaviors, including variables involving a variety of cooperation and conflict event data. Both authors were unaware of each other, which is understandable. But neither tried to learn from, reference, or index in their studies the similar analyses of Cattell (published in 1949 and 1952), Bruce Russett, Brian Berry, myself, and many others: the analyses were done as though none had gone before. Such isolated work is scientifically ridiculous and wastes crucial resources. They should be subject to strong scientific criticism.

Considering accumulations as convergence on stable or reliable knowledge, this, too, has been one of my missions. A major line of investigation is never considered to be completed unless the results are systematically compared with the relevant findings of others. Evidence of this are Chapter 10 of *Dimensions of Nations*, the article in Singer's *Quantitative International Politics*, the comparison of all domestic conflict analyses in my *General Systems Yearbook* paper on field theory, and Tanter's DON-supported replication of my conflict dimensions. More important, DON's ten years encompass a concerted and programmatic building on the literature, on the systematic comparison with others' results, and on DON's continually growing, in-house experience. What has been described variously as a factory analysis machine, as a narrow focus, as exploiting the same old data, or as a love affair with aggregate data, simply has been this kind of accumulation within a broad area of knowledge on the problem of war.

Out of all this, what can I point to as particular *accumulated* findings? These divide into those concerning methodology, data, substance, and theory. Regarding methodology, recall that when DON's research began in 1962 factor analysis had never been applied to international *relations or behavior*, although Cattell, Berry, and Schnore had published applications to cross-national variation in attributes or characteristics. There were some scattered multiple regression analyses, but not canonical analyses, no discriminate analyses, no multidimensional scaling; although applied here and there, the correlation coefficient was still a strange animal indeed. And *APSR* articles wasted pages explaining the nature of the chi square and its application to a simple fourfold table. In this context I undertook a concerted effort to determine the usefulness and applicability of multivariate methods and particularly factor analysis in analyzing international relations. *Applied Factor Analysis* was one fruit of that effort.

This *research on research* encompassed studying the appropriate mathematics, scanning all the relevant methodological literature, experimenting with a variety of permutations of a variety of techniques on a variety of transformed and untransformed data, and so on. From this experience and the hundreds of multivariate regression analyses, factor analyses, canonical analyses, and so on, I have done over ten years, sufficient evidence has accumulated for the following.

First, and in broad brush, international relations as an area of research is more appropriate for multivariate methods than are sociology and psychology. Second, factor analysis *understood as a broad set of models* will be a central quantitative methodology for international relations in future decades. I realize the latter opinion is unpopular and that I am probably the only one among the participants in our conference to hold it. You should realize, however, that broadly understood factor analysis includes *principal components or axes, component analysis, image analysis, similarity transformation, canonical analysis, discriminate analysis, multi-dimensional scaling* (which is to component factor analysis what integration is to differentiation in calculus), *multiple regression* (a special case of canonical analysis) and *partial correlation*. In this comprehensive sense which could be shown mathematically, factor analysis incorporates the major mathematical models being used in econometrics, psychometrics, theoretical physics and quantum physics.

Turning now to data, from the beginning I have been accumulating a core set of data whose characteristics would be well known and understood through a variety of analyses, and would thus be most generally useful. In collecting my data I have made sure that they were always in a form immediately usable by others. This entailed, in the style of Singer and Russett, giving explicit definitions, coding rules, and so forth. These data are now all being transferred to the Michigan Consortium, and should provide a good base for others to accumulate upon. Little more need be said on this subject; if DON is known for anything, it is for data. To strike at one stereotype, however, I do collect other data than that on conflict events from the *New York Times*; event data comprises only about five percent of my total collection.

Moving on to substantive accumulation, as still meaning a convergence on stable and reliable findings, based on a decade of intensive, programmatic quantitative research and on continuous comparison with the results of others, I offer the following generalizations. International relations is highly structured: the treaties, trade, aid, threats, GNP per capita, defense expenditures, literacy, riots, and so forth of nations are organized into very stable and powerful patterns. No other area of human interaction manifests such strong structure. To illustrate, consider that psychologists, who are noted for perceiving psychology as a systematic science involving clear relationships and structure, are comfortable with correlation coefficients between 0.20 and 0.30. They believe it phenomenal to account for 40 or 50 percent of the variance in their criteria variables. And yet, in IR correlations over 4.9 and indeed ranging to 0.98 and 0.99 are commonplace; I for one now refuse to interpret correlation coefficients below 0.50 because so many are above this level.

On this contrast between psychology and IR, a recent conversation I had with Raymond B. Cattell may be enlightening. For over two decades and with millions of dollars Cattell has been programmatically delineating the major personality dimensions explaining behavior. I asked him therefore, at most how much variance in individual behavior could be accounted for by his resulting scales, tests, and so on. Clearly satisfied with the achievement, he said that he could now explain between 25 and 50 percent of behavioral variation. I was surprised: similar work on nations enables us to account for around 90 percent of the variance in a variety of behaviors. In one study (reported in the Russett, *Peace, War, and Numbers*) power parity between the U.S. and object nations statistically accounted for 88 percent of the variation in U.S., Western European and deterrence behaviors towards 117 nations, including such different object nations as Yemen, India, Japan, USSR, and China. Eventually, the implications of this strong IR structure will seep through the profession. The point here is that the fact of such structure is now core knowledge based on accumulated scientific research.

Now for a second generalization. I find that the major *dimensions* accounting for national variation in attributes concern wealth, politics, and power (or size). Nations can be generally characterized as rich or poor, democratic or totalitarian, powerful or weak. *Every* study which has included appropriate variables has shown that wealth, politics, and size are dimensions of social and political groups, whether nations, regions, provinces, cities, small groups, and so on. The stability in findings on wealth, politics, and size is so consistent that their existence can be phrased as social laws.

Moreover, the two or three dozen analyses having the relevant variables delineated Catholic culture, foreign conflict behavior, domestic conflict behavior, and density as secondary national dimensions, even though these studies involved different time frames, researchers, and designs. I therefore believe quantitative analysis has converged on a stable and reliable set of dimensions for characterizing nations, and in which we can place confidence as empirical concepts for understanding and explaining modern international behavior.

How do these dimensions link to such behavior? Consistently through dozens of quantitative analyses, some involving all U.S. dyadic behavior, some involving all Chinese dyadic behavior, some involving samples of Soviet, Brazilian, Indonesian, Indian, Japanese, Cuban, Dutch, English, Israeli, Egyptian, and Polish behavior, some involving cross-sectional data, and some involving longitudinal data, I find that wealth, power, and politics are the most important dimensions in statistically account for behavior. Furthermore, the degree of power parity between two nations best explains statistically their dyadic conflict behavior; cooperation is best explained statistically *in relation to conflict* and on the basis of wealth, politics, and power distances jointly. Here I do not mean the usual social science multiple correlations between 0.30 and 0.50; I mean correlations explaining around 90 percent of the variance and with the odds of actually being zero exceeding a million to one.

Another set of substantive findings has to do with conflict behavior alone. Through my analyses and comparisons with others, I consistently found domestic conflict behavior for nations as a whole to involve a turmoil dimension (of riots and demonstrations) statistically independent of revolution and guerilla warfare dimensions (a finding first published in 1963 and subsequently well illustrated by American domestic turmoil). Moreover, I consistently found that for all nations domestic and foreign conflict behavior atre statistically independent, whether I was analyzing events data in isolation, whether partialing out different levels of wealth, power, or density, or whether holding constant different qualities such as Catholic culture, Western-pluralistic democracy, or communism. Domestic conflict does not statistically help to explain foreign conflict neither do the other national characteristics. Generalizing across several dozen separate studies, to account for foreign conflict quantitatively requires analyzing conflict dyadically. It requires bringing in dyadic differences in wealth, power, politics, and culture, and geographic distances.

Turning finally to theory, my results have consistently converged with those of others in establishing the explanatory and integrating value of field theory. Most find this a strange assertion and there are rumblings that field theory is an unsuccessful paradigm. But this always occurs with a new paradigm; its value is rejected out of hand, at least until evidence for it percolates through the profession, its methods become familiar, and it proves able to resolve some outstanding issues.

Regarding the evidence for field theory we now have, however, I can say this. Results accumulated across perhaps fifty different and independent analyses clearly show field theory (the Model II version) can explain statistically the linkages between nation attributes and dyadic international behavior. Second, the theory synthesizes within itself such a variety of ideas and results in a variety of fields that I see it as the general or broad-gauge scientific IR theory for which we have been searching.

So much for my accumulation. I realize its controversial nature; it is immodest, perhaps arrogant, surely dogmatic. I apologize, but also ask that you realize that a decade of work is condensed into a few generalizations. I cannot surround them here with the necessary qualifications, justifications, and evidence. All this is eventually forthcoming and many details have been established in the books and reports mentioned before.[19]

In his post-Workshop memo Robert North also noted that many of the findings of his project with Choucri highlighted the importance of domestic variables, especially with respect to population, economic, and technological growth. Indeed, in some instances North characterized some of these findings as 'persistent,' albeit derived from a 'limited number of cases':

1. Inferring from cases studied, it is probably characteristic of states and empires, as well as of other societal systems, that quite different causal 'paths' and sequences may lead to the same or similar outcomes. [Strong inference from empirical findings.]
2. Inferring from cases studied, many different public and private motivations and interests will contribute in various proportions to any given national policy or act. Some of these motivations and interests will be economic, some will be strategic, some will be matters of prestige and

[19] Letter dated August 1, 1973.

status, and so forth. Some are likely to be more important in one situation; others will be more important in other situations. [Strong inference from empirical findings.]

3. In cases studied, a country's levels and patterns of external conflict and violence are closely associated with domestic growth on critical dimensions. [persistent empirical finding in limited number of cases.]
4. Levels and rates of increase in population density and in domestic economic and technological growth contribute strongly to the expansion of a country's external activities and interests in cases studies. [Empirical finding in limited number of cases.]
5. In cases studied, collisions and crises involving two or more countries are explained in considerable part by the expansions of the interests and activities of those countries beyond their legal frontiers. [Empirical finding in limited number of cases.]
6. The levels and rates of change of a country's military expenditures in the past are frequently among the strongest predictors of that country's military expenditures in the future. This seems to be explainable to a large extent in terms of bureaucractic processes and effects. [Persistent empirical finding in limited number of cases.]
7. In cases studied, increases in arms expenditures and the arms race phenomenon are best explained by domestic factors within the competing countries, and only after that by interactions between them. A country's own arms expenditures are likely to be accounted for by its own bureaucratic demands and processes and by its own technological and economical growth, and then by the military expenditures of its rivals. [Empirical finding in limited number of cases.]
8. The growth of a country's military establishment (measured in terms of defense expenditures) contributes strongly to that country's collisions with the activities and interests of other countries in cases studied. [Empirical finding in limited number of cases.]
9. Collisions of interests and activities between Country *A* and Country *B* are best explained in cases studied by *A*'s defense expenditures and *B*'s violence behavior (and vice versa). [Empirical finding in limited number of cases.]
10. According to circumstances, a country's alliance commitments (1) may increase as the strength of its military establishment declines relative to the military establishments of its rivals; (2) may decline as the strength of its military establishment increases; or (3) may increase (or decrease) as the strength of its military establishment increases (or decreases). In general, a country is likely to make up for a relatively weak military establishment by seeking alliances or remedy its weak alliance position by strengthening its military establishment or, if need be and it can, attempt to strengthen both.
11. In cases studied, a country's alliance formation is best explained by the defense expenditures of its rivals. [Empirical finding in limited number of cases.]
12. A country's alliance formation tends to be positively associated with its technological and economic growth in cases studied [Empirical finding in limited number of cases.]
13. The relationships between a country's short-term interest and long-term interests are frequently inverse. [Inference from empirical findings.][20]

[20]Memo dated July 2, 1973, on 'Some Findings and Inferences from a Study

In reflecting on the substantive cumulation achieved by the Yale Political Data Program for his post-Workshop memo, Russett also focused on the strength of domestic variables as sources of the external behavior of states:

> I think one of the best examples of cumulation in our work involves our examination of the determinants (*other than* the interactive, 'arms race' ones) of national levels of military expenditure.
>
> In his intensive and extensive review of the arms race literature drawing on the Richardson tradition, Peter Busch (in Russett, 1970a) noted some of the severe deficiencies in work to that point. Among them were data of poor quality, data of very limited quantity for any particular set of interactions (and hence a severe limitation in the degrees of freedom available for statistical analysis), and perhaps most important, serious theoretical deficiencies. The latter was manifested both in frequent rather mechanical and politically uninformed borrowings from physical and economic models, and in a relative neglect of intra-national influences on arms acquisition, especially on the ways other nations' arms expenditures would be perceived. Furthermore, he noted that even in the best empirical arms race studies, no more than about half the *variance* in arms expenditures was explained, and the *levels* around which the variance occurred were explained hardly at all. This conclusion has led us to a variety of efforts to explore the effect of other possible determinants of arms spending, focusing primarily on the United States but frequently using other nations' experience as a basis for comparison:
>
> 1. Attempted international explanations of military spending have focused largely on conflict interactions, to the neglect of intra-alliance bargaining and burden-sharing. General rather atheoretical cross-national studies of military expenditure levels have shown a consistent relationship between nations' size and the share of their resources devoted to military efforts (Russett, 1964 and Russett et. al., 1964, Part B.1.) Some work, however, has been done on alliance burden-sharing from the perspective of collective goods theory, notably by Olson and Zeckhauser (in Russett (ed.), 1968) and by Pryor, Ypersele de Strihou, and Burgess and Robinson (refs. in Russett, 1970a). They have shown that in certain kinds of alliances the theory predicts, and is confirmed by empirical evidence, disproportionate military spending by the various states in the alliance, whereby the larger states spend even more than would be predicted from the relatively larger size of their economies. Russett (1970a, ch. 4) further develops the theory to specify what kinds of alliances it can be expected to apply to (deterrence, not defense or warfighting alliances) and the kinds of states which would, despite the alliance, spend greater-than-predicted amounts on military goods (where they lacked confidence in the big power's deterrent resolve or ability, where military spending provided them with important particular benefits not provided by the alliance (internal security, research and development, control of colonies), or where they are coerced to greater efforts by the big power in control of the defense policies of the alliance members). Empirical results using data gathered at Yale (Taylor and Hudson, 1972) showed that disproportionate large-power expenditure occurred in those alliances meeting

of the Major Powers, 1970–1914,' from Nazlie Choucri and Robert C. North, *Nations in Conflict: National Growth and International Violence* (San Francisco: W.H. Freeman and Co., 1975).

the conditions for application of the theory (NATO, recent Warsaw Pact experience and, with modifications, SEATO and the Rio Pact) and failed to occur in those alliances not meeting the specifications of the theory (CENTO and the Arab League). Recent work by a former member of the Data Program (Starr, 1972) has confirmed and strengthened our findings for the Warsaw Pact.

2. Several scholars (including Huntington, Gray and Gregory, and Cobb; refs. in Russett 1970a) had examined the role of the legislature, and specifically the differential rewards to various legislative constituencies in stimulating or maintaining high levels of military expenditure. The results of these studies were indeterminate, due largely to methodological difficulties I discussed in Russett, 1970b. Further analysis, however, (Russett, 1970a, chs. 2 & 3), showed clearly that legislators from districts with high proportionate military employment (but *not* military contracting) were more likely to favor high levels of military spending than were other legislators. Moreover, and more interesting, such legislators were more likely to approve of a variety of 'hawkish' foreign policy acts than were legislators from districts of low military employment. This finding has been challenged (Cobb, 1973), but has been reconfirmed by further studies at Yale (Moyer, 1973 and in progress) and elsewhere (Clotfelter, 1970). An additional very important finding has emerged from this work of Moyer: Legislators' positions on issues of military spending and foreign policy are much better explained by their general ideological perspectives than by the military dependence of their districts. While the latter variables typically explain about 5 percent of Congressional voting on foreign policy issues, the former typically explain about half the variance. In recent years at least (since 1967) various indices of conservatism on domestic issues (e.g., civil rights, civil liberties, welfare) are very powerful in explaining foreign policy voting. This finding of a relative unidimensionality, and hence polarization in the political system, does not apply to earlier post-World War II years, but there is some indication that a similar pattern existed in the 1930s. This has led us to studies of change over time in military spending in districts of members of selected legislative committees (Arnold, 1973), further supporting the initial finding about the effect of military employment and strengthening the causal inferences, and to a major study of changes in ideology and consensus in American politics over a 35-year period (Rosenberg, in progress). The result has been cumulation in theory, methodology, and findings.
3. Study of the domestic sources of support and opposition to arms expenditure also requires examination of the relative economic gains and losses from military spending accruing to various segments of the economic system. In Russett 1970a, chs. 5 & 6, I found that in the United States the proportion of the GNP devoted to military spending varied in important degree inversely with expenditures for fixed capital formation and for governmental expenditure on social capital (health and education). Similar but less sharp or consistent tradeoff patterns were found in other Western countries examined (Britain, Canada, and France), and I suggested some tentative theoretical explanations of these differences. Again, these results have been challenged on methodological grounds (Hollenhurst and Ault, 1971), but have been further confirmed by our work at Yale (Russett, 1971 and Lee, 1973).
4. These results have encouraged us in further explorations of various

influences, other than conflictful arms race interactions, on military spending. One of these is my study, using public opinion data over a 30-year period, of attitudes among the American populace toward military spending (Russett, 1972). This shows a very sharp recent change in the level of support for military spending, especially a reversal of attitudes among the attentive public, and tests various hypotheses in an effort to account for the change. Another is our study (Hanson and Russett, 1973) of the response in the stock market to various escalatory and deescalatory events in the Korean and Vietnam Wars. Here we tested various hypotheses derived in large-part from neo-Marxian theory about attitudes in the business community. In general we failed to confirm those hypotheses, and even for the later years of the Vietnam war found evidence to disconfirm some of them. These results have led us now to a major study, employing interviews, questionnaires, content analysis, and event data, of key American elite groups, notably major corporation executives and senior military officers.[21]

In his post-Workshop memo Charles Hermann not only shared the view that a number of findings had highlighted the importance of domestic factors as sources of foreign policy, but he also identified three other islands of cumulation:

(1) the effect of size, wealth, and political orientation on the external behavior or states;
(2) the relationship between internal conflict of states and their external conflict;
(3) the nature of the differences and biases of various sources providing accounts of international activity;
(4) some effects of externally generated crises.

There are, of course, a number of other substantive topics that could be added to this list, but these represent the topics with which I feel familiar and in addition share the following characteristics, (1) findings have been established by more than one investigator, (2) some, if not all, of the research on the topic has built upon the work of others, and (3) different data and research techniques have been utilized.

Let me comment briefly on each. First, the size, wealth, and political orientation properties of nations and their effect on state behavior has been identified in a number of factor analytic studies by Cattell, Rummel, Tanter, Sawyer and others. Rosenau has attempted to use these dimensions as a basic typology for classifying nations. He and his students have reaffirmed the importance of these variables in accounting for broad categories of cooperative and conflictful foreign behaviors. So also have studies with events data in which the behavioral variables have been dimensions other than generalized conflict and cooperation (e.g., Salmore and Hermann, Salmore, East and Hermann). These last group of studies (each with different data, time periods, and dependent variables), however, cast serious doubt on the utility of using those three dimensions as an eightfold typology for nations with theoretical implications for their foreign policy. Remarkably, little has been done to offer a theoretical explanation for the reoccurring importance of these variables, and with few exceptions (e.g., East) those scholars writing about economic

[21] Memo dated July 5, 1973. The references for this memo can be found at the end of Bruce M. Russett, 'Apologia pro Vita Sua,' in James N. Rosenau (ed.), *In Search of Global Patterns*, pp. 31–37.

development or physical size have not acknowledged the existence of this pattern of empirical findings.

The second topic — the relationship between internal conflict and external conflict — also has a part of its genesis in the Dimensionality of Nations project. Unlike the first mentioned topic, however, the basic relationship appears to have been anticipated from several theoretical orientations, e.g., the 'scapegoat' hypothesis, the 'frustration-aggression,' hypothesis. The initial factor analytic studies by Rummel and others were surprising because no trace of the expected relationship was detected. Wilkenfeld and later Wilkenfeld and Zinnes have demonstrated the role of alternative political systems as an intervening variable that at least partially identifies the conditions under which internal conflict is associated with external conflict. To my knowledge, no one has conducted a study that will test among the alternative theoretical explanations which could account for the findings.

The third topic — the nature of differences and biases of various sources of international activity — must be regarded as the primary product to date of the events data research. Research done two or more years ago only recently began to appear in the journals (e.g., Burrowes, Azar, McGowan, Hermann, Doran, Pendley and Autunes.) A number of findings seem to be reappearing in these studies, although no one has done a systematic catalog of them. For example, data sources more removed from the acting nation (such as the so-called global sources or sources published in another geographical region from the actor) tend to report proportionately more of the acting nation's conflictful behavior than of its cooperative behavior. Comparable diplomatic events are more likely to be reported by most sources outside the actor's country if the initiating nation is widely acknowledged as a global or regional power. I have a haunting suspicion that findings such as these may represent another case of rediscovering the wheel. A check of the journalism literature might demonstrate that these differences have been empirically documented for some time. The duplication, if indeed it is, may have its origin in the need for those of us collecting events data to produce some publications when the data are not yet sufficiently developed to allow more substantive work.

Finally, the effects of crisis represent an area of empirical research in which recent accumulation has been as much conceptual and theoretical as empirical. We have had for some time the repeated documentation of certain consequences of crisis such as the tendency for decisions to be made by small groups, the reduction of perceived alternatives relative to adversaries, and the tendency for escalatory hostile responses. Such findings emerge from content analysis studies, interviews with participants, simulations, and comparative case studies. However, there also have been some disturbing exceptions to these patterns. Recent books by Holsti and by Hermann have not only distinguished different definitions of crisis but also alternative aspects of crisis, each producing different effects. Hence some of the exceptions to the noted effects of crisis reported by such scholars as North, McClelland, Paige, Robinson, Zinnes, Schwartz, Milburn, Glenn Snyder, Siverson, and Young are attributable to looking at different aspects of the same general phenomena. The explicit recognition of these different components and the effort to articulate the assumptions associated with each represents an important advance.

Three trends may be underway which reduce the future study of crises on foreign policy, just when important new work should be expected. First, the study of crisis behavior no longer seems to be 'in vogue' either among government agencies (who funded much of the research) or political scientists. As the cold war recedes and the actual incidence of international crisis with the potential of military conflict decreases in frequency, the urgency of the problem declines. Second, crisis studies have been criticized as too narrow and focusing on only a small aspect of international behavior. One might be tempted to say as a rejoinder that it is a research problem with manageable boundaries, but it would be interesting to see how many former contributors to the study of crisis have moved on to projects that concern a more comprehensive range of foreign behaviors. Finally, much of the crisis research has focused on the effects of crises on the decision makers and the organizations in which they operate or, at the other extreme, on the long-run stability of the international system. Missing to a considerable degree have been the studies that linked these consequences to the likelihood of war or other immediate outcome behaviors.

For each of the four topics, I have attempted to identify the substantive developments, some (but not all) of the contributors, and one or two problems that must be overcome if further accumulation in these areas is to proceed. Let me say in closing that another strategy which I toyed with in writing this report was the enumeration of empirically discovered 'puzzles' in international relations. In other words, observations recently established for which we now need an explanation. One example, might be the apparent reversal in the effects of alliances found by Dave Singer and his associates when comparing 19th and 20th century data. The lack of association between internal and external conflict (when such an association had been widely assumed to exist) was another example until Wilkenfeld's contribution. I believe that a fair number of these puzzles exist and that a simple inventory of them might launch considerable research among younger scholars casting about for a problem of significance.[22]

Anther island of cumulative research was underscored by Ole Holsti, who in his post-Workshop reflections called attention to the growth of knowledge about the effects of stress on the performance of foreign policy-makers. In order to outline this area of inquiry, Holsti submitted Table 1 which summarizes a lengthy analysis he co-authored with Alexander George.[23] The three columns of Table 1 suggest that work in this area has resulted in at least three different islands rather than just a single one.

Azar's post-Workshop memo cited cumulating knowledge at still another level of analysis. Instead of stressing what had been learned about the actions of states or the behavior of foreign policy officials, he focused on 'some of the more interesting findings' of his project relative to the interactions of states that he sees as convergent with findings developed by other researchers:

[22] Memo dated July 30, 1973.

[23] Ole R. Holsti and Alexander L. George, 'The Effects of Stress on the Performance of Foreign Policy-Makers,' in G.P. Cotter (ed.), *Political Science Annual, Vol. VI: Individual Decision-Making* (Indianapolis: Bobbs-Merrill, 1975), pp. 255–319.

Table 1. Summary of Three Perspectives on Decision-Making under Stress

Conceptualization of decision-making	*Decision-making as the result of individual choice*	*Decision-making as the product of group interaction*	*Decision-making as the resultant of bargaining within bureaucratic organizations*
Sources of theory insight, and evidence	Cognitive psychology Dynamic psychology	Social psychology Sociology of small groups	Organization theory Sociology of bureaucracies Bureaucratic politics
Premises	Importance of subjective appraisal and cognitive processes	Most decisions made by elite groups Group is different from the sum of its members Group dynamics affect substance and quality of decisions	Central organizational values are imperfectly internalized Organizational behavior is political behavior Structure and SOPs affect substance and quality of decisions
Constraints on rational Decision-making	Cognitive limits on rationality Information processing distorted by cognitive consistency dynamics Individual differences on abilities related to decision-making, e.g.: Problem-solving ability Tolerance of ambiguity Defensiveness and anxiety Information seeking Cognitive dissonance (post-decision phase)	Groups less effective for some decision-making tasks Pressures for conformity Risk-taking propensity of groups (?) Quality of leadership	Imperfect information, resulting from: Centralization Hierarchy Specialization Organizational inertia Conflict between individual and organizational utilities Bureaucratic politics and bargaining dominate decision-making
Intervening variables	Reduced span of attention Cognitive rigidity Time perspective	Size of decision unit Frequency and intensity of interaction Group cohesion	Level of decision-making Size of decision unit Level of information entry Access to decision-makers by special interests
Range of variation in performance under high stress	Low variation	Medium variation	High variation

Table 1. *Cont.*

Primary sources of variation in performance under high stress	Personality traits (e.g. manifest anxiety)	Quality of leadership	Nature or source of stress (e.g. international crisis)
Effects of stress on (Modal performance): Search	More stereotyped definition of the situation Search for information likely to be more active but less productive General erosion of creativity	Less accurate definition of the situation Reduced breadth and quality of search for information on the situation and alternatives	Higher quality information on the situation and policy alternatives available Both positive and negative effects on aspects of search
Evaluation	Evaluation likely to be dominated by primitive criteria (black and white, zero sum, etc.)	Less critical evaluation of alternatives Likely to be dominated by group pressures for conformity ('groupthink'), premature closure	Likely to be based on better general knowledge Decision-makers have access to better expertise and analytical skills
Choice	Choice likely to be dominated by short-run consideration and by previously established patterns of coping, whether appropriate or not	Choice likely to be dominated by parochial values; for example, 'what is best for the group' Tend to overgeneralize past experience	More likely to result from analysis by advocates of general values, rather than bargaining by proponents of parochial ones Quality takes precedence over consensus
Feedback	Less sensitive	Less sensitive	More sensitive
Prognosis: decisions made under stress vs. under 'normal' (i.e. low stress) circumstances	Quality: Lower Acceptance: Not applicable Time: Faster Resources expended: Higher in short time period	Quality: Lower Acceptance: Higher Time: Faster Resources expended: Variable to lower	Quality: Higher Acceptance: Uncertain-lower Time: Faster Resources expended Greater in short time, but a different mix

1. There is sufficient empirical evidence to suggest that differential reporting of events data in public sources calls for the necessity to utilize more than one source in gathering inter-nation events data. The number and identity of such sources must be determined empirically by the investigator. This is influenced by the reputation, accessibility and resourcefulness of the sources used in gathering newsworthy events. (This finding is supported by the evidence established by Robert Burrowes, George Antunes and Charles Doran, Walter Corson, and others.) Finding reported in *International Studies Quarterly* (Sept., 1972).
2. When two symmetrical (in capabilities) parties enter a conflict situation, they tend to escalate their hostile actions towards one another a) symmetrically; b) reduce the chronological time intervening between their consecutive hostile signals or actions; and c) exhibit rigidity in their demands or conflict objectives. When they engage in conflict reduction, they tend to exhibit d) asymmetrical hostile interactions and e) increase the chronological time (or temporal distance) between consecutive hostile actions. (These findings are supportive of the research of Charles McClelland, Robert C. North, Charles Hermann and others). Findings reported in *Journal of Conflict Resolution* (June, 1972).
3. Voluntary political unification (a form of integration) takes place between two or more nation-states which i) have a similar cultural base; ii) have trustworthy decision-makers; and iii) have a tradition of sufficiently cooperative immediate past. Such a union will collapse when the following stress on the system occurs: iv) distrust among decision-makers increases and becomes publicly known; v) the relative frequency of cooperative events between the decision-makers of the former states decreases; and vi) incongruencies between articulated preferences of elites and decision-makers who established the union begin to develop and are not satisfactorily corrected or reduced. (These findings are supportive of the work on international integration conducted by Karl Deutsch, Ernst Haas, Amitai Etzioni and others). Findings are reported in *Peace Research Reviews* (November, 1970).
4. In general, data on conflict reduction activities are not easily found in public sources (particularly when compared with conflict events). Reported in *Papers of the Peace Research Society* (International), Vol. 15 (1972)[24]

In addition to noting these substantive findings, Azar's post-Workshop memo stressed the methodological cumulation that had occurred through the generation and use of events data. He noted that

> Events researchers are found in such centers as Stanford University, Michigan State University, The Ohio State University, Cornell University, Syracuse University, Massachusetts Institute of Technology, the U.S. Department of State, the Universities of Southern California, North Carolina at Chapel Hill, Hawaii, Minnesota, and Michigan and many others.
>
> In the 1960s group members had generally similar interests and produced papers and other works at about the same rates. (This is a highly interactive group.) The 1969, 1970, and 1971 conferences which I organized at Michigan State University led to increasing research on data quality control and source coverage problems. Findings showing that an events researcher should avoid

[24] Memo dated July 6, 1973.

Table 2. Characteristics of Events Research Papers*

	Type						*Number of Authors*			
	journal article	*book chapter*	*conference presentation*	*technical report*	*dissertation*	*total*	*1*	*2*	*3*	*4+*
1972	13	17	18	16	0	64	40	16	8	0
1971	0	3	13	17	1	34	22	9	1	1–7
1970	3	2	17	18	6	46	31	11	3	1–4
1969	14	3	11	15	3	46	35	8	1	1–4, 1–5
1968	5	5	0	6	0	16	10	6	0	0
1967	4	3	1	6	0	14	12	0	0	2–5
1966	7	3	1	0	0	11	8	3	0	0
1965	5	2	0	0	0	7	4	3	0	0
1964	5	0	0	1	0	6	5	0	1	0
1963	0	0	0	0	0	0	0	0	0	0
1962	0	0	0	0	0	0	0	0	0	0
1961	3	0	0	0	0	3	3	0	0	0
1960	0	0	0	0	0	0	0	0	0	0
TOTAL	58	38	61	79	10	247	171	56	14	6 [2–4s, 3–5s, 1–7]

*Based on bibliographies from Philip M. Burgess and Raymond W. Lawton, *Indicators of International Behavior: An Assessment of Events Data Research*, Sage Professional Papers in International Studies (Beverly Hills: Sage Publications, 1972) and Edward E. Azar and Joseph Ben-Dak, eds., *Theory and Practice of Events Research: Studies of Internation Actions and Interactions* (New York: Gordon and Breach, forthcoming). Compiled by Thomas Havener, University of North Carolina at Chapel Hill.

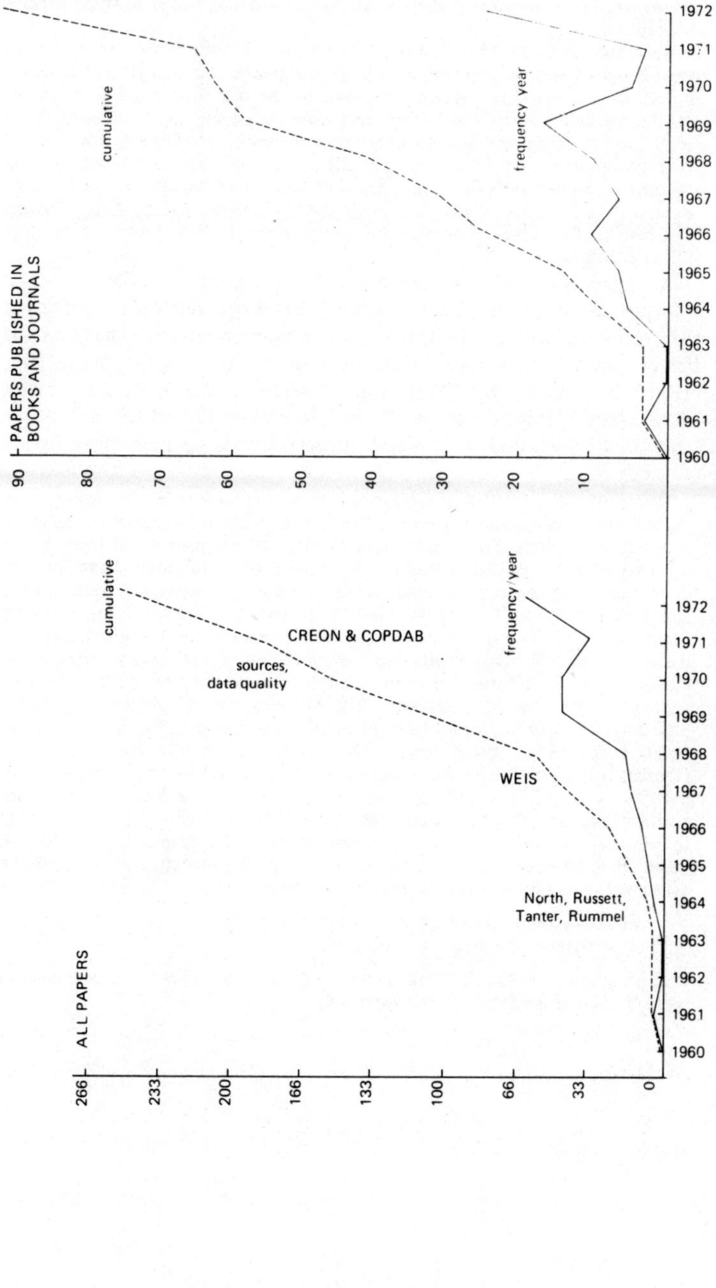

Figure 1. Production of Events Research

Prepared by Thomas Havener.

relying on a single source for data making and that he/she must use a reliable set of sources were presented by a number of scholars found in these centers of learning.

Interests and efforts of group members have overlapped considerably with those of comparative foreign policy researchers and students of reaction processes (international system patterns). In the last four years, the number of interlocking research programs increased, presaging major developments in theory building and methodological innovation. In addition, the cost of data production became an acute problem, and the sharing of data sets has become a central concern. Comparisons of data sets have already begun (e.g., Rosenau) and further sharing of events data is increasing (e.g., Azar, Choucri and North). Indicators of growth are shown in the table [2] and graph figure [1] that follow.[25]

Like Azar, Richard Rosecrance noted that cumulation had occurred with respect to interaction, but his post-Workshop memo also identified two other islands of cumulation which together constitute what he calls a 'three variable paradigm.' Furthermore, picking up a theme that recurred often during the Workshop, Rosecrance explicitly recognized that the several islands had yet to be adequately linked to each other and he thus concluded with some suggestions as to how they might be bridged:

> There was a good deal more agreement represented at the Workshop than might have been evident (1) before the fact; and (2) during some of the more contentious sessions. Specifically, there seems to be agreement in three areas: (a) that changes in infrastructure do influence international behavior and interaction. Differences between states in terms of economic development and modernization do affect the kinds of policies they pursue in international interaction. On the other hand, changes in infrastructure do not simply and rigorously predict international interaction. Part of the variance has to be explained on other bases. (b) Patterns of interaction themselves may influence subsequent patterns of interaction. The bipolarity, multipolarity, unipolarity phenomenon is to be found here, as is the arms race process. After a certain point, moreover (c) belief systems have to be taken into account. Anglo-German beliefs may have been the last to be affected by the Anglo-German pattern of interaction. Still at some point, they were affected as the competition between the two states was perceived in public and international terms. One long-time student of international affairs gave substance to this when he mentioned that when he was a boy in England after the turn of the century, the aphorism was increasingly repeated:
>
> In nineteen hundred and ten
> The Germans will conquer us then!
>
> It is of course true that all three factors influence each other, thus a triangular pattern of interrelation could be specified:

[25] Ibid.

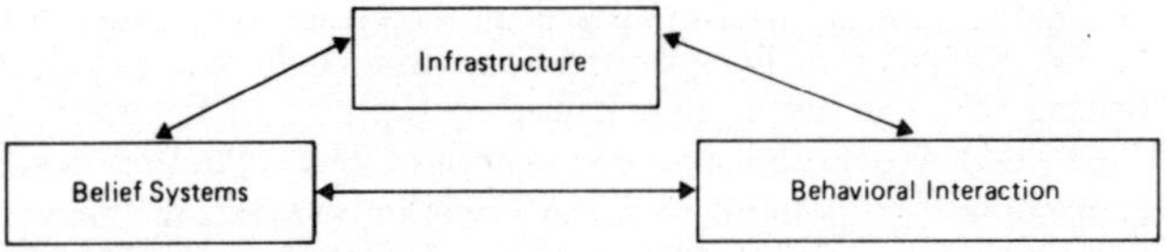

But the most sensitive and profitable linkages are likely to be more limited and more precise.

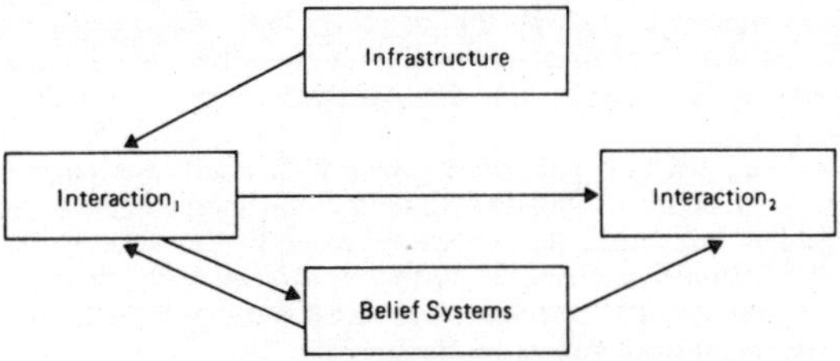

The hypotheses involved here assume that infrastructure (in the short run at least) is not affected by belief systems; that belief systems both affect and are affected by interaction patterns. And that the patterns of interaction at one stage may affect patterns of interaction at another. There may, however, be changes in belief systems that will also affect patterns of interation at a subsequent stage.

One of the difficulties of current research strategies is that investigators tend to concentrate on a single type of data (perhaps a single time period) and a single linkage. North and Choucri, Wallace, Bremer and Singer have worked on linkages between infrastructure and interaction. Alker is focusing on arms race models in which interaction (1) together with infrastructure determines interaction (2). George and Holsti have worked in the belief system area, Azar in the interaction (1) interaction (2) area. Instead of each investigator continually replicating and extending his research within the context of a *single* linkage, it would be much more desirable if investigators who have worked particularly on one pattern of linkage could extend their work to cover another pattern as well. This could be done either through new data formats in the research of one investigator, or it could be done in terms of collaboration with another investigator who has emphasized a different linkage pattern. In other words, projects which emphasize an extension of the linkages in their paradigm should receive particular consideration. Not only will given investigators broaden their own research and extend their horizons in such a manner, it is possible that new conclusions may emerge. As we argued continually at the Workshop, one of the crucial areas is system change or a change in structure. Since any given element of the three variable paradigm cannot explain all the variance, the others must be brought in. It is precisely when an investigator realizes that his approaches must be broadened to take into account additional factors that the most may be learned.

A further suggestion for more fruitful research: investigators in the physical sciences regularly exchange working papers, even those most tentatively elaborated. The information exchange occurs much more rapidly than takes place in international relations. If all those present at the conference were to agree to exchange data and papers on their most recent research foci, it is possible that more could be derived from efforts even on the existing basis.[26]

Noting that the findings generated by her project had been included in North's post-Workshop memo (see above), Nazli Choucri nevertheless felt compelled to submit a brief, overall evaluation because, like Rosecrance, she concluded retrospectively that the deliberations at Ojai underestimated the degree to which researchers had build upon each other's work:

> . . . it seems to me that there is more cumulativeness in systematic international relations than was expressed at the meeting. Particularly with respect to developments in (a) theoretical approaches to conflict and integration (b) data compilations and banks (c) data analysis and (d) interdisciplinary orientations.
>
> If you contrast what is published today with what was current in the early sixties, it is apparent that we have become increasingly sophisticated in our handling of data and in the procedures employed for analysis (statistical, functional, simulational, and also in terms of forecasting). These issues were not brought up sufficiently, nor was there an attempt to evaluate how far we have gone in the analysis of quantitative material.
>
> Our 'findings' have also been cumulative: not so much in the strict sense of adding information bit by bit, but in terms of taking off from previous work and employing each other's analyses as points of departures or at least as points of reference. In this regard, much has indeed been cumulative.
>
> In the area of (a) belief systems (content analysis and analysis of cognitions and perceptions), (b) interaction and events data, and (c) aggregate and attribute data analysis, the developments have also been cumulative. I am distressed, however, by the fact that in our face to face communications at Ojai we have not been as articulate in making these explicit as much as we ought to have.[27]

Not all of the retrospective evaluations, however, were as optimistic about the dynamics of cumulation in the field. Perhaps the most skeptical assessment was submitted by John Mueller, who found it useful to distinguish between short- and long-run cumulative processes:

> International relations research is typified by a sequence of swells, it seems to me: an idea, concept, or method takes hold for a while, is rather thoroughly investigated over a number of years, then gradually abandoned. While it has its day in the sun, short-term cumulation is considerable as scholars, anxious to contribute to the latest hot debate, build and elaborate and criticize and re-think. Looked at in longer range perspective, however, one may have cause to wonder what the excitement was about since little or none of the research has had any lasting significance — in other words, little has managed to be cumulative in the long term.
>
> An example might be the debate in the early 1950s over the concepts of power and realism and national interest. We are probably too close to the quantitative 'revolution' of the 1960s to judge such things but I am unable to detect that much is being done with Stanford-style content analysis any more after a decade of enormous effort and expense and I seem to be aware that there are a number of disillusioned simulators around. Some of my

[26] Memo dated July 2, 1973.
[27] Letter dated July 10, 1973.

skepticism about the events approach is an extrapolation from such historical observations, but hopefully the analogy will prove to be inappropriate.

At the same time, if a researcher happens to be ahead of his time, he will not, by definition, be in the research mainstream, will not have imitators and developers and therefore will not, in the short term, see his research cumulate except insofar as he builds on it himself. Perhaps the work of L.F. Richardson is an example.

Looking at international relations scholarship from the perspective of, say 1955, and applying the test of cumulativeness, one might conclude that power and realism was the wave of the future because of the interest it had generated and because of its apparent cumulativeness, while Richardson's efforts to build arms race models were an eccentric flash in the pan. From a longer term perspective, however, one might well reverse the conclusion (although I should add, that, while I find some richness in the arms race analyses, I am considerably less optimistic than Hayward Alker is about its even longer term significance).

Thus at any point in time it should be easy to generate a number of examples of substantial cumulation, but, if the examples were short term, this would be an inadequate indicator of research quality. If one asks only for long term examples, a much better indicator, I rather feel embarrassed for the field. There are bright spots in almost all areas, but little long term cumulation, I feel. As for quantitative or 'scientific' research, which is what the conference was to focus on, it is, I suppose too early to tell: only short term examples are possible. Nevertheless, as suggested above, we may already be seeing the demise of quantitative approaches thought by many only 10 years ago to carry vast promise.

It may well be the case that international relations is in no worse shape in this respect than most other political science fields; perhaps, as suggested at the conference, it is better off than comparative government — faint praise indeed. I don't know where in political science substantial long term cumulation can be pointed to, but perhaps there are a few areas such as the voting studies.[28]

Although not as explicitly dubious about the cumulativness of research in the IR field, Alker's post-Workshop reflections, hastily penned while returning to a teaching assignment in Chile, reiterated the conviction that cumulation was the central issue and emphasized what he perceived as the broader context of the deliberations:

If I were to try and summarize the major 'messages' I saw at our Ojai Workshop through colored glasses (my own), several points come repeatedly to mind. They belong in a final report even when there is not a 'manifesto' quality to it.

1. The characterization of what we know more than we knew before must be in sociology of knowledge, processual philosopical, historical and contextual terms: (a) *what were the big issues* (causes of war, the design of voluntaristic integration systems, the adequacy of Cold War institutions for weathering crises, the quality of the determinants of foreign policy, the efficacy and worth of the Balance of Power, collective security, etc.): (b) *what were the contending often value-linked views* (otherwise the triviality of 'plausible' results is *very* uninteresting); (c) *what has been the development of paradigms, model sequences, new ways of seeing associated methodologies, etc.* (surely the *historical* characteristics of

[28] Memo dated August 2, 1973.

the development are important); (d) *what was the historical context of social/political events and phenomena that produced the orientations taken* (U.S. IR science has been *often big power IR science*: in the majority of cases either a Superpower global perspective or a great power war/conflict/integration focus is very evident, *by constrast* with Latin American IR which focuses *much more* on *dependency and imperialism* with heavy emphasis on the Lahn context for obvious reasons). Etc., etc.

2. A *positivistic philosophy of science is clearly no longer dominant* even if *it ever was*. A more explicit value-oriented/policy-oriented (often from the U.S. perspective) philosophy of political analysis (similar to Lasswell's) is much more clearly evident. *It is not* anti-scientific.
3. The most interesting topics to Americans are becoming foreign policy belief systems and global systems (in Russia there is great interest in the latter; in Chile in neither). Radical Americans (or anti VN war types) and foreigners from 3rd world countries are more likely (unless totally assimilated) to be interested in imperialistic aspects of these policies (considered as ideologies) and systems.
4. There are several areas of relatively sustained growth; quite a lot of areas that have stagnated, other pieces of work not integrated into cumulative traditions. There is considerable *unevenness* in developments at large. Lots of 'preparadigm work.'
5. The kind of growth that has occurred has often been associated with methodological advance. Thus I sharply disagree with any assessment of simulation that takes a dim view of its potential. Holsti, Rummel, Russett, Rosecrance were all very interested in it, not to mention the Northwestern world. Deutsch is too.
6. Organizational problems of sustaining growth are increasingly serious.
7. *More money can hurt/help science in various ways*! I would like it tied to cumulation oriented institutions and practices, but with a premium on critical work re anomalies, and always some support of new paradigm candidates.[29]

VI. CUMULATION RECONSIDERED

The foregoing evaluations raise as many questions as they answer. Most generally, they encourage a reconsideration of the concept of cumulation. More particularly, they provoke concern as to the nature of the evidence necessary to justify a conclusion that knowledge has been cumulated. The theme that cumulation has occurred stands out, but it is not supported by extensive illustrations of such progress. Simply to assert that various practitioners are building on each other's work is not to demonstrate that in fact one set of findings clarifies or extends a prior set. To note that such recent collections of research on specific topics as those edited by Hermann, Russett, and

[29] Memo dated July 5, 1973.

Wilkenfeld[30] are marked by 'cross-fertilization'[31] among the articles is not to identify the content of the knowledge base that has been constructed. To stress widespread use of the same data banks is not to say that the same data are used in similar ways for similar purposes. To call attention to a growing number of propositional inventories about such important topics as foreign policy, crisis, and alliances[32] is not to indicate that the propositions have been subjected to proper empirical tests or, if they have, that the results are cumulative.[33] To elaborate on a method for cumulating case studies is not to identify generalizable results from a series of such studies.[34]

To be sure, it is unreasonable to expect that the hundreds, and in many cases thousands, of printed pages that contain the findings and ramifications of the research projects at issue could be adequately identified and summarized in the short papers and three days of discussion available to the Workshop participants. And certainly it is the case that the proliferation of collections of empirical essays on particular problems, the emergence of widely used data banks, the advent

[30] Charles F. Hermann (ed.), *International Crises: Insights from Behavioral Research* (New York: Free Press, 1972); Bruce M. Russett (ed.), *Peace, War, and Numbers* (Beverly Hills: Sage Publications, 1972); Jonathan Wilkenfeld (ed.), *Conflict Behavior and Linkage Politics* (New York: David McKay, 1973).

[31] The term is Russett's.

[32] Patrick J. McGowan and Howard B. Shapiro, *The Comparative Study of Foreign Policy: A Survey of Scientific Findings* (Beverly Hills, Cal.: Sage Publications, 1973); Charles F. Hermann and Linda P. Brady, 'Alternative Models of International Crisis Behavior,' in Hermann, *International Crises: Insights from Behavioral Research* pp. 281–303; and Philip M. Burgess and David W. Moore, 'Inter-Nation Alliances: An Inventory and Appraisal of Propositions,' in James A. Robinson (ed.) *Political Science Annual: An International Review, Vol. 3 - 1972* (Indianapolis: Bobbs-Merrill, 1972), pp. 339–83, and Ole R. Holsti, P. Terrence Hopmann, and John D. Sullivan, *Unity and Disintegration in International Alliances: Comparative Studies* (New York: Wiley, 1973), pp. 1–47.

[33] For a compendium of tested propositions that are not easily viewed as cumulative, see Susan D. Jones and J. David Singer, *Beyond Conjecture in International Politics: Abstracts of Data-Based Research* (Itasca, Ill.: F.E. Peacock, 1972).

[34] The elaboration of a method for cumulating case studies was provided by Alexander George (see his 'Bridging the Gap Between Theory and Practice, in J.N. Rosenau (ed.), *In Search of Global Patterns*, pp. 114–16), who subsequently expressed the view that this query as to whether such a method leads to generalizable results is 'misleading'. It fails to recognize that such studies have led to the formulation of '*conditional* generalizations.' Perhaps you do not think that conditional generalizations qualify as cumulation; if so, I would strongly disagree with you. The development of conditional generalizations, I would argue, is a particularly sophisticated approach to cumulation. It is naive to assume that the scientific knowledge we seek must be couched exclusively in the form of universal generalizations. Conditional generalizations are a way of establishing the *boundaries* for empirically derived generalizations. I belabor this point because I think that knowledge in the form of conditional generalizations (rather than, for example, in the form of probabilistic generalizations) is of particular value in an action context.' (Letter dated January 2, 1974.)

of narrowly focused and sophisticated propositional inventories, and the increasing availability of scientific abstracts of IR studies are evidence of momentum, of persistent efforts to probe the mysteries of international life more systematically and penetratingly. But are these evidence of cumulation? The answer is not clear. One would be less uncertain if the growing literature included inventories of research outputs (i.e., findings) as well as of research inputs (i.e., propositions, quantified data, and case studies). And one's certainty would be increased even further if the concrete instances of interdependent findings that were noted in the post-Workshop comments had reflected primarily inter- rather than intra-project cumulation. Most of the specific examples offered came out of the same project, which of course indicates progress in that project, but raises doubts about the generalizability of its findings. For one researcher and those associated with him in a project to build each of his investigations upon previous ones is, as Rummel, Russett, and Singer have amply demonstrated, to fashion a storehouse of knowledge. But, it may not be cumulative knowledge if other researchers who are not associated with the project and its particular concerns do not use the findings as the basis for their own work. It could be argued that the ultimate test of cumulativeness is whether researchers have sufficient confidence in the findings of other studies to use them as givens in their own work. His 0.9 correlations notwithstanding, Rummel's findings on the importance of size, political accountability, and wealth have not been treated as 'social laws' by researchers not associated with the DON project and one can find few other studies that proceed from these findings.[35] Similarly, one would be hard pressed to find many studies undertaken by researchers not associated with the Correlates of War Project that assume and build upon Singer and Small's finding that nineteenth century alliances were negatively correlated with the onset of war while twentith century alliances were weakly but positively associated with the subsequent war levels.[36] Or, to cite a more striking example, I have recently replicated my own finding that internal variables are considerably more powerful than external ones in the determination of foreign policy, using *three different*

[35] One notable exception here is Bruce M. Russett, *International Regions and the International System* (Chicago: Rand McNally, 1967), which accepts and builds on the work of the DON project, especially in Chapters 2 and 3. Although other exceptions could be noted (see pp. 220–21), these are hardly so numerous as to demonstrate a widespread consensus on the lawful nature of these three national attributes.

[36] J. David Singer and Melvin Small, 'Alliance Aggregation and the Onset of War, 1815–1945,' in J. David Singer (ed.), *Quantitative International Politics: Insights and Evidence* (New York: Free Press, 1968), pp. 247–86.

data sets,[37] but I still lack sufficient confidence in my own results to treat them as givens in future inquiries.

There are probably a number of reasons why the confidence that sustains cumulation has not accompanied the growth of scientific IR research, but a prime reason is undoubtedly the absence of a widely shared paradigm. As many of the Workshop papers note, the field does not have an overarching theoretical perspective — a perspective that specifies the central phenomena to be explained and offers an overall basis for explaining them. It may not be an exaggeration to assert that the field does not even have a number of competing paradigms. Alker goes so far as to suggest that 'there are indeed few research paradigms that have so *galvanized* and sustained the aspirations of a community of 50+ scholars *consensually* to follow the lead of exemplary studies.' The field, in short, is still in a preparadigmatic stage, which constitutes and advance over the nonparadigmatic, atheoretical circumstances that surrounded IR research prior to the advent of scientific inquiry, but which partly accounts for both the paucity of cumulative findings and the disinclination to generate them. If a comprehensive and internally consistent paradigm were ever to capture the imagination of researchers in the field — or, more accurately, when such a paradigm captures the field — the task of cumulation will become compelling and a solid knowledge base will quickly develop.

To be sure, a convergence around a shared paradigm could result in an overly narrow preoccupation with a limited set of phenomena. As Singer notes, 'Our paradigms should help us make discoveries, rather than make us prisoners of our hunches and hopes.'[38] Yet the risk of becoming entrapped by our own paradigm seems much less than the preparadigmatic price of non-cumulation. For it is not improbable that once a shared paradigm emerges it will, in turn, foster competing paradigms, and the processes of competition among them are likely to intensify cumulation as the adherents of each paradigm seek to demonstrate the greater utility of their formulations through empirical studies that build upon each other.

But, it may be asked, has not a shared paradigm already begun to emerge? Is this not what the aforementioned convergence around the events data movement represents? And what about Rosecrance's conclusion that a 'three variable paradigm' can be discerned in the research of the Workshop members? Are not these indicators of movement beyond the preparadigmatic stage? Probably not, if by an

[37] James N. Rosenau and George R. Ramsey, Jr., 'External and Internal Typologies of Foreign Policy Behavior: Testing the Stability of an Intriguing Set of Findings,' in Patrick J. McGowan (ed.), *Sage International Yearbook of Foreign Policy Studies, Vol. III* (Beverly Hills, Ca.: Sage Publications, 1975), pp. 245-62.

[38] Letter dated November 28, 1973.

overarching paradigm is meant an explanatory scheme. Neither the events data movement nor the three master variables cited by Rosecrance are linked together by anything resembling an explanatory conception. Researchers in the events data movement are linked by a common methodology for generating data. What the actors depicted by the data do and why they act as they do, however, is subject to virtually as many interpretations as there are events data analysts. Likewise, Rosecrance's three variables are linked in the sense that most researchers consider the interaction among them to be central, but there is little agreement as to how, when, and why they interact.

VII. THE CONCERN FOR VALUES AND POLICY

As revealed by the initial resistance to the concept of cumulation, not all of those who participated in the Workshop are greatly distressed about the preparadigmatic state of the field. Some, like McClelland, are prepared to 'let theory take care of itself' on the grounds that 'it emerges when the right time comes without more than a little nudging.' Others, like George, are interested in applying the results of scientific inquiry to policy problems and are thus more anxious to hasten the development of design theory than of overarching paradigms. Still others, like Rummel and the many able scholars engaged in peace research, are so committed to trying to shed light on the dynamics of conflict that they do not find the construction of abstract paradigms that encompass nonwar phenomena an especially compelling task. Indeed, the pre-Workshop project autobiographies are striking for the large degree to which they show value consideractions to have underlain the origin and sustained the evolution of the projects. Like any science, IR is not so much value-free as it is value-explicit, and the project autobiographies make it plain that IR scientists aspire to having the results of their efforts contribute to a saner and less conflictful world. As indicated by George's estimate of the potentialities of design theory, they also believe that it is possible to be both scientifically rigorous and policy relevant.

This is not to say that the concern for values and policy applications will prevent the field from moving beyond its preparadigmatic state. The efforts of peace researchers, design theorists, and others with one or another applied purpose may, perhaps unintentionally, pay off in terms of paradigm maturation. It may even be that their endeavors will have greater consequences for theory building than for real-world institution building. It seems likely, however, that paradigm maturation will not occur as rapidly as would be the case if the commitment to knowledge cumulation was as intense as the commitment to policy relevance.

In other words, it could be argued that values would be at least equally served by sustained attention to the construction of feasible paradigms and the subsequent cumulation they would facilitate as by a preoccupation with policy relevance. The project autobiographies reveal intense frustration over the unresponsiveness of the policy world to the results of the projects. Alker, for example, complains about the 'confused and/or hostile' reactions of the State Department to the results of his collaboration with Russett on U.N. voting. Likewise, Guetzkow notes plaintively that his simulation project had 'little impact,' even with respect to 'rudimentary aspects of methodology,' on military policy-makers, 'despite the many briefings given and continuous communication maintained with personnel in the Joint War Games Agency . . . in the Office of the Joint Chiefs of Staff.'[39]

In part, of course, the unresponsiveness of officials stems from a lack of respect for social scientific modes of analysis.[40] Partly, too, it arises out of the fact that frequently the research products submitted to officials run counter to what they want to hear. As often as not, government agencies sponsor or solicit outside research in order to bulwark their commitment to ongoing policy programs, thus leading them to pay scant attention to findings and briefings that undermine their *a priori* positions. Whatever the reasons why officials and publics lack sufficient confidence in the products of scientific IR research to adapt them to their needs when they are deliberately tailored to be relevant, might not the time and resources invested in making the products available and palatable be put to better use?

VIII. ORGANIZATION FOR RESEARCH

Cognizant of the rapid proliferation of scientific IR research and the multiple purposes that it has served and aware that the resulting progress has been disjointed and the growth uneven, members of the

[39] It should be noted that not all the participants are frustrated over the unresponsiveness of policy-makers. Russett argues that they can be reached through indirect routes: 'Rather than measure the relevance of our work by the interest and understanding shown by officials, concentration on 'counter-elites' and attentive publics is often a better route to policy influence.' (Letter dated November 5, 1973).

[40] For an elaboration of this point, see James N. Rosenau, *International Studies and the Social Sciences: Problems, Priorities and Prospects in the United States* (Beverly Hills, Cal.: Sage, 1973), pp. 80–90.

Workshop were more than ready to endorse Guetzkow's plea to organize and coordinate more effectively the diverse efforts of the expanding community of IR scholars. A full session of the Workshop devoted to the problem yielded a number of suggestions, ranging from structures for pooling resources to mechanisms for increasing the degree of interaction among projects. Compelling as many of the suggestions were, however, enthusiasm was tempered by the realization that they had often been advanced in the past but had rarely been implemented. The recent history of the field is strewn with *ad hoc* committees that seldom meet and impressive schemes for exchanging personnel, data, and findings that never got launched. Most notably, despite wide-ranging agreement on the need for research on research — i.e., on the necessity of periodic assessments of the state and structure of the field — a concerted attempt to undertake such inquiries has never materialized. Thus, for example, we still do not have even the beginnings of an answer to the questions posed in Guetzkow's pre-Workshop paper: '. . . whether or not a net of close communication is useful among investigators, so that their work may dovetail more adequately, or does such a social structure among scholars tend to diminish innovation?' Indeed, as Guetzkow also notes, we do not even have any solid evidence on whether large, team-centered projects are likely to carry the field forward more effectively than small, individual-centered projects.

The persistent failure of efforts to organize the field and the inability to institute penetrating assessment procedures is perhaps another reflection — as well as perhaps a source — of the preparadigmatic state of research. Surely an infrastructure facilitating research and self-assessment would have developed long ago if findings had begun to pile up on each other. Organizational tinkering cannot insure the cumulation of knowledge, but a continuous flow of overlapping and interdependent research results seems bound to create the need for procedures to absorb, sort, and assess the convergent findings.

IX. LEADERSHIP IN THE FIELD

Despite, or perhaps because of, the difficulties of organizing the work of IR researchers, leadership needs to be exercised in the field. The goals of research, the values attached to scientific inquiry, and the desirability of developing a body of cumulative findings are not issues that can be determined in a marketplace. Nor do the separate efforts of individual scholars cohere spontaneously into a meaningful whole. Research goals and priorities have to be set, and this leadership function can either be performed by private foundations and governmental agencies or it can be carried out by the community of IR scholars themselves. If the community does not clarify its purposes, then those who provide funds and other rewards will point the way.

Because the goal-setting function has to be performed, it is perhaps a cause for concern that a manifesto did not emerge from the deliberations at Ojai. It is true that those present at the Workshop did not perceive themselves as presenting constituencies or as otherwise charged with leadership responsibilities. Yet it was not modesty about their own leadership potential, or reluctance to arrogate to themselves the tasks of leadership, that accounts for the fact that the possibility of issuing a manifesto for the field was not mentioned after the first session of the Workshop. It seems clear in retrospect that the idea did not surface again because consensus about appropriate goals and modes of research did not exist among the participants. Even the question of exercising leadership would doubtless have evoked some disagreement if it had been discussed. Mueller, for example, concluded his post-Workshop reflections with the question of whether manifestos that chart research paths for the future are desirable:

> The principal reason for this conclusion stems from the observation that so many promising avenues have proved to be blind alleys in the past. Thus it almost seems arrogant to suppose one can suggest before the fact which areas of exploration are likely to be most productive. Nor do I see any way to point to areas in which research is particularly 'needed': *good* research is so obviously needed in all areas that I can't imagine how one can conclude that everything has been wrapped up in one area so that scholars should move on to other ones. Even warnings about apparent blind alleys may be unwise since a good study might find a way out.
>
> The real problem it seems to me, is that there are never at any point in time very many really fine scholars and, for their talents to be most productive, they should be encouraged to work in whatever area they are best at regardless of current 'needs' or research fads. An area is only as good as the people working in it. For example, I am interested in following developments in the 'operational code' area, but the principal attraction is that Alexander George is doing the developing — a fine scholar doing something he does well. Should he go into something else, my interest in following the operation code area would diminish greatly.
>
> 'Whither IR?' manifestos can do positive damage if they encourage able scholars to follow fads into areas they are relatively weak in. A good data maker is not necessarily a good data analyst or a good theorist, and vice versa, and suggestions, for example, that we 'need' better theory more than we need better data (how can one possibly know that anyway?) seem to me potentially mischievous in their consequences.
>
> The fashionableness of quantitative international relations research in some quarters in the last decade has, I feel often been detrimental in leading scholars fully capable of doing sound historical or legalistic studies into pastures where they promptly got mired down. We would have been much better off if they had produced tedious historical descriptions of the Bosnian crisis of 1908 that would still be worth reading 100 years from now instead of expensively producing stacks of naive numbers that can be made to say nothing.

> In addition 'Whither IR?' statements may often merely reflect topical substantive whims: the developing areas were places to know about when independence tremors were gaining headlines but are no longer now that they have settled into a more normal state; arms control was a big thing in the late 1950s and early 1960s when it was a major subject of political debate (though realistically almost unattainable), but is not now despite reasonable prospects for success.
>
> From these kinds of thoughts I am led to suggest that exercises in direction-pointing, summing-up, and manifesto-promulgating are likely to be at best futile and at worst damaging.[41]

The difficulty with Mueller's observations is that they are founded on an empirically insufficient premise and contain a conspicuous omission. The insufficient premise is that in the past the community of IR scholars has performed the function of self-consciously determining and enunciating its goals. There is no evidence that manifestos will do damage or that they will reflect mere whims. The tendency to follow fads has occurred in the absence of deliberate and self-conscious leadership, not because of it. It can be readily argued that historical descriptions of the Bosnian crisis are lacking not because of a leadership that urged avoidance of such inquiries, but because the *laissez-faire* conditions Meuller champions have prevailed.

What Mueller's comments ignore is the high probability, noted above, that the goal-setting task will be performed. In an era of limited resources, IR scholars will not be free to undertake any research they please if it requires support from funding agencies. Some projects will be favored over others, and the norms and standards that determine which get favored and which get rejected will, to repeat, be set by some group. Presumably it is preferable that these norms and standards emanate from the research community rather than from elsewhere. To be opposed to goal-setting for IR research may be to espouse a luxury that is no longer possible.

X. SUMMARY

The papers and deliberations of the Workshop indicate clearly that a decade of scientific IR research has been marked by *both* successes and failures. The failures include the slow, unproductive pace of theoretical development, the persistence of communication gaps over the meaning of cumulation, the lack of consensus on the nature and tasks of a science of IR, the scarcity of widely accepted findings, the inability to either impress the policy-making world or to define an appropriate

[41] Memo dated August 2, 1973.

role with respect to it, and the absence of feedback procedures for facilitating and assessing progress.

But the Workshop also pointed up a record of accomplishment. Recent years have witnessed considerable growth in the number of individuals and projects backed by large-scale funding. Both substantively and methodologically, the field has advanced well beyond where it was a decade ago. Islands of cumulation have surfaced, a multimethod orientation has emerged, the events data movement has taken hold, and the legitimacy of scientific and quantitative inquiry has been established. These are no small accomplishments for a fledgling science and, most importantly, there is no reason to believe that development will stop or even slow down. On the contrary, the advent of new generations of researchers, equipped with more sophisticated intellectual tools and burdened by fewer ambivalences than their predecessors, makes it seem likely that the record of progress will be extended and quickened. The link to the future lies not in the failures of the past, but in its successes — in the fact that the present study of IR is virtually unrecognizable in comparison to what it was but a few short years ago and that, as a consequence, we now know much more about international phenomena than ever before. That there is still a great deal to learn constitutes a challenge to hard work, not a basis for despair.

10 Of Syllabi, Texts, Students, and Scholarship in International Relations: Some Data and Interpretations on the State of a Burgeoning Field*

There is no shortage of introductory textbooks in international relations (IR). Here we present the results of a systematic content analysis of 26 volumes published between 1966 and 1973,[1] but many more could have been subjected to scrutiny if we had not confined our conception of a text to *single- or co-authored works that purport to offer a comprehensive overview of the 'basics' of the field*. Had we expanded this conception to include works in international organization, international law, and American foreign policy, we could easily have tripled our sample. Indeed, had we developed a conception of a text that allowed for the inclusion of those works that IR teachers treat as worthy of purchase by their students and/or of multiple assignments in their courses — particularly paperbacks that are explicitly and exclusively confined to a thorough and systematic examination of one central aspect of IR (such as diplomacy, game theory, crises, or foreign policy decision making) — our sample would probably have been enlarged more than a hundredfold.[2]

As it is even the narrow conception of texts which we did employ proved troublesome, partly because we could not include data on 8 such works that have been published since we completed our content analysis in 1974.[3] and partly because definitions differ as to what

*Written with Gary Gartin, Edwin P. McClain, Dona Stinziano, Richard Stoddard, and Dean Swanson. An earlier version of this chapter was published in *World Politics*, Vol. XXIX (January 1977), pp. 263-341. Reprinted with the permission of Princeton University Press.

[1] The 26 texts are hereafter identified by their authors; see Table 1.

[2] In this connection, see Tables 2 and 3 below.

[3] Robert D. Cantor, *Introduction to International Politics* (Itasca, Ill.: F.E. Peacock 1976); Ira S. Cohen, *Realpolitik: Theory and Practice* (Encino, Cal.:

constitutes the 'basics' of IR and how thorough an overview of them must be to achieve comprehensiveness. What is basic to one scholar is peripheral to another; what one considers comprehensive, another views as limited or superficial. In constructing our sample of 26, therefore, we had to proceed in terms of somewhat crude notions of basic and thorough coverage, erring on the side of including those works whose scope was broad enough to be assigned throughout an entire course.

Whatever criteria may be used to identify them, it is instructive to ask *why* there are so many texts. Is it because the IR field is so inchoate that only a multitude of works can serve all the approaches and emphases to which students are exposed in what may be more than 2,000 introductory IR courses given throughout the country in any given year?[4] Because every respectable publisher of political science texts, aware that the market is a big one, feels that his list must include one or more entries covering the IR field, and therefore persuades one or more teachers of IR to write their own texts even though they themselves may be satisfied with the one they have been using? Because the training and capabilities of undergraduates vary so greatly among the nation's colleges and universities that publishers believe there are several IR markets that can only be served by having several texts on their list, some aimed at the Ivy League schools, others at state universities, and still others at junior colleges? Because some teachers need to supplement their income, add to their scholarly credentials, or are otherwise motivated to enhance their work by writing texts? Because others are so thoroughly dissatisfied with the available texts that they seek to elevate the field by preparing their own? Or because teachers have such varied conceptions of what they want to accomplish in their introductory courses?

Probably an affirmative answer to all these questions is warranted. The scope of the field is vast, and diversity does mark its contents. Publishers do seek to uncover and tap all potential markets.[5] Students

Dickenson Publishing Co. 1975); David J. Finlay and Thomas Hovet, Jr., *7304: International Relations on the Planet Earth* (New York: Harper & Row 1975); Robert A. Isaak, *Individuals and World Politics* (North Scituate, Mass.: Duxbury Press 1975); Ralph Pettman, *Human Behavior and World Politics: An Introduction to International Relations* (New York: St. Martin's Press 1975); Steven J. Rosen and Walter S. Jones, *The Logic of International Relations* (Cambridge, Mass.: Winthrop Publishers 1974); Richard W. Sterling, *Macropolitics: International Relations in a Global Society* (New York: Alfred A. Knopf 1974); and Michael P. Sullivan, *International Relations: Theories and Evidence* (Englewood Cliffs, N.J.: Prentice-Hall 1976).

[4] The estimated figure of 2,000 was given to us by several publishers' representatives.

[5] The role of publishers in the processes whereby knowledge is passed on to new generations of students is highlighted by the extent to which several have turned to market research techniques in order to guide the actual writing of

do vary in their skills and interests from one type of institution to another. Academics do need to supplement their incomes, and they do have images of what students should learn.

Whatever the full explanation of the plethora of texts, collectively they offer valuable insights into the state of the field and the way in which successive generations of students are trained to comprehend it. Our purpose here is to tease such insights out of the welter of available introductory materials. The essentials of a field are perhaps best distilled in the knowledge and methods that are passed on to those who enter it, and it is these essentials we seek to uncover. We assume that the patterns and disparities uncovered in a large sample of texts can serve as measures of the coherence and diversity of IR. We aspire to providing such measures, to portraying the images of IR that are widely shared and the methodologies that are widely practiced. And, in so doing, we hope to provide an assessment that can serve as useful feedback — if not as the basis for revising prevailing assumptions and perceptions, at least as a means for taking stock, for pondering whether the dominant images and practices are taking those in the field in the directions they wish to travel. We also hope that in the process our analysis provides sufficient information about each of the content-analyzed texts to assist those teaching IR courses to make adoptions consistent with their images of the field and the analytic skills they want their students to acquire.

There is another major purpose that motivated us to undertake this inquiry. We want to demonstrate the virtues of systematic assessment. As noted at greater length elsewhere, we believe that the same criteria of evidence and methodological rigor should be applied in evaluating IR materials as are used in IR research itself.[6] Most reviews of texts and most assessments of research consist of analytic essays in which the reviewers offer impressionistic interpretations of the central tendencies that underlie the materials under review. Often, to be sure, these analytic essays are insightful and pervaded with useful observations about the state of the field, where it has been, and where it seems to be

introductory texts. Consider, for example, the following account, told with considerable enthusiasm and pride to the senior author by the responsible editor, of how one large publishing firm brought an introductory text in anthropology into being. First the firm circulated a questionnaire to those teaching introductory courses in the field, asking them to indicate the main topics they covered in their courses and offering them three books from the publisher's list in exchange for the information. The returned questionnaires were then content-analyzed, computerized, and an average chapter outline, along with the main themes of each derived therefrom. At this point the firm scoured the field to find an author to write the book that the market research techniques had, in effect, created. As the editor put it, 'We needed to find someone to flesh out the chapter outline!'

[6] James N. Rosenau, 'Assessment in International Studies: Ego Trip or Feedback?' *International Studies Quarterly*, XVIII (September 1974), 339–67.

going.[7] But in the absence of systematic data supporting the interpretations and depicting the extent of their relevance, such assessments fail to provide the bases for corrective measures. One can never be sure whether the trends and practices asserted to be at work are pervasive, whether they are a function of particular outlooks and training, or whether they are overreactions on the part of reviewers with axes to grind. Thus, in the hope of generating materials that are not founded on impressions and that cannot readily be dismissed as axe-grinding, we have dared to undertake an assessment marked by rigor and precision. In so doing we have resisted the temptation to sprinkle our analysis with quotes from the various texts that exemplify the absurdity of the practices we deplore or that uphold the orientations we favor. Given the amount of material we have examined, it would be easy indeed to proceed from quotation to quotation as a means of demonstrating the wisdom of our biases. But our commitment here is to rigorous analysis, and we have therefore confined our interpretations to commentary about the quantitative patterns we have uncovered. We do not claim to have prepared a definitive review, but we do contend that the ensuing analysis rests on solid empirical foundations as well as an aspiration to provoke thought about the problem of introducing students to IR.

I. THE USES OF A TEXTBOOK

To evaluate the merits of any text is to have notions about the purposes it must serve. Instructors differ in this regard — partly because they have different conceptions of the nature and state of IR knowledge, partly because they have different images of their students' capabilities, and partly because they must cope with different limitations as to the size of their courses, the adequacy of their libraries, the availability of teaching assistants, and the traditions of their institutions. For various reasons, therefore, some instructors organize their courses exclusively around assignments in a text and/or book of readings; others use texts to provide coherence for their courses while at the same time assigning a number of paperbacks and/or selections

[7] For some stimulating essays in which IR texts are insightfully assessed, see Kenneth E. Boulding, 'The Content of International Studies in College: A Review,' *Journal of Conflict Resolution*, VIII (March 1964), 65-71; Charles B. Neff, 'The Study of International Relations: New Approaches to a Familiar Subject,' *World Politics*, XV (January 1963), 339-53; Richard C. Snyder, 'Toward Greater Order in the Study of International Politics,' *World Politics*, VII (April 1955), 461-78; Fred A. Sondermann, 'The Study of International Relations: 1956 Version,' *World Politics*, X (October 1957), 102-11; and Dina A Zinnes, 'An Introduction to the Behavioral Approach: A Review,' *Journal of Conflict Resolution*, XII (June 1968), 258-67.

from a variety of other sources; and still others do not use a text at all, relying instead on their course outlines and/or lectures to infuse a coherence into assignments from a wide range of diverse materials.

Conceptions of the state of knowledge about IR are relevant to these various uses of a textbook: instructors seem more likely to rely exclusively on a text if they believe that the field has achieved a consensus as to what constitutes the basic facts and concepts that ought to serve as an 'introduction' to the course of world affairs. Teachers of IR who perceive the field as having yet to evolve an overarching paradigm that identifies the basic facts and concepts, or who adhere to scientific criteria of evidence and consider the accumulated knowledge of the field to be more impressionistic than reliable, seem likely to look beyond the available texts to materials that are consistent with either the particular conceptualization of the field or the criteria of evidence to which they subscribe.

Conceptions of the motivations and talents that students bring to the course are relevant to the way in which texts are used: instructors seem more likely to adopt a text if they are convinced they have found one that is consistent with their image of what their students are willing and able to do. If instructors believe their students lack analytic skills and require simplified syntheses in order to comprehend the basics of the field, they are likely to seek out texts that treat IR knowledge as established, rely on gross definitions, offer unqualified explanations, recite historical facts, ignore nuances, and eschew references to the methodologies whereby the knowledge, explanations, and facts presented were developed. If, on the other hand, they see their students as curious and capable of grasping complexity, they are likely to employ texts that stress alternative conceptualizations and explanations, treat knowledge as tentative and dependent on the methodology employed, and otherwise challenge their readers to form their own conclusions. These two types of instructors are also likely to differ in the degree to which they rely on a text to infuse structure into their courses. Those that tend to view their students as unmotivated and incompetent seem likely to rely more exclusively on a text than those with a more favorable image of students, since the latter will probably look to supplemental materials to insure a wider range of alternative formulations, contradictory findings, and innovative mthodologies.

The varying consequences of the varying conceptions of the field and students will probably be reinforced by the circumstances under which instructors must offer their courses. Those who have huge numbers of students and/or poor libraries seem more likely to view the field as synthesizable into an overall, established paradigm that can be captured in a single text than are those whose classes are small and whose libraries have multiple copies of many books and the funds for placing duplicated materials on reserve shelves. Moreover, the greater the number of students enrolled in their courses, the more instructors are likely to perceive the 'average' student as limited in both curiosity and competence.

All the foregoing considerations, of course, may be as operative for those who write texts as for those who adopt them. If IR knowledge is perceived as established and integrated, texts are likely to be compendia of historical facts and conventional concepts; writers who are less sure of the field's base of knowledge are more likely to take note of alternative explanations, conceptual nuances, evidential sources, and methodological underpinnings. Similarly, if textwriters see themselves as synthesizing materials for mediocre and unmotivated students, the knowledge they present is likely to be cast in language that simplifies complexity and that otherwise caters to the perceived need for clear-cut facts and explanations.

The more one ponders the uses of a textbook, in short, the clearer it becomes that texts are more than a reflection of the state of a field, more than a synthesized product of a complex knowledge-building process. They are also contributors to that process, embedded in it as both mirrors and sources of the ways in which researchers, teachers, publishers, and students go about their respective tasks. The dynamics of building and disseminating IR knowledge thus involve a vast feedback system in which texts can play a major role. The interdependence of this system is set forth in Figure I, an earlier version of which served to clarify and limit our inquiry at the outset. At that time we recognized that we could not explore all the relationships identified in Figure I and that we were compelled to confine ourselves mainly to what the 26 texts revealed about the state of the field and the capabilities ascribed to students. At the same time it seemed clear that even such a limited assessment requires recognition of the various ways in which texts shape and reflect the learning of IR perspectives and knowledge.

We were also aware that, although we wanted to undertake as detached and objective an assessment as possible, we were not lacking in judgments as to what a 'good' text ought to contain. So that the ensuing analysis can be fairly evaluated, it is perhaps useful to explicate our values in this regard. Indeed, since we consciously built our basic values into some of our content-analytic categories, we owe our readers an initial summary of our conception of the prevailing state of the field and the general orientations of the undergraduates who seek (or otherwise submit to) an introduction to it. We see the field as in disarray, as lacking any consensus as to the nature, sources, and consequences of international processes. Thus, whether it is

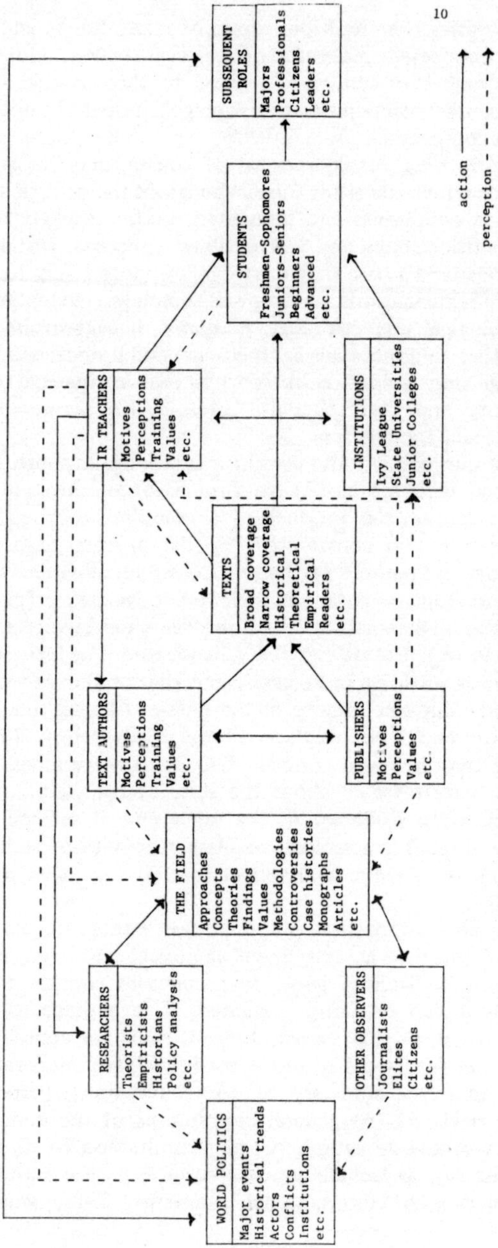

FIGURE 1. THE STRUCTURE OF THE IR FIELD AND THE ROLE PLAYED BY TEXTBOOKS

designed for exclusive use in a course or for use with other materials, we believe the 'ideal' text should, even as it presents a comprehensive picture of world politics, take note of alternative approaches and explanations, be explicit about the concepts on which the analysis is founded, be precise about the links between causes and effects, be sensitive to the need for evidence in support of assertions made about the motives, dynamics, and ramifications of the actions and interactions examined, and be permeated by phrases that convey the probabilistic, tentative, and qualified nature of the interpretations and conclusions that it offers.

These qualities seem all the more compelling to us because they are also consistent with our conception of students and the pedagogical goals that texts ought to serve. In our experience, students are not so lacking in curiosity and capabilities that they have to be spoon-fed. Rather, we believe that they are more talented than either they or their instructors think; that their curiosities are susceptible to arousal; that they are able to cope with the notion that IR knowledge is elusive, fragmented, and open to multiple interpretations; that they can abandon dependence on sheer description and will thrive on the joys of analysis if given a chance to do so. We *do* recognize the great variability in the orientations and capabilities of students, both within and across institutions, and thus we appreciate that some concessions in style and simplifications of content may be necessary; but we do not accept the premise that the limitations of beginning students necessitate the writing of texts that eschew analysis, avoid complexity, minimize methodology, and rely on historical narration and unverified description.

If the foregoing perspectives seem unduly repeated throughout the ensuing analysis, it is not only because of the importance we attach to them. The repetitiveness can also be viewed as a reflection of the many ways in which the philosophical assumptions that textwriters make about the nature of the field and the ability of students pervade their analyses.

II. ARE TEXTBOOKS USED?

As we began to appreciate the various ways in which texts could be used in a course, it became increasingly clear that we ought not content-analyze the 26 texts under review without first ascertaining whether they were being used. Convinced that practitioners in the field were far from agreement on the nature of IR, and aware that introductory courses could be organized around paperbacks and collections of readings, it seemed absurd to probe lengthy, comprehensive, and single or co-authored texts for insights into the state of the field if in fact teachers were not relying on them and students were not being exposed to them. This realization led us to send a request, in February 1973, to 146 colleges and universites located in various parts of the country and designed to serve a variety of types of students, for copies of syllabi used in "any and all introductory undergraduate courses in 'International Relations' (or 'World Politics,' or whatever title may be used) given by different instructors using differing syllabi in your Department during 1972–73." Our request yielded an astonishing degree of cooperation: 178 different syllabi for courses defined as introductory were received from 106 different institutions.[8]

[8] In addition to the 178 syllabi that were usable for our purposes, we also received scores of syllabi for more advanced courses, partly because the inclination to cooperate was high and partly because some institutions do not differentiate between introductory and advanced courses. We are grateful to colleagues in the following institutions for their help in creating the sample of 178 syllabi: University of Alabama: Amherst College: Appalachian State University; University of Arizona; Barnard College; Boston University; Brandeis University; Brown University; University of California (Berkeley); University of California (Los Angeles); University of California (Riverside); University of California (Santa Barbara); California State University (Hayward); Carleton College; Case Western Reserve University; Catholic University of America; University of Cincinnati; Claremont Men's College; Colorado College; Columbia University; Cornell University; Dartmouth College; Denison University; DePauw University; Douglass College; Drew University; Eastern Kentucky University; Emory University; Franklin and Marshall College; George Washington University; University of Georgia; Hamilton College; Harvard University; Hobart & William Smith Colleges; University of Illinois; University of Illinois at Chicago Circle; Indiana State University; Indiana University; University of Iowa; Johns Hopkins University; Kansas State University; Kent State University; University of Kentucky; Forrest College; Lehigh University; Livingston College; Louisiana State University; Marshall University; University of Maryland; Massachusetts Institute of Technology; McGill University; Miami University (Ohio); University of Michigan; Michigan State University; Middlebury College; University of Missouri (St. Louis); New Mexico State University; State University of New York (Albany); State University of New York (Binghamton); State University of New York (Buffalo); State University of New York (College of Arts and Letters at Geneseo); State University of New York (Stony Brook); New York University; University of North Carolina (Chapel Hill); Northwestern University; Ohio University; University of Oklahoma; Oklahoma State University; University of Oregon; University of Pennsylvania; Pennsylvania State University (Capital Campus); University of Pittsburgh; Pitzer College; Pomona College; Purdue University; Queens College (New York); University of Richmond; University of Rochester; Roosevelt University; Rutgers University (Camden); Rutgers University (Newark); Rutgers University (New Brunswick); Scripps College; University of South Carolina; Stevens Institute of Technology; Syracuse University; University of Texas (Austin); University of Texas (El Paso); Texas Tech University; Union College; Vanderbilt University; University of Virginia; Virginia Polytechnic Institute & State University; Wayne State University; West Virgina University; Western Kentucky University; College of William & Mary in Virginia; University of Windsor; University of Wisconsin (Madison); University of Wisconsin (Milwaukee); Wittenberg University; College of Wooster; Xavier University; Yale University; Youngstown State University.

The senior author of this assessment personally coded all 178 syllabi in terms of 62 variables that, taken together, provided an overview of the extent to which texts serve as the basis on which world politics is reconstructed for students in introductory IR courses. In addition, so as to depict the breadth of the nontextual materials to which students are exposed, a separate tally was made of every reading assigned or suggested in the 178 syllabi.

The results of this preliminary inquiry provide ample justification for both an intensive and a qualified investigation of the 26 texts under review. An intensive probing is warranted because 136 of the 178 courses (or 76 percent) made assignments from one or more of the 26 texts;[9] the mean number of chapters from the books in our sample that the students taking these 136 courses were required to read was 20. A further indication of the substantial reliance on texts is evident from the fact that 29 of the 178 syllabi listed one or more of the 26 texts under 'suggested reading'; 67 assigned chapters from texts not in our sample;[10] and 30 included other texts among the suggested readings. Justification for an intensive analysis of an extensive sample of texts can also be seen in a breakdown of the 26 texts in our sample by the number of courses in which each was assigned. This is presented in Table 1, where it can be seen that none of the texts dominates the field. To be sure, those by Holsti, Morgenthau, Deutsch, and Coplin were adopted substantially more than any of ther others,[11] but none of these was used in more than 13 percent of the courses. This finding surely suggests that a wide range of texts must be examined if the prevailing tendencies and crosscurrents in the field are to be uncovered.

Thus, there are sound reasons to undertake a content analysis of the 26 texts in our sample; there are, however, equally good reasons why the results of the investigation must be carefully qualified. Several aspects of the data make it clear that instructors of introductory IR courses do not rely exclusively on comprehensive texts by single

[9] Of the 178 syllabi, 55 percent required reading in only one of the 26 texts, 14 percent required chapters in two of them, and 7 percent assigned three or more.

[10] Of the 42 syllabi that did not assign a text in our sample, 19 were among the 67 requiring reading in other texts, most of them in the fields of American foreign policy, international organization, or international law. All in all, 155, or 87 percent, of the 178 syllabi contained assignments in one or another text — a proportion that is quite consistent with the results of another survey of 553 IR professors, also conducted in 1972-1973, in which some 94 percent were found to rely on texts. Cf. Jerilee Grundy, 'CLEP: International Relations Survey,' *International Studies Notes*, I (Winter 1974), 19.

[11] Comparisons of the figures in Table 1 must be made with caution, since there was substantial variation in the number of months and years for which the texts had been available for adoption. Indeed, several that appeared in none or in only one of the syllabi had been published in the year in which we conducted our survey, and thus could not possibly have been used in a number of courses.

authors. In addition to the fact that in 42 courses none of the texts in our sample were assigned, and that in 23 courses no text whatsoever was used, the analysis of the syllabi yielded a variety of findings that point to a tendency to carry the exposure of students well beyond textbooks:

(a) If teachers placed exclusive reliance on texts, their syllabi would have listed only one source in which assignments were explicitly made. However, that pattern obtained in only 4 percent of the cases. The dominant pattern was one of assignments in a variety of sources (books and articles), with the median figure for all 178 syllabi being 6 different sources, and the mean being 10 sources.

(b) Suggested as well as assigned readings were listed in 33 percent (59) of the syllabi, so that the median for all the sources listed was 8 items and the mean was 19.

(c) Assignments from books of readings were made in 62 percent (110) of the syllabi.

(d) Assignments from nonfiction books other than texts, articles, or compilations of readings were made in 77 percent (137) of the syllabi, with the median number of such books assigned being 3 and the mean 6.[12]

(e) Assignments from the same book more than once during the course were made in 75 percent (133) of the syllabi; 70 percent (125) cited at least one book only once as an assignment (with the mean of books cited only once being 7 and the median 2).

(f) Students were required to purchase at least two books by 82 percent (146) of the syllabi; the average syllabus listed 4 items to be purchased[13]

In short, any central tendencies uncovered in the 26 texts cannot be automatically treated as indicative of the way researchers and teachers in the field perceive and assess the structure and dynamics of global politics. The wide use of the texts suggests that they are representative of the perspectives of more than 26 authors, but clearly teachers in the field do not regard them as sufficient syntheses of the fundamental concepts and facts to which introductory students ought to be exposed.

A tally of the number of syllabi that listed duplicated preprints or government reports suggests that this sense of insufficiency with respect to the available texts does not stem from a conviction on the part of instructors that the texts are short on recent research findings. As will be seen, there is little evidence that the work conducted on the frontiers of research gets fed back into textbooks quickly, but this does not seem to be a limitation that instructors attempt to overcome. Only 3 percent of the 178 syllabi assigned preprint materials, and only 1 percent listed them among the suggested reading; for government reports

[12] In addition, 50 syllabi listed a mean of 26 nonfiction books as suggested readings.

[13] That this trend toward multiple-book courses is not confined to IR and has become sufficiently widespread and pronounced to trouble textbook publishers can be readily seen in Ray W. Vanderhoef, 'College Textbook Crisis of the 1970's,' *Publishers' Weekly*, Vol. 200 (October 4, 1971), 24–25.

Table 1. Number of Syllabi for 178 Introductory IR Courses in Which Assignments Were Made from the 26 Texts Subjected to a Systemic Content Analysis in 1973-74

Text	*Number of Syllabi in Which Assigned*
Axline, W. Andrew and James A. Stegenga, *The Global Community: A Brief Introduction to International Relations* (New York: Dodd, Mead, 1972), 196 pp.	5
Bobrow, Davis B., *International Relations: New Approaches* (New York: Free Press, 1972), 95 pp.	1
Coplin, William D., *Introduction to International Politics* (Chicago: Markham Publishing, 1971), 391 pp.*	21
Crabb, Cecil V., Jr., *Nations in a Mutipolar World* (New York: Harper & Row, 1968), 702 pp.	3
Deutsch, Karl W., *The Analysis of International Relations* (Englewood Cliffs, N.J.: Prentice-Hall, 1968), 214 pp.	27
Dougherty, James E. and Robert L. Pfaltzgraff, Jr., *Contending Theories of International Relations* (Philadelphia: J. B. Lippincott, 1971), 416 pp.	3
Duchacek, Ivo D., *Nations and Men: An Introduction to International Politics* (2nd ed.; New York: Holt, Rinehart & Winston, 1971), 560 pp.*	4
Edwards, David V., *International Political Analysis* (New York: Holt, Rinehart and Winston, 1973), 366 pp.	0
Frankel, Joseph, *International Politics: Conflict and Harmony* (Baltimore: Penguin Books, 1973), 265 pp.	1
Hartmann, Frederick H., *The Relations of Nations* (4th ed.; New York: Macmillan, 1973), 715 pp.	2
Holsti, K. J., *International Politics: A Framework for Analysis* (2nd ed.; Englewood Cliffs, N.J.: Prentice-Hall, 1972), 532 pp.	32
Hopkins, Raymond F. and Richard W. Mansbach, *Structure and Process in International Politics* (New York: Harper & Tow, 1973), 498 pp.	0
Jordan, David C., *World Politics in Our Time* (Lexington, Mass.: D. C. Heath, 1970), 426 pp.	1
Legg, Keith R. and James F. Morrison, *Politics and the International System: An Introduction* (New York: Harper & Row, 1971), 369 pp.	6
Modelski, George, *Principles of World Politics* (New York: Harper & Row, 1973), 498 pp.	0
Morgan, Patrick M., *Theories and Approaches to International Politics: What Are We to Think?* (San Ramon, Calif.: Consensus Publishers, 1972), 282 pp.	2
Morgenthau, Hans J., *Politics Among Nations: The Struggle for Power and Peace* (5th ed.; New York: Alfred A. Knopf, 1973), 617 pp.	33
Organski, A. F. K., *World Politics* (2nd ed.; New York: Alfred A. Knopf, 1968), 509 pp.	12
Palmer, Norman D. and Howard C. Perkins, *International Relations: The World Community in Transition* (3rd ed.; Boston: Houghton Mifflin, 1969), 799 pp.	0

Puchala, Donald James, *International Politics Today* (New York: Dodd, Mead, 1971), 379 pp.	12
Rosecrance, Richard, *International Relations: Peace or War?* (New York: McGraw-Hill, 1973), 334 pp.	1
Schuman, Frederick L., *International Politics: Anarchy and Order in the World Society* (7th ed.; New York: McGraw-Hill, 1969), 751 pp.	1
Spanier, John, *Games Nations Play: Analyzing International Politics* (New York: Praeger, 1972), 457 pp.*	13
Sprout, Harold and Margaret Sprout, *Toward a Politics of the Planet Earth* (New York: Van Nostrand Reinhold, 1971), 499 pp.	6
Stoessinger, John G., *The Might of Nations: World Politics in Our Time* (4th ed.; New York: Random House, 1973), 461 pp.*	3
Van Dyke, Vernon, *International Politics* (3rd ed.; New York: Appleton-Century-Crofts, 1966), 541 pp.	2

*A subsequent edition was published between 1974 and 1976.

the corresponding percentages were 5 and 2. These figures suggest that the gap between teaching and research may be as wide as the lag between the generation of findings and their formal publication (or, perhaps more accurately, between their generation and their republication in books of readings).[14]

The degree to which texts are relied upon and/or supplemented was not found to be a function of class size. The syllabi for large classes were found not to differ from those of small ones in terms of their length, the number of sources from which assignments were made, the number of items assigned or suggested, the number of assigned books cited more than once, the number of texts assigned, the number of books of readings assigned, the number of nonfiction books assigned other than texts or readers, or the number of books students were required to purchase.[15]

Our data suggest that the inclination to supplement the textbook with a diverse range of materials arises partly out of a pedagogical concern for varying the stimuli to which students are exposed and partly — and probably much more importantly — out of the absence of an underlying consensus about the nature of IR, its major concepts,

[14] To some extent, of course, this gap may be narrowed through the verbal presentations instructors make in class. Yet it seems doubtful to us whether many teachers report extensively to their students on what they read in preprints and journals or hear at professional meetings; else they would be inclined to make more assignments from these sources.

[15] These comparisons were based on a chi square test using a .05 level of significance, with the 32 syllabi for which class size was not known being omitted from the analysis. Of the remaining 146 courses, 19 had 25 or fewer students, 41 had between 26 and 50, 43 had between 51 and 75, 17 had between 76 and 100, and the remaining 26 had over 100, with 10 of these exceeding 200 students.

its methodological premises, and its empirical foundations. If IR was a field in which one or two major paradigms predominated, the number of sources listed as assigned and suggested on syllabi would surely not be as great as indicated above. Indeed, altogether the 178 syllabi listed 2,038 *different* sources as either assigned or suggested. As can be seen in Table 2, only 147 (8 percent) of these appeared on 5 or more syllabi. More than 1,400 books or articles appeared on only one syllabus. Of the 29 works that appeared in 11 or more syllabi, moreover, less than half were systematic inquiries into a selected topic. As can be seen in Table 3, which lists these 29 books, 8 are texts in our sample, one (Wolfers) is an IR text not in our sample, one (Claude, *Swords Into Plowshares*) is a text in international organization, 5 are books of readings, and one (Kennedy) is an autobiographical account of a crisis. This leaves 13 conceptual or empirical inquiries, none of which appeared in more than 14 percent of the syllabi, among the 29 used most frequently.

Surely the patterns evident in Tables 2 and 3 would not prevail in a field that was marked by widespread agreement as to what materials constitute the basic — or introductory — notions out of which a more advanced, penetrating understanding must evolve. The resort to such a diversity of materials can only mean that, as a realm of inquiry, IR is at present so lacking in structure as to permit anyone who teaches it to define the field in any way he or she wants. Anything goes, the syllabi seem to say, so long as it takes place on two sides of national boundaries.

Table 2. Number of Syllabi in Which 2,038 Sources Assigned or Suggested in 178 Syllabi Appeared

Number of Syllabi	*Number of Assigned or Suggested Sources*
1	1,418
2	281
3	119
4	73
5	44
6	25
7	15
8	12
9	11
10	11
11-20	22
21 or more	7
Total	2,038

Table 3. The 29 Assigned or Suggested Sources That Appeared in 11 or More of the 178 Syllabi

Source	*Number of Syllabi in Which Listed*
H. J. Morgenthau, *Politics Among Nations**	50
K. J. Holsti, *International Politics**	39
J. N. Rosenau (ed.), *International Politics and Foreign Policy*†	36
K. W. Deutsch, *The Analysis of International Relations**	33
I. L. Claude, *Power and International Relations*	26
W. D. Coplin, *Introduction to International Politics**	26
K. N. Waltz, *Man, The State, and War*	26
E. H. Carr, *The Twenty Years' Crisis*	19
T. C. Schelling, *Arms and Influence*	18
A. Wolfers, *Discord and Collaboration*	18
A. F. K. Organski, *World Politics**	17
G. T. Allison, *Essence of Decision*	16
T. C. Schelling, *The Strategy of Conflict*	16
J. G. Stoessinger, *Nations in Darkness*	16
I. L. Claude, *Swords Into Plowshares*	15
R. L. Pfaltzgraff (ed.), *Politics and the International System*†	15
W. D. Coplin and C. W. Kegley (eds.), *A Multi-Method Introduction to International Politics*†	14
R. F. Kennedy, *Thirteen Days*	14
H. Magdoff, *The Age of Imperialism*	14
D. J. Puchala, *International Politics Today**	14
S. Hoffmann (ed.), *Contemporary Theory in International Relations*†	13
C. A. McClelland, *Theory and the International System*	13
J. W. Spanier, *Games Nations Play**	13
Q. Wright, *A Study of War*	13
D. H. Meadows and others, *The Limits to Growth*	12
R. N. Rosecrance, *Action and Reaction in World Politics*	12
M. A. Kaplan, *System and Process in International Politics*	11
S. Spiegel and K. N. Waltz (eds.), *Conflict in World Politics*†	11
H. and M. Sprout, *Toward a Politics of the Planet Earth**	11

*Text in our sample †Book of readings

From a pedagogical point of view, of course, the diversity that springs from dissensus can be readily applauded. Students have an opportunity to explore various perspectives and, if they are so inclined, can avoid the restlessness that the organization of a single text may engender. There is some evidence in the syllabi that instructors supplemented text assignments partly as a means of catering to this restlessness. Or at least the fact that term papers were assigned in 48 percent of the courses, that 26 percent of these involved literature reviews, and that 19 percent of the syllabi listed participation in a simulation as a course requirement suggests an inclination to vary the learning stimuli.

But it would be erroneous to treat the lack of consensus and the concern for student motivation as equally powerful explanations of the number and variety of books and articles to which students are exposed. The syllabi also contained considerable evidence that most instructors were not inclined to appeal to the curiosity of their students; much less to provide opportunities for its expression. Indeed, even the briefest perusal of the paragraphs in the syllabi describing the conduct of the course[16] conveyed the impression that few instructors are ready to concede confusion over, or curiosity about, international phenomena. Even fewer are inclined to treat knowledge of IR as tentative and subject to variation as conceptualizations and methodologies are varied; instead, most know exactly what they want their students to read and are unwilling to initiate a self-sustaining learning process by allowing their students to choose among alternative assignments. These impressions were amply confirmed by the quantitative data: in only 2 syllabi was more than one week explicitly set aside for a discussion of the nature of knowledge and the methodologies avilable for its generation, and only 27 percent devoted at least a week to the subject; 68 percent of the syllabi included no suggested readings; only 10 percent contained at least one assignment in which students were offered a choice among two or more readings; and only 26 percent offered any kind of choice as to the nature of the term paper that had to be written. Perhaps most important (and, for us, most disquieting), only 12 percent of the syllabi included any wording in their descriptions of the course and its conduct that could be interpreted as suggesting to students that the study of IR is unique, complicated, and/or challenging. Indeed, only 49 percent indicated the goals of the course for which the syllabus was designed.

Pedagogical concerns, therefore, can hardly be seen as the prime source of the diversity of the materials to which students are exposed. The structure of most introductory IR courses appears to be too rigid to attribute the diversity to the performance of the teaching function. Instead, the tendency to supplement text assignments appears best explained by the lack of agreement on the nature of the field. Pedagogical concerns may reinforce this tendency, but most of the evidence from the syllabi makes it seem likely that the absence of a shared paradigm serves to free instructors to pursue whatever intellectual orientations they regard as important.

[16] At least one page of 38 percent of the syllabi was devoted to specifying the purposes and/or procedures of the course; most of the rest devoted only a paragraph or two to such matters.

An insight into the extent of the dissensus over the basic nature of IR is provided by the way in which the syllabi subdivided the field. In 89 percent of them, the assignments and lectures were organized in terms of topical categories — 31 percent exclusively through major (Roman-numeral type) headings, and 49 percent breaking the headings down further into subheadings; the remaining 9 percent merely attached subheadings to each week of the course. But it is the number of headings and subheadings used that suggests the lack of fundamental agreement. As can be seen in Table 4, IR teachers did not follow a common practice when they broke their courses up into basic components: no more than 14 percent agreed on the number of major headings under which to organize the materials of the field; as many used more than 10 headings as used 4. As might be expected, the figures on the use of subheadings revealed an even wider degree of divergence, but even here the range of subcategorizing tendencies was notably large.

To stress the lack of shared perspectives, however, is to run the risk of overlooking faint signs of convergence. One such sign, turned up by the analysis of the syllabi, bears noting. It concerns the degree to which the teaching of IR is organized around current events. Where earlier generations of students in introductory IR courses were said to have been required to keep abreast of the news,[17] only 13 percent of the syllabi listed such a requirement.[18] A reasonable interpretation of this datum is that, while practitioners in the field have yet to agree about the nature of its discipline and contents, they have at least come to share the view that an appropriate comprehension of international phenomena does not depend centrally on a familiarity with day-to-day developments. If earlier generations of introductory students were as widely exposed to newspaper reading as is alleged, this finding may be of more than passing interest. It may signify movement toward the emergence of an IR discipline; or at least it could be argued that to rely heavily on the presentation of current events is to proceed wholly without discipline, and that any movement away from such a reliance could not occur unless the broad outlines of a discipline were becoming manifest to most of those in the field. Admittedly, a commitment to treat knowledge as more stable than the vagaries of daily events is hardly the same as possessing a disciplined mode of inquiry, but surely it is a necessary first step. One might wish that additional steps had been taken as a consequence of the postwar behavioral revolution in

[17] Grayson Kirk, *The Study of International Relations in American Colleges and Universities* (New York: Council on Foreign Relations 1947).

[18] Interestingly, all but one of 23 of the syllabi listing this requirement indicated that it should be performed through the printed rather than the electronic media.

Table 4. Classification of 178 Syllabi by the Number of Substantive Headings and Subheadings Used to Organize the Course Materials (in Percentages)

(1) *Number of Headings or Subheadings Used*	(2) *Proportion of Syllabi Using Specified Number of Headings*	(3) *Proportion of Syllabi Using Specified Numbers of Subheadings*
0	19	40
2	4	1
3	11	1
4	12	1
5	14	1
6	8	2
7	7	2
8	5	4
9	3	5
10	4	4
11	2	4
12	2	6
13	2	4
14	2	4
15	2	2
16	0	2
17	1	2
18	0	1
19	0	2
20	0	1
21	0	2
22	0	1
23	0	1
24	0	2
25	1	1
26 or more	1	4
	100	100

the social sciences; but at least some concrete evidence of disciplinary development can be discerned.[19]

In sum, the 178 syllabi of introductory courses point up the utility of intensively analyzing the texts used in the field, even as they

[19] Further evidence that IR teachers have some sense of working in a discipline can be found in the proportion of courses in which movies or items of fiction were listed among the assignments: only 3 percent of the syllabi listed movies, and only 4 percent assigned items of fiction. On the other hand, the limited extent to which the behavioral revolution may have had an impact on the teaching of IR is perhaps indicated by the fact that only 3 percent of the syllabi assigned, or allowed for, the writing of a term paper in which the student was required to develop a research design, and only 8 percent called for a paper that involved the processing and/or analysis of quantitative data.

also depict a field marked by considerable diversity, if not disarray. Indeed, all the major tendencies uncovered in the syllabi — the lack of interest in recent research findings, the absence of shared paradigms, the apparent disinterest in methodology and the variable nature of knowledge, the limited concern for student motivation and curiosity — can be discerned and even more elaborately in the texts. It is to the content analysis of these that we now turn.

III. TEXTBOOKS AS FACILITATORS OF LEARNING

Our content analysis was conducted in two stages. In one, we employed knowledgeable undergraduates to make simple counts of countries mentioned, maps, charts, footnotes, and other structural dimensions of the texts; in the other, we took on the task of tracing 49 more thematic variables through a content analysis of one-tenth of the paragraphs in each chapter of each text. The first procedure involved an examination of 11,020 pages; the second necessitated the analysis of 2,91[illegible] paragraphs. We are satisfied that in both instances we adhered to the appropriate methodological canons and that our findings are reasonably reliable.[20] Taken together, the two sets of data

[20] To some extent, of course, the simple-count data set is more reliable than the thematic data set — partly because it does not involve sampling procedures, and partly because intercoder reliability is bound to be higher when the mere appearance of a word or format entity is counted than when complex themes have to be recognized and aggregated. The simple-count data set is free of sampling problems because it consists of the entire population; i.e., the analytic units were tallied each time they appeared on every page of every text. High intercoder reliability was sought with respect to this set by working closely with the coders to insure common use of the few categories that were subject to multiple meanings (such as whether the mention of a city constituted reference to the country in which it is located), and by then spot-checking their work to prevent systematic error.

In the case of the thematic data set, on the other hand, we did not have the time to content-analyze each paragraph of every text (as it was, roughly ten minutes were required to code the 49 variables for each paragraph), and thus were compelled to focus on a sample of them. This we did by consulting with statisticians, who assured us that an analysis of 10 percent of the paragraphs was sufficient to achieve a representative sample, and by selecting the paragraphs through a table of random numbers (with transition paragraphs in which the author locates moves from one topic to another being skipped over in order to maximize the analysis of substantive content). The selection process was carried out within each chapter so as to insure coverage of the entire text. Four procedures were used to enhance intercoder reliability in the use of the thematic categories. First, we spent a full twenty weeks (approximately eighty hours) during the winter and spring of 1973 (at Ohio State University) meeting together as a group, identifying, clarifying, pre-testing, and revising the thematic variables. In so doing, we considerably narrowed our differences over the meaning of concepts and the rules for tracing them in the paragraphs. Second, for none of the texts were the paragraphs coded by only one or two of us; rather, the paragraphs for each book were distributed among us for coding, thereby minimizing the degree to which any one of us might introduce systematic error. Third, so as to further prevent systematic bias and achieve uniformity in the coding, the senior author checked the coding of every paragraph and altered those codes for particular variables that appeared to stem from one or two coders holding conceptions of the variables that deviated from that shared

allowed us to organize our inquiry under three broad headings: texts as facilitators of learning, texts as stimuli to learning, and texts as expressive of knowledge.

Texts can facilitate learning in three basic ways: by being written in a clear, concise, and readable style that sustains interest; by being organized in a format that allows the reader to move easily through the written material; and by providing the intellectual tools and skills that are needed to acquire further knowledge and interpret future events. Our data permitted us to evaluate only the last two of these attributes directly. Techniques for assessing style and readability of texts have been developed in the field of psychology,[21] but the constraints of time did not allow us to apply these to the books under review.

Indirectly, however, inferences about style can be drawn from some of our data on the format, skills, contents, and orientations around which the various texts are organized. Indeed, there is obviously considerable overlap — and there are even some contradictions — among the various attributes and dimensions around which we have cast our analysis. Skills shape format and format shapes skills, and both shape and are shaped by content. In so doing, moreover, certain formats and contents are often precluded by the skills a textwriter seeks to highlight. The style and format of a text that stresses factual material and historical narrative, for example, is likely to be quite

by the rest of the group. Fourth, because two aspects of the paragraphs — their 'prime units' (i.e., their central foci) and six cause-and-effect variables — proved especially resistant to convergence during the pre-testing, only the senior author identified the prime unit in every paragraph which served as the basis for assessing the other variables, and alone coded the variables that required judgments about cause and effect.

Ideally, of course, we ought to have also used a fifth technique to insure reliability: that of having a substantial sample of the paragraphs coded by all the coders and then calculating the degree of agreement or disagreement among us on each variable. Early in the coding process we did carry out this procedure on twelve paragraphs. By the time we realized that we had not subjected a sufficient number of paragraphs to this test, several of us had left Ohio State; it proved impossible to reconvene the group in order to carry out further intercoder reliability checks. The results on the initial twelve paragraphs were not discouraging, however. Several variables were found to be troublesome, but most yielded high intercoder reliability scores. (A score exceeding .90 was recorded on 38 of 43 variables, and the mean score for these 43 variables was .95.) In checking the coding of each paragraph, the senior author was especially attentive to those variables that had earlier failed to yield high scores.

In sum, we are confident that our procedures minimized the presence of systematic bias in the thematic data set. Any such bias that remains is that of the senior author who explicitly exercised it in the context of the consensual judgment of the other authors.

[21] See, for example, Rudolf Flesch, *How to Test Readability* (New York: Harper and Brothers 1951); and Barry Gillen, 'Readability and Human Interest Scores of Thirty-Four Current Introductory Psychology Texts,' *American Psychologist*, XXVIII (November 1973), 1010-11.

different from one that emphasizes conceptual precision and methodological rigor; it may well be that the two types are so contradictory in their goals that the style of one cannot possibly be achieved in the other. Thus, despite the lack of direct measures of style, we hope that the ensuing discussion will provide insights into the readability of the texts.

FORMAT

The basic data on the structure and format of the 26 texts are listed in Table 5. The picture presented is mostly that of substantial variability across a wide range. Some of the texts reconstruct the politics of the world in short compass; others are lengthy tomes. They average 17 chapters and 424 pages, but these figures are misleading, since 11 have more than 450 pages and 8 have frewer than 350. Indeed, the books also differ so much in the size of their pages, the size of their type, and the average number of words on each page that we sought standardization by using a per-25,000-words-of-text unit to present the data in Table 5.

The variability in visual presentations is no less than that which marks the length of the books. Table 5 reveals that some texts rely on tables and diagrams to depict the patterns considered important, while others are conspicuously lacking in such techniques for summarizing data and concepts. Substantially more uniformity is evident, on the other hand, with respect to the visual depiction of geographic patterns. There are no maps whatsoever in 17 of the texts, and only 6 have as many as one map per 25,000 words of text. In general, the texts with maps tend to have few tables or diagrams and, as will be seen, they also tend to be among those most historical in their orientation. It is almost as if a geographic-historical approach precludes the use of tabular and diagrammatic materials and vice versa — a distinction that no doubt reflects different conceptions of the nature of knowledge, and that is also probably another indication of the impact of the behavioral revolution on IR. Much as one might regret and resist the tendency to treat the knowledge contained in maps and narrative histories and that aggregated in tables and conceptualized in diagrams as mutually exclusive, it is certainly the case that interpretation of the latter requires, more than does the former, the kind of analytic skills emphasized by the behavioral revolution.

The extent to which the texts acknowledge dependence on a prior body of knowledge is hardly less variable. Table 5 reveals a wide disparity in the practice of footnoting the sources from which the materials are drawn: where 4 of the texts were found to have

Table 5. Format Characteristics of 26 Texts

	Absolute Number			*Number per 25,000-Word Units*							
Text	(1) *Paragraphs Analyzed*	(2) *Chapters*	(3) *Text Pages*	(4) *Chapters*	(5) *Pages*	(6) *Maps*	(7) *Tables*	(8) *Diagrams*	(9) *Footnotes*	(10) *Headings*	(11) *Subheadings*
Axline-Stegenga	36	5	184	3.2	119.48	0.0	0.0	0.0	0.0	12.9	9.7
Bobrow	31	13	94	11.3	81.74	0.0	1.7	9.6	0.0	17.4	15.7
Coplin	93	12	360	2.4	71.29	0.0	2.0	1.8	36.6	12.9	13.3
Crabb	166	20	652	1.4	45.79	0.0	0.3	0.0	75.0	3.9	15.5
Deutsch	62	18	202	4.4	49.39	0.0	2.9	3.7	7.6	10.8	5.1
Dougherty-Pfaltzgraff	88	13	398	2.1	64.93	0.0	0.0	0.3	157.6	15.5	16.0
Duchacek	128	15	543	1.5	52.87	0.0	0.0	0.0	37.6	7.7	13.1
Edwards	71	15	366	2.7	65.83	1.4	0.0	1.1	22.1	13.7	17.4
Frankel	59	10	265	3.9	103.11	0.0	0.4	0.4	23.3	15.1	1.9
Hartmann	216	31	642	2.2	46.29	1.1	0.5	0.4	29.7	14.6	0.0
Holsti	112	16	515	1.7	55.44	0.0	1.2	0.2	45.4	10.6	8.1
Hopkins-Mansbach	158	23	466	2.1	42.60	0.0	3.7	5.9	28.7	9.8	10.8
Jordan	78	28	287	4.9	50.00	2.8	0.2	0.0	44.8	23.5	1.4
Legg-Morrison	67	8	346	1.6	71.49	0.0	3.7	0.6	5.2	8.7	6.8
Modelski	106	17	362	2.7	58.29	0.2	5.2	1.0	37.2	17.7	1.3
Morgan	65	10	275	2.2	59.78	0.0	2.6	1.7	79.2	12.3	2.6
Morgenthau	147	32	552	3.1	52.87	0.2	0.3	0.9	38.3	9.3	12.2
Organski	174	19	490	1.7	43.56	0.0	1.2	0.3	12.9	8.3	13.7
Palmer-Perkins	272	25	770	1.4	42.73	0.9	0.9	0.3	60.2	8.2	25.2
Puchala	78	15	364	2.7	65.82	0.4	3.6	1.1	35.2	10.8	12.3
Rosecrance	77	21	320	3.4	52.12	0.0	0.8	9.6	19.4	15.6	8.6
Schuman	148	15	687	0.9	42.51	2.6	0.1	0.0	10.6	5.1	7.6
Spanier	80	13	429	1.8	58.29	0.0	0.1	0.7	82.1	7.3	0.5
Sprout-Sprout	163	19	468	2.0	48.45	0.9	3.5	0.9	20.0	12.9	6.0
Stoessinger	98	14	541	1.3	51.67	0.0	0.1	0.0	22.4	12.1	3.1
Van Dyke	142	24	442	2.5	47.02	0.0	0.1	0.0	36.4	13.5	22.3
Mean	112	17	424	2.7	59.36	0.4	1.4	1.2	37.2	11.9	9.6

more than 75 footnotes per 25,000-word unit, 4 also have less than 10; the standard deviation from the mean of 37 footnotes is 33. Clearly, the capacity of students to appreciate that the prevailing conception of IR stems from a tradition of previous inquiry is differentially encouraged by the various texts. On the other hand, given the absence of a shared methodological paradigm and a widespread agreement about the nature of IR, it is hardly surprising that textwriters vary widely in their inclination to cite prior findings and theories.[22]

It might be argued that this interpretation is offset by the greater uniformity among the texts in the number of headings and subheadings used to organize the written materials, that a modicum of agreement about the nature of the field is reflected in the fact that the standard deviation from the mean of 12 headings per 25,000-word unit was only 4. Such a conclusion is unwarranted, however, because this uniformity (depicted in column [10] of Table 5) is probably more a consequence of the marketing views shared by the publishers than the views of the field held by the writers. Publishers believe that the interest of readers is best sustained by regularly and frequently breaking up the text into subsections, and using bolder-type leads that anticipate the ensuing paragraphs. Headings and subheadings do facilitate learning from texts but (unlike in syllabi) it is doubtful whether their use also reflects the degree to which observers agree about IR knowledge and its categorization.

PROVISION OF TOOLS AND SKILLS

Presumably, one of the main purposes of any introductory course is to provide students with the capacity to undertake more advanced work in the field or, if they take no further courses, to comprehend the world scene long after they have graduated from college. An introductory course that leaves no residue of competence, no tools and skills with which to interpret and assess the subsequent course of events, is time wasted for all concerned. The facts and issues will change with the passage of time, rendering obsolete and unusable those studied in the introductory course, but the concepts, perspectives, and techniques through which facts and issues are given meaning will continue to be serviceable. It is this basic intellectual equipment that is not dependent on time or place which, hopefully,

[22] It is noteworthy that a similar pattern, perhaps also stemming from the license which the absence of a dominant paradigm affords, was discovered with respect to the inclination of textwriters to provide their readers with lists of additional sources to consult for more thorough treatments of the major topics covered by each chapter: while 15 of the texts contain such lists, 11 did not facilitate learning through the use of this device.

introductory courses make available to those who take them. Although the provision of the tools and skills necessary to the comprehension of world politics in the future is probably best undertaken primarily in lectures and class discussions, it is a task that textwriters cannot ignore. Even if they choose not to organize their materials in terms of the intellectual equipment they deem necessary to an enduring capacity for sound interpretation, they inevitably contribute to or detract from this capacity by the way in which they present their materials — by the extent to which they define their terms, the clarity and nature of the concepts they employ, the degree of their caution in interpreting motivations and consequences, the degree of explicitness about their own values, the links they draw between their conclusions and the methods used to drive them, their readiness to draw on a variety of disciplines for insights and concepts, and the levels of abstraction at which they cast their analyses. Implicitly as well as explicitly, in short, introductory texts provide tools and skills on which their readers may rely for years as they seek to understand the unfolding international scene.

As will be seen, virtually all the 49 variables probed in our content analysis of the 26 texts under review are relevant to the provision of tools and skills. Hence we will have occasion to take note of the way in which the texts perform this task in all the sections that follow. Here, however, we want to focus on six variables that are more exclusively concerned with the provision of intellectual equipment. Table 6 presents the basic findings relevant to these six variables for each text. Here it can be seen that the texts do not vary much in their provision of five of these tools or skills, largely because they do not provide them. In each case, however, at least one text stands out as an exception.

Perhaps the most interesting pattern in Table 6 concerns the degree to which the textwriters *explicitly* indicated their own values about the materials they present.[23] In only 4 texts did the authors explicate their own judgments in more than 5 percent of their paragraphs; in only 2 of these cases (Axline-Stegenga and Schuman) was this practice followed in more than 10 percent of the paragraphs. On the other hand, only one text (Coplin) totally avoided the practice: 25 of the 26 texts had at least a few paragraphs in which the writers' values are readily discernible — a finding that suggests either that they are not committed to value-free analysis or that they are not entirely successful in maintaining such a commitment.

[23] Our coding rule for the identification of explicit values was to ask, 'Does the paragraph contain any explicit indication of the textwriter's values?' A simple affirmative or negative response was recorded in each case; any doubt was resolved in favor of a negative answer.

Table 6. Proportion of 2,915 Paragraphs from 26 Texts in Which 6 Types of Analytic Tools and Skills Were Employed (in Percentages)

Text	*(n)*	(1) *Textwriters' Values Explicit*	(2) *Use of Other Disciplines*	(3) *Data Generation Techniques*	(4) *Data Analysis Techniques*	(5) *Definitions Prime Unit*	(6) *Location in Time or Space*
Axline-Stegenga	(36)	14	6	0	0	25	17
Bobrow	(31)	3	10	29	26	26	13
Coplin	(93)	0	2	2	1	34	6
Crabb	(166)	2	5	2	0	19	51
Deutsch	(62)	7	5	2	8	29	20
Dougherty-Pfaltzgraff	(88)	2	18	5	6	23	19
Duchacek	(128)	3	4	1	0	17	25
Edwards	(71)	3	6	0	0	27	6
Frankel	(59)	3	2	0	0	20	15
Hartmann	(216)	4	2	0	1	16	58
Holsti	(112)	2	1	0	0	40	24
Hopkins-Mansbach	(158)	3	3	3	5	16	30
Jordan	(78)	5	0	0	1	22	44
Legg-Morrison	(67)	3	0	0	0	24	13
Modelski	(106)	7	3	0	0	24	9
Morgan	(65)	9	3	12	2	23	5
Morgenthau	(147)	1	2	0	1	16	26
Organski	(174)	2	2	1	2	13	15
Palmer-Perkins	(272)	1	2	0	1	21	58
Puchala	(78)	1	5	0	1	17	9
Rosecrance	(77)	3	0	1	0	12	30
Schuman	(148)	14	3	0	0	18	56
Spanier	(80)	5	4	0	0	20	45
Sprout-Sprout	(163)	3	5	0	1	16	23
Stoessinger	(98)	2	0	0	0	6	56
Van Dyke	(142)	2	2	1	0	17	13
Mean		4	4	2	1	20	31

Our view is that we are practitioners of a value-explicit discipline. We therefore do not fault the textwriters for failing to achieve a 100 percent record of detachment with respect to their own values. Indeed, we tend to be critical of them for not explicating their values in a higher proportion of their paragraphs. Exactly what proportion would be appropriate, however, is difficult to assess, since much of the content of any text is necessarily devoted to sheer description and definitional analysis. Some might argue that the small percentages indicated in column (1) of Table 6 are sufficient to any text that purports to provide a balanced and detached analysis. But we tend to be critical on the grounds that the values of textwriters probably underlie their observations more extensively than these figures indicate; the texts may thus not convey to beginning students an adequate appreciation of the degree to which our understanding of the world is a function of how we perceive and evaluate it. As will be seen, the pervasive disinclination to explicate values is only the first of several indications that IR textwriters tend to treat the world they describe as an objective reality.

A similar pattern was discovered with respect to the extent to which the texts explicitly drew (in either the text or the footnotes) on disciplines other than political science and international relations.[24] Column (2) of Table 6 shows that only 4 texts explicitly cited another discipline as the source of the concepts and/or data presented in more than 5 percent of their paragraphs, and that only one (Dougherty-Pfaltzgraff) did so in more than 10 percent. Data not presented in Table 6 reveal this pattern even more starkly: in 17 of the texts, not one of the sample paragraphs drew upon economics; the equivalent figure for psychology was 19 texts, for sociology and geography 21, for psychiatry 24, and for anthropology 26. Indeed, for disciplines other than the social sciences, the figure was much more impressive — there were only 9 texts with no paragraphs coded in this residual category — as if drawing upon concepts and data from the physical and biological sciences generated a felt obligation — not experienced with respect to the social sciences — to be explicit about the borrowing process. To be sure, the coding requirement that the other disciplines had to be explicitly mentioned means that these findings underestimate the degree to which the textwriters are in fact dependent on other disciplines. But we would argue that an appreciation of the unity of knowledge and the resulting inclination to seek insight and evidence across disciplinary boundaries is a skill that needs to be nurtured in students; the most effective way to do so is to acknowledge directly each and every step that is taken back and forth across the boundaries that allegedly separate the various disciplines.

With only one conspicuous exception (Bobrow), a uniform pattern of avoidance also marks the way in which the textwriters *explicitly*

[24] Our coding rule for differentiating between explicit and implicit recourse to the materials of other disciplines read as follows: 'The paragraph or footnotes must indicate that it is drawing on other knowledge bases rather than simply using or citing these bases (e.g., a discussion of international trade would be coded as [no recourse to another discipline] unless it is noted that the discussion depends on or draws from economic theory or data).'

drew upon quantitative techniques for generating and analyzing data.[25] As can be seen in columns (3) and (4) of Table 6, only two texts referred explicitly to one or another technique for generating data in more than 5 percent of their sample paragraphs, and only three exceeded this proportion in their explicit references to one or another technique for analyzing quantitative data. Fifteen texts made no references whatsoever in their sample paragraphs to the data generation techniques and thirteen cited no data analysis techniques. Again, it might be contended that our coding requirement — that the recourse to quantitative techniques be explicit — is too stringent, that the provision of these tools and skills can be accomplished simply by using them. We demur. Even if such techniques were frequently used (and below we cite evidence that they have not been), their existence and importance must be highlighted for beginning students, else they will have little basis for coming to appreciate that data do not converge and speak for themselves, that data have to be made and interpreted by observers. However one may feel about the utility and appropriateness of quantitative techniques, surely students in introductory courses are entitled to know of their availability. We can only conclude that textwriters do not share this view. Their reasons, at best, may be that they feel their readers are incapable of coping with a conception of IR as founded on a variable knowledge base; at worst, they may perceive IR as an objective reality which they have undertaken to depict for their readers. In this sense, we see their insensitivity to quantitative techniques as stemming from the same sources as their disinclination to explicate their own values and to wander across disciplinary boundaries.

Although hardly less uniform in their practice, the textwriters are not nearly as inclined to avoid specifying definitions as they are to explicate their values and the disciplinary or quantitative sources from which they derived their observations. As can be seen in column (5) of Table 6, all of them explicitly defined the 'prime unit' of each paragraph[26] in at least 5 percent of the cases, and 18 of them included

[25] Our coding rule for distinguishing an explicit recourse to such techniques read as follows: 'The technique must be specifically identified. Code as [reference to technqiue not made] if the results of the use of a technique are given, but the technique itself not specifically identified. Simply to use a technique is not to refer to it.' Separate subcategories for generating (content analysis, simulation, survey research, etc.) and analyzing (correlational methods, factor analysis, etc.) techniques were included in the coding scheme, but so few paragraphs were coded in them that the results did not seem worthy of presentation in Table 6.

[26] The prime unit of each randomly selected paragraph served as the basis for coding virtually all the variables discussed hereafter. It might be a person, a role, a process, a concept, a country, an event, an international organization — that is, whatever constituted the main subject or concern of the paragraph (as determined by the senior author on the basis of a close reading of the paragraph and, where

such a definition in between 16 and 25 percent of their paragraphs. Plainly, the standard admonition of teachers to students, 'define your terms,' is widely accepted by those who write texts. The fact that definitions tend to be used in only one out of approximately 5 paragraphs should not be interpreted as an insufficient acceptance of the standard. Rather, it is an indication of the degree to which defined terms are then used in exposition — as if the introduction of a new term requiring definition tended to occur on an average of about every fifth paragraph. Whether the definitions presented are appropriately incisive and elaborate, of course, is another matter, and one that cannot be inferred from our use of the definition variable. Some insight into the question, however, can be derived from the discussion, below, of the level of abstraction at which the prime units were analyzed.

Whereas essential uniformity marks the percentages presented in the first five columns of Table 6, the same can hardly be said of column (6). Here the first sign of extensive variability among the texts is evident in the degree to which the prime units of their sample paragraphs were specifically located in historical time or geographic space.[27] Indeed, a bimodal distribution of the texts is plainly manifest in the case of this variable: 7 placed the unit in time or space in 44 or more percent of their paragraphs, while 19 did so in only 30 percent or less. The bimodality of this distribution can be seen even more sharply by noting that the mean percentages for the clusters of 7 and 19 were, respectively, 53 and 17 percent. The distinction between these two clusters is, in effect, the distinction between the

necessary for clarification, the preceding three paragraphs).

If a paragraph contained a definition of a phenomenon not identified as the prime unit, it was coded as not having a definition. Similarly (to give one other illustration of the centrality of the prime unit to our analysis), in our effort to trace the degree to which the textwriters were concerned with the outcomes of behaviors or situations, we included a 'consequences' variable and a paragraph was coded as citing a consequence only if the prime unit was posited as giving rise to it. Consequences caused by entities other than the prime unit were not coded. Originally we sought to develop a scheme in which our variables were applied to every actor or entity mentioned in a paragraph, but this proved much more unmanageable and unreliable than focusing on what the textwriter seemed to treat as the main subject of the paragraph.

[27] The data on this variable were created by affirmative or negative responses to the question, 'Is the prime unit of the paragraph [explicitly or implicitly] identified *in and of itself* in time or space?' Four coding rules were employed to reach a decision in each case: (a) References to times and places that were not part of the prime unit were ignored, since the coding judgment pertained only to the prime unit 'in and of itself.' (b) 'For the unit to be located in space, mention must be explicitly made of an event, person, or place that a narrative historian or political geographer could specifically identify in an account or on a map.' (c) 'For the unit to be explicitly located in time, mention must be made of a day, month, year, decade, century, etc.' (d) 'Implicit time involves specified events without specific time frames (e.g., if the unit is linked to the Korean War without the fact that the conflict occurred in the early 1950s being mentioned).'

tendency to engage in more abstract or more concrete analysis. The 19 that recorded the mean of 17 percent tend toward a more abstract form of presentation in the sense that their mode of analysis does not require them to locate their prime units in time or space; the 7 that recorded the mean of 53 percent cast their analysis in such a way that often the prime unit could not be specified without the inclusion of one or the other of these concrete dimensions.

We regard this distinction as so central to the kinds of tools and skills a text provides that later in the ensuing analysis we note how the texts in the two clusters — which we refer to as the More Abstract and the More Concrete texts — differ in their treatment of certain substantive aspects of IR. It will become clear that the more abstract mode of analysis leads the observer to very different kinds of questions, formulations, and observations than does the more concrete mode. For the present, however, it is sufficient to note that while it may be desirable that students be familiar with certain moments and locales in history, it is quite probable that most 'facts' are not retained as working knowledge. Repeated exposure to the practice of abstracting from particular times and places, on the other hand, tends to foster an enduring skill that can be applied under a variety of circumstances. We shall have occasion to return to this point when we look more closely at the specific data on the times and places cited in the sample paragraphs (Tables 13, 15, and 16).

IV. TEXTBOOKS AS STIMULI TO LEARNING

The acquisition of the tools and skills necessary to an enduring comprehension of world affairs does not ensure the will to use them. The capacity for cogent analysis does not automatically give rise to cogent analysis. Students must be motivated to apply their talents, to probe the dynamics of IR in systematic and creative ways; else they may well fall back on conventional and simplistic modes of thought. Much — indeed, most — of this motivation originates elsewhere than in texts. The way IR is presented and discussed in the classroom, and the attitudes toward learning acquired earlier in life, are obviously more significant sources of motivation than the books that are assigned week after week. Yet, at least texts can be cast in such a way as not to contribute to the attenuation of curiosity, and conceivably they may even serve as stimuli to learning by reinforcing and enlarging the motivations acquired elsewhere. They can make such a contribution, that is, if they approach knowledge about IR cautiously, treating it as tentative and uncertain rather than as given and self-evident; as subject to alternative explanations rather than as susceptible to only one interpretation; and as constantly undergoing revision whenever the dialogue within the community of observers leads to new understandings and changing degrees of consensus. Students are more likely to be stimulated to use their analytic tools and skills, we believe, if international phenomena are not treated as objective realities that teachers and textwriters are revealing for the benefit of those who seek an introduction to the subject. Curiosity is provoked and sustained by what is unknown and yet knowable, by an assurance that the use of analytic tools and skills will yield greater insight and better understanding. To confront students with a body of knowledge that needs to be absorbed rather than pondered is, it seems to us, to dampen the will to learn.

Fortunately, our view of what stimulates learning is entirely consistent with our conception of the field. We believe that knowledge about IR, like that about any other subject, can never be objective, that inevitably it consists of evolving and shifting intersubjective consensuses among those who observe the world, consensuses that evolve and shift as new techniques of observation and new findings lead to new and revised assessments of how and why events unfold as they do.[28] Thus, to expose students to the practice of viewing international phenomena probabilistically and cautiously, of viewing them as subject to variation and alternative explanation, and consequently as the products of varying degrees of intersubjective agreement, is to stimulate learning. The practice also serves to stress crucial methodological and philosophical premises about the nature of the field. The stimuli to learning become, in effect, learning itself.

In addition, the various practices inherent in probabilistic thinking and the various philosophical premises inherent in treating knowledge as varying degrees of consensus constitute tools and skills that enhance incisive analysis. The textwriter who founds his chapters and paragraphs on such practices and premises is providing training as well as substantive knowledge and the motivation to continue learning. The ensuing analysis focuses on six variables included in our content analysis in order to uncover the use of these practices and premises, their relevance to texts as stimuli to learning, and their bearing on the preceding finding that a preponderance of the texts provides little by way of analytic tools and skills.

Although a few exceptions can be noted with respect to some of the variables, the 26 texts are no more praiseworthy as stimuli to learning than as providers of tools and skills. The overall picture derived from the six measures used in this regard is more one in which

[28] For an extensive attempt to elaborate this approach to knowledge, see Rosenau, *The Dramas of Politics: An Introduction to the Joys of Inquiry* (Boston: Little, Brown 1973).

knowledge of IR is posited as objective and unvarying than as consensual and tentative. Perhaps the most clear-cut indication that the textwriters tend to treat the materials they present as objective reality is provided by the distributions that resulted from coding the sample paragraphs in response to the query 'Is the status of the knowledge about all or some of the content specified?' Four possible answers to the question were coded and, as can be seen in Table 7, in virtually

Table 7. Degree of Intersubjective Consensus about the Knowledge Presented in 2,915 Paragraphs from 26 Texts (in Percentages)

Text	*(n)*	(1) *Wide Intersubjective Consensus*	(2) *General Agreement with Some Dissent*	(3) *Subject of Controversy*	(4) *No Degree of Consensus Specified*
Axline-Stegenga	(36)	3	0	0	97
Bobrow	(31)	3	0	3	94
Coplin	(93)	0	2	5	93
Crabb	(166)	1	1	0	98
Deutsch	(62)	3	0	0	97
Dougherty-Pfaltzgraff	(88)	0	1	16	83
Duchacek	(128)	1	0	3	96
Edwards	(71)	1	1	3	95
Frankel	(59)	2	3	5	90
Hartmann	(216)	1	1	1	98
Holsti	(112)	0	1	4	95
Hopkins-Mansbach	(158)	0	0	6	94
Jordan	(78)	0	1	3	96
Legg-Morrison	(67)	2	2	2	95
Modelski	(106)	0	0	2	98
Morgan	(65)	0	5	11	84
Morgenthau	(147)	0	0	1	99
Organski	(174)	0	1	1	98
Palmer-Perkins	(272)	1	1	5	93
Puchala	(78)	1	0	5	94
Rosecrance	(77)	0	0	0	100
Schuman	(148)	1	0	1	98
Spanier	(80)	0	1	3	96
Sprout-Sprout	(163)	2	4	5	89
Stoessinger	(98)	1	0	1	98
Van Dyke	(142)	0	1	0	99
Mean		1	1	3	95

every text the preponderance of the paragraphs did not treat the materials they present as the product of greater or lesser degrees of intersubjective consensus. An average of 95 percent of the paragraphs for the 26 texts contained *no* specification of the status of the knowledge proffered.

In other words, except for a few methodological passages in their introductory chapters that note the existence of various approaches to the field, the texts offer virtually no hint that what they present is other than objective reality. To be sure, given the paucity of findings and interpretations that have cumulated in the field, it is understandable that an average of only 1 percent of the paragraphs was coded as specifying the existence of a wide intersubjective consensus in support of the observations they make, or that an identical mean was uncovered with respect to the proportion of paragraphs that posited 'a general agreement with some dissent.' But it is incomprehensible, at least to us, that the average proportion of paragraphs indicating the existence of controversy over the 'meaning, validity, and/or utility' of the knowledge presented was only 3 percent. Only in the two texts explicitly organized in terms of the contrasts between different approaches and concepts — those by Dougherty-Pfaltzgraff and Morgan — did we record a noticeable proportion of paragraphs in which differences of opinion over the observations offered was acknowledged, and even in these cases the proportions seem considerably smaller than might have been expected.

Surely the field is pervaded by much greater dissensus over the facts, concepts, foci, and perspectives regarded as basic than the data in Table 7 reveal — and yet this equally basic characteristic of the field is kept essentially hidden from students in introductory courses, as if they were incapable of coping with ambiguity and of understanding that knowledge is an ever-evolving process. Probably none of the textwriters is as certain about his understanding of IR as the paragraphs he writes imply, and probably all of them are cautious and probabilistic in their discussions with colleagues on the subject. But somehow, beginning students are considered to be different (as if they were too young to know that knowledge is tentative), so that the rhetoric of certainty and objective reality is reserved for them even as it is eschewed with peers.

Another indicator of such rhetoric is presented in Table 8, which contains the distributions of the data for another variable used to probe the conceptions of knowledge employed by the textwriters. These distributions result from coding each of the sample paragraphs in each text in response to the question, 'Is any content of the paragraph explicitly treated as self-evident?'[29] The resulting distribution

[29] Our coding rules cited the appearance of the following phrases as examples

Table 8. Proportion of 2,915 Paragraphs from 26 Texts in Which the Contents were Treated as Self-evident, either with or without an Authority Cited (in percentages)

Text	*(n)*	(1) *Assertions of Self-Evidence With Authority Cited*	(2) *Assertions of Self-Evidence Without Authority Cited*	(3) *Self-Evidence Not Asserted*
Axline-Stegenga	(36)	0	17	83
Bobrow	(31)	3	10	87
Coplin	(93)	0	6	94
Crabb	(166)	3	8	89
Deutsch	(62)	0	3	97
Dougherty-Pfaltzgraff	(88)	1	1	98
Duchacek	(128)	4	9	87
Edwards	(71)	0	7	93
Frankel	(59)	2	13	85
Hartmann	(216)	1	21	78
Holsti	(112)	0	7	93
Hopkins-Mansbach	(158)	2	4	94
Jordan	(78)	0	9	91
Legg-Morrison	(67)	0	6	94
Modelski	(106)	0	8	92
Morgan	(65)	2	9	89
Morgenthau	(147)	0	18	82
Organski	(174)	0	14	86
Palmer-Perkins	(272)	2	7	91
Puchala	(78)	0	14	86
Rosecrance	(77)	1	22	77
Schuman	(148)	1	17	82
Spanier	(80)	2	10	88
Sprout-Sprout	(163)	2	15	83
Stoessinger	(98)	0	11	89
Van Dyke	(142)	1	7	92
Mean		1	11	88

suggests that while the texts varied somewhat in this regard, a large number of them resorted to assertions of self-evidence in more than an isolated paragraph. Such assertions were found in more than one-tenth of the paragraphs of more than half the texts; in all 26 cases,

of contents being treated as self-evident: 'obviously,' 'quite clear,' 'there can be no doubt that . . .' and 'In fact, of course, . . .'

only a very small proportion of the assertions of self-evidence were accompanied by a citation of the authority for them. Admittedly, a preponderance of the paragraphs in all the texts were free of the rhetoric of self-evidence (the mean for the negative answer to the question was 88 percent), but we would argue that the paragraphs in which such a rhetoric was discerned are higher than is warranted by either the demands of logic (i.e., in paragraphs that elaborate definitions), the facts (i.e., the degree to which anything is self-evident in IR), or the requirements of sound pedagogy (i.e., the need to sustain the curiosity of students).

If a paragraph does not assert that its observations are self-evident, what kind of support, if any, does it offer for them? We sought an answer to this question in two ways. In one we simply asked, 'Does the paragraph identify the source(s) for any observations it offers?'; in the other we sought to classify the nature of the source(s) by asking, 'Is the prime unit discussed or analyzed in terms of, or does it consist of, one or more historical examples, mathematical or formal theories, hypothetical or generalized examples (without specific historical references and not mathematically derived), [and/or] quantitative findings created through manipulation?' Tables 9 and 10 present the results of these inquiries. Despite considerable variability among the texts, in both tables it can be seen that the authors were essentially disinclined to draw upon an explicit body of knowledge when they made observations that were not described as self-evident.

The sources and their identification are found in Table 9: Although 3 texts (Dougherty-Pfaltzgraff, Morgan, and Crabb) did offer a source in a preponderance of their sample paragraphs, 19 texts were recorded as not doing so in more than two-thirds of their paragraphs. When they did cite sources, moreover, half the texts generally did so by citing an authority (i.e., another observer or a document) in the body of the paragraph itself rather than by citing the findings of other studies in a footnote — hardly a surprising tendency if IR is conceived to be a field that has yet to cumulate a large body of findings around which wide intersubjective consensuses have formed. Indeed, Table 10 reveals that virtually all the texts worked through their observations by recourse to historical, hypothetical, or general examples to the extent they offered support for them at all. Not only do examples not constitute proof, as has often been noted, but they are also insufficient as a means of encouraging students to approach IR as an emerging, ever-shifting, consensual body of knowledge. On the contrary, historical examples seem likely to serve in great measure as supplements to the rhetoric of certainty and objective reality, since they appear to be unqualified affirmations of whatever points they are intended to exemplify.

Table 9. Proportion of 2,915 Paragraphs from 26 Texts in Which the Source(s) for their Observations were Identified (in Percentages)

Text	*(n)*	(1) *Source(s) Identified In Paragraph*	(2) *Source(s) Identified In a Footnote**	(3) *Source(s) Identified In a Display†*	(4) *Source(s) Not Identified*
Axline-Stegenga	(36)	11	0	0	89
Bobrow	(31)	19	0	0	81
Coplin	(93)	6	9	0	85
Crabb	(166)	11	51	1	37
Deutsch	(62)	10	4	2	86
Dougherty-Pfaltzgraff	(88)	35	43	1	21
Duchacek	(128)	22	22	3	53
Edwards	(71)	10	13	1	76
Frankel	(59)	10	2	0	88
Hartmann	(216)	8	6	2	84
Holsti	(112)	10	19	3	68
Hopkins-Mansbach	(158)	9	27	5	59
Jordan	(78)	15	7	1	77
Legg-Morrison	(67)	3	0	2	95
Modelski	(106)	3	13	6	78
Morgan	(65)	40	25	3	32
Morgenthau	(147)	10	6	1	83
Organski	(174)	2	4	2	92
Palmer-Perkins	(272)	16	21	3	60
Puchala	(78)	9	14	3	74
Rosecrance	(77)	6	4	3	87
Schuman	(148)	18	10	1	71
Spanier	(80)	16	38	0	46
Sprout-Sprout	(163)	7	7	1	85
Stoessinger	(98)	12	6	0	82
Van Dyke	(142)	17	14	1	68
Mean		12	16	2	70

*Includes paragraphs in which the source(s) were also identified in the content of the paragraph.

†Includes paragraphs in which the source(s) were also identified in the content of the paragraph and/or a footnote.

The fact that most of the textwriters relied on hypothetical or generalized examples to reason through their observations in one-third or more of their paragraphs might be interpreted as offsetting the tendency to posit an objective reality, as indicating a readiness to concede the tentative, variable, and anything but self-evident nature of IR knowledge. However, such would be the case only if hypothetical

Table 10. Proportion of 2,915 Paragraphs form 26 Texts in Which Different Types of Evidence were used to Analyze their Prime Units (in Percentages)

Text	*(n)*	(1) *Historical Examples*	(2) *Mathematical or Formal Theories*	(3) *Hypothetical or Generalized Examples*	(4) *Quantitative Findings*	(5) *No Evidence Offered*
Axline-Stegenga	(36)	19	0	38	0	43
Bobrow	(31)	6	6	25	9	54
Coplin	(93)	25	2	48	2	23
Crabb	(166)	55	0	33	0	12
Deutsch	(62)	16	3	48	7	26
Doughtery-Pfaltzgraff	(88)	13	3	41	1	42
Duchacek	(128)	34	0	45	2	19
Edwards	(71)	23	0	31	0	46
Frankel	(59)	29	0	27	0	44
Hartmann	(216)	49	0	25	1	25
Holsti	(112)	39	0	46	3	12
Hopkins-Mansbach	(158)	32	1	50	2	15
Jordan	(78)	44	0	37	0	19
Legg-Morrison	(67)	3	0	57	0	40
Modelski	(106)	24	0	35	2	39
Morgan	(65)	17	1	33	1	48
Morgenthau	(147)	32	0	34	1	33
Organski	(174)	32	1	24	1	42
Palmer-Perkins	(272)	46	0	32	2	20
Puchala	(78)	18	0	48	2	32
Rosecrance	(77)	34	0	45	3	18
Schuman	(148)	55	0	31	0	14
Spanier	(80)	48	0	38	0	14
Sprout-Sprout	(163)	20	0	44	1	35
Stoessinger	(98)	81	0	5	0	14
Van Dyke	(142)	39	0	11	3	47
Mean		36	1	35	1	27

or generalized examples were worked through in a probabilistic context, with alternative explanations and differing likelihoods being used to elaborate that which was being exemplified. Unfortunately, as noted below, such a probabilistic context was not a pervasive characteristic of any of the texts, so that it seems reasonable to conclude that the evidence provided by textwriters does not adequately serve as a balance to those of their observations that were offered as self-evident. Whatever the texts may teach about IR, they hardly seem conducive to to teaching the basic canons of evidential reasoning and sound analysis.

In order to probe the degree to which the texts were cast in a probabilistic context, we included a variable that required each sample paragraph to be coded in terms of a simple affirmative or negative response to the question, 'Are alternative explanations of the prime unit presented?'[30] The results are presented in Table 11, and again they fall short of what we deem proper and desirable. In one text (Morgan), roughly one-third of the paragraphs were coded affirmatively, and in another 7, roughly one-quarter were so coded; but even these proportions are discrepant with our thinking on the extent to which any observation about international phenomena can be alternatively explained or formulated. The finding that no more than 15 percent of the paragraphs in half the texts were coded affirmatively would seem to be particularly out of line with the multiplicity of possible interpretations.

Data on still another variable relevant to the orientations of the textwriters are presented in Table 12. In this instance we asked, 'Is the prime unit described or analyzed in cautious or probabilistic terms?' Two forms of an affirmative response, as well as a negative response, were coded. One was used for 'specified probabilities' and the other for 'unspecified probabilities or cautious terms,' by which we meant "phrases such as 'seems,' 'in a sense,' 'possibly,' 'likely,' 'more often than not,' and other terms of cautious observation."[31] Once again we find the results disappointing. Although the texts varied widely in their record in this respect, the degree of caution exercised by their authors hardly seems consistent with either a probabilistic approach to knowledge or a sensitivity to the need to stimulate and sustain the curiosities of students in introductory courses. To be sure, given the ambiguities and dearth of quantitative studies that presently mark the field, it is understandable that, in virtually all the texts, more paragraphs were coded with unspecified than with specified probabilities. But this finding seems trivial in comparison to the fact that in all but 3 of the texts at least two-thirds of the paragraphs were coded as lacking cautious or probabilistic terms, and that the overall average of such paragraphs was 81 percent.

[30] In order to maximize the chances of finding alternative explanations, our coding rules required an affirmative response 'if the same prime unit is coded in the three previous paragraphs and alternative formulations of it offered.'

[31] Following the practice used in coding all the variables, each sample paragraph was coded only once in response to the question; explicit rules favored the extreme alternatives being employed whenever a paragraph contained wording that was applicable to both the middle (unspecified probabilities) alternative and one of the extremes. If, for example, a cautious term such as 'possibly' was used along with an incautious one such as 'certainly,' the paragraph was coded in terms of the latter.

Table 11. Proportion of 2,915 Paragraphs from 26 Texts in Which Alternative Explanations of their Prime Units were Offered (in Percentages)

Text	*(n)*	(1) *Alternative Explanation Offered*	(2) *Alternative Explanation Not Offered*
Axline-Stegenga	(36)	3	97
Bobrow	(31)	26	74
Coplin	(93)	24	76
Crabb	(166)	14	86
Deutsch	(62)	0	100
Dougherty-Pfaltzgraff	(88)	29	71
Duchacek	(128)	16	84
Edwards	(71)	25	75
Frankel	(59)	24	76
Hartmann	(216)	7	93
Holsti	(112)	14	86
Hopkins-Mansbach	(158)	23	87
Jordan	(78)	21	79
Legg-Morrison	(67)	18	82
Modelski	(106)	11	89
Morgan	(65)	32	68
Morgenthau	(147)	11	89
Organski	(174)	15	85
Palmer-Perkins	(272)	13	87
Puchala	(78)	13	87
Rosecrance	(77)	13	87
Schuman	(148)	9	91
Spanier	(80)	25	75
Sprout-Sprout	(163)	12	88
Stoessinger	(98)	16	84
Van Dyke	(142)	18	82
Mean		16	84

It is perhaps noteworthy that the inclusion of a probabilistic rhetoric is one of only two pedagogical and methodological variables on which the 19 More Abstract and the 7 More Concrete texts differed noticeably. No more than 3 percentage points separated the overall performance of the two groups with respect to their explication of their own values, their reliance on other disciplines, their use of quantitative techniques, their inclusion of definitions, their tendency to note the degree of intersubjective consensus, their inclination to treat their observations as self-evident and/or to cite sources for them, and their

Table 12. Proportion of 2,915 Paragraphs from 26 Texts in Which Different Probabilities were used to Analyze their Prime Units (in Percentages)

Text	*(n)*	(1) *Specified Probabilities*	(2) *Unspecified Probabilities (or Cautious Terms)*	(3) *Probabilistic (or Cautious) Terms Not Used*
Axline-Stegenga	(36)	11	6	83
Bobrow	(31)	10	42	48
Coplin	(93)	4	30	66
Crabb	(166)	1	5	94
Deutsch	(62)	2	13	85
Dougherty-Pfaltzgraff	(88)	3	16	81
Duchacek	(128)	5	20	75
Edwards	(71)	13	32	55
Frankel	(59)	7	15	78
Hartmann	(216)	4	3	93
Holsti	(112)	17	15	68
Hopkins-Mansbach	(158)	8	31	61
Jordan	(78)	4	23	73
Legg-Morrison	(67)	3	24	73
Modelski	(106)	7	4	89
Morgan	(65)	2	20	78
Morgenthau	(147)	1	3	96
Organski	(174)	3	9	88
Palmer-Perkins	(272)	1	11	88
Puchala	(78)	4	20	76
Rosecrance	(77)	0	12	88
Schuman	(148)	2	5	93
Spanier	(80)	4	10	86
Sprout-Sprout	(163)	5	21	74
Stoessinger	(98)	9	3	88
Van Dyke	(142)	9	14	77
Mean		5	14	81

proclivity for alternative explanations; but 13 percentage points differentiated the proportion of their paragraphs that were found to lack cautious or probabilistic terms. In the More Abstract group, 77 percent were so coded, whereas the comparable figure for their More Concrete counterparts was 90 percent — a difference that is readily explicable when it is appreciated that knowledge tends to seem increasingly variable as one moves up the ladder of abstraction.[32]

Even the greater caution exercised by the More Abstract group, however, hardly offsets the central finding that a probabilistic rhetoric does not mark the texts. The More Abstract texts used such a rhetoric to a greater degree than their More Concrete counterparts, but it did not pervade their writing (or even appear in at least one out of every four paragraphs).

Most textwriters, in other words, are inclined to assert that phenomena are either present in an unchanging state, or absent — without allowing for variations under changing circumstances. We suspect that they are much less absolutist in their research and teaching, if only because variability appears to be a prime characteristic of international phenomena. Yet shomehow they tend not to allow variables to vary in their texts, treating them more as constants, as unwavering, as givens in what thus emerges as a static world scene. Such a tendency concerns us, to repeat, not only because it violates our notion of the need for probabilistic perspectives on IR, but also — and primarily — because it contradicts what we believe to be the best way to stimulate and train those who enter the field. If students do not acquire the rhetoric of probabilistic analysis at an early stage, if their observations are not pervaded by 'it seems as if' or 'it is likely that,' what will bring them to appreciate the variabilities of world politics or the excitement that can be derived from studying the subject? If they are not exposed to variables that vary, how can they be expected to allow their minds to play with ideas and their curiosities to be provoked by the mysteries of causation?

V. TEXTBOOKS AS EXPRESSIVE OF KNOWLEDGE

Perhaps it seems absurd to assess the substantive materials presented by the 26 texts after having raised so many philosophical and methodological doubts about how the knowledge they offer is developed. Our analysis thus far suggests that none of them can be relied upon as a compendium of accumulated and shared findings. Yet they may be expressive of the trends and crosscurrents at present extant in the field. As indicated in Figure I, textwriters tend to be consumers

[32] The other substantial difference between the two groups on a methodological variable concerns the types of evidence on which they relied to develop their observations: the More Concrete group used historical examples in 53 percent of their paragraphs, and hypothetical or generalized examples in 20 percent; the comparable figures for the More Abstract group are 27 and 31 percent. These differences can also be easily understood in terms of the distinction between concrete and abstract analysis. Interestingly, again the two groups did not differ by more than 3 percentage points in the extent to which they cited quantitative findings in support of their observations.

rather than producers of research. Although important exceptions could be noted (such as Organski's notions about 'the power transition'), the texts probably reflect and reinforce rather than elaborate and contribute to the prevailing trends and crosscurrents, through both their conceptions of the central variables that shape and sustain international phenomena and their organization of these into chapters that derive from their exposure to the literature of the field. If this is so, and if allowance is made for the way in which their assumptions about the capabilities of students lead to the simplification and objectification of the concepts, data, and interpretations they present, then it is reasonable to treat the texts under review as a shortcut to insights about the state of the field, its substantive perspectives and empirical insights. Our analysis thus proceeds by examining data descriptive of their conceptions of time, space, actors, action, issues, and causation as key aspects of world affairs.

CONCEPTIONS OF TIME AND HISTORY

We noted earlier that a bimodal distribution marked the way in which the texts located the prime units of their paragraphs in time and place, with 19 of them tending to be more abstract in this regard, while 7 tended to specify concretely one or another of these dimensions. In order to probe these tendencies more extensively, as well as to investigate whether the historical sensitivities of the textwriters were confined to the immediate past, we coded each sample paragraph (as well as its prime unit) in terms of whether it 'explicitly' contained 'any mention of points in time located' in any one of seven historical eras. Both the beginning and ending of the time periods mentioned were coded, so as to pick up observations about historical sequences that spanned one or more of our 7 categories. Table 13 presents the distributions of the data for both points in time (with those for the ending dates in parentheses); here again it can be seen that the texts differed considerably in the extent to which they cast their analyses in a historical content. In at least two-fifths of their paragraphs, 10 did so, while another 10 identified a time period in fewer than one-quarter of their paragraphs. Equally clear is the tendency, both for those that stressed historical context and those that did not, to cite developments in the recent past more elaborately than those in the nineteenth and earlier centuries. In 21 of the texts, more references were made to historical periods that ended after 1946 than to periods ending prior to that date. Yet it would be erroneous to interpret this finding as an excessive preoccupation with immediate events. Only 10 texts made more references to historical periods that began after

Table 13. Proportion of 2,915 Paragraphs from 26 Texts that Mentioned Beginning and (in Parentheses) Ending Dates in 7 Historical Eras (in Percentages)

Text	(*n*)	(1) *Pre-1815*	(2) *1815-1914*	(3) *World War I*	(4) *1919-1939*	(5) *World War II*	(6) *1946-1960*	(7) *1961-1972*	(8) *Dates Not Mentioned*
Axline-Stegenga	(36)	6 (3)	3(0)	3(3)	0(0)	3(3)	11(14)	6 (8)	68(69)
Bobrow	(31)	0 (0)	13(7)	0(3)	0(0)	0(0)	0 (3)	10(10)	77(77)
Coplin	(93)	0 (0)	2(1)	0(0)	2(0)	2(2)	6 (3))	8(14)	80(80)
Crabb	(166)	1 (0)	7(3)	2(1)	9(6)	7(4)	25(18)	15(34)	34(34)
Deutsch	(62)	5 (3)	1(0)	1(2)	3(3)	1(2)	10 (6)	5(11)	74(73)
Dougherty-Pfaltzgraff	(88)	6 (4)	9(5)	1(1)	4(6)	2(2)	0 (1)	0 (3)	78(78)
Duchacek	(128)	5 (1)	4(3)	4(2)	5(1)	11(5)	2 (5)	12(19)	57(64)
Edwards	(71)	0 (0)	0(0)	1(0)	1(0)	1(1)	9 (4)	3(10)	85(85)
Frankel	(59)	7 (3)	7(2)	2(3)	3(0)	0(0)	5 (2)	5(19)	71(71)
Hartmann	(216)	10 (2)	10(6)	3(1)	9(8)	5(6)	20(18)	11(21)	32(38)
Holsti	(112)	14(11)	4(1)	1(0)	7(2)	3(4)	5 (5)	8(17)	58(60)
Hopkins-Mansbach	(158)	6 (5)	3(2)	1(1)	2(2)	1(1)	9 (3)	9(16)	69(70)
Jordan	(78)	3 (1)	1(3)	0(0)	9(5)	3(1)	10 (7)	10(19)	64(64)
Legg-Morrison	(67)	8 (8)	3(0)	1(1)	5(0)	1(1)	0 (0)	3 (9)	79(81)
Modelski	(106)	17(13)	2(0)	0(1)	5(1)	3(4)	3 (5)	4 (9)	66(67)
Morgan	(65)	3 (0)	2(0)	2(0)	1(0)	3(5)	1 (1)	2 (8)	86(86)
Morgenthau	(147)	15 (6)	6(5)	5(2)	7(8)	2(7)	3 (2)	2 (8)	60(62)
Organski	(174)	3 (1)	3(1)	2(0)	3(2)	3(3)	6 (4)	2(11)	78(78)
Palmer-Perkins	(272)	3 (1)	7(4)	4(1)	7(5)	6(4)	22(20)	8(22)	43(43)
Puchala	(78)	3 (0)	0(0)	1(0)	12(1)	4(3)	5 (2)	1(17)	74(77)
Rosecrance	(77)	17 (9)	16(8)	5(8)	3(4)	1(4)	6 (5)	8(16)	44(46)
Schuman	(148)	16 (9)	6(4)	3(2)	11(6)	7(7)	24(26)	10(20)	23(26)
Spanier	(80)	3 (1)	1(2)	9(0)	3(1)	6(8)	16(11)	10(22)	52(55)
Sprout-Sprout	(163)	5 (1)	6(4)	2(3)	3(1)	4(4)	7 (3)	3(14)	70(70)
Stoessinger	(98)	5 (2)	5(3)	1(0)	6(3)	7(5)	23(17)	14(31)	39(39)
Van Dyke	(142)	3 (0)	2(1)	1(0)	7(5)	2(2)	8 (6)	4(13)	73(73)
Mean		6 (3)	5(3)	2(1)	6(3)	4(4)	11 (9)	7(17)	59(60)

1946 than to periods beginning at an earlier point in time. Indeed, exactly half of the texts mentioned periods beginning prior to World War I. These apparent discrepancies between the data for the beginning and ending dates can be readily interpreted: since every text mentioned both dates whenever they placed a paragraph in a historical context (i.e., since their proportions in the last column of Table 13 were virtually identical), the greater frequencies in the left-hand columns for the beginning dates and in the right-hand columns for the ending dates reflect a practice of casting analysis in sweeping historical contexts, extending across two or more of the time boundaries through which periodicity is usually introduced into modern history. Stated differently, to the extent historical context was employed, the text-writers tended to look well into the past for explanations of the present rather than focusing exclusively on current events. Just as course syllabi were found not to rely on newspapers for information, so most texts seemed to eschew reliance on the prevailing scene for guidance and insight.

Whatever their use of history as an explanation for the present, however, the texts clearly seemed to be unconcerned with it as a guide to the future. We also coded every paragraph in terms of whether they 'explicitly mentioned structures or trends that may exist or unfold in the future, or cease to exist in the future, or continue to exist in the future.' As can be seen in Table 14, virtually every text shied away from a future context. More than half made such references in

Table 14. Proportion of 2,915 Paragraphs for 26 Texts that Mentioned Developments that may occur in the Future (in Percentages)

Text	*(n)*	(1) *Future Mentioned*	(2) *Future Not Mentioned*
Axline-Stegenga	(36)	11	89
Bobrow	(31)	0	100
Coplin	(93)	4	96
Crabb	(166)	5	95
Deutsch	(62)	8	92
Dougherty-Pfaltzgraff	(88)	5	95
Duchacek	(128)	7	93
Edwards	(71)	1	99
Frankel	(59)	0	100
Hartmann	(216)	3	97
Holsti	(112)	3	97
Hopkins-Mansbach	(158)	4	96
Jordan	(78)	4	96
Legg-Morrison	(67)	7	93
Modelski	(106)	3	97
Morgan	(65)	2	98
Morgenthau	(147)	3	97
Organski	(174)	8	92
Palmer-Perkins	(272)	9	91
Puchala	(78)	9	91
Rosecrance	(77)	8	92
Schuman	(148)	6	94
Spanier	(80)	10	90
Sprout-Sprout	(163)	15	85
Stoessinger	(98)	3	97
Van Dyke	(142)	4	96
Mean		6	94

less than 5 percent of their sample paragraphs and only one (Sprout-Sprout) stands out as having noticeable concern for developments that lie ahead. We confess to being disappointed by this finding, not only because our scientific orientations lead us to an interest in prediction, but also because our concern for motivating and training students leads us to presume that by more frequent exposure to analyses that project and extrapolate into the future, students will develop a keener sense of the variability and dynamics of IR.

CONCEPTIONS OF SPACE

In this section we present the results of a separate content analysis of every mention of a country, continental region, or international organization on every page of every text.[33] We do so not by way of investigating the way in which the textwriters approach questions of geography. Rather, our purpose is to use the pattern of geographic references as a means of exploring their perceptions of the hierarchical structure of the international system. We presume that the more frequently textwriters refer to a country, region, or organization, the more importance do they attach to it as an international actor. Thus, for example, by comparing the relative frequency of references to the United States, the Soviet Union, China, Japan, and the Common Market countries with those to the nations of Asia, Africa, and Latin America, one can develop an insight into the status- and issue-orientations of the textwriters. In addition, the relative frequency with which they refer to the United States (or, in the case of Frankel, to Great Britain), can serve as a good indication of the extent to which ethnocentric bias underlies their analysis. The extent to which the various texts differed in the frequencies of their references to specific actors, moreover, provides a measure of how they vary in terms of the levels of abstraction at which their analyses are cast.

Table 15 presents the mean number of references to political entities at the national level (or, as in the case of Berlin or divided countries, at the subnational level with some claim to statehood or special status) per 25,000-word unit in the 26 texts. The countries

[33] The unit of measurement used in the analysis and in Table 15 is mentions per 25,000 words. This ratio is based not on a sample of paragraphs, but rather on every mention in every paragraph (except those in book titles, prefaces, appendices, footnotes, or tables). Mentions of capital cities used as a shorthand for countries (such as 'Washington' or 'Moscow') were coded as a country reference. The geographic categories used to code the data were those developed in Bruce M. Russett, J. David Singer, and Melvin Small, 'National Political Units in the Twentieth Century: A Standardized List,' *American Political Science Review*, Vol. 62 (September 1968), 932–51.

Table 15. Frequency of References to National and Subnational Political Entities (Ranked by Mean Number of References per 25,000-Word Unit for 26 Texts)

Country	*Mean*	*Country*	*Mean*	*Country*	*Mean*
U.S.	74.43	Burma	.71	El Salvador	.09
U.S.S.R.	64.76	Iraq	.71	Zambia	.08
Great Britain	27.96	Philippines	.70	Maldive Islands	.08
China	24.06	Brazil	.69	Hong Kong	.08
France	23.28	Laos	.67	Costa Rica	.08
Pre-WWII Germany	19.96	Syria	.67	Trinidad & Tobago	.07
Japan	9.37	Malaysia	.66	Gabon	.07
India	7.18	Cyprus	.66	Monaco	.07
Cuba	6.48	Ghana	.64	Madagascar	.07
Israel	5.76	Tanzania	.63	Mozambique	.07
United Arab		Cambodia	.61	Mauritania	.07
Republic (Egypt)	5.37	Bulgaria	.60	Togo	.06
Italy	5.12	Morocco	.60	U.S. Pacific Trust	.06
Vietnam	4.33	Albania	.56	Senegal	.06
Pakistan	4.25	Thailand	.54	Chad	.06
Korea	3.59	Caribbean West Indies	.53	Liechtenstein	.06
Czechoslovakia	3.54	Dominican Republic	.50	Jamaica	.06
Austria	3.51	Luxemburg	.49	Greenland	.06
Berlin	3.24	Argentina	.47	Oceania	.05
Poland	3.03	Lebanon	.46	Panama Canal Zone	.05
Greece	2.64	Saudi Arabia	.43	Malawi	.05
Spain	2.44	Denmark	.39	Bhutan	.05
North Vietnam	2.24	Persian Gulf	.36	Upper Volta	.05
Federal Republic		Ireland	.35	Sierra Leone	.04
of Germany	2.21	Ivory Coast	.34	Lesotho	.04
Switzerland	2.19	Norway	.33	Cameroon	.04
Yugoslavia	2.17	New Zealand	.33	Central African Republic	.04
Indonesia	2.08	Guatemala	.32	Malta	.04
Canada	2.05	Mongolia	.31	Fiji Islands	.04
South Vietnam	2.00	Chile	.30	Southern Yemen	.04
Turkey	1.96	Venezuela	.30	Nauru	.03
Hungary	1.88	Yemen	.29	Western Samoa	.03
Congo (Brazzaville)	1.82	Afghanistan	.27	Quemoy-Matsu	.03
Belgium	1.71	Peru	.26	Guam	.03
Union of South Africa	1.66	Sudan	.25	Virgin Islands	.03
Netherlands	1.58	Kenya	.23	Niger	.03
Taiwan	1.25	Libya	.22	Barbados	.03
Democratic Republic		Sri Lanka	.21	Burundi	.02
of Germany	1.24	Colombia	.21	Bahamas	.02
North Korea	1.21	Panama	.19	Rwanda	.01
Portugal	1.13	Kuwait	.18	Guyana	.01
Rumania	1.12	Liberia	.17	Bahrain Islands	.01
South Korea	1.06	Somalia	.16	Macao	.01
Algeria	1.05	Iceland	.14	Gambia	.01
Iran	.97	Singapore	.13	Mauritius	.01
Nigeria	.91	Mali	.12	Bermuda	.01
Jordan	.90	Uganda	.12	Martinique	.00
Bangladesh	.88	Uruguay	.12	St. Lucia	.00
Finland	.88	Angola	.12	Zaire	.00
Ethiopia	.81	Paraguay	.11	Grand Cayman	.00
Sweden	.78	Puerto Rico	.11	Antigua	.00
Tunisia	.77	Nepal	.10	St. Vincent	.00
Australia	.76	Nicaragua	.10	Netherlands Antilles	.00
Rhodesia	.75	Ecuador	.09	British Honduras	.00
Mexico	.73	Haiti	.09		
Palestine	.72	Honduras	.09		

are listed in rank order. Here it becomes dramatically evident that the textwriters have a highly stratified conception of the international system. Where 12 countries had a mean in excess of 5.0 units, more than 60 had one of less than 0.5 units. Stated differently (and in terms of data not in Table 15), only 13 countries were mentioned in every text, and only 55 were mentioned in as many as 20 texts. Even among the entities cited most frequently, moreover, the degree of stratification is considerable, with the U.S. and the U.S.S.R. being referred to more than twice as often as any other country. These are followed by another cluster of four — Great Britain, China, France, and pre-World War II Germany — that were mentioned more than twice as often as any of the others. At that point in the ranking, neither great- or major-power status, nor even regional leadership, appears to be the prime basis for the frequency of mentions. Rather, a goodly number of the remaining countries near the top of Table 15 consist of those around which major crises of the cold-war period centered. For example, while such regional leaders as Brazil and Ghana appear well down on the list, 7 of the top 20 — Cuba, Israel, Vietnam, Korea, Czechoslovakia, Berlin, and Greece — presumably achieved their relatively high status because they have been the foci of major world issues rather than because of the capabilities they bring to the international arena.

For the textwriters, in other words, importance as an international actor is not simply a matter of power and respect. They may conceptualize status in terms of such variables as size and industrial capacity, but aside from the few great powers, the countries to which they refer most frequently are likely to be those that get caught up in major international conflicts. Their time frame for status is thus a narrow one; any comparable ranking derived from texts available twenty years from now is likely to be very different from the one in Table 15. We are distressed by this finding. It can be viewed in several ways, only one of which strikes us as conducive to either the presentation of sound knowledge or the basis for good pedagogy. The narrow, issue-oriented time frame can be interpreted (a) as an indication that the texts continue to be mainly concerned with current events; (b) as an indication that the writers are disinclined to rely on quantified events data to depict the recurrent patterns and hierarchical structure of world politics and therefore fall back on analyzing those major crises for which there is considerable documentation; (c) as a sign that the texts are cast at abstract levels of analysis and use the more dramatic events of recent times to illustrate their analytic distinctions; or (d) as a measure of the large extent to which textwriters are so preoccupied with superpower politics and confrontation that they focus more on the arenas of conflict than on the evidences of hierarchical structure. The third of these interpretations is perhaps the most persuasive and encouraging, especially as we shall present some evidence below that more than a few of the texts do cast their analyses at sufficiently high analytic levels to need to cite concrete situations only for illustrative purposes. Even so, we are disturbed by the possibility that major crises have inadvertently come to serve as the bases for moving up the ladder of abstraction rather than as empirical examples of conceptual distinctions derived from an independent understanding of the world's stratification system. Perhaps the catastrophic conflicts that mar history do reveal the hidden structures of international politics; but we suspect that this may not be so and that there are more reliable ways — such as events data — of uncovering underlying patterns.

The data in Table 15 do not allow for the conclusion that the textwriters have an ethnocentric concern with the United States. It is ranked first in terms of the mean number of references, but the Soviet Union is such a close second that the data can more plausibly be interpreted as reflecting a preoccupation with superpower politics than as an expression of ethnocentrism. Indeed, as can be seen in Table 17, 8 texts refer to the Soviet Union more frequently than to the United States.[34]

On the other hand, a pronounced orientation toward industrial and Western societies can be discerned in the rankings of Table 15. Leaving aside the countries that ranked high because they were the foci of cold-war crises, we find that the nations of the Third World were, with few exceptions, conspicuously located toward the lower end of the ranking, while those of the industrial regions could be found mostly in the upper half of the ranking.

An insight into the relative degrees of concern for developed and developing nations is provided by the frequency of references to the various geographic entities to which observers tend to resort when summarily analyzing activities in a whole region or continent. These data are presented in Table 16, and here it is plainly evident that the textwriters are not oblivious to the Third World. Europe was the highest-ranking region, with Africa, Asia, and South America following; in the case of Africa and Asia, the number of references exceeded all but 7 countries, and in the case of South America, all but 11. The countries of the developing world, it would seem, are considered important as aggregates, but not as differentiated entities. Perhaps because they have a more detailed understanding of the inner workings and problems of Western nations, the textwriters are more inclined to identify them directly, while relying on regional generalizations

[34] Furthermore, Frankel, the author of the one text prepared originally for distribution in England, resists ethnocentric temptations and refers to the United States considerably more often than to Great Britain (again see Table 17).

Table 16. Frequency of References to Regional and Continental Entities (Ranked by Mean Number of References per 25,000-Word Unit for 26 Texts)

Region	*Rank*	*Mean Number*	*Region*	*Rank*	*Mean Number*
Europe	1	21.02	Middle East	7	2.96
Africa	2	8.96	Southeast Asia	8	2.18
Asia	3	7.92	North America	9	1.57
South America	4	5.35	Central America	10	1.34
Western Europe	5	3.91	Scandinavia	11	.22
Eastern Europe	6	3.89	Polar Region	12	.14

when their analysis concerns other parts of the world.

Turning to the degree to which the texts vary in the importance they attach to various entities at the national level, in Table 17 we present the rankings, for each text, of the 20 countries with the highest average number of references per 25,000-word unit. Here it can be seen that the rankings of most of the countries were quite stable across the 26 texts, with the level of agreement on the 5 highest being especially conspicuous. Some exceptions can be found in almost every column, but the overall pattern suggests considerable consensus about both the way in which the global system is stratified and the importance that is attached to major international conflicts.

A finding that will become even more evident in the next section is that the frequency of references to international organizations and other supranational political entities (Table 18) does not reflect an intense preoccupation with this level of world politics. To be sure, a comparison of Tables 15 and 18 reveals that the mean number of references to the United Nations exceeded the comparable figure for all but three countries, and that the League of Nations, COMECON, and NATO were referred to more often than several of the top 20 entities at the national and subnational level. Beyond these few exceptions, however, the world portrayed in the texts is not pervaded with supranational institutions. Table 18 lists 29 institutions, of which 23 were referred to less often than once every 25,000 words. Similarly, a comparison of Tables 16 and 18 reveals that 10 of the 12 regional entities were referred to more often than all but 5 of the supranational institutions, one of which (the League of Nations) no longer exists. Persumably the League appears high on the list because the textwriters feel compelled to analyze the weaknesses of international organizations as well as to describe the historical antecedents of the United Nations.

In sum, the texts tend to portray the world as centered around nation-states and as sustained by industrialized and Western actors, particularly the United States and the Soviet Union. For reasons

Table 17, Part I. Ranking for Each Text of the 20 Entities at the National or Subnational Levels with the Highest Average Number of References per 25,000-Word Unit (Rankings run from 1 for the highest to 20 for the lowest)

Text	*U.S.A.*	*U.S.S.R.*	*Great Britain*	*China*	*France*	*Pre-WWII Germany*	*Japan*	*India*	*Cuba*	*Israel*
Axline-Stegenga	2	1	4	3	4	7	10	6	13	8
Bobrow	2	4	6	8	8	7	8	14	3	13
Coplin	1	2	3	5	4	6	10	9	7	8
Crabb	2	1	4	3	5	8	10	6	11	9
Deutsch	1	2	3	6	4	5	7	10	9	14
Dougherty-Pfaltzgraff	1	2	3	6	4	4	7	9	11	12
Duchacek	2	1	6	3	5	4	7	8	12	16
Edwards	2	1	6	7	7	9	12	14	5	19
Frankel	1	2	3	4	7	6	14	8	13	5
Hartmann	2	1	5	3	7	4	6	11	16	18
Holsti	2	1	6	4	5	3	9	13	12	18
Hopkins-Mansbach	1	2	3	6	4	5	8	13	7	9
Jordan	2	1	6	4	3	11	9	17	5	7
Legg-Morrison	1	2	4	3	4	6	8	12	10	10
Modelski	1	5	2	4	3	6	7	8	18	15
Morgan	1	2	7	3	6	7	11	14	4	9
Morgenthau	1	2	3	9	4	5	8	11	12	17
Organski	1	2	3	4	5	6	7	8	10	13
Palmer-Perkins	1	2	3	5	4	6	8	7	16	13
Puchala	1	2	5	3	4	6	9	7	13	15
Rosecrance	1	2	5	9	3	4	8	17	7	10
Schuman	1	2	3	6	4	5	7	12	18	10
Spanier	1	2	4	3	5	6	10	12	11	18
Sprout-Sprout	1	2	3	4	5	7	6	8	13	12
Stoessinger	2	1	3	4	5	7	11	6	17	8
Van Dyke	1	2	3	5	6	4	7	10	19	16
All 26 Texts	1	2	3	4	5	6	7	8	9	10

Table 17, Part II

Text	*Egypt (U.A.R.)*	*Italy*	*Vietnam*	*Pakistan*	*Korea*	*Czechoslovakia*	*Austria*	*Berlin*	*Poland*	*Greece*
Axline-Stegenga	10	16	12	9	18	16	20	15	19	14
Bobrow	5	15	8	1	15	15	15	12	15	15
Coplin	12	18	14	17	11	15	15	13	20	19
Crabb	7	16	12	14	13	17	20	18	15	19
Deutsch	14	8	12	16	11	17	20	19	17	17
Dougherty-Pfaltzgraff	8	12	17	15	13	18	18	16	20	10
Duchacek	15	13	11	17	14	9	20	19	10	13
Edwards	19	14	11	3	10	14	12	4	18	14
Frankel	20	12	9	14	10	16	17	19	17	11
Hartmann	13	8	19	17	11	14	9	15	10	20
Holsti	11	10	19	14	17	7	15	16	20	8
Hopkins-Mansbach	10	11	12	19	14	16	18	17	15	20
Jordan	14	16	12	14	13	17	20	18	15	9
Legg-Morrison	17	19	7	13	13	13	19	18	13	9
Modelski	11	9	10	17	13	12	16	20	18	14
Morgan	16	13	5	19	10	14	16	11	19	18
Morgenthau	16	7	20	19	13	14	6	17	10	15
Organski	11	9	15	20	12	18	19	15	14	17
Palmer-Perkins	9	10	20	12	11	18	13	19	17	15
Puchala	10	8	12	20	10	18	15	18	11	14
Rosecrance	13	11	12	19	20	14	6	16	17	15
Schuman	9	8	16	19	16	15	13	20	11	14
Spanier	13	17	7	19	9	14	20	8	15	16
Sprout-Sprout	9	10	11	18	13	15	20	19	15	15
Stoessinger	9	18	16	13	15	9	18	12	14	19
Van Dyke	19	8	12	20	15	12	14	17	10	17
All 26 Texts	11	12	13	14	15	16	17	18	19	20

Table 18. Frequency of References to International and Supranational Political Entities (Ranked by Mean Number of References per 25,000-Word Unit for 26 Texts)

Entity	*Mean*	*Entity*	*Mean*
United Nations (UN)	26.72	International Labour Organisation (ILO)	.25
Council for Mutual Economic Assistance (COMECON, CMEA)	6.01	General Agreement on Tariffs and Trade (GATT)	.25
League of Nations	5.53	Food and Agriculture Organization (FAO)	.24
North Atlantic Treaty Organization (NATO)	3.53	International Monetary Fund (IMF)	.18
European Economic Community (Common Market, EEC)	2.42	European Atomic Energy Community (EURATOM)	.17
Organization of American States (OAS)	1.02	International Bank for Reconstruction and Development (World Bank, IBRD)	.16
International Court of Justice (ICJ)	.91	United Nations Children's Fund (UNICEF)	.11
United Nations Educational, Scientific and Cultural Organization (UNESCO)	.77	United Nations Conference On Trade and Development (UNCTAD)	.10
Warsaw Treaty Organization (Warsaw Pact)	.72	International Red Cross	.08
'Free World'	.67	Council of Europe	.08
South-East Asia Treaty Organization (SEATO)	.63	United Nations Development Program (UNDP)	.07
European Coal and Steel Community (ECSC)	.47	World Court	.05
Organization of African Unity (OAU)	.33	International Atomic Energy Agency (IAEA)	.04
World Health Organization (WHO)	.31	United Nations High Commissioner for Refugees (UNHCR)	.02

elaborated below, we are concerned about this underlying structure. Nation-states may be the prime actors, and the industrial superpowers do dominate, but is the imbalance as great as the foregoing data imply? Will such a perspective continue to be appropriate to an increasingly interdependent world?

CONCEPTIONS OF ACTORS

Our preoccupation with the levels of abstraction at which IR texts are cast led us to code each sample paragraph in terms of whether it 'explicitly contains any mention' of each of 8 types of actors, 4 of them being concrete actors and 4 being analytic at 4 levels of analysis: (1) 'an individual person,' (2) 'a specific role filled or fillable by a concrete person,' (3) 'a concrete group less encompassing than a nation-state or national society,' (4) 'a generalized group less encompassing than a nation-state or national society,' (5) 'a concrete nation-state or nation-states,' (6) 'a generalized nation-state or nation-states,' (7) 'a concrete governmental or nongovernmental international organization,' and (8) 'a generalized governmental or nongovernmental international organization.'[35] Table 19 presents the percentage of each type of actor found in the sample paragraphs of each text. Here several patterns could be discerned. One of them affirmed the earlier finding that texts can differ considerably in their emphasis on concrete and analytic phenomena. Whereas 6 of the texts, for example, cited an equal or higher proportion of generalized actors at all 4 levels of analysis, 4 mentioned concrete actors more frequently at each level. Similarly, another 5 included generalized actors in as many or more paragraphs at 3 of the 4 levels, while 5 mentioned concrete actors in more paragraphs at 3 levels. The percentage differences in both directions, moreover, were often sizable, running as high as 69 points in one case (Stoessinger at the national level) and exceeding 20 points in more than a few cases. Stated differently, the bimodal distribution resulting from the opposite tendencies toward concrete and analytic formulations left only 6 texts with more paragraphs containing generalized actors at 2 levels and more concrete actors at the other 2 levels. It might be said that these 6 texts are the only ones that achieve a balance in identifying the generalized and concrete actors, but we would be more

[34] Perhaps the best way to summarize our coding rules for these categories is to give an example or two of actors coded in each: (1) 'Winston Churchill'; (2) 'the American presidency' or 'the voter'; (3) 'the Nixon Administration' or 'the Labor Party'; (4) 'bureaucracies' or 'dissident factions'; (5) 'Albania'; (6) 'superpowers'; (7) 'the United Nations' or 'IBM'; and (8) 'transnational professional societies' or 'multinational corporations.'

Table 19. Proportion of 2,915 Paragraphs from 26 Texts in which mention was made of 8 Types of Actors at 4 Levels of Analysis (in Percentages)

		Individuals		*National Subgroups*		*Nation-States*		*International Organizations*	
Text	*(n)*	*Concrete (1)*	*Analytic (2)*	*Concrete (3)*	*Analytic (4)*	*Concrete (5)*	*Analytic (6)*	*Concrete (7)*	*Analytic (8)*
Axline-Stegenga	(36)	8	39	6	25	31	69	8	14
Bobrow	(31)	3	10	7	6	26	13	0	0
Coplin	(93)	8	45	5	30	41	68	11	14
Crabb	(166)	47	26	25	20	80	35	31	5
Deutsch	(62)	13	24	10	40	40	56	11	11
Dougherty-Pfaltzgraff	(88)	21	22	6	25	23	42	3	9
Duchacek	(128)	36	36	20	27	50	56	14	7
Edwards	(71)	8	6	1	6	24	32	9	1
Frankel	(59)	8	5	5	14	41	58	14	5
Hartmann	(216)	32	8	3	10	68	46	23	5
Holsti	(112)	14	25	16	33	56	62	17	10
Hopkins-Mansbach	(158)	34	36	19	24	50	36	15	7
Jordan	(78)	22	18	10	15	58	45	8	6
Legg-Morrison	(67)	6	16	7	36	22	61	10	10
Modelski	(106)	4	17	3	23	27	55	5	9
Morgan	(65)	9	25	9	28	15	38	9	8
Morgenthau	(147)	18	16	3	15	49	51	19	4
Organski	(174)	5	11	5	16	45	65	9	5
Palmer-Perkins	(272)	27	23	3	16	61	45	42	7
Puchala	(78)	14	32	6	26	31	62	13	5
Rosecrance	(77)	14	17	9	23	53	73	9	7
Schuman	(148)	50	29	33	30	68	36	17	4
Spanier	(80)	40	22	31	39	74	60	13	5
Sprout-Sprout	(163)	10	28	7	31	33	59	6	4
Stoessinger	(98)	32	5	12	9	84	15	49	3
Van Dyke	(142)	11	11	4	16	43	61	24	8
Mean		22	21	12	22	50	50	18	6

inclined to conclude that they are the only ones that lack a perspective on this important issue.

A second pattern that becomes evident in Table 19 is that, within the texts, striking differences prevail between the way in which subnational groups and international organizations are presented. The former tend to be treated as generalized actors, while the latter are identified in concrete terms. Of the 26 texts, 22 recorded a higher proportion of paragraphs with generalized subnational groups; the same number mentioned concrete international organizations in as many or more of their paragraphs. It is as if the role of subnational actors has yet to be adequately researched, and thus their activities and importance are understood only at the conceptual level, whereas the role of international organizations is historically clear but conceptually obscure. One 'knows' that subnational actors exert influence on foreign policy, but it is an influence that is difficult to trace empirically, and few case studies that do so are available. On the other hand, one 'sees' international organizations at work almost daily, but whether and how they perform a central role in the dynamics of world politics is hard to derive from the welter of observations. In addition, the relative neglect of international organizations at more abstract levels may stem from the tendency (elaborated below) of the textwriters to organize their materials around a nation-state-centered world. In such a world, empirical note must be taken of how international organizations facilitate, hinder, or otherwise serve as a backdrop for the activities of nation-states, but the need to locate them conceptually is not considered important inasmuch as their role is considered to be slight. Whatever the reasons for the sharp discrepancy in the treatment of subnational and international actors, they do not obtain with respect to national and individual actors. In both these instances, more texts cite the generalized actor as or more often than its concrete counterpart, but the discrepancy is not so pronounced (17 to 9 in the case of national actors, and 14 to 12 in the case of individual actors).

The most clear-cut pattern in Table 19 involves the nation-state orientations of the textwriters. All 26 pay as much or more attention to this type of actor than any other, *both* conceptually and empirically. Indeed, the mean figure for the proportion of paragraphs mentioning a national actor was exactly 50 percent for both the generalized and concrete categories, and this figure is more than twice the size of the average for any of the other actors in either category. If the deeper structures of the international system are undergoing profound change, as some assert, the recognition of such processes does not appear to have surfaced at the textbook level. Notwithstanding occasional paragraphs that acknowledge the process whereby technological change has fostered the emergence of new actors, issues and transnational relationships, the student is introduced to a world pervaded by the nation-state.

In like manner, perhaps for reasons already suggested, all 26 texts paid the least attention to international organizations as generalized actors. On the other hand, 13 mentioned them as much or more as concrete actors than they did subgroups or individuals; only 7 refer to them less often than to any of the other concrete actors.

Aside from their shared preoccupation with nation-states and their minimal interest in generalized international organizations, the texts do not exhibit any uniformity with respect to their relative treatment of the other actors. Generalized subgroups were mentioned second-most frequently by 16 of the texts; at the concrete level only 3 did so, and 14 referred to them least often. Generalized individual actors were cited second-most frequently in 11 texts and third-most frequently in the remainder. The comparable figures for concrete individual actors were 12 and 12, with the remaining 2 citing them least often.

CHARACTERISTICS AND VARIABILITY OF ACTORS AND ACTION

Whatever the actor and whatever the level of abstraction at which it is depicted, how do the texts tend to conceive of it? As goal-oriented? As motivated? As subject to variation? As being shaped or influenced by causes? As giving rise to consequences? As engaging in behavior, either interactively with other actors or independently without reference to them? Our content analysis included variables designed to shed light on these questions. More accurately, we coded each sample paragraph in terms of whether the prime unit was associated with any or all of these characteristics.[36] In the case of most of these variables, moreover, we recorded whether or not the paragraph described them as varying.

The first four columns of Table 20 present data on the goals and motives ascribed to the prime units, with goals being defined as 'in order to' statements about the unit, and motives being viewed as 'because of' characterizations. That is, paragraphs were coded as referring to goals when their units were described as being oriented toward — either through planning or through action — some future

[36] Although often the prime units were individual, subgroup, national, or international actors, a number of them were not: thus there is need for caution against treating the data in Tables 20-24 as exclusively descriptive of actors. They also depict the characteristics of situations, wars, crises, schools of thought, and the other topics that constitute the main focus of a paragraph. An insight into the way in which the texts conceptualize actors is best achieved by comparing the columns in Tables 20-24 rather than by interpreting the absolute figures.

Table 20. Proportion of 2,915 Paragraphs from 26 Texts in Which Goals, Motives, and Independent Behavior were Ascribed to their Prime Units and Variations in them were Depicted (in Percentages)

Text	*(n)*	*(1) Goals*	*(2) Goal Variation*	*(3) Motives*	*(4) Motive Variations*	*(5) Independent Behavior*	*(6) Behavior Variations*
Axline-Stegenga	(36)	14	3	11	3	22	8
Bobrow	(31)	10	3	0	0	3	3
Coplin	(93)	27	7	6	3	27	16
Crabb	(166)	35	10	12	3	20	13
Deutsch	(62)	31	13	6	2	23	14
Dougherty-Pfaltzgraff	(88)	20	7	8	4	23	12
Duchacek	(128)	16	2	5	1	19	8
Edwards	(71)	25	11	10	6	20	16
Frankel	(59)	25	12	2	2	10	7
Hartmann	(216)	25	6	10	5	37	19
Holsti	(112)	53	18	26	16	51	38
Hopkins-Mansbach	(158)	33	13	6	1	33	18
Jordan	(78)	30	11	10	2	24	15
Legg-Morrison	(67)	37	14	2	0	24	13
Modelski	(106)	17	1	4	3	22	15
Morgan	(65)	14	1	5	2	15	5
Morgenthau	(147)	20	4	12	4	20	15
Organski	(174)	27	4	10	2	20	6
Palmer-Perkins	(272)	31	7	9	3	31	15
Puchala	(78)	28	9	13	8	19	4
Rosecrance	(77)	35	14	6	0	23	13
Schuman	(148)	30	15	11	7	35	20
Spanier	(80)	42	9	10	1	44	16
Sprout-Sprout	(163)	10	1	2	1	9	4
Stoessinger	(98)	24	5	14	3	13	4
Van Dyke	(142)	30	6	9	4	18	7
Mean		27	8	9	3	25	13

state of affairs, thus necessitating the use of 'in order to' language (or its equivalent) to depict the plans or action. Paragraphs were coded as referring to motives when the present plans, actions, or circumstances associated with their prime units were assessed in terms of past or present states of affairs, thereby compelling the textwriters to use some equivalent of 'because of' language.[37] Table 20 reveals that the textwriters are much more interested in the goals than in the motives of actors. Indeed, all 26 texts were found to have a higher proportion of paragraphs with goals than with motives; in 23 instances the former were more than twice the number of the latter. We interpret this finding as indicating the degree to which the field of IR has both moved away from the orientations of historians and eschewed those of social psychologists. If historical narration were still an overriding concern,

[37] For an elaboration of this distinction between 'in order to' and 'because of' statements, see Richard C. Snyder, H. W. Bruck, and Burton Sapin, *Foreign Policy Decision-Making: An Approach to the Study of International Politics* (New York: Free Press 1962), 144.

the ratio of motive-to-goal characteristics would presumably be larger for most of the texts. And it seems likely that this would also be the case if the field had replaced a tendency toward narrative history with one in which the psychological sources of behavior were considered central. Instead, the ratios evident in Table 20 suggest that the field proceeds mainly from a political and/or policy perspective in which actors and their activities are conceived to be goal-oriented. Such a perspective, moreover, appears to be operative irrespective of whether textwriters cast their analyses at concrete or abstract levels. A comparison of the 7 More Concrete texts with the 19 classified as More Abstract, in terms of the degree to which they attributed motives and goals to the units, yielded virtually no differences: only 3 and 5 percentage points, respectively, separated the two groups along the motivation and goal dimensions.

Although the texts are uniformly inclined to focus more on goals than on motives, they differ considerably in the extent to which they portray units as goal-oriented. In at least one-third of their paragraphs, 5 made goal attributions, whereas 8 did so in no more than one-fifth of their paragraphs. The political model may be more prevalent than the historical and psychological ones, but it is hardly accorded equal attention by the various texts.

On the other hand, uniformity does mark their inclination to allow for variation on the part of the goals they ascribe to the units. As can be seen in Table 20, only one text (Schuman) depicted goals as varying in half of the paragraphs where goals are identified, while 12 texts allowed for such variability in less than one-quarter of their goal-oriented paragraphs. Stated differently, on the average the texts had goal attributions in 27 percent of their paragraphs, but the mean for the proportion of varying goals was only 8 percent. And the same disinclination to portray variability was equally manifest in the attribution of motives, with the comparable means being 9 and 3 percent. Such tendencies are, of course, not surprising in view of the earlier findings that most textwriters tend not to cast their analysis in cautious or probabilistic terms or to offer alternative explanations of the phenomena they investigate. Indeed, the data on variability in Table 20 are a particular expression of the earlier findings. Nevertheless, we cannot help but record again our dismay over the apparent insensitivity to both the intellectual and pedagogical need to treat the key variables in world affairs for what they are: variables and not constants.

To be sure, the lack of sensitivity along this line is probably exaggerated in Table 20, since conceivably the textwriters occasionally assess the variability of the identified goals and motives in the paragraphs that follow those that were selected as part of our sample. It seems doubtful, however, whether the practice of extending the analysis of goals and motives beyond a single paragraph fully accounts for the discrepancies in Table 20. If the impulse to depict variability dominated textwriters to the extent we think it should, the identification of a goal or motive would be followed sufficiently closely by an indication of alternative goals or motives to appear in the same paragraph more often than is the case according to our data. In our judgement, a goal or motive is not properly identified until its variability is simultaneously indicated — a rule of procedure that would surely result in a much narrower gap between the percentages in columns (2) and (4) of Table 20 on the one hand, and their counterparts in columns (1) and (3) on the other.

That a greater dispostion toward discerning and depicting variability is possible can be seen in the way in which the textwriters portray and assess behavior apart from its sources, attributes, and consequences. Each sample paragraph was coded in terms of a positive or negative answer to two questions on the presence of behavior in other than interactive situations: 'Is the prime unit explicitly posited as engaging in behavior without reference to the reactions of another actor?' 'If behavior is identified on the part of the prime unit, is it posited as varying in some way?' The resulting data are presented in the last two columns of Table 20. Here it is evident that although most of the texts devote roughly the same amount of attention to behavior as to the goals it is designed to serve, they are much more prone to treat the former as variable than the latter. In contrast to the one text noted above that depicted goals as varying in half of the paragraphs in which goals are identified, 16 texts described variations in independent behavior in more than half of the paragraphs where such behavior was ascribed to the prime unit. Indeed, in one text (Bobrow) such variation was portrayed each time independent behavior was identified. All told, an average of 25 percent of the sample paragraphs in all the texts were coded as containing prime units that engaged in independent behavior; the mean for those containing variations in this behavior was 13 percent.

It is not difficult to develop an explanation for the greater tendency to associate variability with behavior than with its goals or motives. One can observe behavior directly, whereas goals and motives must be inferred from behavior. Hence it is much easier to perceive variations in behavior and record them with confidence. Even the inferential derivation of one goal or motive involves a tentative and uncertain analytic exercise, so that to derive ways in which the goal or motive might vary or be part of a multiplicity of goals or motives is to undertake an especially tenuous task. But this, of course, is precisely our point. Analysis ought not to be confined to that which is readily observed. If the dynamics of world politics are to be uncovered and explained, imagination and venturesomeness must be invoked. The variability that constitutes the dynamics of the field is at least partially rooted in inferential phenomena, in the sources and consequences of behavior; any analysis that avoids probing variability at these levels seems destined to fall short of a substantial addition to understanding.

This is not to say, however, that the textwriters are unconcerned with the sources and consequences of behavior. As can be seen in columns (1) and (3) of Table 21, all but one text 'discussed or analyzed' the prime unit 'in terms of consequences or outcomes it causes' in at least one-third of their paragraphs.[38] Indeed, a comparison of these columns with column (5) in Table 20 reveals that the proportion of paragraphs that ascribed sources and consequences to the prime unit is higher for, respectively, 21 and 25 of the texts than is the equivalent figure for independent behavior.

Yet, to discern sources and consequences is not equivalent to fully carrying out the task of inferring from observed behavior. One can hardly avoid taking note of causes and effects if one is operating with a model of political behavior rather than a commitment to historical narration. Such inferences, we believe, must be supplemented with an analysis of (i.e., further inferences about) the ways in which the sources and consequences perceived to be operative can or do vary. And in this respect the texts are no more exemplary than in their handling of variation in goals and motives. Columns (2) and (4) of Table 21 depict the extent to which they allowed the identified sources and consequences to vary, and here it is evident that again variables tended to be treated as constants. Only one text (Rosecrance) depicted both the sources and consequences as varying in more than half the paragraphs in which these characteristics were identified. On the other hand, 10 texts identified variable sources less than one-quarter of the time, and 8 others did so less than one-third of the time. Similarly, 14 and 4 texts portrayed varying consequences in, respectively, one-quarter and one-third of their paragraphs where that characteristic was identified. On the average, the texts ascribed sources in 38 percent of their paragraphs and variable sources in 11 percent, while the comparable means for consequences were 42 and 10 percent.

Given this degree of insensitivity to the variability of international phenomena, it is hardly surprising that only a very small proportion of the paragraphs in most of the texts linked variation in sources to variations in consequences. The last column in Table 21 lists the proportion of paragraphs in which such a linkage was found. Here we uncovered what we regard as perhaps the most important finding of our inquiry: 15 texts linked varying causes and effects in fewer than 5 percent of their paragraphs, and 7 others did so in fewer than 10

[38] The quoted words are taken from our rules for coding each variable.

Table 21. Proportion of 2,915 Paragraphs from 26 Texts in which Sources and Consequences were Ascribed to their Prime Units and Variations in them were Depicted (in Percentages)

Text	*(n)*	*(1) Sources*	*(2) Source Variation*	*(3) Consequences*	*(4) Consequence Variation*	*(5) Links Between Varying Sources and Consequences*
Axline-Stegenga	(36)	39	11	47	19	6
Bobrow	(31)	23	7	26	3	0
Coplin	(93)	55	23	46	20	14
Crabb	(166)	30	7	43	5	1
Deutsch	(62)	47	23	48	16	11
Dougherty-Pfaltzgraff	(88)	30	9	38	14	6
Duchacek	(128)	34	4	34	5	3
Edwards	(71)	44	18	44	6	4
Frankel	(59)	42	10	44	3	2
Hartmann	(216)	27	7	37	7	2
Holsti	(112)	48	28	62	30	21
Hopkins-Mansbach	(158)	45	16	34	16	9
Jordan	(78)	36	5	47	9	3
Legg-Morrison	(67)	52	16	42	18	9
Modelski	(106)	35	8	35	9	4
Morgan	(65)	37	12	34	9	5
Morgenthau	(147)	37	11	48	9	6
Organski	(174)	40	8	44	6	3
Palmer-Perkins	(272)	29	4	37	5	1
Puchala	(78)	46	23	38	13	8
Rosecrance	(77)	69	36	57	34	27
Schuman	(148)	31	2	37	1	1
Spanier	(80)	60	11	54	11	6
Sprout-Sprout	(163)	36	14	49	14	4
Stoessinger	(98)	36	0	52	5	0
Van Dyke	(142)	31	9	37	5	1
Mean		38	11	42	10	5

percent. This strikes us as a crucial finding because such links are, in effect, at the center of any intellectual effort in which independent and dependent variables are analyzed. They are the very nature of hypotheses, not to mention the materials out of which theories are developed. And the data in the last column of Table 21 plainly indicate that IR texts are conspicuously lacking in this central dimension of the knowledge-building enterprise. It would seem that either the field is barren of hypotheses that textwriters feel comfortable in passing on to those taking introductory courses, or that they are afraid to appear wrong by casting the knowledge that has cumulated in hypothetical form. Both interpretations are probably accurate, but in either event we find it difficult to imagine how the field can move from its present impressionistic knowledge base to a reliable, ever-expanding one if its practitioners and textwriters avoid seeking and proposing links between the independent and dependent variables that are deemed important.

CONTEXTS OF INTERACTION

Although students of IR have yet to develop a widely accepted explanatory paradigm, they have long shared the basic premise that comprehension of the field requires an understanding of the dynamics of interaction among actors, as well as the sources and nature of their behavior. To be able to explore why actors do what they do is not to grasp what happens subsequently, as their actions precipitate and sustain the sequences of interaction through which the situations, crises, and relationships of world politics are established, maintained, and transformed. These interaction sequences, most analysts seem to agree, are more than the sum of the actions of the parties to them; accordingly, they need to be conceptualized and probed separately even as the actors and actions that sustain them are subjected to scrutiny. Thus, bifurcation has tended to mark the field, with some investigators exploring phenomena at the action level and others casting their analyses at the interaction level — emphases that have come to be seen as the distinction between foreign policy and international politics.

Our content analysis took account of these two levels through the inclusion of several key interaction variables. With respect to each of the paragraphs we asked, first, whether 'the prime unit is explicitly discussed or posited as an interaction sequence.'[39] We then proceeded to record whether it is 'discussed or analyzed in a context where the presence of 'force,'[40] of 'conflict,'[41] of 'cooperation,'[42] of 'bargaining,' and of the 'distribution of power' are 'explicitly noted.' The resulting data on these 6 variables are presented in Table 22. Here it can readily be seen that the texts faithfully reflect the tendency to emphasize both the action and interaction levels. Column (1) depicts 17 texts as positing interaction sequences in more than one-quarter of their paragraphs; half of them had at least one-third of their paragraphs so coded. Indeed, a comparison of the data in this column with those in column (5) of Table 20 yields the finding that interaction phenomena tended to be emphasized somewhat more than those pertaining to action: 21 texts had a higher proportion of their paragraphs coded in the former category than the latter. Taken together, the 26 texts associated the prime unit with an interaction sequence in 32 percent of their paragraphs,

[39] Our coding rules required that at least 'two parties' had to be explicitly identified for a prime unit to be treated as an interaction sequence. If the existence of a second actor had to be inferred from the description of the sequence, it was not coded as interaction.

[40] The coding rule here specified, 'by force is meant the use of arms.'

[41] 'Conflict refers to differences of opinions, goals, etc., among parties to a situation (including interpersonal and intergroup conflict as well as nonviolent and violent conflict).'

[42] 'Cooperation refers to compromise, accommodation, concerted effort, etc.'

Table 22. Proportion of 2,915 Paragraphs from 26 Texts in which the Prime Unit was Analyzed in the Context of 6 Interaction Variables (in Percentages)

Text	*(n)*	*(1) Interaction Sequences*	*(2) Conflict*	*(3) Cooperation*	*(4) Force*	*(5) Bargaining*	*(6) Power Distribution*
Axline-Stegenga	(36)	25	62	22	50	6	36
Bobrow	(31)	10	19	3	16	7	3
Coplin	(93)	52	52	33	24	24	25
Crabb	(166)	45	65	32	33	3	29
Deutsch	(62)	37	42	21	31	13	18
Dougherty-Pfaltzgraff	(88)	35	56	14	36	5	12
Duchacek	(128)	38	66	21	39	10	27
Edwards	(71)	34	42	18	30	4	13
Frankel	(59)	17	42	20	20	2	17
Hartmann	(216)	24	63	23	49	7	20
Holsti	(112)	32	72	37	42	5	33
Hopkins-Mansbach	(158)	45	59	24	38	10	22
Jordan	(78)	35	62	15	37	5	31
Legg-Morrison	(67)	25	51	21	18	3	22
Modelski	(106)	18	40	9	26	0	29
Morgan	(65)	21	32	12	22	0	6
Morgenthau	(147)	24	60	9	44	8	35
Organski	(174)	25	42	10	28	6	41
Palmer-Perkins	(272)	34	56	28	34	5	21
Puchala	(78)	24	47	22	27	10	23
Rosecrance	(77)	43	83	26	56	9	22
Schuman	(148)	34	70	22	46	9	28
Spanier	(80)	41	76	15	56	1	39
Sprout-Sprout	(163)	21	36	10	28	2	24
Stoessinger	(98)	45	50	30	33	8	27
Van Dyke	(142)	22	42	15	33	5	18
Mean		32	55	20	36	6	25

while the average at the action level was 25 percent.

The other columns of Table 22 also reveal some clear-cut tendencies. Perhaps most noticeable are the sizable differences in the extent to which the textwriters focused on conflict on the one hand and cooperation on the other. Although empirical data are available that indicate the processes of conflict and cooperation may be equally prevalent in world politics,[43] such a balance was not evident in any of the texts. All 26 were found to have a higher proportion of paragraphs depicting conflict than cooperation; 23 of them had more than twice as many paragraphs coded in the conflict than in the cooperation category; and 7 had more than 4 times as many conflict as cooperation paragraphs.[44]

The fact that force was found to be present in a higher proportion of paragraphs than bargaining in all 26 texts is, of course, quite consistent with the tendency to place greater emphasis on conflict than on cooperation. The exercise of force is one form of conflict, while bargaining may be an expression of a readiness to cooperate. Indeed, the inclination to stress conflict was even more pronounced in a comparison of the data on force and bargaining in Table 22: all texts but one (Coplin) were found to place at least twice as many paragraphs in a force context than in a bargaining context, and 13 texts had at least 6 times as many paragraphs coded in the force than in the bargaining category.

Much the same can be said about the data on the variable we have labeled 'power distribution' in column (6) of Table 22. Coded here were sample paragraphs in which the prime unit is 'discussed or analyzed in a context where the distribution of power and authority is explicitly noted.''[45] We included this variable in order to identify the degree to which the textwriters are sensitive to hierarchical distinctions, which we conceive to be another possible indicator of a preoccupation with the conflict dimension of interactive phenomena. Thus, it is not surprising that a comparison of the data on power distribution more closely resembled those on force than those on bargaining. To be sure, all but 3 texts had a higher proportion of their paragraphs coded in a

[43] Charles A. McClelland and Gary D. Hoggard, 'Conflict Patterns in the Interactions Among Nations,' in Rosenau, ed., *International Politics and Foriegn Policy: A Reader in Research and Theory* (rev. ed.; New York: Free Press 1969), 711–24.

[44] These findings are consistent with the impressions of Boulding (fn. 7) and Snyder (fn. 7) recorded more than a decade ago. Both authors decried the imbalance between conflict and cooperation and urged textwriters to pay more attention to integrative processes. Apparently their advice has yet to be taken seriously by the authors of textbooks.

[45] Our coding rules allowed for distributions of power and authority that 'may involve superiors, subordinates, or equal parties,' as well as those within 'domestic' settings (such as, for example, 'the President is more powerful in foreign affairs than Congress').

force than in a hierarchical context, but at the same time all but 2 placed at least twice as much emphasis on power distribution than on bargaining; in 11 cases the stress on hierarchical distinctions was at least 6 times greater. Indeed, as indicated by the mean figures for columns (3) and (6) in Table 22, the texts even tended to pay slightly greater attention to the distribution of power and authority than to processes of cooperation.

This imbalance in the direction of conflict, force, and hierarchy is easier to explain than to justify. The advent of World War II led to a great stress on 'realism' in the study and teaching of IR, on recognizing that international actors are often aggressive and self-serving in their behavior, and the cold-war period of the 1950's and 1960's perpetuated and legitimized the presumption that the central tendencies in world politics move toward conflict. Indeed, one of the texts in our sample (Morgenthau) was a major stimulus to the ascendency and continued dominance of the realist school. Published first in 1948 and periodically republished in revised editions (the one in our sample is the fifth), *Politics Among Nations* so explicitly and cogently espoused 'the theory of realism' and so effectively managed to place all the seemingly relevant phenomena of world politics in a realist framework that it came to dominate introductory teaching in the field, reportedly being used far more widely than any other text throughout the 1950's and most of the 1960's. Our survey of syllabi reveals that this primary reliance on Morgenthau's text has come to an end, but the data in Table 22 make it no less clear that the influence of realist thinking continues to prevail.

Though the imbalance in the direction of conflict and force is thus understandable, it cannot be readily justified. Whatever the accuracy of the realist model in the past, it seems increasingly discrepant with the course of events. The cold war has abated and the interdependence of nations had increased considerably, thereby emphasizing the cooperative and bargaining processes through which international actors relate to each other. To be sure, nations still conflict and they still resort to force, but the dynamics of technology have shrunk the social, economic, and political distances that separate them, and have given rise to a vast array of new issues requiring cooperation over the conservation and distribution of resources. In recent years, the scope of world politics has been extended upward to the biosphere and downward to the ocean bottom, and in the process the realist model appears increasingly obsolete. Or at least it seems clear that students of IR will need as incisive a comprehension of the processes of cooperation as of the processs of conflict if they are to grasp either the immediate issues or the long-term trends of world affairs.

ARENAS OF ACTION AND INTERACTION

Additional evidence of the predominance of the realist model is provided by comparisons of the extent to which the texts 'explicitly discussed or analyzed' the prime unit 'in the realm of diplomacy,' in 'the military realm,' in 'the economic realm,' and in 'the realm of nongovernmental international relations.' The data for these variables are presented in Table 23. Here it can be seen that much more attention is devoted to diplomatic and military issues or processes than to economic and nongovernmental questions. In roughly half the texts, more of the sample paragraphs were coded in the military than in the diplomatic realm, but in 22 a higher proportion was recorded in both of these realms than in the economic category. In all 26, more paragraphs were coded in these two realms than in the nongovernmental realm. More often than not, in fact, the proportions in the military and diplomatic categories were two and three times larger than those in, respectively, the economic and nongovernmental arenas. The key to these comparisons, it seems to us, is the relatively high degree of attention paid to the military aspects of IR. The attention devoted to diplomatic aspects could have been anticipated, given the viability of nation-states and their need to interact with each other through governmental channels,[46] but the equally extensive concentration on military matters seems inappropriate to a world in which economic and social interdependencies are mounting and attempts to achieve military resolutions of conflict are lessening. Such an imbalance, however, is quite consistent with the realist model, and thus leads us again to wonder whether the available texts in the field are not somewhat out of phase with the emerging parameters of world politics.

Our content analysis also includes two domestic realms of action and interaction. One is a general arena in which paragraphs were coded in terms of whether the prime unit is 'explicitly discussed or analyzed in the context of sociopolitical processes internal to nation-states.' Internal governmental processes were excluded from this category but were included in a second domestic variable that differentiated paragraphs in terms of whether they 'explicitly contain any mention of a policy-making process or a decision-making process.'[47] At least two clear-cut tendencies became apparent in the data on these two variables. As can be seen in Table 24, most textwriters devoted more attention to internal nongovernmental processes than to governmental

[46] Indeed, one survey reports a slow but continuous growth between 1921 and 1970 of the space that IR textbooks devote to diplomacy. Cf. Elmer Plischke, "Treatment of 'Diplomacy' in International Relations Textbooks," *World Affairs*, xxxv (Spring 1973), 328–44.

[47] Our coding rules defined 'policy making' as involving 'interaction among role occupants of a specified unit designed to chart a course of action.'

Table 23. Proportion of 2,915 Paragraphs from 26 Texts in which the Prime Unit was Analyzed in 4 Realms of Action and Interaction (in Percentages)

Text	*(n)*	*(1) Diplomatic*	*(2) Military*	*(3) Economic*	*(4) Nongovernmental*
Axline-Stegenga	(36)	39	39	8	11
Bobrow	(31)	3	6	0	3
Coplin	(93)	59	32	26	11
Crabb	(166)	47	31	19	9
Deutsch	(62)	14	31	11	3
Dougherty-Pfaltzgraff	(88)	24	23	5	8
Duchacek	(128)	45	34	9	10
Edwards	(71)	23	21	6	14
Frankel	(59)	19	22	17	12
Hartmann	(216)	44	41	15	2
Holsti	(112)	42	39	21	6
Hopkins-Mansbach	(158)	52	35	22	13
Jordan	(78)	36	39	14	10
Legg-Morrison	(67)	36	30	22	27
Modelski	(106)	24	24	7	22
Morgan	(65)	15	15	0	5
Morgenthau	(147)	38	39	9	9
Organski	(174)	19	29	24	4
Palmer-Perkins	(272)	43	30	28	12
Puchala	(78)	33	27	30	13
Rosecrance	(77)	43	49	16	6
Schuman	(148)	46	41	24	9
Spanier	(80)	29	59	31	10
Sprout-Sprout	(163)	25	26	28	17
Stoessinger	(98)	29	32	20	1
Van Dyke	(142)	22	25	15	4
Mean		35	33	18	9

policy making. Not only did more paragraphs of 23 texts qualify for coding in the former than in the latter category, but 16 recorded at least twice as high a proportion in the nongovernmental arena as in the policy-making realm. This is perhaps a surprising finding, given the long-standing interest in foreign policy decision making and the recent prominence of bureaucratic models of policy making. On the other hand, it is quite consistent with the aforenoted tendency of the text-writers to place somewhat greater stress on interaction at the international level than on action at the national level. Indeed, a comparison of the data in Table 24 with those in columns (1) and (2) of Table 23 reveals that in 20 texts more paragraphs were coded in the

Table 24. Proportion of 2,915 Paragraphs from 26 Texts in which the Analysis was Cast in Terms of 2 Domestic Arenas (in Percentages)

Text	*(n)*	*(1) Internal Nongovernmental Processes*	*(2) Internal Policy-Making Processes*
Axline-Stegenga	(36)	28	11
Bobrow	(31)	19	13
Coplin	(93)	9	15
Crabb	(166)	25	9
Deutsch	(62)	24	10
Dougherty-Pfaltzgraff	(88)	15	15
Duchacek	(128)	22	15
Edwards	(71)	13	13
Frankel	(59)	17	3
Hartmann	(216)	13	5
Holsti	(112)	20	6
Hopkins-Mansbach	(158)	13	20
Jordan	(78)	18	4
Legg-Morrison	(67)	22	10
Modelski	(106)	11	0
Morgan	(65)	12	15
Morgenthau	(147)	17	7
Organski	(174)	22	2
Palmer-Perkins	(272)	18	4
Puchala	(78)	26	3
Rosecrance	(77)	25	13
Schuman	(148)	32	13
Spanier	(80)	27	16
Sprout-Sprout	(163)	26	13
Stoessinger	(98)	7	4
Van Dyke	(142)	18	1
Mean		19	9

diplomatic realm than in either the internal nongovernmental or policy-making arenas, and that the comparable figure for the military realm was 24 texts. In many instances, moreover, the proportions for the diplomatic and military realms were more than twice those recorded for either or both domestic arenas.[48]

[48] These findings are also consistent with the impressions of Boulding and of Snyder, recorded a number of years ago. The former (fn. 7, p. 68) admonished textwriters for not concentrating more attention on internal sociological processes; the latter (fn. 7, pp. 473-75) stressed the need for more extensive consideration of foreign policy decision-making processes. Again their advice appears to have gone largely unheeded.

VI. SOME SUMMARIZING DATA

It seems clear that our data lend themselves to several interpretations; different readers planning to adopt IR texts will doubtlessly reach different conclusions as to which ones are most appropriate for their courses. So as to facilitate such choices, we have developed a simple additive index that summarizes our data and provides a basis for comparing and evaluating the 26 texts. Our index is founded on 24 data points (listed in the Appendix, along with the weights used for each item). These are subdivided in terms of the three main dimensions around which the preceding analysis has been organized, i.e., the provision of tools, the stimuli to knowledge, and the expression of knowledge. The 24 data points comprise roughly half of our indicators, and we believe that they offer a good composite picture of each dimension as well as of the three taken together.

The data generated by the index are summarized in Table 25.[49] In it, the weighted scores (expressed in percentages) for each dimension are presented along with the overall score for each text. The texts are rank-ordered in terms of their overall scores.

It is important to stress at the outset that interpretation of the index scores must be in comparative rather than in value terms. The range of 0 to 100 offers a standardized yardstick for comparing the quality of the 26 texts in our sample, but it does not allow for judgments based on absolute criteria. Theoretically the 'ideal' text would record a score approaching 100 percent. Plainly, it is unrealistic to expect scores at such a high level (since it would be unwieldy to an extreme to write paragraphs that contain all 24 components of the

[49] The index was constructed according to the following formula:

$$\frac{\sum_{p=1}^{N}\left[\frac{\sum_{i=1}^{4} T_i}{4}+\frac{\sum_{j=1}^{5} S_j}{5}+\frac{\sum_{k=1}^{15} E_k}{15}\right]}{3N}\times 100$$

where T is the sum of all the 'tools' variables across all paragraphs, S is the sum of all the 'stimuli' variables across all paragraphs, E is the sum of all 'expression of knowledge' variables across all paragraphs, and N is the number of paragraphs sampled from the text. We chose to construct the index in this fashion for three reasons. First, we wanted the index scores for each of the three dimensions to range from 0 to 100. The index scores are therefore an average of percentages for each dimension relative to the number of paragraphs. Second, the index treats each of three major components of an IR text as equal by dividing by the number of items that make up each category. Some may view this as a questionable assumption, but it is quite difficult if not impossible to make a case for differential weighting of the three categories. Third, we controlled for book length by dividing the index score by $3N$, thereby avoiding unintentional weighting of variables according to the number of items included in the index.

index); at the same time it is not feasible to specify exactly what scores would constitute a desirable level (since styles can vary as to the length and scope of paragraphs).

On the other hand, comparisons among the texts and the three dimensions can be readily undertaken on the basis of the index scores. To be sure, the overall scores have a narrow range, from a high of 35 percent to a low of 15 percent (giving rise to a standard deviation of 4.2). In some respects, of course, this narrow range constitutes a major finding on which we shall shortly comment. At the same time, despite the narrowness of the differences, we are persuaded that our index has yielded enough variability to allow for several useful summarizing observations. It is interesting, for example, to compare the index scores and the syllabi data on usage presented in Table 1. Of the 4 texts most frequently assigned, 2 (Holsti and Coplin) rank among the top 3 on the index and one (Coplin) ranks highest. Of the 3 next most frequently used texts, 2 (Spanier and Puchala) are also among those near the top of the rankings. In other words, although text usage in the field is far from dominated by one or two texts, those that rank high on our index tend to be among those most widely used by IR instructors. This finding is further supported by a comparison of the index scores and the data in Table 3, where a similar pattern can be discerned. Of the top 9 texts, 4 are among the 29 assigned or suggested sources that appear in 11 or more of the 178 syllabi.

Turning now to the three components of the index, the scores on individual tools, stimuli to learning, and expression of knowledge are quite instructive. Consider, first, the tools section. We believe that the ideal introductory text in IR should provide the student with a capacity to do more advanced work in the field and to understand world affairs long after graduating from college. To our minds, it is more important to present concepts and perspectives through which 'facts' are given meaning rather than to present the 'facts' alone. Thus the provision of analytic tools is quite central to our evaluation. Practically all 26 texts received relatively high scores on this indicator. The mean (27 percent) for the provision of analytic tools was higher than that of the other two components of our index. Indeed, 15 texts registered a score above the mean. And the standard deviation (5 percent) was the lowest recorded. Two reasons come to mind as helping to explain these comparatively high scores. We noted earlier that text-writers tend to take seriously the admonition often directed toward students — 'Define your terms.' This tendency toward explicit definitions increased the score for tools. Also, two important tools — 'Are there data generation and analysis techniques cited?' — were omitted from the composite index because we presumed that these techniques may be learned in other disciplines and in more advanced IR courses.

Table 25. Composite Index Scores for 26 IR Texts Along 3 Dimensions and Overall (in Percentages)

Text	*Number of Paragraphs Sampled*	*Rank*	*(1) Overall Scores*	*(2) Individual Tools*	*(3) Stimuli to Learning*	*(4) Expression of Knowledge*
Coplin	(93)	(1)	35	34	37	32
Dougherty-Pfaltzgraff	(88)	(2)	29	31	28	21
Holsti	(112)	(3)	28	31	17	35
Spanier	(80)	(3)	28	23	21	34
Morgan	(65)	(5)	26	33	27	18
Axline-Stegenga	(36)	(6)	25	33	14	27
Edwards	(71)	(6)	25	33	21	20
Hopkins-Mansbach	(158)	(6)	25	24	22	30
Puchala	(78)	(6)	25	32	16	27
Duchacek	(128)	(10)	24	27	18	23
Deutsch	(62)	(11)	23	29	13	28
Legg-Morrison	(67)	(11)	23	29	11	29
Bobrow	(31)	(13)	22	34	21	10
Crabb	(166)	(13)	22	21	19	26
Frankel	(59)	(13)	22	31	14	21
Rosecrance	(77)	(13)	22	26	8	32
Sprout-Sprout	(163)	(13)	22	29	16	23
Modelski	(106)	(18)	21	31	11	21
Van Dyke	(142)	(18)	21	28	15	20
Jordan	(78)	(20)	20	22	16	26
Schuman	(148)	(20)	20	21	12	28
Morgenthau	(147)	(22)	19	28	9	20
Organski	(174)	(22)	19	28	8	22
Palmer-Perkins	(272)	(22)	19	18	13	26
Hartmann	(216)	(25)	16	20	7	21
Stoessinger	(98)	(26)	15	15	10	19
	$\bar{x}$	=	23	27	16	25
	SD	=	4	5	7	6

Had these variables been included, undoubtedly they would have reduced the tools scores, since we found them to be conspicuous by their absence from the texts (with the striking exception of Bobrow). Even without the benefit of these indicators, it is noteworthy that Bobrow's text shared, with Coplin, the highest score on tools.

Whereas the tools section received relatively high scores, the opposite is true for the indicators on stimuli to learning. With Coplin as a major exception, the texts scored uniformly low on the elusive but important learning-stimuli indicators. Of course, the argument can readily be made that the acquisition, reinforcement, and enlargment of motivations for learning is not easily accomplished through the medium of an IR text. Many might even say that it is futile to rely on texts as a means of raising aspirations. We dissent. As stated earlier, we believe that to ponder knowledge and its inexactness, rather than to memorize it, will result in more curiosity about how and why events unfold as they do. Apparently, however, ours is a minority position. Our index indicates that the majority of writers of IR texts assume that their introductory students are sufficiently motivated and curious about IR phenomena. How else can one explain the strikingly low stimuli scores? Here the mean score (16 percent) was considerably below the other mean scores. Only 10 texts received a score above the mean.

It is interesting to speculate why the score of Coplin's text is considerably higher than the others on the learning-stimuli indicators. One possible explanation of Coplin's concern with the motivation and curiosity of students may lie in the fact that his text, in manuscript form, was subjected to fairly extensive pre-testing in a number of introductory IR classes before publication. Indeed, one of this article's junior authors participated in an introductory IR class in which the Coplin manuscript was used. Students were encouraged to provide feedback as to their impressions of the text's adequacy, and many did so. The argument can be made, then, that Coplin's text, as a result of the pre-testing, is more in touch with the realities of the classroom environment and the lack of interest in IR on the part of many students. This speculation, of course, does not account for the relatively low scores registered by the other texts since, among other things, we do not know the extent to which they were extensively pre-tested. Our only recourse, at this time, is to re-emphasize the alarming neglect of motivational considerations.

As for the third component of our index, scores for expression of knowledge were noticeably higher than those for stimuli to learning, but slightly lower than those for tools. That is not surprising. After all, we might expect that the provision of substantive materials would be a primary objective of many IR textwriters. The scores of 13 texts were above the mean, and the standard deviation (6 percent) indicated a relatively close grouping. While no single text dominated this category, there is one (Bobrow) that scored exceedingly low. This is surprising, given Bobrow's scores on tools and stimuli; but perhaps it is understandable in view of the 'new approaches' orientation of his text. In general, however, the restricted range and relatively low index scores, in conjunction with our earlier findings, support the arguments (1) that

IR texts vary slightly in terms of emphasis on substantive materials, and (2) that a cumulated body of established findings and shared understandings remains beyond our current grasp.

The above observations concerning the lack of variability, the relatively low component scores, and the small mean values for individual index elements apply to the composite index as well. The overall mean score (23 percent) reemphasizes, once again, our central contention that the 26 IR texts, when reviewed systematically along a variety of dimensions, fall far short of the ideal. The lowest-scoring text (Stoessinger) was separated by 20 percentage points from the highest-ranked text (Coplin). The top ten texts were separated by only 11 percentage points. The scores, in short, suggest that the 26 texts, with some notable exceptions, just do not differ from one another in any appreciable degree with respect to our terms of reference. Our analysis clearly indicates that the IR instructor in search of a good text has a small field from which to choose. No one text suffices. Rather, our analysis would recommend the use of various combinations of texts that maximise certain desirable qualities. Some instructors, for example. may choose to assign a text such as Spanier's, which scored comparatively high (34 percent) on the expression of knowledge variables, in conjunction with Bobrow's brief but succinct 'new approaches' text, while others may simply choose one of the highest-ranked texts and augment it with relevant outside reading.

These examples are offered as suggestive of how our analysis and index can be utilized, and should not be interpreted as saying that a combination of Spanier and Bobrow is best for use in the IR classroom. On the contrary, notwithstanding the many value judgments offered throughout the analysis, we recognize that there is no single best way to teach IR or to write a text about it. Our inquiry discloses that all is not well in the teaching of IR, but improvement can be achieved in a variety of ways, and thus we are not so presumptuous as to conclude with pronouncements as to which texts ought to be favored. Rather, we derive satisfaction from having raised more questions than we have answered and, in so doing, having called attention to some of the premises and promises that teachers and textwriters alike may want to follow or avoid as they go about their respective tasks.

APPENDIX

24 Variables (and the Weights attached to the Responses) included in the Composite Index for 26 IR Texts

I Acquisition of Tools and Skills
- A. value explicitness
  - 1 yes
  - 0 no
- B. other disciplines
  - 1 yes
  - 0 no
- C. prime unit defined
  - 1 yes
  - 0 no
- D. time or space
  - 0 yes
  - 1 no

II Stimuli to Learning
- A. status of knowledge
  - 1 yes
  - 0 no
- B. content self-evident
  - 0 yes
  - 1 no
- C. sources presented
  - 1 yes
  - 0 no
- D. alternative explanations
  - 1 yes
  - 0 no
- E. probabilistic terms
  - 1 yes
  - 0 no

III Expression of Knowledge
- A. prime unit has consequences
  - 1 yes
  - 0 no
- B. prime unit behavior
  - 1 yes
  - 0 no
- C. prime unit behavior varies
  - 1 yes
  - 0 no
- D. interaction sequence
  - 1 yes
  - 0 no
- E. presence of goals
  - 1 yes
  - 0 no
- F. goals vary
  - 1 yes
  - 0 no
- G. prime unit has causes
  - 1 yes
  - 0 no
- H. cooperation present
  - 1 yes
  - 0 no
- I. economic realm
  - 1 yes
  - 0 no
- J. nongovernmental realm
  - 1 yes
  - 0 no
- K. internal processes
  - 1 yes
  - 0 no
- L. policy-making process
  - 1 yes
  - 0 no
- M. future cited
  - 1 yes
  - 0 no
- N. history present
  - 0 yes
  - 1 no
- O. individuals, subnational groups nation-states, international organizations — generalized
  - 1 yes
  - 0 no

Bibliography of James N. Rosenau

1951

The Roosevelt Treasury

Editor. New York: Doubleday; xvi plus 461 pp.

1958

The Nomination of 'Chip' Bohlen

New York: Henry Holt; 16 pp.

1959

'Senate Attitudes Toward a Secretary of State'

in J. C. Wahlke and H. Eulau (eds.), *Legislative Behavior* (New York: Free Press), pp. 333–346.

1960

*'The Birth of a Political Scientist'

PROD 3 (January): 19–21.

1961

Public Opinion and Foreign Policy: An Operational Formulation

New York: Random House; vi plus 118 pp.

International Politics and Foreign Policy: A Reader in Research and Theory

Editor. New York: Free Press; 511 pp.

KEY TO SYMBOLS:

* Also in *The Scientific Study of Foreign Policy* (2nd edn.).

† Also in *The Study of Political Adaptation.*

‡ Also in *The Study of Global Interdependence.*

1962

'Consensus, Leadership and Foreign Policy'
SAIS Review 6 (Winter): 3-10.

'Consensus-Building in the American National Community: Some Hypotheses and Some Supporting Data'
Journal of Politics 24 (November): 639-661. Reprinted in John E. Mueller (ed.), *Approaches to Measurement in International Relations: A Non-Evangelical Survey* (New York: Appleton-Century, 1969).

'Convergence and Cleavage in the Study of International Politics and Foreign Policy'
Journal of Conflict Resolution VI (December): 359-67.

1963

**Calculated Control as a Unifying Concept in the Study of International Politics and Foreign Policy*
Research Monograph No. 15, Center of International Studies, Princeton University; 58 pp.

National Leadership and Foreign Policy: A Case Study in the Mobilization of Public Support
Princeton, N.J.: Princeton University Press; xvii plus 409 pp.

'The Functioning of International Systems'
Background 7 (November): 111-117.

1964

International Aspects of Civil Strife
Editor. Princeton, N.J.: Princeton University Press; vii plus 322 pp.

'Internal War as an International Event'
in J. N. Rosenau (ed.), *International Aspects of Civil Strife*; 45-91. Reprinted in George A. Kelly and Clifford W. Brown, Jr. (eds.), *Struggles in the State: Sources and Patterns of World Revolution* (New York: Wiley, 1970).

'Meticulousness as a Factor in the Response to Mail Questionnaires'
Public Opinion Quarterly XXVIII (Summer): 312-314.

1965

'Behavioral Science, Behavioral Scientists, and the Study of International Phenomena'
Journal of Conflict Resolution IX (December): 509-520.

1966

*'Pre-Theories and Theories in Foreign Policy'

in R. B. Farrell (ed.), *Approaches to Comparative and International Politics*, Evanston: Northwestern University Press, 27–92. Reprinted in W. D. Coplin and C. W. Kegley (eds.), *Analyzing International Relations: A Multimethod Introduction* (New York: Praeger, 1975).

'Transforming the International System: Small Increments Along a Vast Periphery'
World Politics XVIII: 525–545. Reprinted in Henry S. Kariel (ed.), *The Political Order: A Reader in Political Science* (New York: Basic Books, 1970).

1967

Of Boundaries and Bridges
Research Monograph No. 27, Center of International Studies, Princeton University, 66 pp.

Domestic Sources of Foreign Policy
Editor. New York: Free Press; xvi plus 340 pp.

*'Foreign Policy as an Issue Area'
in J. N. Rosenau (ed.), *Domestic Sources of Foreign Policy*, 11–50.

*'The Premises and Promises of Decision-Making Analysis'
in J. C. Charlesworth (ed.), *Contemporary Political Analysis* (New York: Free Press), 189–211.

*'Games International Relations Scholars Play'
Journal of International Affairs XXI (Summer): 293–303.

'Compatability, Consensus and an Emerging Political Science of Adaptation'
American Political Science Review LXI (December): 983–88.

1968

The Attentive Public and Foreign Policy: A Theory of Growth and Some New Evidence
Research Monograph No. 31, Center for International Studies, Princeton University; 48 pp.

'Political Science 221: Douglass College'
Vincent Davis and Arthur N. Gilbert (eds.), *Basic Courses in International Relations: An Anthology of Syllabi* (Beverly Hills: Sage Publications); 84–90.

*'Moral Fervor, Systematic Analysis, and Scientific Consciousness in Foreign Policy Research'
in A. Ranney (ed.), *Political Science and Public Policy* (Chicago: Markham), 197–236.

'Political Theory as Academic Field and Intellectual Activity'
Co-authored with Neil McDonald, *Journal of Politics* 30 (May);

311–44. Reprinted in Marian Irish (ed.), *Political Science: Advance of the Discipline* (New York: Prentice-Hall, 1968).

'Comparative Foreign Policy: Fad, Fantasy, or Field'
International Studies Quarterly 12 (September): 296–329

'The Concept of Intervention'
Journal of International Affairs XXII (Summer): 165–76.

*'The National Interest'
International Encyclopedia of the Social Sciences. New York: Crowell-Collier, Vol. 11, 34–40.

*'Private Preferences and Political Responsibilities: The Relative Potency of Individual and Role Variables in the Behavior of U.S. Senators'
In J. D. Singer (ed.), *Quantitative International Politics: Insights and Evidence* (New York: Free Press), 17–50.

1969

**Race in International Politics: A Dialogue in Five Parts*
Monograph Series in World Affairs, University of Denver, Vol. 7, No. 2, 50 pp.

Linkage Politics: Essays on the Convergence of National and International Systems
Editor. New York: Free Press; xii plus 352 pp.

Contending Approaches to International Politics
Editor with Klaus Knorr. Princeton, N.J.: Princeton University Press; v plus 297 pp.

*'Toward the Study of National-International Politics'
in J. N. Rosenau (ed.), *Linkage Politics*, 44–63.

'Tradition and Science in the Study of International Politics'
Co-author with Klaus Knorr, in K. Knorr and J. N. Rosenau (eds.), *Contending Approaches to International Politics*, Chap. 1.

*'Intervention as a Scientific Concept'
Journal of Conflict Resolution XII (June): 149–71. Reprinted in Richard A. Falk (ed.), *The Vietnam War and International Law*, Vol. 2 (Princeton, N.J.: Princeton University Press, 1969).

International Politics and Foreign Policy: A Reader in Research and Theory
Editor. Revised edition, New York: Free Press; xx plus 740 pp.

1970

*†*The Adaptation of National Societies: A Theory of Political Behavior and Its Transformation*
(New York: McCaleb-Seiler); 28 pp.

'Adaptive Strategies for Research and Practice in Foreign Policy'
in Fred W. Riggs (ed.), *A Design for International Studies:*

Scope, Objectives, and Methods (Philadelphia: American Academy of Political and Social Science), 218–245.

'Foreign Policy as Adaptive Behavior: Some Preliminary Notes for a Theoretical Model'
Comparative Politics 2 (April): 365–89.

'Public Protest, Political Leadership, and Diplomatic Strategy'
Orbis XIV (Fall): 557–71.

'Field and Environmental Approaches to World Politics: Implications for Data Archives'
Co-author with Raymond Tanter. *Journal of Conflict Resolution* XIV (December): 513–26.

1971

The Scientific Study of Foreign Policy
New York: Free Press: xv plus 472 pp.

'Public Opinion, Foreign Policy, and the Adaptation of National Societies'
Societas I (Spring): 85–100.

1972

The Attentive Public in an Interdependent World: A Survey of Theoretical Perspectives and Empirical Findings'
Columbus, Ohio: Mershon Center; 116 pp.

‡†'Adaptive Polities in an Interdependent World'
Orbis XVI (Spring): 153–73.

'Dissent and Political Leadership'
Dialogue 5: 36–45.

Foreword
Davis B. Bobrow, *International Relations: New Approaches* (New York: Free Press), vii–xv.

The Analysis of International Politics
Editor with Vincent Davis and Maurice A. East.
New York: Free Press; xii plus 397 pp.

*'The External Environment as a Variable in Foreign Policy Analysis'
in J. N. Rosenau, V. Davis, M. A. East (eds.), *The Analysis of International Politics*, 145–165.

1973

International Studies and the Social Sciences
Beverly Hills: Sage Publications; 147 pp.

The Dramas of Politics: An Introduction to the Joys of Inquiry
New York: Little, Brown; xiii plus 250 pp.

†'Paradigm Lost: Five Actors in Search of the Interactive Effects

of Domestic and Foreign Affairs'
Policy Sciences 4 (December): 415–36.

'Mobilizing the Attentive Citizen: A Model and Some Data on a Neglected Dimension of Political Participation'
(A paper presented at the Annual Meeting of the American Political Science Association, New Orleans.)

‡'Theorizing Across Systems: Linkage Politics Revisited'
in J. Wilkenfeld (ed.), *Conflict Behavior and Linkage Politics* (New York: David McKay), 25–56.

'International Studies in the United States: Some Problems and Issues of the 1970s'
Yearbook of World Affairs, 1973: 401–16.

*'The Adaptation of Foreign Policy Research: A Case Study of an Anti-Case Study Project'
Co-author with Philip M. Burgess and Charles F. Hermann. *International Studies Quarterly* 17 (March): 119–44.

1974

Citizenship Between Elections: An Inquiry into the Mobilizable American
New York: Free Press; xxxii plus 526 pp.

Comparing Foreign Policies: Theories, Findings, and Methods
Editor. Beverly Hills: Sage Publications; xi plus 442 pp.

†'Foreign Intervention as Adaptive Behavior'
in John Norton Moore (ed.), *Law and Civil War in the Modern World* (Baltimore: Johns Hopkins University Press), pp. 129–151.

The Transnationalization of Urban Communities: Some Data on Elites in a Midwestern City
Columbus, Ohio: Mershon Center; 43 pp.

‡*Success and Failure in Scientific International Relations Research*
Final Report, National Science Foundation; 79 pp.

'The Final Examination as a Group Process'
Teaching Political Science 2 (October): 65–77.

‡'The Coming Transformation of America: Resistance or Accommodation?'
World Studies I (Spring): 1–26.

‡'Assessment in International Studies: Ego Trip or Feedback?'
International Studies Quarterly 18 (September): 339–67.

'Comparing Foreign Policies: Why, What, How'
in J. N. Rosenau (ed.), *Comparing Foreign Policies*, 3–22.

'Foreign Policy Behavior in Dyadic Relationships: Testing a Pre-Theoretical Extension'
Co-author with Gary D. Hoggard in J. N. Rosenau (ed.), *Comparing Foreign Policies*, 117–150.

1975

*'Comparative Foreign Policy: One-Time Fad, Realized Fantasy, and Normal Field'
in C. W. Kegley, Jr., A. G. Raymond, R. M. Rood, and R. A. Skinner (eds.), *International Events and the Comparative Analysis of Foreign Policy* (Columbia: University of South Carolina Press), 3–38.

*'External and Internal Typologies of Foreign Policy Behavior: Testing the Stability of an Intriguing Set of Findings'
Co-author with Goerge R. Ramsey, Jr., in P. J. McGowan (ed.), *Sage International Yearbook of Foreign Policy Studies*, Vol. III (Beverly Hills: Sage Publications), 251–68.

1976

World Politics
Editor with Gavin Boyd and Kenneth Thompson. New York: Free Press; xii plus 754 pp.

In Search of Global Patterns
Editor. New York: Free Press; ix plus 389 pp.

'Perspectives on World Politics'
in J. N. Rosenau, A. Boyd, K. Thompson (eds.), *World Politics*, 1–11.

'The Study of Foreign Policy'
in J. N. Rosenau, A. Boyd, K. Thompson (eds.), *World Politics*, 15–35.

‡'Capabilities and Control in an Interdependent World'
International Security 1 (October): 32–49.

'The Restless Quest'
in J. N. Rosenau (ed.), *In Search of Global Patterns*, 1–9.

'Restlessness, Change, and Foreign Policy Analysis'
in J. N. Rosenau (ed.), *In Search of Global Patterns*, 369–376.

'The Lessons: of Vietnam: A Study of American Leadership'
Co-author with Ole R. Holsti. (A paper presented at the 17th Annual Meeting of the International Studies Association, Toronto, Canada.)

'Vietnam Revisited: A Comparison of the Recollections of Foreign Service and Military Officers of the Lessons, Sources and Consequences of the War'
Co-author with Ole R. Holsti. (A paper presented at the Xth Congress of the International Political Science Association, Edinburgh, Scotland.)

‡'International Studies in a Transnational World'
Millenium 5 (Spring): 1–20.

'Intellectual Identity and the Study of International Relations, or Coming to Terms with Mathematics as a Tool of Inquiry' in D. A. Zinnes and J. V. Gillespie (eds.), *Mathematical Models in International Relations* (New York: Praeger), 3-9.

1977

'Comparative Politics'
Co-author with Robert R. Kaufman, in Donald M. Freeman (ed.), *Political Science: History, Scope, and Methods* (New York: Free Press), 45-83.

'Teaching and Learning in a Transnational World'
(A paper presented at the First Assembly of the Institute for the Advancement of Teaching and Learning, California State University, Northridge.)

'Problem Recognition: Belief Systems of American Leaders'
Co-author with Ole R. Holsti. (A paper presented at the Annual Conference of the International Studies Association/South, Columbia, South Carolina.)

'The Meaning of Vietnam: Belief Systems of American Leaders'
Co-author with Ole R. Holsti. *International Journal* XXXII (Summer): 452-74.

†'The Adaptation of Small States'
(A paper presented at the Conference on Contemporary Trends and Issues in Caribbean International Affairs, Institute of International Relations, University of West Indies, Trinidad.)

*'Puzzlement in Foreign Policy'
The Jerusalem Journal of International Relations I (Summer): 1-10.

‡'Of Syllabi, Texts, Students, and Scholarship in International Relations: Some Data and Interpretations on the State of a Burgeoning Field'
Co-author with Gary Gartin, Edwin P. McClain, Dona Stinziano, Richard Stoddard, and Dean Swanson. *World Politics* XXIX (January): 263-342.

1978

'Decision-Making Approaches and Theories'
Alexander de Conde (ed.), *Dictionary of the History of American Foreign Policy* (New York: Charles Scribner's Sons), Vol. I, 219-228.

'Cold War Axioms in the Post-Vietnam Era'
Co-author with Ole R. Holsti. (A paper presented at the Annual Meeting of the International Studies Association, Washington, D.C.; revised for publication in Alexander George, Ole R. Holsti, and Randolph M. Siverson [eds.], *International Systems Change*, Westview Press.)

‡'The Tourist and the Terrorist: Two Extremes on the Same Transnational Continuum'
(A paper presented at the Annual Meeting of the International Studies Association, Washington, D.C.; translated into French and published in *Études Internationales* X (June), 219–52.)

1979

'America's Foreign Policy Agenda: The Post-Vietnam Beliefs of American Leaders'
Co-author with Ole R. Holsti in Charles W. Kegley, Jr., and Patrick J. McGowan (eds.), *Challenges to America: United States Foreign Policy in the 1980s*, Beverly Hills: Sage Publications, 231–268.

'Public Opinion and Soviet Foreign Policy: Competing Belief Systems in the Policy-making Process'
Co-author with Ole R. Holsti. *Naval War College Review* XXXII (July–August), 4–14.

†'The United States in (and Out of) Vietnam: An Adaptive Transformation?'
Co-author with Ole R. Holsti. *Yearbook of World Affairs*, 1979.

'Thinking Theory Thoroughly'
in K. P. Misra and R. S. Beal (eds.), *International Relations Theory: Western and Non-Western Perspectives* (New Delhi: Vikas Publishing House, Ltd.), Chap. 1.

*'Muddling, Meddling, and Modeling: Alternative Approaches to the Study of World Politics in an Era of Rapid Change' in K. P. Misra and R. S. Beal (eds.), *International Relations Theory: Western and Non-Western Perspectives*, Chap. 3, and *Millennium: Journal of International Studies* 8 (2).

'Vietnam, Consensus, and the Belief Systems of American Leaders'
Co-author with Ole R. Holsti, *World Politics* XXXII (October), 1–56.

‡'The Concept of Aggregation and Third World Demands: An Analytic Opportunity and an Empirical Challenge'
(A paper prepared for the Conference on Constancy and Change: The Political Economy of Global Differentiation, Ojai, Ca.)

1980

The Dramas of Political Life: An Introduction to the Problems of Governance
North Scituate, Mass.: Duxbury Press; 282 pp.

The Scientific Study of Foreign Policy (Revised and Enlarged Edition)
London: Frances Pinter Publishers, Ltd.; 564 pp.

The Study of Political Adaptation
London: Frances Pinter Publishers, Ltd.
The Study of Global Interdependence: Essays on the Transnationalization of World Affairs
London: Frances Pinter Publishers Ltd.; 334 pp.
‡'Toward a New Civics: Teaching and Learning in an Era of Fragmenting Loyalties and Multiplying Responsibilities'
Comparative Political Analysis, Vol. I, No. 1 (Fall).
Does Where You Stand Depend on When You Were Born? The Impact of Generation on Post-Vietnam Foreign Policy Beliefs
Co-author with Ole R. Holsti. *Public Opinion Quarterly*, Vol. 44 (Spring 1980), 1–22.

Index